I0814141

The Map of Wilderland

The Map of Wilderland

Ecocritical Reflections on Tolkien's Myth of Wilderness

Amber Lehning

The Kent State University Press
KENT, OHIO

ISBN 978-1-60635-442-1
Manufactured in the United States of America

Cataloging information for this title is available at the Library of Congress.

26 25 24 23 22 5 4 3 2 1

Contents

Introduction

In wildness is the preservation of the world.
—Thoreau, *Civil Disobedience, and Other Essays*, 61.

The idea of wilderness is an essential component of the way modern humans conceive of their relationship with the natural world. It is also an idea that resists easy definition so successfully that Thoreau's famous (and famously precise) epigram is generally absorbed without comment into its vast and indeterminate compass. Strictly speaking, the wildness mentioned by this patron saint of environmentalism should be considered as a character of a place, while wilderness is the place itself, characterized by wildness. The difference is subtle, but in some ways it lies at the root of understanding how and why human beings relate the way they do to the nonhuman world. Such an understanding is becoming dangerously important as the planet continues its unfaltering march into a new Anthropocenic age.

While today's environmental crisis has many roots, some of the most important reach deeply into the myths and stories peoples develop as they seek to understand the wilderness and their place within it. There are many destructive stories behind the behaviors of modern civilization that have precipitated the current and ongoing devastation of the planet; Christian dominion theology, American Manifest Destiny, and the clockwork universe of the nineteenth century are just a few of these. These stories form the mythic basis behind an unconscious but widely held belief that the clear open sky, endless sprawling forests, and uncountable miles of crystal-clear waters on this planet are an inexhaustible resource. They also underscore an intellectual separation between humanity and the natural world that can justify the worst of environmental excesses. The current desperate ecological situation—melting glaciers, increasing temperatures, and violently destructive hurricanes and winter storms across the world—is beginning to demonstrate just how wrong those destructive myths truly are.

Unlike concrete, scientific problems with empirical ecological solutions, this separation cannot be fixed in any physical way. The only way to counter these destructive stories is to shift some of the deep belief they command into new, positive, good stories. "We need a powerful new story that we are a part of nature and not separate from it," says Richard Schiffman. "We need a story that properly situates humans in the world—neither above it by virtue of our superior intellect, nor dwarfed by the universe into cosmic insignificance."[1] If poor stories created the human actions that destroyed the environment, then better ones should be able to at least begin to create actions that will help humanity mitigate the consequences of that previous devastation. There are certainly many stories that might prove positive and powerful in this way. One that stands out in all measures, from popularity to longevity to actual mythic influence that could truly allow humans to change the way they interact with the natural world, is the vast legendarium created by the father of fantasy literature, J. R. R. Tolkien.

Tolkien's Middle-earth cycle is certainly a powerful story that, when examined carefully, turns out to be a positive and proenvironmental one. It is also a widely beloved story. Despite the critical disdain heaped upon Tolkien by the mainstream literary establishment, his books have proved so enduringly popular that a huge survey in 1997 voted *The Lord of the Rings* the "Book of the Century" by a large margin and placed *The Hobbit* at number nineteen, making him not only the first-placed author but one of only two writers to have two books in the top one hundred.[2] When Peter Jackson's critically acclaimed films brought Tolkien's mythic cycle to the silver screen at the turn of the twenty-first century, the story became more well known and entered the mythological consciousness of even more people than the wildly successful books had managed to do.

The power of Tolkien's great tale lies in its skillful storytelling, of course, but it also draws on its resonance with many diverse cultural spectra across the world. Although he may have conceived of his masterwork as a "mythology for England,"[3] as he revised and rethought his legendarium "his works outgrew their original purpose to become the mythology of an entire world, rather than of a single country or people."[4] Citizens of countries from China to Chile have read Tolkien's stories in translation and used them as inspiration and mythic instruction, often with great impact on the way they interact with their communities and the natural world. This study will examine Tolkien's masterwork from several different angles, including source criticism, direct ecocriticism of his texts, and consideration of the ways his mythic story has continued to develop since his death into something that resonates strongly with the most current ideas in modern wilderness philosophy.

Why is wilderness so important? Humans are creatures of their environment, physical animals who, even in modern cities, are subject to the same climactic laws that govern the wild lands far away. As David Abram observes, the city of New York remains "an island settlement in the Hudson River estuary. . . . For all the international commerce that goes on within its glassy walls, Manhattan could not exist without its grounding amid the waters with their tidal surges. Meanwhile, the inhabitants of Los Angeles awaken, often enough, to the trembling power of their own terrain."[5] But, despite the human dependence on the natural processes of the places where they live, it is not self-evident why people should care about places where no humans are. Why should they work to protect wild areas, outside of those cities, or the vast machine-worked farms where the food is grown to sustain all those city-dwellers?

The study of environmental ethics has proposed several dozen answers to this question, all of which are colored by the crisis of global climate change, which has become an inescapable part of any postmodern discussion of the natural world. Edward Abbey, the father of radical environmentalism, links wilderness to hope: one could be "a lover and defender of the wilderness without ever in his lifetime leaving the boundaries of asphalt, powerlines and right-angled surfaces. We need wilderness whether or not we ever set foot in it. We need a refuge even though we may never need to go there. . . . We need the possibility of escape as surely as we need hope."[6] This is, as *The International Encyclopedia of Ethics* points out, a sort of "psychotherapy at a distance" where "it is importantly psychologically therapeutic just knowing areas of wilderness exist, whether we visit them or not."[7] Mark Jenkins points out that "the very idea of wilderness acts as a balm on the psychic scrapes and bruises that inevitably come with navigating this modern world."[8] The other answers stretch from resource-based and utilitarian, to sociological and pedagogical, to philosophical and ontological, and all are worth considering as solid arguments for the importance of wild places.

One of the most interesting of these arguments recognizes that mythology is as important as biology to the human relationship with nature. Max Oelschlaeger suggests that "the idea of wilderness in postmodern context is . . . a search for meaning—for a new creation story or mythology—that is leading humankind out of a homocentric prison into the cosmic wilderness."[9] This argument dates to the earliest days of humanity, and yet it manages to touch on the very root of both the problem and the solution of the current environmental crisis.

Archetypal psychology explains that humans are reasoning creatures whose psyches seek patterns in the world around them and use those patterns to form meaning. The natural world was obviously the main source of such patterns for early humans, and even today—as archetypes continue to arise out of the patterns humans encounter in natural environments—"these environments evoke powerful emotions and take on a profound significance for the individual."[10] Such significance, such meaning, provided the emotional energy behind the first human spiritual practices. Early in the pursuit of mythology as a study in itself, nineteenth-century thinkers developed many competing nature-based theories of myth. "If one phenomenon seemed to be preferred, it was taken as the center of the mythological system," from the terrifying thunder of Adalbert Kuhn to the lovely daybreak of Max Müller.[11] Although these older theories have since deservedly collapsed under the ethnocentric weight of their overly universalistic enthusiasm, they remain on the historical mythological studies record as a testament to the way the shape of the local natural world has had an enormous impact on how humans connect with and relate to it.

Whether in the vast open deserts of the Middle East or in the deep forests of central Europe, for humans, "wilderness—what we think the concept means and our attitude toward that concept—is a powerful reflection of our overall relationship with nature."[12] Unfortunately, in today's world, the existence of wilderness is no longer a given. The change human activity has wrought upon the climactic patterns of the planet will ensure for centuries to come that there is no place on the Earth that is not affected by the choices and consequences of *Homo sapiens sapiens*. In the early days, prehistoric humans were the ones who were endangered by the seemingly insurmountable powers of the wilderness; weather, wild animals, and the unforgiving march of the seasons were deadly enemies whose vagaries could wipe out entire tribes. The agricultural revolution taught humans the benefits of first taming the wilderness and then shaping it to their purposes. By the time of the Industrial Revolution, humans were actually using the wilderness, which came to be viewed as a vast store of natural resources to be mined and exploited. Today, in the postmodern Information Age, that exploitation has emptied the stock of those seemingly endless resources and that once-infinite wilderness is now in danger of disappearing forever.

This trend undoubtedly troubled Tolkien. The world he lived in was being rather brutally reshaped by the modern industrial forces that characterized the early twentieth century, and he felt the resulting loss of natural places keenly; he once stated in a letter that he was "much in love with plants and above all trees" and that he found "human maltreatment of them as hard to bear as some find ill-treatment of animals."[13] Noted Tolkien critic Tom Shippey speaks often of the deep connection with trees and forests, which "would come to be seen as Tolkien's 'Green' ideology."[14] Other scholars have noted the "putting together of various elements to shape an ecologically deep environmental vision" as "one of the things that J. R. R. Tolkien accomplished supremely well."[15] This case should certainly not be overstated; there is no doubt that—unlike explicitly nature writers such as Henry David Thoreau or Aldo Leopold—Tolkien was first and foremost a storyteller, and not a crusader for some sort of proto-Green movement as modern environmentalists would perhaps seek to claim. But his "Green ideology" nevertheless remains an important presence in his stories.

An affinity for green and growing things, as contrasted with the smoke and clanging of modern industry, is pervasive in both the plots and themes of the works of the Middle-earth legendarium. The strong vein of antimodernism visible in Tolkien's treatment of wilderness clearly resonates with postmodern readers concerned with environmental issues today. Careful examination of that treatment, both in the ancient legends that Tolkien so admired as well as in his own fictional world, has the potential to help the millions of people who love Middle-earth use that resonance to positively shift their own stories about themselves and their relationship to the real natural world around them.

Part I: "The Myth of Wilderness" considers wilderness and the portrayal of the natural world as presented in some of Tolkien's most important medieval sources. Its three chapters examine British medieval literature from the early Germanic period (*Beowulf*), through the Celtic tales of the High Middle Ages (*Mabinogion*), and into the late medieval Middle English period (*Sir Gawain and the Green Knight*). Each chapter lists some of the source-critical evidence for the work's influence on Tolkien's academic and creative life, and then uses ecocritical techniques to tease out the relationship between humanity and the wild natural world as presented in the cultural milieu for which the work is considered representative. Three distinct but related concepts of wilderness arise from these three works, and those concepts form the basis for examining Tolkien's Middle-earth in part II.

Part II: "The Lands of Arda" is an ecocritical and mythological examination of Tolkien's own portrayal of wilderness and the natural world throughout the Middle-earth legendarium. Chapter 4, "Rangers in the Mountains," examines Tolkien's use of the Germanic concept of wilderness as a harsh and dangerous place, the abode of monsters and the arena for heroic actions. Chapter 5, "Elves in the Forest," explores how Tolkien borrowed the Celtic concept of wilderness as a place of perilous and uncanny beauty, a haven where worthy heroes can find rest and recuperation from their labors. Chapter 6, "Hobbits in the Shire," considers a place of less wildness but broader accessibility, the somewhat idealized pastoral concept of the English wilderness as a friendly place of pleasant recreation. This part explores, reviews, and builds upon existing Tolkien ecocriticism, and develops the wilderness concepts highlighted in part I to establish a framework to serve as the basis of the analysis in part III.

Part III: "The Wilderness of Myth" looks at what Tolkien's vision means for wilderness today. In this Information Age, pressured on all sides by physical changes in the climate and the increasingly urban status of global civilization, how can Tolkien's great modern myth help postmodern people develop a more sustainable and healthy relationship with wilderness and the natural world? Chapter 7, "Tolkien and American Wilderness Philosophy," examines the strong resonance between Tolkien's ideas of wilderness and some important ones in American Wilderness Philosophy. Chapter 8, "Tolkienian Wilderness in the Information Age," considers a few New Media adaptations of the Middle-earth legendarium, and touches on the presence of Tolkien's work in the mythic guidance of environmental activists. Chapter 9, "Tolkienian Courage and Wilderness Today," explores what mythic instruction Tolkien's three wilderness concepts might offer to ordinary people seeking to wrestle with today's dire and despair-inducing environmental situation.

Before people can begin to change their stories about their relationship to the natural world, they will need to find new stories that move them in deeply personal ways, ways powerful enough to encourage them to change their behavior. Tolkien's modern myth, with its deep roots in the past and its potential for universal and continuing applicability in the future, is uniquely positioned to serve as such a catalyst. With careful consideration of the mythic instruction and ethical lessons to be learned within its pages, Tolkien's great masterwork may prove a powerful aid in the quest of those who recognize the importance of wilderness, and who seek to create a new story about it that will help to reunite the sundered physical bodies and mental constructs of the postmodern human soul.

PART I
THE MYTH OF WILDERNESS

It seemed that he was learned in old lore,
as well as in the ways of the wild.
—Tolkien, *Lord*, 185

Learned in Old Lore

This is a work of mythological studies. Although source criticism and eco-criticism will figure prominently in the following pages, and although this first part will focus nearly exclusively on the examination of three famous works of literature, it is important from the outset to understand that this study is not one of a strictly literary nature. Instead, it is deeply concerned with the archetypal power of story and the ways that narratives shape human perceptions of and behavior in the world. If the concept of myth resides at the point where the overlapping studies of religion, folklore/literature, and archetypal psychology meet, then this particular work lies deep in the domain of the literary aspect of myth, partially within the domain of the psychological one, and just skirts along the borders of the religious one.

Joseph Campbell famously described myth as "the secret opening through which the inexhaustible energies of the cosmos pour into human cultural manifestation" and "the living inspiration of whatever else may have appeared out of the activities of the human body and mind."[1] While Campbell's grandly universal concepts revolutionized the study of myth, they are rooted mostly in the religious realm and serve more as a starting point than a trajectory for this study. At another extreme, archetypal psychology can sometimes focus on a single person's individual story: "a myth is a fantasy, a preferred lie, a foundational story, a hypnotic trance, an identity game, a virtual reality, one that can be either inspirational or despairing. It is a story in which I cast myself, it is my inner cinema, the motion picture of my inner reality."[2] The stories chosen as mythic instruction to give meaning to events can undoubtedly have a dramatic impact on a person's life, but deeply private and personal stories should not be the sole powers under consideration for those seeking narrative weapons against the worldwide ecological crisis. "The depth psychologist is generally concerned with how the fantasies or wishes of the unconscious affect the personality and behavior of a single human being," Walter Odajnyk has observed; "the mythologist, by contrast, is interested in how the fantasies appear in the wider community and affect that community's perception of itself and its surrounding world."[3] The relationships between humankind and the natural world are both cosmological and personal, certainly, but they are also cultural and communal, and it is to this middle ground of myth that this study will try and keep.

The power of stories in a cultural context is a compelling starting point from which to approach the work of J. R. R. Tolkien. His tales are "deliberately complex and multi-layered, drawing on many traditions, even interacting with them in a kind of mythic literary conversation,"[4] and his own thinking on myth is arguably not too divergent from positions taken by most modern mythological studies scholars: "I believe that legends and myths are largely made of 'truth,' and indeed present aspects of it that can only be received in this mode; and long ago certain truths and modes of this kind were discovered and must always reappear."[5] Joseph Campbell would not likely disagree.

Still, Tolkien's attitude toward the study of comparative mythology later popularized by Campbell was admittedly dismissive at best. In an essay lamenting the fact that England had no collection of mythic songs such as the Finnish *Kalevala*, Tolkien worried that, even if such a thing existed, it would prove a "playground of anthropologists and comparative mythologists,[6] where they luxuriate mightily awhile—but however good and interesting in its own way their sport and hunting may be (I fear I am often sceptical) it is as foreign to my present purpose as would be the processes of the manufacture of cheese."[7] Tolkien's purpose was, as in nearly all of his writing, to advance the consideration of a work on its own merits and for its own sake, and this study will try and do the same as much as possible.

Tolkien was similarly dismissive of another critical technique fundamental to this book. Anyone considering Tolkien's legendarium in the light of its sources must bump up against their author's professed dislike of, even contempt for, source criticism. "I fear you may be right that the search for the sources of *The Lord of the Rings* is going to occupy academics for a generation or two," he grumbled in a letter, plaintively lamenting, "I wish this need not be so."[8] Tom Shippey offers an in-depth and spirited defense of the practice in an essay titled "Why Source Criticism?," where he observes that "all literary works bear some relation to the milieu in which they are composed and received, but we often do not realize how quickly elements of those milieux are forgotten. . . . The knowledge may be important, and has a fair chance of being interesting."[9] As a renowned philologist and professor of Anglo-Saxon at Oxford, Tolkien certainly knew the milieux of his old stories as well as he knew the stories themselves; there is also no doubt that, as he was writing his new one, he quite consciously tapped into his store of older ones, mining them for everything from single words to entire narrative arcs.

Tolkien himself admitted to feeling strongly "the fascination of the desire to unravel the intricate knotted and ramified history of the branches on the Tree of Tales."[10] Anyone approaching Tolkien's work cannot help but experience some of the same fascination, but such unraveling turns out to be a fraught and difficult exercise. Considering how often Tolkien himself provides clear statements in his writings about the exact works that influenced him, it can feel rather more difficult than it should.

A large part of the problem is that Tolkien read so very widely. As Shippey points out, the breadth of Tolkien's intellectual appetite

> is often disguised by the fact that he read "outside the syllabus," and had a habit of minimizing his reading, but his education . . . would have left him with at least as much grasp of Greek and Latin as a modern Classics major (probably, in these degenerate days, far more), and a very good understanding of the Bible (the same comment applies); while his whole professional life, not least as a lexicographer, depended on using all the information one could gather, unimpeded by any notion of "canonicity." All was grist that came to the philological mill.[11]

Conceivably, any work with even the remotest relation to the Western canon could legitimately be put forth for investigation as a source for Tolkien's work—and, as anyone familiar with the explosion of source criticism in Tolkien studies over the past two decades or so can attest, sometimes it can feel like most of them have.

This wide casting of the influence net is not necessarily a bad thing. Following M. M. Bakhtin, E. L. Risden points out that "'source' need not imply direct borrowing, but merely the stimulation or inflection of response. Source criticism thus becomes not just a multifaceted search for direct influences, but a nearly endless attention to background noise, generating innumerable mysteries, resonances, problems."[12] Mythological influence can be visualized as a braided river making its way slowly through a floodplain; waters join, mingle, flow together for a while, and then the mingled waters split and go separate ways, where they eventually join other flows. Those other flows may or may not have originated in the same stream as the first ones, but even if they did, they would have mingled and split in different ways and proportions during their individual upstream journeys. Some of these mythic flows are huge and strong, drawing immense amounts of creative energy along in their wake, and others are mere trickles that wander in tiny ribbons around large eyots before rejoining the main stream. The complexity of these flows is something that can never fully be unraveled. The most any scholar can hope to do is gaze a while at a particularly beautiful spot, carefully examine the water to see where it might have come from, and perhaps speculate on where it might be going.

It important to remember, in the midst of such scholarly speculation, that the nature of water is not at all exclusive. If through deep examination of one theme or character or incident a scholar spots clear traces of an earlier one, such recognition does not obviate the presence of other influences or other flows. As an example, since it is certain Tolkien knew both the *Völsunga Saga* and *The Song of Hiawatha*, from a mythological perspective there is no reason Smaug cannot draw on Fáfnir and Megissogwon both, and still allow for other upstream dragon ancestors such as the great nameless one who proved Beowulf's bane. Describing *The Hobbit* in a letter, Tolkien explained that the tale is "derived from (previously digested) epic, mythology, and fairy-story."[13] The digestion process can be seen as a creative and artistic one; it takes older beautiful things, breaks them down, and then recombines them into new and newly beautiful things. Tolkien's distaste for the academic predilection to search for and overvalue the predigested inputs can be plainly seen in yet another metaphor: "In Dasent's words I would say: 'We must be satisfied with the soup that is set before us, and not desire to see the bones of the ox out of which it has been boiled.' . . . By 'the soup' I mean the story as it is served up by its author or teller, and by 'the bones' its sources or material—even when (by rare luck) those can be with certainty discovered. But I do not, of course, forbid criticism of the soup as soup."[14] Nevertheless, it is (in Tom Shippey's words) "true, as they say, that you do not have to have the recipe to appreciate a cake: but it is also true that you can learn a lot from seeing what a great cook has in his kitchen."[15] Part I of this study, with its mythological purpose, will—with all due deference to Professor Tolkien—seek to appreciate the soup itself, as manifested in three specific historical moments in British literature, while simultaneously considering the amount and quality of the ingredients, how they might have interacted, and how they may interact in other combinations. To stretch Shippey's metaphor a bit, when a meal turns out to be especially delicious and healthful, analyzing the great cook's tools and techniques is a valuable exercise for those seeking to increase the overall enjoyment and health of future meals.

Tolkien's work draws on the entire spectrum of Western myth, legend, and literature, from Neolithic epics to twentieth-century spy novels, but a major feature of his fiction (and of the fantasy genre it would go on to inspire) stems from its medieval character. The ecocritical menu that follows, therefore, presents for analysis three well-known monuments of British medieval literature: the tenth-/eleventh-century Anglo-Saxon *Beowulf*, the twelfth-/thirteenth-century Middle Welsh *Mabinogion*, and the late fourteenth-century Middle English *Sir Gawain and the Green Knight*. Each of these works contributes a significant amount of mythical energy to the development of Tolkien's own tale, and each is a reasonably representative example of its own cultural milieu.

There is a great deal of excellent source criticism extant on Tolkien's relationship to these three works, as well as a growing amount of ecocriticism examining the works themselves. Rather than replowing old furrows, the analysis in part I will rely on such existing work. Each chapter will open with a general overview of current scholarship discussing the historical and cultural influence of the literary source on Tolkien's thinking, and then conduct an ecocritical examination of each source from a perspective specifically focused on the relationship between humans and the wild natural world.

In medieval Europe, this relationship was at a point of shocking transition. From one perspective, it was the culmination of more than five thousand years of human historical experience. In the grand sweep of history this is a minuscule amount of time, of course; Paleolithic humans wrote no epics but occupied the planet without significantly affecting it for forty thousand years. But after the Neolithic Revolution, everything changed. Soon the Sumerians had to range far afield for timber,[16] the Athenian navies so thoroughly denuded the trees from the islands of Greece that Plato himself comments on the deforestation in *Critias*,[17] and the Roman hunger for wheat arguably created the desert that is North Africa today.[18] From another perspective, though, the European mythological river had in medieval times not yet plunged over the Cartesian cliff. Nature was no longer divine in herself, but was still imbued with divine power. The varied conceptions of the human relationship to that power would shift, flow, and combine into something that would eventually become the inescapably ambiguous modern idea of wilderness.

But that is the concern of later chapters. For now, it is better to look backwards, toward the end of the first millennium CE, and focus attention on a few temperate islands rising out of the northeastern corner of the Atlantic Ocean.

CHAPTER ONE

Germanic Wilderness

Visualize the river of Western culture as it plunges around these islands, flowing past Celtic- and Germanic-speaking monks toiling away at insular monasteries. Imagine their stories as the provincial accoutrements of Classical Roman civilization crumble around them and Europe descends into the ages scholars would later refer to as Dark.

Tolkien knew as much about these ages as anyone reasonably could. Although his fiction eventually became a worldwide sensation, he was first and foremost a medievalist and an expert in Old and Middle English philology. He was a reader in English language at the University of Leeds, published a Middle English dictionary, collaborated on a scholarly edition of *Sir Gawain and the Green Knight,* and served as professor of Anglo-Saxon at Oxford University for nearly forty years. While he was deeply familiar with the entire corpus of Old and Middle English literature, it is clear that the most important work, both within that corpus and as part of the intellectual landscape of Tolkien's own life, was the Old English poem *Beowulf.*

There is zero critical disagreement about how large *Beowulf* loomed in Tolkien's world. It "was Tolkien's lodestar. Everything he did led up to or away from it."[1] He was considered "the first-ranked *Beowulf* scholar of his generation."[2] His landmark 1936 lecture to the British Academy is hailed as a watershed event in the history of *Beowulf* criticism, an "important monument of literary history,"[3] which is now "widely accepted as the starting point (i.e., the beginning) of literary criticism of *Beowulf.*"[4] What made

Tolkien's approach different from his predecessors was the fact that he "took for granted the poem's integrity and distinction as a work of art and proceeded to show in what this integrity and distinction inhered."[5] Before Tolkien, *Beowulf* was either falsely esteemed or unjustly censured for being "something that it was not," whether that thing was "primitive, pagan, Teutonic, an allegory (political or mythical), or . . . an epic" or "a heathen heroic lay, a history of Sweden, a manual of Germanic antiquities, or a Nordic *Summa Theologica*."[6] After Tolkien, literary criticism of the poem focused on the literary values of the poem *as a poem*. Had he written nothing else, "*Beowulf*: The Monsters and the Critics" would have been enough to rank Tolkien among the great critical thinkers of Western literature—and that fact that he did write something else has actually doubled back from his popular work to tremendously enrich his academic field, as today many of the most accomplished Tolkien scholars (Tom Shippey, Jane Chance, and Michael Drout, among others) are also renowned experts in Old English studies.

It would be only natural to find the themes and images of *Beowulf* present among the most significant mythic influences on Tolkien's fiction, and source critics overwhelmingly agree that this is the case. Verlyn Flieger implies that the *Beowulf* poet was the undisputed primary influence on Tolkien and refers to "Tolkien's master, the poet of *Beowulf*."[7] Tom Shippey is even more explicit in his statement that "the single work which influenced Tolkien most was obviously the Old English poem *Beowulf*."[8] Tolkien himself was conscious of the importance of the poem to his work; he claims directly—in an answer to a letter from a nonscholar fan asking about the obvious correspondences between *Beowulf* and *The Hobbit*—that "*Beowulf* is among my most valued sources."[9] In contrast to the numerous dissenting critical voices whose spirited argument about many other works of Western literature so enlivens the Tolkien studies field, the chorus of agreement regarding the influence of *Beowulf* on Tolkien's Middle-earth is nearly unanimous.

The direct correspondences between *Beowulf* and Tolkien's legendarium are too numerous to catalog exhaustively, so a few of the most obvious examples will have to suffice. The first, of course, is the clear parallel between Beowulf's dragon and Smaug in *The Hobbit*. "It is widely recognized that Tolkien drew the main outlines of the plot of the episode of the dragon's rampages from the plot of the final third of *Beowulf*,"[10] and specific details such as the theft of the cup and the dragon's deadly response solidly support this argument.

Another quite obvious correspondence between Middle-earth and the *middan-geard* of *Beowulf* is the culture of the Rohirrim. Tom Shippey observes that the chapter in book III of *The Lord of the Rings* titled "The King of the Golden Hall" is "straightforwardly calqued[11] on *Beowulf.* When Legolas says of Meduseld, 'The light of it shines far over the land,' he is translating line 311 of *Beowulf, lixte se léoma ofer landa fela.*"[12] The language of the Rohirrim is the Mercian dialect of Old English, and their culture is a careful and layered combination of the Anglo-Saxons of *Beowulf* and the "great lost romance" of the horse-loving Goths into "a people that never were, but that press closer and closer to the edge of might-have-been."[13] A list of point-by-point comparisons, from the exact procedure of approaching an audience with a king to the presence of an untrustworthy adviser sitting at that king's feet, is unnecessary here, although Thomas Honegger's interesting observation that "the more desperate the situation gets, the more Anglo-Saxon the Rohirrim become"[14] is worth noting as an indication that Tolkien was perhaps drawing more on his professional expertise as the action of his tale quickened.

In some ways Tolkien's concept of the *Beowulf* poet "was a version of himself, and his authorial person in creating *The Lord of the Rings* was a version of that *Beowulf* poet,"[15] with whom he "felt more than continuity . . . he felt a virtual identity of motive and of technique."[16] Of all of the works considered here, this oldest of English poems provides what might arguably be the clearest glimpse into Tolkien's view of his work and the artistic processes that created it. In a very real way, there would be no Middle-earth without *Beowulf.* This means that any insights that might be gained from examining the relationship between humankind and the natural world in this work are likely to be especially valuable when it comes time to examine Tolkien's own work in part II.

Certainly there is another Germanic influence on Tolkien nearly as strong as that of *Beowulf,* one flowing from the cold Scandinavian and Icelandic rivers of the Norse sagas. In his early schoolboy days at King Edward's School, Tolkien was already delivering papers on the *Völsunga Saga.*[17] He read and taught Old Norse language and literature during most of his academic life. He explicitly states that the names of the dwarves in *The Hobbit* (not to mention that of the great wizard Gandalf) are lifted verbatim from the Icelandic *Poetic Edda,* and he just as explicitly acknowledges both the clear debt that his dragon Smaug owes to Fáfnir and the one owed by his tragic dragonslayer Túrin Turamabar to Fáfnir's killer Sigurd.[18] Unfortunately, from the point of view of this study, the sagas in general and the *Völsunga Saga* in particular offer considerably fewer depictions of direct interaction between humankind and the natural world than are available in Old English poetry.

In one lecture on the *Poetic Edda,* Tolkien argued that "to a large extent the spirit of these poems which has been regarded as (a branch of) the common 'Germanic spirit'—in which there is some truth: Byrhtwold at Maldon would do well enough in Edda or Saga—is really the spirit of a special time,"[19] a time and spirit that are shared between the Old Norse and Old English worlds. While there are certainly rich cultural differences between the Icelandic settlers and the Anglo-Saxons, the extant Old English literature is actually older than the Norse,[20] and the similarities in their approaches to the natural world are close enough that any specific examination would likely prove repetitive. Christopher Tolkien wrote of the *Völsunga Saga* that his father "did not hold the author's artistic capacity in high regard."[21] This evident disdain, set against the obvious deep reverence he held for the *Beowulf* poet and his own belief in their common spirit, makes the Old English poem the natural choice for a text representative of the medieval Germanic world.

At the very beginning of his book *Wilderness and the American Mind,* Roderick Nash observes that the modern English word *wilderness* actually has its ultimate etymological origins in *Beowulf.*[22] In line 1430 of that poem, the words "*wyrmas ond wil-dēor*"[23] appear "in reference to savage and fantastic beasts inhabiting a dismal region of forests, crags, and cliffs."[24] Tolkien renders these words[25] as "serpents and beasts untamed,"[26] and Seamus Heaney uses "serpents and wild things."[27] So, although the fully developed modern word "'wild-dēor-ness,' the place of wild beasts"[28] would admittedly have to wait for the Middle English of Laȝamon's thirteenth-century Arthurian poem *Brut,* the seed of the idea has already sprouted here in the Old English of *Beowulf.* The wildness of the beasts becomes in this early word a characteristic of the representations of the whole of the natural world throughout Old English poetry.

On initial contact, in both Old English poetry in general and *Beowulf* in particular, wild nature is presented as unfriendly at best. Nash remarks that throughout *Beowulf* "the uninhabited regions are portrayed in the worst possible light—dank, cold, and gloomy."[29] Other scholars note how the mood of *Beowulf* is "unrelentingly Northern—brutal, cold, heroic, and severe,"[30] and observe that most of the described landscapes "are hostile and threatening: humankind is surrounded by desolate moors and fens, and the symbol of its life of civilization is not 'domesticated' landscape but the hall building in the stronghold, withstanding both human enemies and the menace of the wilderness."[31] This reflects a general perception regarding the early Germanic concept of the world as a gloomy unending forest of "hunger and cold, howl of wolf, grinding of ice, exile and misery of friendless men, bitter toil on a wintry ocean."[32] The people who inhabited this dark place in pre-Christian days are represented by the figure of "man alien in a hostile world, engaged in a struggle which he cannot win while the world lasts," as Tolkien himself puts it.[33] *Beowulf,* as one of the earliest surviving examples of extant Germanic literature, is certainly responsible for a good portion of this forbidding historical impression.

Examples abound in the text. At the first victory feast celebrating Beowulf's defeat of Grendel, the king's poet sings a heroic lay, in which he describes the winter endured by the Anglo-Saxon hero Hengest in the court of his enemies (lines 1127–35):

> But Hengest remained
> through the death-stained winter. . . .
> . . . . he thought of his homeland
> but he could not steer his ring-prowed ship
> on the cold sea; the deep heaved in storms,
> dark under wind; the waves froze
> in chains of shore-ice till the next year came.[34]

The coming of spring after this dark and brutal winter, although described in imagery somewhat more friendly than the icy fastnesses of the preceding season, represents neither joy nor relief but only the opportunity for revenge (lines 1135–41):

> Winter was gone,
> the lush fields fair. The exile departed,
> the guest, from the court; he thought more of vengeance,
> total and utter, than departure by sea,
> how to drive the matter to a full grief-meeting,
> that the Frisians be deeply remembered by sword.[35]

Gummere's observation how the Germanic "fierceness of delight in battle and slaughter makes the only contrast"[36] to the inhospitability of the land is fully on display here. It is not so much that there is no beauty present—any visitor to the Nordic countries in the springtime is quite likely to encounter pleasant spring meadows and budding trees perfectly analogous to those anywhere else in the world—it is that such beauty seems to receive only passing attention in the poetry of this coldly Northern place.

Another famous example of forbidding landscape in *Beowulf* is Hrothgar's description of the approach to the lake where Beowulf must do battle with Grendel's mother (lines 1357–76):

A secret land they guard, high wolf-country,
windy cliffs, a dangerous way
twisting through fens, where a mountain torrent
plunges down crags under darkness of hills,
the flood under the earth. Not far from here,
measured in miles, lies that fearful lake
overhung with roots that sag and clutch,
frost-bound trees at the water's edge.
. . . . Not a pleasant place!
Tearing waves start up from that spot,
black against the sky, while the gloomy wind
stirs awful storms till the air turns choking,
the heavens weep.[37]

At the mere, the king's predictions of a hostile land are proven true (lines 1413–16):

suddenly he came
upon stunted firs, gnarled mountain pines
leaning over stones, cold and gray,
a joyless wood. The water beneath
was stirred with blood.[38]

These lines are some of the most studied in *Beowulf*, and it is not without justification that they serve as a shortcut for the modern understanding of the Germanic concept of the natural world as grim and unforgiving.

An important Classical literary-historical parallel to this passage is the description of the "vaporous black lake near a deep cave"[39] marking the approach to the underworld in book VI of Virgil's *Aeneid*. Throughout the entire Old English period in Britain, "Virgil held a solid place in the schools" and "readers sought enlightenment about both specific particularities and global interpretation of their cherished poet."[40] As Magennis argues, "the literary pedigree for the kind of set-piece natural description in a narrative poem exemplified in *Beowulf* would be represented most familiarly for the educated early medieval readers by the epic verse of Vergil."[41] There are also significant parallels between these foreboding lines and St. Paul's vision of hell as described in another Old English composition, a loose translation of the Latin *Visio St. Pauli* recorded as sermon 17 of the tenth-century *Blickling Homilies.*[42] Although the question of whether one Old English work influenced the other or whether both derive from an unknown predecessor is also somewhat contested, this parallel argues that, to the newly Christianized Anglo-Saxons, "the landscape of the mere symbolizes Hell. It is a Garden of Evil, in which one of the race of Cain dwells, freezing in sin."[43] Here *Beowulf* clearly demonstrates some of the solid mythic resonances between the Germanic pagan heritage and the Classical and Christian imagery inherited from Rome.

The truth is that *Beowulf* is not a purely "Northern" work, and Tolkien understood this better than most. His own position on any direct influence of Latin epic on *Beowulf* is an uncertain one; he remarks that "the smaller points in which imitation might be perceived are inconclusive" but then suggests a "deeper likeness" based on the similar cultural and historical situations of Virgil and the Anglo-Saxon poet: "the great pagan on the threshold of the change of the world; and the great (if lesser) Christian just over the threshold of the great change in his time and place."[44] Indeed he nearly argues for the sort of loose mythological influence generally advocated in this study when he famously describes *Beowulf* as "a poem from a pregnant moment of poise, looking back into the pit, by a man learned in old tales who was struggling, as it were, to get a general view of them all, perceiving their common tragedy of inevitable ruin, and yet feeling this more *poetically* because he was himself removed from the direct pressure of its despair."[45] Tolkien is describing here a point in time when the Classical Christian and Northern heathen branches of the Western river had just begun to join and flow together. Without the literacy of Christianity, with its roots in the Near East and its trunk and lower branches growing out of Greece and Rome, very little indeed of Germanic mythic thought would have survived into modern times.[46] Acknowledging the presence of such mythological links to the Classical tradition also underlines some glimmers of hopeful light at other places in the *Beowulf* text, which may help to illuminate the cold

Northern darkness and break the icy grip of unrelenting grimness so associated with Old English poetry.

The most obvious such glimmer comes early in the poem, when in lines 92–98 the poet describes the "clear song of the scop," who in "melodious chant"

> told how the Almighty   had made the earth,
> this bright shining plain   which the waters surround;
> He, victory-creative,   set out the brightness
> of sun and moon   as lamps for earth-dwellers,
> adorned the green fields,   the earth, with branches,
> shoots, and green leaves;   and life He created,
> in each of the species   which live and move.[47]

This description of the Christian Creation seems to present a vision of the natural world somewhat more kindly than those encountered in later lines—but once the ice (so to speak) is broken, once the possibility of a respite from the icy Northern wastelands is recognized, it becomes clear that the poem is not quite so implacably dark as it is often portrayed.

There actually are pleasant landscapes in *Beowulf*. They are, to be sure, generally "landscapes inhabited by humankind, or friendly to the purposes of humankind,"[48] with the light and security of the hall sharply contrasted with the dark dangers of the wilderness. When Beowulf and his warriors land on the Danish shore, they head immediately for Hrothgar's bright hall at Heorot, described with imagery familiar to any reader of Tolkien (lines 306–11):

> The warriors hastened,
> marched in formation,   until they could see
> the gold-laced hall,   the high timbers,
> most splendid building   among earth-dwellers
> under the heavens   —the king lived there—
> its gold-hammered roofs   shone over the land.[49]

The dark and dangerous fenlands may be full of monsters, but where the king lives all is bright and splendid—until the sun goes down.

Images of light characterize positive encounters with the environment elsewhere in the poem, as well. In lines 222–23 Beowulf and company celebrate the end of their sea voyage when they see Denmark's "silvery sea-cliffs" and "high rocky shores, / broad headlands."[50] The brightness of these *brim-clifu blīcan*—in Tolkien "the cliffs beside the ocean gleaming"[51] or in Heaney "sunlit cliffs"[52]—highlights a landscape feature that feels downright cheerful, so cheerful it prompts gratitude from the adventurers in lines 227–28; they "gave thanks to God" that "the wave-road was smooth" and "had been easily crossed."[53] This is a clear incident of a positive rather than a negative experience of humans in their environment.

This experience is closely mirrored at the end of Beowulf's description of his harrowing swimming contest with Breca. After a legitimately grim passage full of dark seas crawling with sea monsters and bloody tides, his victory is heralded by light (lines 569–72):

> Light came from the east,
> God's bright beacon, and the seas calmed,
> till I saw at last the sea-cliffs, headlands,
> the windy shore.[54]

To further underscore the relationship between brightness and victory, Beowulf's boast to free the Danes from Grendel's darkness promises joy at the return of the light (lines 603–6):

> Whoever pleases
> may walk brave to mead once a new day,
> Tomorrow's dawn, the sun clothed in light
> shines from the south on the sons of men.[55]

The *sunne swegl-wered*—in Tolkien's words "the sun in skiey robes"[56] or Heaney's "scarfed in sun-dazzle"[57]—is the key imagery in Beowulf's vow to end the reign of Grendel's darkness.

While light and darkness are important tools used by the poet to characterize positive and negative human experiences of the wilderness, there is another contrast in the poem that even further muddies the waters of the general unfriendliness of the Old English natural world. The contrast lies within the boundaries of the concept of wilderness itself. As Magennis observes, the wilderness in *Beowulf* is conceived of "both as fenland and as mountainous moors, these being landscapes hostile to humankind. Forests and woods, on the other hand, feature in the symbolic landscape of the poem primarily as places of escape and retreat."[58] Close examination of the text supports this rather subtle distinction; in general, when threatened the monsters flee to their homes in the cold sea or dank and swampy fens, while humans seek their shelter in the embrace of the forest. In lines 2596–99, Beowulf's companions abandon him for the safety of the trees:

> But not at all did the sons of nobles,
> hand-picked comrades, his troop stand round him
> with battle-courage: they fled to the wood
> to save their lives.[59]

They do not come out until after the battle is over, in lines 2846–47, where the poet characterizes them as "faith-breaking cowards" who "gave up their forest."[60] In both instances, the Old English word *holt,* defined as "a wood, a copse,"[61] is used for the shelter among the trees to which the cowards flee. Beowulf uses his same word in lines 1392–94 for his promise that Grendel's avenging mother will "find no escape / in the depths of the earth, nor the wooded mountain (*fyrgen-holt*), / nor the bottom of the sea."[62] The same word also appears in the "safe cover" (*holt-wudu*) sought by the hunted stag in line 1369.

A modern mind, accustomed to lumping all uninhabited spaces into a loosely defined concept of "wilderness" that would include fens and forests both, might easily lose such a distinction among the numerous conceptual casualties of the translation process. But such distinctions can be solidly grounded in cultural and historical understanding of Northern peoples. Gummere notes that the land of the Germanic tribes "was one vast forest, broken by swamp or meadow, with here and there a stretch of open land."[63] Tacitus famously complained of the land of the Germanic tribes that it "either bristles with forests or festers with swamps,"[64] perhaps reflecting a certain characteristically Roman mistrust of forests. But, while pretty much everyone regarded marshy fens as unfriendly places, it is generally accepted that "the German loved his forest; and trees are everywhere near to his heart."[65] The concept of taking refuge in the forest resonates strongly in Western literature, both before and after the Anglo-Saxon period, and it appears several times in Tolkien's own work. As an example, in book III of *The Lord of the Rings,* Merry is faced with the choice between a frightening dark wood or an impending bloody clash between Orcs and men, and remarks that "the forest seems better to me, all the same, than turning back into the middle of a battle" before fleeing with Pippin into Fangorn.[66] But, despite its later presence in the Western imagination, this idea does not feature in Near Eastern or Classical myth. It is a generally Northern concept, and its beginnings can be glimpsed here, hidden and often lost among the references to the unfriendly *wyn-lēasne wudu* of *Beowulf*.[67]

It seems that the blanket characterization of "hall Good/wilderness Bad" usually attributed to Old English literature does not quite hold up under close scrutiny. The truth is that "Old English poetry presents not one, derivative representation but multiple, contradictory and often lively representations of 'the natural world.'"[68] A certain ambiguity surrounding the relationship between humans and their environment is found to some extent in all Western literature; it appears in the earliest Near Eastern Neolithic epics, and is quite a distinctive characteristic of Classical thought. But this northern expression of ambiguity departs from such earlier examples in its clear and remarkably complete foregrounding of the human experience. In parts of *Beowulf* the characterization of landscape sometimes actually seems to depend wholly on the mood of the humans passing through it.

This variance is demonstrated most convincingly in the differing depictions of the road that leads to the lair of the Grendelkin. Magennis observes in these differences the "completeness of the poem's subjection of physical reality to the expression of mood."[69] A modern conception of landscape is usually externally defined by certain unchanging physical characteristics, but the physical details of this particular road vary depending on the state of mind of the humans who happen to be traversing it at any given time. After following the blood trail of the dying Grendel to the dark lake, Hrothgar's men find the celebratory return trip a pleasant one (lines 853–56):

> Then home again the tried retainers,
> The young men too, gay as a hunt,
> came from the mere, joyful on horseback,
> well-mounted warriors.[70]

This is a good road, good enough that

> At times the warriors made their horses rear,
> let fine dark steeds go racing in contest
> wherever the footing was straight and firm,
> the paths well known.[71]

As Magennis observes, here there is "no hint of a sinister aspect to the scene."[72] And yet, when Beowulf and his men travel the same road to the same mere in preparation for the hero's battle with Grendel's mother, they find the landscape quite different. It is unquestionably the same way:

> The creature's tracks
> were plainly visible through the wood-paths,
> her trail on the ground; she had gone straight
> Toward the dark lands.[73]

One envisions the blood trail of the murdered Æschere mingling with that of Grendel along the path. But instead of a road "suitable for carefree horse-racing,"[74] lines 1408–11 describe how Beowulf and his men

> climbed up high
> into stony hills, the steep rock-lands,
> through narrow files, an unknown way,
> dangerous cliffs over water-snakes' caves.[75]

Essentially, the landscape is "inextricably involved with its inhabitants, and the fear it inspires depends on who is lurking in it: for the Danes joyfully following Grendel's bloody tracks in the sunshine ... it holds no terror, but for a similar group anticipating Grendel's mother it appears frightening and inhospitable."[76] On the last victorious trip home, bearing Grendel's head in victory, the path is once more experienced as a *cúþe strǣte,* "road well-known."[77] Neville proposes that this kind of changing landscape can "be read as less an external than an internal topography, a description of 'men's imaginative and psychological response to Grendel' rather than an actual physical place."[78] This kind of relativistic experience describes a world in which the separation between humans and their environment reaches levels nearly bordering on the solipsistic.

Nearly, but not completely. Just as the landscape of *Beowulf* is grim but not quite unrelentingly grim, it is not quite completely psychological either. While the natural world is undoubtedly defined by human experience in the poem, it also simultaneously defines the humans who experience it, or at least sets the boundaries around what is often considered the highest Northern value: heroism. Tolkien's spirited defense of the monsters reclaimed the poem from its mischaracterization of a "heroic lay" as defined by later Germanic literature such as the sagas, and his construction results in a conception of Beowulf as a far greater hero than any nonsupernatural human conflict could ever create. There is a reason that Beowulf's adventures are still current today, while very few can name the deeds of, say, Ingeld son of Froda[79]—and that reason is tied to the monsters who inhabit these changing landscapes. As Tolkien himself observes, "Grendel is an enemy who has attacked the centre of the realm, and brought into the royal hall the outer darkness, so that only in daylight can the king sit upon the throne. This is something quite different and more horrible than a 'political' invasion of equals."[80] That which makes Grendel such a terrible foe is the same thing that makes Beowulf such an admirable hero, and this elusive thing is tightly bound up in the ambiguities of the relationship between the Danes and their unfriendly world.

Much critical disdain has been heaped upon Hrothgar and his people for their twelve years of helplessness in the face of Grendel's depredations. However, as Neville proposes, if Grendel is conceived of as a personification of the uncontrollable natural world, then his "easy domination merely reflects humanity's normal limits, since the natural world's power inevitably exceeds that of the human race. . . . the nobility in Hrothgar's court hinders Grendel's destruction of life and property no more effectively than it could halt a thunderstorm."[81] In the face of this uncontrollability, the magnitude of Beowulf's heroism becomes apparent.

> Beowulf's interactions with the natural world similarly reveal his singularity, his distinction from normal humanity. From his first presentation of himself to Hrothgar to his choice of burial place, Beowulf is circumscribed—both "written about" and limited—by the natural world. . . . Beowulf not only enters but characteristically immerses himself—alone—in the natural world. . . . The implication is that success in battle is not enough to distinguish Beowulf from other strong warriors. Such distinction requires success against the natural world's superior power.[82]

Neville's characterization here wraps up the various complex strands of the representation of the natural world in *Beowulf* into a neat package that highlights an almost fully modern ideological separation of humans from their environment.

If the very physical details of an environment depend upon the human experience of it, and yet the destructive power of that environment remains as uncontrollable as a thunderstorm, it is little wonder that the world is largely described as cold and unfriendly and that the heroes of humankind are the ones who can face its power without fear. As Neville describes, "the apparently similar hostility with which the natural world faces humanity . . . reveals inconsistencies: having defined humanity as helpless before forces too powerful for it to oppose, the natural world is still available to define human society as a potent defence, necessary for survival in the face of such forces."[83] If Germanic literature in general, and *Beowulf* in particular, says anything about the natural world, it is that most human beings are helpless in the face of its power, but also that renown follows from having the strength and fortitude to oppose it, even knowing that such opposition will mean the hero's inevitable death.

This deeply Germanic idea is one of the strongest elements in modern English literature. But if the modern English differ in their mythic world view from their Continental or Scandinavian cousins, the difference likely stems from the point where the river of Old English cultural experience first plunged into the isle of Britain. There it encountered another flow, one vastly different in its conception of the wild natural world—different, but no less powerful.

CHAPTER TWO

Celtic Wilderness

When Tolkien's beloved Anglo-Saxons came to Britain, they did not find the island uninhabited. The Celtic-speaking peoples from whom the British take their name had a unique Insular culture shaped by the archipelagic environment, the turbulent years of Roman occupation and subsequent abandonment, and an early conversion to Christianity that expanded the benefits of literacy to include some of the common people much earlier than in many places on the Continent. The cultural ideas of these Britons mingled with those of the Angles, Saxons, and Jutes to form the basis of what Tolkien thought of as the true (i.e., pre-Norman) English cultural experience.

While the supremely Teutonic *Beowulf* is universally recognized for its importance to Tolkien's work, the influence of the Celtic world is a bit more critically contested. The arguments against it rest largely on the evidence of a letter Tolkien sent in response to a somewhat unflattering review given by a publisher's reader of an early version of the *Quenta Silmarillion.* That letter criticized the *Silmarillion*'s "eye-splitting Celtic names" and "mad, bright-eyed beauty that perplexes all Anglo-Saxons in face of Celtic art."[1] Tolkien's response is characteristically testy: "I am sorry the names split his eyes. . . . They are coherent and consistent and made upon two related linguistic formulae. . . . Needless to say they are not Celtic! Neither are the tales. I do know Celtic things (many in their original languages Irish and Welsh), and feel for them a certain distaste: largely for their fundamental unreason. They have bright color, but are like a broken stained glass window reassembled without design."[2] This apparently unequivocal statement has done a lot to discourage critics from the investigation of Tolkien's Celtic sources over the years.[3] Like many things Tolkien said in letters, however, it is not even fully consistent with things he said in other letters. When his irritated statement is set alongside his later assertion that his Elven language Sindarin (undeniably one of the "related linguistic formulae" he described) was "deliberately devised to give it a linguistic character very like (though not identical with) British-Welsh . . . because it seems to fit the rather 'Celtic' type of legends and stories told of its speakers,"[4] he even begins to appear a bit disingenuous.

More recent scholarship on Tolkien's Celtic sources has identified a much more nuanced picture of possible influences than his 1937 letter might indicate.[5] Dimitra Fimi argues that Tolkien's attitude toward the Celtic cultural world was fairly complex and proposes that the distaste he expressed in this letter and elsewhere was more directed at a somewhat misleading "romantic idea of 'Celticness,'" than at actual "things Celtic."[6] Similarly, J. S. Lyman-Thomas suggests that Tolkien's testy letter should be considered "more the rebuke of a layman by a professional scholar" than a blanket disavowal, and that "the disparagement of 'Celtic things' that for so long discouraged scholars from investigating his use of Irish, Welsh, and other so-called Celtic material was based on a fundamental misinterpretation."[7] Tolkien taught courses on Medieval Welsh at Leeds, and he stated many times in his writings that he found "an abiding linguistic-aesthetic satisfaction" in the Welsh language.[8] More tellingly, in an indication of the high level of expertise in Celtic studies perceived in him by his distinguished colleagues, he served as Oxford's "first speaker of the prestigious O'Donnell lectures . . . established to discuss the Celtic element in the English language."[9] In that lecture, published later under the title "English and Welsh," Tolkien asserted that "Welsh is of this soil, this island, the senior language of the men of Britain; and Welsh is beautiful," and confirmed that *The Lord of the Rings* "contains, in the way of presentation that I find most natural, much of what I personally have received from the study of things Celtic."[10] Considering that Tolkien delivered "English and Welsh" the day after *The Return of the King* was published,[11] the lecture's attitude toward "things Celtic" seems to reflect more accurately on the ideas of his work than the irritated (and much earlier) letter quoted above.

Once the stream of influence from the non-Germanic branches of the British world is acknowledged, mythological parallels between Celtic ideas and Tolkien's work are not hard to find. The fierce army of fighting trees in the Welsh poem *Cad Goddeu* thunders into battle very much in the manner of Treebeard and his Ents, while the "perilous forests of Welsh legend echo in Tolkien's Mirkwood and Lothlórien."[12] Supplementing the Norse and Anglo-Saxon lore that went into the creation of Smaug is another a detail regarding that worthy dragon's home in the Lonely Mountain: "whereas neither the *Beowulf* dragon nor the Norse Fáfnir is associated with a mountain in this way, the White and Red Dragons of Welsh tradition are associated with Snowdon, the highest mountain in Wales."[13] Tom Shippey sees Welsh influence in *The Silmarillion* as well: "the hunting of the great wolf [in "Of Beren and Lúthien" in the *Quenta Silmarillion*] reminds one of the chase of the boar Twrch Trwyth in the Welsh *Mabinogion*."[14] A reasonably contemporary review of *The Lord of the Rings* notes that "the marriage of Aragorn and Arwen is mainly Celtic in conception—it might be a clear statement of the mightily confused situation of Pwyll, or Manawyddan, and Rhiannon in the *Mabinogion*," opines that the Elves' immortality is "very like the Gaelic *Tir na nOg*," and suggests that "the elves are Celtic in language and fate."[15]

This 1957 review captures an early glimpse of what has since become recognized as perhaps the most obvious (and certainly the most critically commented upon) connection between Celtic myth and Tolkien's legendarium: his Elves. In his tradition, they are "sages and warriors and lovers," a characterization that is found less in early Germanic literature than in "medieval works such as *Sir Orfeo*, the *Mabinogion*, certain Arthurian romances, and the legends of the Tuatha de Danaan,"[16] all of which have obvious Celtic connections.[17] Fimi observes that the "things Celtic" present in Tolkien's Middle-earth are "mainly associated with the Elves and Valinor" and notes how "for anyone familiar with medieval Irish literature, there is a striking similarity between the Noldor, the Elves that rebelled against the Valar and abandoned Valinor to return to Middle-earth, and the Tuatha Dé Danann, the semi-divine creatures of Irish mythology and ultimately of Irish folklore."[18]

Verlyn Flieger quips that "Tolkien's immortal Elves—the Vanyar, the Noldor, the Teleri, the Sindar, the Wood-elves in all their hidden kingdoms and Elven fastnesses of Doriath and Gondolin and Nargothrond and Lórien and the Undying lands—are as faërian, as otherworldly, as dangerously beautiful and typically Celtic a bunch as any who ever came out of a fairy mound, or peopled the haunted woodlands and enchanted keeps and castles of the Arthurian world."[19] Similarly, Alfred Siewers cites "the overlay landscape of the Elven realms in Tolkien's fantasy" as its "most distinctive Celtic element, echoing the Otherworld common to both early Welsh and Irish literatures."[20] While some elements of Tolkien's Elven cultures do have parallels in later English, early Germanic, or even Mediterranean myth, the greatest debt they owe is to these Celtic ideas. Their presence firmly establishes that traces of the Celtic streams flowing into the river of what would become medieval England are worthy of study for their influence on the lands and peoples of Middle-earth.

In selecting a medieval Celtic text to examine here, the two clearest choices are the Irish Ulster Cycle with its central text of the *Táin Bó Cúailnge* (generally known in English as *The Cattle Raid of Cooley*) and the collection of stories in Middle Welsh known today as the *Mabinogion*. These roughly contemporaneous texts are prose epics that "present culturally foundational 'retro' narratives that resist aspects of rising Western European culture in the twelfth century."[21] These two mythological cycles share some cognate names and appear to be loosely related (although scholars differ on any directions or sharing of influence). While there is no doubt that Tolkien knew both works, in deference to his aesthetic antipathy to the Irish language[22] and his oft-professed love of Welsh, this study will focus on the *Mabinogion*, which can ably serve as a text representative of the medieval Celtic world.

Tolkien's familiarity with the *Mabinogion* is well attested. In their exhaustive three-volume *J. R. R. Tolkien Companion and Guide*, Christina Scull and Wayne G. Hammond note several opportunities for Tolkien to have attended lectures at Oxford delivered by the noted Welsh scholar Sir John Rhys.[23] Tolkien's copy of Lady Charlotte Guest's famous translation of the work "includes marginal annotations that show he read it alongside the Welsh text, correcting Guest's version and noting where she had made omissions."[24] It is also generally accepted that the hobbit manuscript known as the *Red Book of Westmarch*, which Tolkien identifies as the "most important source for the history of the War of the Ring" in his prologue to *The Lord of the Rings*,[25] is actually a "small scholarly joke"[26] echoing the *Red Book of Hergest*, one of the two surviving manuscripts in which the stories of the *Mabinogion* are collected.

The *Mabinogion* is, to modern sensibilities, a difficult text. The eleven stories it collects "comprise an ensemble of rather heterogeneous parts," as one translator wryly puts it.[27] They are somewhat nonlinear and have the repetitive-feeling formulaic character of oral poetry jumbled together with the narrative sweep of prose without any apparent direction. The first four stories, generally known as the "Four Branches of the *Mabinogi*" because of their similar last lines, alternate in location between south and north Wales and are loosely organized around a dynasty of legendary semidivine Welsh rulers. The other seven tales in the cycle resist even this rudimentary classification. Five are Arthurian; three of these site Arthur's court at Caerleon and tell tales familiar to readers of Chrétien de Troyes's famous French romances, one portrays an unusually robust and dynamic King Arthur on a wild quest to help one of his vassals gain a bride, and the last can be described as "satirizing not only the elaborate descriptions of Arthurian knights, their horses, and their trappings, but also the structure of medieval romance itself."[28] The two remaining tales deal with Romano-British material that seems to link Welsh culture to that of a (pre–Anglo-Saxon) golden age in Roman Britain. With all this seeming "fundamental unreason," readers unfamiliar with this kind of storytelling often find themselves empathizing with Tolkien's metaphor of a brightly colored but poorly assembled "broken stained glass window" described above.

Many nineteenth-century critics, even those supportive of Celtic literature, responded to this difficulty with condescension, sometimes even describing the unknown Welsh author as "pillaging an antiquity of which he does not fully possess the secret; he is like a peasant building his hut on the site of Halicarnassus or Ephesus" using stone "of an older architecture,[29] greater, cunninger, more majestical."[30] It was not until the later part of the twentieth century that scholars seriously began to dispute this characterization as the "confused rubble of a ruined mythological system."[31] The problem, similar to that railed against by Tolkien as he castigated the *Beowulf* critics for demanding that poem be something it is not, is that in considering the narrative unity or structure of medieval texts many critics start

> from a false premise, for they seem to assume that a text, even if mediæval and not a product of a Continental-European tradition, must have a unity in the Aristotelian or post-Aristotelian sense, that is, that the story must have a linear progression or sequence of events, a clear narrative thread that proceeds from the exposition through to the conclusion, when the action is satisfactorily resolved, whilst any subsidiary narrative threads contribute directly to the main one. Moreover, it has been tacitly assumed that such a "unity" is synonymous with literary excellence in absolute terms.[32]

Despite their brilliance and color, there is no way that these Welsh tales can meet such a standard—and yet they were, at great expense of money, materiel, and manpower, carefully copied out by hand onto precious vellum several times, a fact that supports the argument that they were "entirely acceptable to the Welsh public in the second half of the Middle Ages" just as they were.[33] In order to appreciate such texts, it is certainly necessary to approach them on their own terms and allow them to shape their own structure.

Of the many different tracks critics have followed in searching for such terms and structure, many have focused on the abiding sense of place that imbues the text. Especially in the case of the Four Branches, readers "have the experience, not often to be had with a medieval romance, of pointing to places that were known by an author nine centuries ago, who used them in the most natural and down-to-earth way as the scenes for wonder, love and the supernatural."[34] Alfred Siewers observes that the cycle of the *Mabinogi* "unfolds a landscape-narrative of Wales that can still be followed on foot and tracked on maps of western Britain," and proposes that the landscape, "in dialogue with the landscape of a larger retrospectively remembered Celtic Britain, becomes the central character.[35] The human is embedded in this landscape."[36] This pure landscape orientation, where the humans are a part of the story of the landscape rather than vice versa, may contribute to the sense of dislocation felt by readers more accustomed to the undisputed centrality of human experience.

This deep rootedness in place is acknowledged in the Welsh character by Celticist John Bollard. "Awareness of the meaning and effect of places, with their multiple layers of history and narrative, runs deep in Wales," he observes; "the place represents the tale, in a sense it *is* the tale, and the tale has something to teach us."[37] The tale of Lleu Llaw Gyffes in the Fourth Branch is a good example.[38] To create a wife for Lleu (who is under a curse "that he will never have a wife from the race that is on this earth at present"), a sorcerer and a ruler "took the flowers of the oak, and the flowers of the broom, and the flowers of the meadowsweet, and from those they conjured up the fairest and most beautiful maiden that anyone had ever seen."[39] Lleu married the beautiful girl and "set up a court in the cantref at a place called Mur Castell, in the uplands of Ardudwy."[40] Unfortunately for the young hero, his bride proved unfaithful to him at the first opportunity, and through a fantastic chain of events her lover struck Lleu with a poisoned spear. He then "flew up in the form of an eagle and gave a horrible scream, and he was not seen again" until he was transformed back into a man and the flower-woman and her maidens fled from his vengeance, "so afraid that they could only travel with their faces looking backwards. And they knew nothing until they fell into the lake and were drowned."[41]

Mur Castell today is a brooding hill with a medieval mound overlooking the ruins of a Roman camp at Tomen y Mur in North Wales.[42] There is a lake about three miles from Tomen y Mur called Llyn y Morynion, "the Lake of the Maidens."[43] Bollard suggests that "if a Welsh man or woman heard this name [Tomen y Mur], not only would the place and the story be called to mind, but also the social consequences of adultery, especially to anyone with adultery on their mind."[44] Modern readers, accustomed to realistic stories set in real-world places, might not notice how unusual this clear physical link between place and tale is for Western medieval literature. Beowulf's grand adventures take place in an area that can only be narrowed to somewhere in southern Scandinavia, the location of Camelot has never been convincingly determined, and even the great city of Troy had to wait for modern archaeology to establish its real-world existence. But people today can visit this Welsh lake, climb the hill, and put their hands on the mossy green mound where the poets say Lleu had his court and his wife took a lover with such disastrous consequences, and the reality of the ancient landscape becomes, in an unusually experiential way, inseparable from the reality of the medieval tale.[45]

But the modern, pragmatic, Western European sensibility objects: the landscape may be real, certainly, but the magical occurrences in the tale are patently not. In the "real" world, women are not conjured from flowers and men do not transform into eagles when struck by poisoned spears, no matter how old or interesting the obscure names assigned to crumbling antiquities at the top of green hills might be. This objection leads to another very important characteristic of the environment in the *Mabinogion,* and one that would later be used to great effect by Tolkien in his own work: there is present an "Otherworld" intertwined with and overlaid upon the normal world of human experiences.

Alfred Siewers describes this Otherworld as "a type of overlay or multiplex landscape that integrates aspects of spiritual, imaginative, and natural realms of human life and the physical environment, including wilderness and animals, and that permits shape-shifting as well as transport through time and space."[46] There are some similarities between this characteristically Celtic idea and the way the natural world is conflated with the supernatural in Old English poetry; in *Beowulf,* sea monsters and wolves, demons and deer "all inhabit the same landscapes and interact with human beings in parallel ways. . . . As a result, on a basic level the Anglo-Saxons did not have a word or expression for the modern conception of the natural world because they did not conceive of an entity defined by the exclusion of the supernatural."[47] Such similarities most likely derive as much from the pre-Thomist intellectual period shared by the two cultures as from any mythic relationship between them, however. Siewers points out that "the linguistic distinction of a supernatural category of life as opposed to the natural only emerged sharply in what is now Western Europe with the flourishing of Scholasticism, shaping 'a particular mental geography in which events could be assigned to particular domains, this natural, that supernatural.'"[48] Both the *Mabinogion* and *Beowulf* are products of times predating this Aristotelian shift in thinking. But, whatever the provenance of the mingling of natural and supernatural in these two works, the influence of the Celtic version on Tolkien is clearly reflected in the Otherworldly yet vitally present status of the Elven realms in Middle-earth.

Consider the magical mound of Gorsedd Arberth, which appears several times in the *Mabinogion;* in the First Branch, it is said that "the strange thing about the mound is that whatever nobleman sits on it will not leave there without one of two things happening: either he will be wounded or injured, or else he will see something wonderful."[49] The danger in this description, although clearly present, is the danger of unknown adventures, not the grim and bloody menace of the fiendish horrors plaguing the hapless king Hygelac. The other-than-human inhabitants of these liminal Celtic realms are "natural though magical beings, reciprocal mirrors of human life setting limits to human behavior," which have not been demonized in the way of the Grendelkin in *Beowulf.*[50] They are wonders, not monsters—although they, like the humans they reflect (and also like Tolkien's Elves, who draw so deeply upon their influence), occasionally act in monstrous ways.

Sometimes in the *Mabinogion* it almost seems like the work is intentionally seeking to distinguish itself through a deep landscape orientation from the Continental European conquerors who controlled Britain at the time. Siewers argues that "implicit in mindfulness of loss throughout the *Mabinogi* . . . is the loss of most of Britain to the Anglo-Saxons and . . . Anglo-Normans."[51] In the Third Branch, another adventure-prefacing visit to Gorsedd Arberth causes a curse of emptiness to fall on Dyfed:

> They heard a tumultuous noise, and with the intensity of the noise there fell a blanket of mist . . . And after the mist, everywhere became bright. When they looked to where they had once seen the flocks and herds and dwelling-places, they could now see nothing at all, neither building nor beast, neither smoke nor fire, neither man nor dwelling-place, only the court buildings empty, desolate, uninhabited, without people, without animals in them; their own companions had disappeared, with nothing known of their whereabouts.[52]

The deep bond between the land and its people has been severed. Only the heroes remain. Siewers makes the important observation that, as opposed to later English or Continental ideas of the Wasteland as an infertile place incapable of sustaining human life, this curse instead "brought not a landscape devoid of nature and animals and fecundity, or even court buildings, but a landscape devoid of other humans."[53] The land is still fertile; the lonely heroes are able to plant three wheat fields in which "the wheat sprang up the best in the world . . . flourishing alike so that no one had seen wheat finer than that."[54] It is the land that is cursed by its loss of humanity, not humans cursed by loss of their land's fertility. Again, the landscape is foregrounded in a somewhat dislocating way.

This cursed Welsh landscape is then explicitly contrasted with other lands; to survive, the royal heroes travel to England and take up trades, only to be chased out of town after town because their saddles, shields, and shoes are so good that the English "townsmen became angry with them and agreed to try and kill them."[55] This narrative characterization "associated England with hostile urban landscapes of commercialism, its people envious of the naturally magical craftsmanship of native heroes,"[56] while the heroes roaming across the Welsh realm of Dyfed "had never seen a place more pleasant to live in, nor better hunting ground, nor land more abundant in honey and fish."[57] Dyfed is consistently portrayed, much like Tolkien's Shire, "as smiling and welcoming country. The author had positive identification with it . . . but not with Scotland, Ireland, or England, all seen more or less negatively in terms of treachery and insecurity."[58] In order to lift the curse, the hero returns to magical Gorsedd Arberth to hang a mouse he had caught stealing his wheat; the "trio of succeeding ecclesiastical personages (clerk, priest, and bishop)" who try to stop his murder of the mouse are likely an "anachronistic association with Norman power . . . in terms of ecclesiastical impositions."[59]

The hero triumphs in the battle of wits against these pesky churchmen (the last of whom turns out to be an evil sorcerer in disguise), and Dyfed is restored to its accustomed beauty and abundance.

The presence of Anglo-Norman influence is at its most overt in the *Mabinogion*'s Arthurian tales, particularly the three stories that demonstrate obvious kinship with the romances of Chrétien de Troyes (and that are accordingly a bit more accessible to modern readers than the Four Branches). Here the landscape is not so deeply rooted in the physical rocks and trees of western Britain. One translator notes both the odd "lack of specific geography," as well as the fact that the tales are "more genteel and romantic" than the earlier ones, "overlaid with continental notions of chivalry and good manners."[60] While it is true that Arthur maintains his court at historic Caerleon-upon-Usk, "there are no clear geographical or political boundaries to his kingdom, and the action takes place in a somewhat unreal, daydream-like world."[61] It is almost as though, in response to the cultural and linguistic pressures of the conquerors in these later tales, the balance of the perfectly blended overlay landscape is tipped in the stories toward the Otherworld and away from the unpleasant reality of occupied Wales.

Consider "Peredur son of Efrog," the tale from the *Mabinogion* that corresponds to the *Perceval* of Chrétien de Troyes. Chrétien names his hero a Welshman, and takes advantage of the French chivalric stereotype that "all Welshmen are by nature more stupid than beasts in the field"[62] to demonstrate young Perceval's foolishness. However, in the Welsh tale Peredur hails not from one of the Welsh kingdoms but from "an earldom in the North,"[63] which might account for the "veneer of French manners" present in the tale.[64] The land of Peredur's travels is much more loosely correlated with "real" places than in the Four Branches. Nevertheless, the Otherworld is just as deeply interlaced with everyday experience, with wonders to be encountered nearly around every corner.

While Peredur's numerous adventures through this landscape of wonder have struck many critics as disconnected or arbitrary, Ceridwen Lloyd-Morgan argues for the presence of several different but carefully integrated themes. One relevant to this study is what she calls the "journey motif," or a "pattern of riding alone through wilderness or forest," which she points out is common to nearly all Arthurian literature[65] (and that is a common pattern in Tolkien's narratives as well, although his tales tend more toward fellowships and companies than solitary wanderers).

The oral character of this particular text provides a specific linguistic formula that is repeated over and over to introduce each new encounter. No less than five times Peredur finds himself in a new place described nearly verbatim as one previously:

> Then he came to a great, desolate forest, and far into the forest he could see a clearing of open ground, and in the clearing he could see a pavilion.[66]

> And finally he came to a great, desolate forest, and at the edge of the forest was a lake, and on the other side of the lake was a large court and a fine fortress around it.[67]

> He came to a great forest, and at the far end of the forest he came to a level meadow, and beyond the meadow he could see a great fortress and a beautiful court.[68]

> Meanwhile Peredur went on his way and came to a great, desolate forest. He could see neither the tracks of men nor herds in the forest, only thickets and vegetation. And when he comes to the far end of the forest, he can see a great, ivy-covered fortress with many strong towers.[69]

> Cross that mountain over there, and you will see a lake, and a fortress within the lake. And it is called the Fortress of Wonders.[70]

Although likely derived from oral poetic formulae, upon closer examination this repetition proves not to be solely formulaic. While the same words are used to introduce each episode, and the basic elements of forest and dwelling are present, the descriptions become more detailed and the locations move up in magnificence as Peredur's character develops. A mere pavilion provides the setting for the young and rather churlish fool, not yet a knight; he then proceeds through encounters with a series of larger and finer edifices as he gains skill, until finally (after fourteen years of rule as the consort of the Empress of Constantinople) he is fit to enter the fantastic Fortress of Wonders. Even under the influence of Anglo-Norman ideas, the landscape still manages to project itself forward, to assert the "reciprocally relational landscape between the Otherworld and the human world," which Siewers identifies as a central organizing principle of these tales.[71] The reflective correlation of hero and land, though less specific than in earlier Welsh literature, is nonetheless still strongly present—and it would go on to have great influence on medieval Western literature in general and on Tolkien in particular.

Siewers concludes his study of the medieval Celtic Otherworld with observations of this far-ranging influence: "The landscapes of the *Mabinogi*, and those of the early Irish Sea zone generally, remain obscured yet still activated tropes of iconographic resistance to the Western tendency to reform nature into interiorized virtual reality. They remain influences on, or at least supporting analogues with, green worlds of English literature to come—through fourteenth-century revival in Chaucer and the *Gawain* poet, to Malory, Spenser, Shakespeare, and beyond."[72] There is no doubt of the influence these landscapes exerted on Tolkien, both directly from the Welsh literature and through the later intermediaries Siewers mentions. As the years passed, the Germanic and Celtic cultural influence of the conquered British citizenry slowly began to seep into the Continental Anglo-Norman world view. By the late fourteenth century, this mingling interaction developed into a literature that is identifiable today as uniquely English.

CHAPTER THREE

English Wilderness

While *Beowulf* is generally accepted as the center of Tolkien's academic and professional life, it only just surpasses the later Middle English texts of the manuscript known today as *Cotton Nero A.x.* This manuscript is the only surviving witness to four poems written by an anonymous fourteenth-century author in a northwest Midlands dialect of Middle English: *Purity, Patience, Pearl,* and the justly famous alliterative Arthurian tale of *Sir Gawain and the Green Knight.* As with the anonymous author of *Beowulf,* critics generally agree that this poet was of extreme importance to Tolkien. He "first encountered *Gawain* at King Edward's School . . . and it remained a lifelong preoccupation and a focus for much of his scholarly activity."[1] Tom Shippey observes that Tolkien's engagement with this material "lasted almost the whole of his professional or writing life," and goes on to explain that "Tolkien had the *Gawain*-poet in mind for at least fifty years. His first work . . . was the joint edition of *Sir Gawain and the Green Knight . . .* [with] his Leeds colleague E. V. Gordon . . . in 1925. It was an enormously successful book, which altered the whole current of English medieval studies—till then heavily Southern and Chaucerian in bias . . . and which is still in 1993 the standard edition."[2] Other critics agree; Flieger describes Tolkien's "long and fruitful association" with the poem.[3] "Excluding his seminal essay on *Beowulf,*" observes Miriam Youngerman Miller, "Tolkien's scholarly efforts were primarily devoted to the *Gawain* poet."[4] Stuart Lee and Elizabeth Solopova point out that "Tolkien's interest in the poem is attested by the volume of research he devoted to it as a medievalist,"[5] and John Rateliff argues that the poem "clearly held his lifelong attention and affection."[6] Tolkien's translations of two of the *Gawain* poet's works (*Sir Gawain and the Green Knight* and *Pearl*) along with another Middle English romance (*Sir Orfeo*) were complete but unpublished at the time of his death; these were edited and published in a single volume by his son Christopher in 1975.

Tolkien clearly held this anonymous West Midlands poet in high regard. In a 1953 lecture in Glasgow, he praised *Sir Gawain and the Green Knight* as "one of the masterpieces of fourteenth-century art in England, and of English Literature a whole," and described it as belonging to "that literary kind which has deep roots in the past, deeper even than its author was aware. It is made of tales often told before and elsewhere, and of elements that derive from remote times beyond the vision or awareness of the poet."[7] Indeed, Miller argues that the "correspondences between *Sir Gawain and the Green Knight* and *The Lord of the Rings* are pervasive and bespeak an absorption on Tolkien's part of the *Gawain*-poet's work which borders perhaps on identification."[8] Shippey expands on this idea of identification: "Tolkien saw the *Gawain*-poet—as he had earlier presented the *Beowulf*-poet—as an artist in vital respects much like himself: someone deeply embedded in a Christian and Catholic tradition, but nevertheless . . . ready to make use of the lost, popular, monster-creating, 'fairy-tale' traditions" of English culture.[9] In Tolkien's own words, the poet was "capable of weaving elements taken from diverse sources" into a unique texture, and also a person who would "have in that labour a serious purpose."[10] The hindsight of half a century of critical work on Tolkien's legendarium make the applicability of such criticism to his own work quite obvious.

Curiously, despite the nearly unanimous critical agreement about the importance of the *Gawain* poet in Tolkien's intellectual life, direct plot parallels in Middle-earth of the sort highlighted in the previous chapters are somewhat thin on the ground in *Sir Gawain and the Green Knight*. At one extreme, Roger Schlobin only just acknowledges that Gawain might serve as a source for Tolkien from "a moral or philosophical perspective," insists that "nothing can be directly proved regarding the influence of *Gawain*" on Tolkien,[11] and finally (if grudgingly) accepts that "within the violence of the epic form and within his interpretation of *Gawain*, Tolkien chooses the kindlier virtues—forgiveness, mercy, pity, learning, nobility, humility, friendship, loyalty—much as the *Gawain* poet does."[12] Other scholars, although more liberal in their allowances, still rely more on thematic and technical arguments than plot parallels to establish a source relationship. John M. Fyler notes that many "familiar thematic patterns" of *Gawain* are present in *The Lord of the Rings*, and argues that the poem "was much on Tolkien's mind[13] when he was writing the trilogy."[14] Miller, after touching on details of the generic quest aspect present in most medieval literature, argues that "Tolkien's most important debt to the *Gawain*-poet . . . is technical, the specific methods used to create and sustain a credible fantasy," and she analyzes the "carefully constructed secondary worlds" and "framework of historicity" within the "provision of enormously detailed technical accounts of their invented worlds."[15] She also notes thematic parallels between the works, including an "emphasis on youth," the presence of morally ambiguous nature figures in the Green Knight and Tom Bombadil, and "many trials of fidelity and courage" for both Gawain and Frodo, who "commence to fulfill their quests, only to find that both have been unaware of the true natures of their tests."[16] In general, despite this dearth of specific shared plot elements, the similarity in tone and theme between Tolkien's work and *Sir Gawain and the Green Knight*—the medieval feel of the modern fantasy as well as the relatively modern ideas of the medieval romance—are compellingly present to even the most casual reader of both works.

Before turning to the text of *Sir Gawain and the Green Knight*, it is important to acknowledge that the *Gawain* poet is certainly not the only great late medieval English author; any discussion that did not at least mention Geoffrey Chaucer would be guilty of a grave omission indeed. Tolkien certainly knew and respected Chaucer's work. He lectured on *The Canterbury Tales* routinely during his time at Oxford, and spent many years of work on a never-completed edition of Chaucer's works for the Clarendon Press.[17] In 1931 he presented a paper to the Philological Society in Oxford, which would be published several years later as "Chaucer as a Philologist: The Reeve's Tale," and on more than one occasion he donned fourteenth-century garb and recited Chaucer from memory as part of the Oxford Playhouse "Summer Diversions" program.[18] However, despite a clear respect, Tolkien sometimes seemed dissatisfied by the prominence of Chaucer's work in Middle English studies, perhaps because he perceived it as championing the Norman-influenced culture of southern England at the expense of that of the more Germanic, Norse-inflected North. In a 1938 letter, Tolkien laments the

> erroneous imagination that Chaucer was the first English poet, and that before and except for him all was dumb and barbaric. That is of course

> not true, and is perhaps . . . rather misleading. I do not personally connect the North with either night or darkness, especially not in England, in whose long 1200 years of literary tradition Chaucer stands rather in the middle than the beginning. I also do not feel him springlike but autumnal (even if of the early autumn) and not kinglike but middle-class.[19]

Importantly, despite his long professional association, Tolkien's only published academic work on Chaucer involved an analysis of that poet's use of northern alliterative dialect. "Chaucer was a great poet," Tolkien admits elsewhere, but then grumbles about how "by the power of his poetry he tends to dominate the view of his time," points out that Chaucer's "was not the only mood or temper of mind in those days," and finally argues that, while the *Gawain* poet "may have lacked Chaucer's subtlety and flexibility," the northern artist demonstrated a "nobility to which Chaucer scarcely reached."[20] Tolkien was even of the opinion that Chaucer "knew *Sir Gawain,* and probably the author also."[21] In light of Tolkien's long-established preference for the northern tributaries of the river of English culture, in selecting a "window of many-coloured glass, looking back into the Middle Ages"[22] the choice of *Sir Gawain and the Green Knight* as a representative medieval English work in this study seems more than justified.

One of the first things to be noted about *Sir Gawain and the Green Knight* is its close kinship to the cold Germanic world of Old English literature. In Lee and Solopova's view, Tolkien "believed that the nearest parallel to *Beowulf* was *Sir Gawain and the Green Knight.*"[23] There are some passages in the latter, particularly ones of gloomy or wintry landscape description, which feel as though they could easily be inserted into the former with only the removal of some French vocabulary and grammar innovations present in Middle English.

As an example, consider the passage describing Gawain's lonely journey in search of the Green Chapel:[24]

> By a mount in the morning merrily he was riding
> into a forest that was deep and fearsomely wild,
> with high hills at each hand, and hoar woods beneath
> of huge aged oaks by the hundred together;
> the hazel and the hawthorn were huddled and tangled
> with rough ragged moss around them trailing,

with many birds bleakly on the bare twigs sitting
that piteously piped there for pain of the cold.[25]

Although Gawain does find rest and respite at a castle in the midst of all this wildness, the day he actually must journey to said chapel dawns a cold and unwelcoming one:

but wild weathers of the world awake in the land,
clouds cast keenly the cold upon earth
with bitter breath from the North biting the naked.
Snow comes shivering sharp to shrivel the wild things,
the whistling wind whirls from the heights
and drives every dale full of drifts very deep.[26]

The approach to the chapel is reminiscent of the trip to the mere of the Grendelkin, frosty cliffs and boiling waters and all:

They go by banks and by braes where branches are bare,
they climb along cliffs where clingeth the cold;
the heavens are lifted high, but under them evilly
mist hangs moist on the moor, melts on the mountains;
every hill has a hat, a mist-mantle huge.
Brooks break and boil on braes all about,
bright bubbling on their banks where they bustle downwards.
Very wild through the wood is the way they must take.[27]

Lee and Solopova remark on how "the realistic description of the mountain and forest scenery in *Sir Gawain* has the same imaginative force as the description of the wilderness in *Beowulf.* The poet emphasizes Gawain's loneliness . . . suffering, harsh and desolate surroundings and the constant presence of danger."[28] Here, in theme and imagery, is a close analogue to the grim, Northern world through which Beowulf made his heroic way, and it mirrors the same tightly coupled relationship between human experience and the landscape itself noticed earlier:

Frequently, this inhospitable and bleak landscape is read as a reflection of Gawain's state of mind . . . as an individual, who is projecting his own feelings of misery on to the landscape. . . . The wilderness itself fades out of focus, as interpretative efforts are brought to bear on the explicitly

> human concerns that the landscape is thus seen to represent. This compulsion to superimpose human reactions onto landscape is particularly marked in the case of wildernesses.[29]

The dwelling of the *wil-dēor* in Old English has now become the *wyldrenesse* of Middle English, and while in this poem the word has not yet attained all the connotations of today's concept of wilderness, it definitely reflects here the more desolate and dangerous ones.

Even the earlier, more pleasant descriptions of the natural world in *Gawain* are, as in *Beowulf*, colored by the way humankind experiences them:

> And so this Yule passed over and the year after,
> and severally the seasons ensued in their turn:
> after Christmas there came the crabbed Lenten
> that with fish tries the flesh and with food more meagre. . . . [30]

Gillian Rudd observes how this passage, and the lyrical and famous stanzas that follow it, "remind us of how much the seasons affect our sense of well-being as much as mark the passing of the year before Gawain must set off."[31] She also notes how the readers are "given little time to rejoice in the new life of spring, the warmth of summer or the plenty of autumn" before being "hustled on to the cold of winter, where the narrative spends most of its time."[32] This handling of landscape imagery closely echoes many of the characteristics of the Old English conception of the natural world discussed above: grim, dangerous, dependent in quality on the psychological mindset of the hero traveling through it. There is obviously a clear continuity between the Anglo-Saxons and the medieval Englishmen who comprised the *Gawain* poet's audience.

But Middle English is not Old English, and the West Midlands of the fourteenth century is neither linguistically nor culturally identical to the kingdoms of Hwicce or Mercia where *Beowulf* could have been composed or recited. Nearly half a millennium of English history—Viking invasions, Norman invasions, the conquests of Wales and Ireland—is evident in the differences between *Gawain* and *Beowulf*, which under examination prove as interesting as the similarities.

The main difference is visible in the courtly presence of the chivalric world. According to Jane Chance, Tolkien believed that the late tenth-century marked the point in time that heralded "the demise of Anglo-Saxon (heroic) values and the birth of Norman French (chivalric) practices"[33] in England. By the time of the *Gawain* poet, several hundred years of Norman occupation had left their indelible mark. Even then, when Edward III was presiding over a strong revival of the English language in public life and invading France to start the Hundred Years' War, the Gallic influence on the knights-and-ladies narrative of *Gawain* is obvious. The poet demonstrates "extensive familiarity with courtly literature, manners, material culture and various aristocratic pastimes, such as hunting and feasting,"[34] which were characteristic of the French-speaking nobility of the time. When that Anglo-Norman chivalric tradition is examined, however, its roots prove to be even more interesting in the context of a cultural examination of English literature; it derives from a mythological cycle that was originally neither Norman nor Anglo-Saxon but would ultimately go on to become characteristically English.

The medieval "Matter of Britain," as the Arthurian cycle would eventually be known (as contrasted with the "Matter of Rome" of Classical myth and the Carolingian "Matter of France"), centered around the heroic King Arthur, whose origins are indisputably Celtic (as evinced by their presence in the *Mabinogion,* discussed in the previous chapter). Tom Shippey points out that, regardless of the *Gawain* poet's belief, "the Arthurian tradition was originally non-English, indeed dedicated to the overthrow of England; its commemoration in English verse was merely a final consequence of the stamping-out of native culture after Hastings, a literary 'defoliation' which had also led to the . . . near-total loss of all Old English heroic tradition."[35] *Sir Gawain and the Green Knight*, whatever affinities it might demonstrate with that lost Anglo-Saxon tradition, owes at least as large a debt to the similarly suppressed Celtic Arthurian world.

The deep mythological river of the Matter of Britain is the result of several hundred years of literary cross-pollination, with the originally Welsh, Cornish, and Breton stories making the switch into French and then eventually back again into English (with a few detours into other medieval Continental languages such as Dutch and German). *Gawain* is justifiably considered "the masterpiece of the Arthurian tradition in English and, arguably in any language," but it is also "at base a Celtic monument,"[36] which includes significant Celtic elements, both broadly thematic—an earlier version of the beheading game is told in the story of Bricriu's Feast in the Irish Ulster cycle—and specifically linguistic.

Jeffrey F. Huntsman points out that the poem is

> marked not just by a richer pattern of alliteration than the paltry two- or three-element structure allowed by Old English prosody but by a complex pattern of alliteration concatenated with a number of other poetic features—rhyme, assonance, consonance, and several types of binding repetition of words and phrases—features for which our English prosody lacks even names. . . . The alliterative poets of the West Midlands wrote within a prosodic convention that replicated, as far as the English language would allow, an ancient Celtic pattern.[37]

The *Gawain* poet was writing "in a borderland between Welsh-speaking and English-speaking regions of Britain," and thematically the poem demonstrates a "distinctive conjunction of themes from the First Branch of the *Mabinogi,*" including "an overlay landscape associated with a mysterious annual ritual contest" and "an otherworldly temptress with natural associations and surprising guises."[38] One of the clearest thematic parallels to the *Mabinogion* is the "strong sense of place" present upon "Gawain's sudden appearance on the north coast of Wales, in a carefully detailed segment of his journey."[39] The poet is clearly "intimately familiar with the terrain that Gawain traverses as he heads towards North Wales, the direction of the British Otherworld."[40] The description of landscape in the poem does demonstrate an ultraspecificity in relationship to actual places in northwest Britain, but such specificity interestingly applies only to Gawain's journey through the Welsh countryside.

The location of Camelot in the poem is not specified, and the rest of the kingdom ruled from the Round Table is as geographically unclear as it was in the Arthurian tales of the *Mabinogion.* But people today can follow the path Gawain takes on his search for the Green Chapel. As Siewers puts it, Gawain at first travels through the "indigenous cultural realms of Wales, from a Frenchified Arthurian court in the unspecified Anglo-Norman space of Camelot," but then the poem "carefully tracks Gawain's geographical route to the realm of the Green Knight, through west Britain"[41] in a way that tightly mirrors the detailed landscapes of the Four Branches of the *Mabinogi:*

> He had no friend but his horse in the forests and hills,
> no man on his march to commune with but God,
> till anon he drew near unto Northern Wales.
> All the isles of Anglesey he held on his left,
> and over the fords he fared by the flats near the sea,

> and then over by the Holy Head to high land again
> in the wilderness of Wirral; there wandered but few
> who with good will regarded either God or mortal.[42]

Although the Wirral peninsula is today no longer *wyldrenesse,* it is neverheless real and easily identifiable on any map of England, separated from northern Wales by the muddy flats of the Dee estuary. Gillian Rudd remarks that the text "flaunts its pseudo-historical setting before sending us off into the enduring and actual wilderness,"[43] and Siewers points out that "the geography of the supernatural 'green world,' in the 'wild' cultural periphery of West Britain's Celtic Fringe, stands out more realistically than the geography and setting of the supposedly 'real' and 'historical' court of King Arthur."[44] The similarities to the way landscape is treated in the *Mabinogion* are quite striking, and clearly betray the influence of the Celtic world on the character of later English literature.

The Green Chapel itself also owes a good deal to Irish and Welsh tales, specifically those of magical fairy mounds:

> Then he halted and held in his horse for the time,
> and changed oft his front the Chapel to find.
> Such on no side he saw, as seemed to him strange,
> save a mound as it might be near the marge of a green,
> a worn barrow on a brae by the brink of a water,
> . . . .
> Then he went to the barrow and about it he walked,
> debating in his mind what might the thing be.
> It had a hole at the end and at either side,
> and with grass in green patches was grown all over,
> and was all hollow within: nought but an old cavern,
> or a cleft in an old crag; he could not it name
> aright.[45]

Huntsman describes this strange mound, located beyond one of the streams that serve as "traditional boundaries for the magical places at which this world and the Otherworld intersect," as a "pre-Celtic tumulus, a burial mound, thought to be an entrance to that Otherworld."[46] It is here Gawain expects to meet the *aluish mon* (elvish man) whom he had beheaded a year earlier, and to receive a retributory ax stroke likely to end his life. Still, bravely, the knight

> With high helm on his head, his lance in his hand,
> he roams up to the roof of that rough dwelling.
> Then he heard from the high hill, in a hard rock-wall
> beyond the stream on a steep, a sudden startling noise.[47]

No semidivine Welsh legend ascending the magical mound of Gorsedd Arberth could have expected to encounter more danger of wound or injury, or to see anything more wonderful.

The Green Knight himself is certainly a marvel, a character as much of Faërie as any in literature. Tolkien observes wryly that "if we are introduced to a green man, with green hair and face, on a green horse, at the court of King Arthur, we expect 'magic,'"[48] and this extravagant character does not fail to meet this expectation. He is human in shape, but far more than human, a "*lusus naturae* in size and colour, conveying to many critics a sense of identification with the wild wintry landscape from which he appears, called by the poet in respectful but uncertain style *an aghlich mayster*, 'a terrible Master.'"[49] There is overwhelming critical agreement that this character, "with his green skin, green horse and holly branch," clearly "represents nature in some way," but in exactly what way—and what he might signify within the Middle English conception of the natural world—is considerably less certain.[50] Huntsman notes his similarity to the *dyn glas* (gray-green man) of Welsh folklore, a "pivotal winter figure who represents simultaneously the dying of the old year and, in the promise of the slumbering earth, the birth of the new."[51] Rudd seems to agree, accepting that the "timing of his entry into Arthur's court . . . suggests connections with the folkloric Green Man who embodies the principle of new life returning after the dead of winter."[52] But Rudd also notes that he is considerably more than an oversized version of the mysterious leaf-faced or vegetation-disgorging carvings common in European cathedrals: "although this person is beyond doubt *a* green man, he is not strictly speaking *the* Green Man."[53] In seeking to determine what he is, and what he represents, readers are confronted with (and sometimes frustrated by) the considerable shrewdness and skill of the medieval poet in creating such a memorable character.

In his Otherworldly *aluish* form, he can easily be typed as an anthropomorphic representation of the *wyldrenesse*. Flieger ties him to Tolkien's Treebeard in this way, as an "archetype of the green world" who "speaks for the spirit of wild, uncultivated life."[54] More subtly, Rudd suggests (following William Anderson) that his appearance, in answer to King Arthur's demand for a "marvel,"

> hints at the distance humans have put between themselves and the rest of the natural world, to the extent that the simple processes of nature have become imbued with an air of the supernatural. . . . As human culture and religion . . . increasingly divided the human from the rest of nature, and as the rational, intellectual and scientific were privileged more and more, the only place left for other modes of apprehension and being, indeed for otherness in general, was that of the supernatural, yet a supernatural conceived of most readily in human form.[55]

This insightful observation certainly rings true for a modern reader, but it feels a bit anachronistic for the *Gawain* poet, simultaneously too early and too late. In the fourteenth century, this process of rational scientification was only in its earliest, pre-Enlightenment stages, and the supernatural anthropomorphic personification of nature (as deities of sky or sea or storm or earth) have been a feature of human culture as long as there has been human culture.

The Green Knight resists such easy identification because he is not just a supernatural figure in the poem; he is also a perfectly civilized Anglo-Norman nobleman, with a fine castle, a refined court, and a very beautiful wife. The appearance of his welcoming home on Christmas Eve in answer to Gawain's fervent prayer is as much a transition from wilderness to human civilization as Gawain's route to the Green Chapel on New Year's Day is a journey in the other direction, and the central figure of both places proves to be one and the same.

Michael George identifies in *Sir Gawain and the Green Knight* a "dual cultural approach to nature,"[56] a multiplicity of competing concepts in a single work that would later leave its mark on many of Tolkien's landscapes as well. The first approach seems to be intrinsically related to the sense in Old English literature that "the human race lives precariously, with only brief moments of respite in places of refuge like the hall, which is surrounded on all sides—besieged even—by the forces of the natural world."[57] This idea results for George in a perception that "the environment is hostile and needs to be ruthlessly conquered,"[58] a viewpoint that he proposes is represented in the poem by the figure of Gawain and his journeys through the threatening wilderness. The other, which George ties to the "direct symbol of the natural world and . . . hybrid of civilization and wilderness" that is the Green Knight, is a "moderated form of dominance, one that promotes care for the natural environment."[59] But even such moderated dominance, useful as it may be for a reader today as a positive example of a medieval relationship between humans and their environment, does not take into account the untamed and untamable aspect of the wilderness, the pure wildness that refuses to submit to stewardship of any kind and yet is (at this medieval point in time) beyond human capacity to destroy.

This is where the Celtic idea of overlay landscape comes in; "from the twelfth-century Welsh *Mabinogi* to Old Irish tales, the heroic *Táin Bó Cúailnge,* and *Sir Gawain and the Green Knight,* a sense of the 'other side' of nature, which humans cannot fully know or control, informs the depiction of landscapes, forests, and countryside."[60] The symbolically named Bertilak de Hautdesert[61] certainly "stands astride the boundary between human and natural world,"[62] but he also bridges the natural and the supernatural, living as much in the blended landscape of Celtic myth as in the hostile Germanic one. He is thus a personification of the human, natural, and supernatural all at the same time.

In truth, there are so many interpretations of the representations of the natural world possible in this medieval work that an ecocritic can generally find support for whatever postmodern point she is trying to make—and this fact is ultimately both a monument to the skill of the *Gawain* poet and a demonstration of the ever-increasing ambiguity of the relationship between humans and their environment already present in late medieval Britain.

When the wilderness concepts in *Beowulf,* the *Mabinogion,* and *Sir Gawain and the Green Knight* are considered together as a whole, an interesting picture arises, one of an odd mixture of continuity and change, shifting and combining. In the medieval British imagination, the generally grim characterization of the natural world in Anglo-Saxon thought seems to have blended with the dangerous but attractive Otherworld of the deep and mysterious Celtic forests to create a uniquely English concept of wild nature where both heroes and the monsters they battled find shelter in the greenwood. This English idea did not so much supplant its predecessors as supplement them; Gawain would have found both Beowulf's and Peredur's ideas about the wild natural world quite understandable, while the reverse is not necessarily true.

Of course, the Western mythological river had flowed over many lands from its origins in Paleolithic prehistory, through the Near East and the Classical world, long before it ever watered the green and pleasant lands of the British Isles. It accordingly carried with it a multitude of conflicting ideas about the natural world, which can be traced all the way back to the dawn of human history. Max Oelschlaeger places the genesis of the idea squarely in the hands of the Neolithic Revolution; he argues that, "viewed retrospectively, the idea of wilderness represents a heightened awareness by the agrarian or Neolithic mind, as farming and herding supplanted hunting and gathering, of distinctions between humankind and nature."[63] These distinctions encouraged value clusters to develop around ideas of the land and the place of the peoples living on it, and those values championed both human action in the face of overwhelming power and the majestic beauty of that power itself.

Those values are still present in the Western mind. The wilderness in human myth has always been a place of trial and transformation; before the British medieval period, Gilgamesh was a foe of the forest, the Hebrews sought their God in the vast expanses of the desert, and the Greek and Roman poets and philosophers both mistrusted the darkness and danger of the deep woodlands and extolled the beauty of the Classical *locus amœnus* whose trees, grass, and water were essential to human happiness. Afterwards, the contradicting English mixture of Germanic harshness and Celtic strangeness would soften further, transmuting into the merry English greenwood of Robin Hood and Shakespeare. By the end of the seventeenth century, one branch of the mythological river would carry these characteristically English ideas onward into vast tracts of untamed land unknown to medieval Europe or its predecessors. There those ideas would mingle with other aspects of the mythic and cultural New World experience and eventually coalesce into the firmly ambiguous concept of wilderness familiar today.

Tolkien's legendarium partakes fully of this modern ambiguity. Middle-earth as a place is dangerous and sheltering, its inhabitants both heroes and monsters. Middle-earth certainly inherits this ambiguous quality from Tolkien's medieval sources (not to mention their own sources in Classical Antiquity and before, with which he was certainly familiar), but it also owes a debt to the violent convulsions and breathtaking destruction that first appeared at an industrial scale in the late nineteenth and early twentieth centuries. These developments only multiplied the conflicting ideas about wilderness in the mind of the industrialized West.

In order to effectively approach Tolkien's great modern myth with an eye to examining how it can help people today shift their stories about their environment, it is helpful to focus on the deft way in which he navigates this morass of ambiguity. Middle-earth is not merely a stage set of painted cardboard, an oversimplified or binary good-bad characterization of place set up as a backdrop to highlight human stories. It is, as Patrick Curry has remarked, "a character in its own right,"[64] and it is fully characterized by all of the conflicting human conceptions of the natural world. This is arguably one of the main reasons Tolkien's work has such power to shape the mythological thinking of readers today. Without taking away from the veracity of his characters or the excitement of his plot, it is not too much to say that it is the lovingly crafted details of the natural world, not to mention the values present in the choice to highlight those details, that make Middle-earth feel so utterly real. Examining these details and their associated values will be the aim of part II.

PART II
THE LANDS OF ARDA

For wild and wide it seemed to them were the lands of Middle-earth.
—Tolkien, *Silmarillion*, 132

Wild and Wide

To many readers of Tolkien, Middle-earth is as real a place as any they might have visited in the mundane world, and arguably more real than some. This is certainly due to the mythic verities permeating his stories, which ring so psychologically true for so many people, but it can also be attributed to the fact that the scope and detail of the world in Tolkien's legendarium is simply astonishing. Indeed, there is so much information to work with that scientist fans have long enjoyed using the tools of their trade to examine, and even write papers about, the imagined empirical aspects of Arda. Environmental researchers at the University of Bristol published a detailed climate model of Middle-earth that examined the rain shadows of the Misty Mountains, noted that the most Shire-like climate in the United Kingdom is centered around Leicestershire and Lincolnshire, and observed that "Los Angeles and western Texas are notable for being amongst the most Mordor-like regions in the USA."[1] A geologist examining Tolkien's maps took issue with the shape of his mountain ranges, describing them as "a geographical car wreck from which I can't look away" and concluding regretfully that Tolkien, while brilliant, "was no connoisseur of geography."[2] Tolkien was admittedly neither a climatologist nor a geologist, but a botanist and artist team examining his descriptions of plant life concluded that he was definitely botanically knowledgeable; they found enough detail in the texts to support an entire book on the flora of Middle-earth, with full botanical treatments of 141 different species, real and imagined.[3] It is a tribute to the power of Tolkien's storytelling that his work attracts, and is detailed enough to support, such examination from people who might be expected to value only the realities of the physical and everyday world.

What is the character of a fictional place with the power to capture even the imagination of botanists? It is a place that manages to embrace the full spectrum of ambiguity in the relationship between humans and their environments. Throughout his work, Tolkien extols natural beauty without disregarding its danger, and his idea of wilderness emphatically includes both of these. From the cruelty and heart-stopping beauty of the Misty Mountains to the rolling grasslands of Rohan, from the crushing ice of the Helcaraxë to the well-tended farmlands and woodlands of the Shire, from the splendor of Lothlórien to the volcanic deserts of Mordor, the construction of Middle-earth includes within its bounds a breathtakingly vast collection of climates and lands. Tolkien's fictional world is big enough, and detailed enough, to encompass the entire bundle of contradictions that is the physical environment of the "real" world.

Under stern examination, however, this sweeping statement only holds fully true for the world as viewed from the perspective of a Western European. For, just as the texts examined in part I are Western, so indeed is the fictional world they influenced. Due to the deep universality woven into the fibers of this mythology, it is a sometimes overlooked fact that every moment of chronicled plot action in *The Hobbit* and *The Lord of the Rings* takes place in a natural and cultural atmosphere that is very specifically that of the European continent.

This is not to say that there are no non-European locales in Middle-earth. Readers are tantalized by travelers' tales like those of Elrond or Aragorn, who had "crossed many mountains and many rivers, and trodden many plains, even into the far countries of Rhûn and Harad where the stars are strange."[4] When asked by a fan about these places, Tolkien pointed out that "Rhun is the Elvish word for 'east.' Asia, China, Japan, and all the things which people in the west regard as far away. And south of Harad is Africa, the hot countries."[5] There are many references to these lands in the legendarium. The numerous enemies from the East, who "sapped the waning strength of Gondor" in its decline, "journeyed in great wains, and their chieftains fought in chariots."[6] Gollum mentions more lands south of Gondor where "the Yellow Face is very hot . . . and there are seldom any clouds, and the men are fierce and have dark faces."[7] While journeying in Ithilien, Frodo and Sam get caught up Faramir's ambush of some of those men. Sam also gets a glimpse of a towering Mûmak, with "great legs like trees, enormous sail-like ears spread out, long snout upraised like a huge serpent about to strike," curving tusks "bound with bands of gold and dripped with blood," and "the ruins of what seemed a very war-tower lay upon his heaving back."[8] Nomadic horse warriors in wagons, dark-skinned peoples who make war with elephants: these imply the presence of Central Asian–like steppes and African-like deserts and jungles, just as the Inuit-like Snowmen of Lossoth (who once rescued one of Aragorn's ancestors) imply polar tundra. But these lands are presented as faraway places, exotic, unquestionably not-home to the people with whom Tolkien's myth spends most of its time.

Tolkien was very conscious of this Western-centric aspect of his work. When asked if Middle-earth was Europe, he replied, "Yes, of course—Northwestern Europe . . . where my imagination comes from,"[9] and he wrote in a letter to W. H. Auden that "if you want to write a tale of this sort you must consult your roots, and a man of the North-west of the Old World will set his heart and the action of his tale in an imaginary world of that air, and that situation: with the Shoreless Sea of his innumerable ancestors to the West, and the endless lands (out of which enemies mostly come) to the East."[10] Tolkien often seems to feel the need to defend himself on this point;[11] in a letter responding to a draft of an article describing Middle-earth's spiritual correspondence to "Nordic Europe," he wrote testily "Not *Nordic*, please! A word I personally dislike; it is associated . . . with racialist theories."[12] He then goes on to argue that

> Auden has asserted that for me "the North is a sacred direction." That is not true. The North-west of Europe, where I (and most of my ancestors) have lived, has my affection, as a man's home should. I love its atmosphere, and know more of its histories and languages than I do of other parts; but it is not "sacred," nor does it exhaust my affections. . . . [In Middle-earth] the North was the seat of the fortresses of the Devil. The progress of the tale ends in what is far more like the re-establishment of an effective Holy Roman Empire with its seat in Rome than anything that would be devised by a "Nordic."[13]

In the same letter he provides specific guidance on how he imagines his locations would map onto the "real" world: "The action of the story takes place in the North-west of 'Middle-earth', equivalent in latitude to the coastlands of Europe and the north shores of the Mediterranean.... If Hobbiton and Rivendell are taken (as intended) to be at about the latitude of Oxford, then Minas Tirith, 600 miles south, is at about the latitude of Florence. The Mouths of Anduin and the ancient city of Pelargir are at about the latitude of ancient Troy."[14] This construction puts Mordor somewhere in Eastern Europe; even the Black Land is a Western one. Although he was born in South Africa, "unlike near-contemporary writers such as Kipling and T. H. White, Tolkien showed little interest in the exotic lands where many British military and civil servants found themselves in the *fin de siècle*. Instead, he clung fiercely to his English roots."[15] The characteristics of the natural world in Tolkien's beloved Shire, foregrounded against the global variety of his world-spanning Middle-earth, unquestionably reflect those roots.

This digression on Eurocentrism should certainly not be read as claiming Middle-earth has nothing to offer non-Western readers. In the same way that the ancient writings of an obscure desert tribe of Semitic nomads today provide deep mythic inspiration to people whose lands and climates in no way reflect that of Canaan, Tolkien's modern myth is full of universal truths about the natural world, which can deeply inform readers of all cultures. But it does explain how the clothing in which Tolkien dresses the central character that is Middle-earth—temperate forests, rolling grasslands, towering mountains, and a steady march of seasons—can be best understood in terms of the natural and cultural environment, which would make such clothing necessary.

Given this unapologetically Western (and specifically English) context, one way to examine how Middle-earth's inhabitants interact with its wild natural world is to use a framework based on three distinct cultural ideas flowing into the stream of the modern English consciousness. Although the correspondence is not exact, the archaic mountain wilderness of the Rangers, the Romantic forest wilderness of the Elves, and the pastoral cultivated wilderness of the hobbits correlate loosely with the medieval Germanic, Celtic, and English ideas examined in part I. The Wilderland of the Rangers draws on the harsh mountainous terrain, grim brooding forests, and inhospitable monster-infested wastelands of *Beowulf* and the Germanic tradition, where wilderness is largely defined as the dark lands stretching for uncountable miles between small bright circles of civilization, lands "empty of all save birds and beasts, unfriendly places deserted by all the races of the world."[16] The dream-like green forestlands of the Elves reflect the dangerously breathtaking beauty of the Otherworldly Celtic woodland realms, where non-Elven visitors find themselves "in a timeless land that did not fade or change or fall into forgetfulness."[17] While the Shire is largely characterized by its fields and farms, it includes a number of friendly woodlands fit for pleasant camping adventures, like the "wild corner of the Eastfarthing" known as the Woody End through which Frodo and his friends journey near the beginning of their tale.[18]

Earlier ecocritical writings on Tolkien have come to similar conclusions, and these are gratefully acknowledged as starting points for this study. Especially influential was Marjorie Burns's observation that "since character and landscape are always closely related in Tolkien's literature, this means there are three basic terrains in his composite Middle-earth: a Northern European-Scandinavian wilderness, a Celtic twilight realm, and an English countryside."[19] Similarly, Dickerson and Evans propose three "environmental domains" in their book: "*agriculture,* which uses the environment for food; *horticulture,* in which the pragmatically 'useless' aesthetic quality of the world is cultivated for the purpose of beauty; and *feraculture,* which sets portions of the environment apart from use to preserve its wild character."[20] From a more human-centered perspective, Susan Jeffers sees in Tolkien's work power dynamics involving a people's interdependent "power with," dialectical "power from," or exploitative "power over" a landscape;[21] while this tripartite construction does not map precisely to the three realms under discussion here, her ideas overlap and interlink with them in useful ways. These works, and others like them, have been instrumental in shaping the examination of Tolkien's texts in the following chapters.

Although each of these three wilderness categories will be considered in its own chapter, the distinctions between them are more conceptual than geographic, and they are not completely discrete entities. Just as the single word *wilderness* in modern English encompasses all of these concepts and more, there is a good deal of conceptual overlap between many of Middle-earth's most memorable wild places. Locations that are located physically in one category but reflect the characteristics of another—mountainous but Otherworldly Rivendell is one example, and the dangerous Old Forest in the Shire is another—will largely be examined in the context of their strongest concept of wilderness, not necessarily just their physical location on the map of Middle-earth, and they may make appearances in more than one chapter below so that their mythic power may be examined in the light of more than one concept.

There is one final methodological note to the approach of part II requiring a bit of explanation. Let an excerpt from *The Lord of the Rings,* which demonstrates many characteristics of Tolkien's landscapes, serve as a starting example: Frodo, from the Seat of Seeing atop Amon Hen in book II, observing a setting the vast sweep of which feels utterly unfathomable to those who may have never left their small Shire-lives.

> Eastward he looked into wide uncharted lands, nameless plains, and forests unexplored. Northward he looked, and the Great River lay like a ribbon beneath him, and the Misty Mountains stood small and hard as broken teeth. Westward he looked and saw the broad pastures of Rohan; and Orthanc, the pinnacle of Isengard, like a black spike. Southward he looked, and below his very feet the Great River curled like a toppling wave and plunged over the falls of Rauros into a foaming pit; a glimmering rainbow played upon the fume. And Ethir Anduin he saw, the mighty delta of the River, and myriads of sea-birds whirling like a white dust in the sun, and beneath them a green and silver sea, rippling in endless lines.[22]

This rolling excerpt masterfully demonstrates the variety of landscape that captures Tolkien's imagination, from the "forests unexplored" to the "Great River," from the mountains to the sea. It also provides a good introduction to Tolkien's expansive, almost overwhelming, descriptive prose style. Any reader of Tolkien soon learns that much of the power of his visual imagery depends on long and thickly ornamented passages, where image builds on image into a powerful whole. Tolkien's poetic prose is notoriously difficult to paraphrase, and extensive quotation is often necessary to fully capture the tone of his representations of the natural world. In this matter, a good amount of indulgence on the part of the reader is requested as this study dives into the details of the wilderness imagery woven throughout Middle-earth.

CHAPTER FOUR

Rangers in the Mountains

The first of Tolkien's wilderness concepts to be considered here is the one that is arguably the oldest: the place of danger, of survival and heroism, of vastly powerful natural forces that can sweep away human lives in an instant. It is the Norse/Germanic concept of the sagas and *Beowulf*, the "settings and scenes that the Norse and Anglo-Saxons carried along with them to England within their mythologies: desolate reaches, vast rolling plains, and mountains of fire and ice."[1] Tolkien speaks of this concept as one of "man alien in a hostile world, engaged in a struggle which he cannot win while the world lasts."[2] It is the concept the earliest English settlers brought with them into the New World, the "hideous and desolate wilderness" of William Bradford, where "the whole country, full of woods and thickets, represented a wild and savage hue."[3] It is, in Roderick Nash's words, that wild place "instinctively understood as something alien to man—an insecure and uncomfortable environment against which civilization had waged an unceasing struggle."[4] The relationship between humans and their natural world in these mythological terms is presented as a battle, even a war: humans versus nature in a zero-sum fight to the death, and the great heroes are the ones who can venture into the wild lands, survive the trials they find there, and return to tell the tale.

For Tolkien, this concept seemed to represent both the draws and dangers of adventure. His blurb for the dust-jacket copy of the original publication of *The Hobbit* promises that, within the pages of the book, the reader would encounter "journeys there and back, out of the comfortable Western world, over the edge of the Wild, and home again" in an ancient time "when the famous forest of Mirkwood was still standing, and the mountains were full of danger."[5] *Mirkwood* itself is a Germanic word, and one that Tolkien knew well; he explains in a letter to his grandson that "Mirkwood is not an invention of mine, but a very ancient name, weighted with legendary associations. It was probably the Primitive Germanic name for the great mountainous forest regions that anciently formed a barrier to the south of the lands of Germanic expansion. In some traditions[6] it became used especially of the boundary between Goths and Huns."[7] These "great mountainous forest regions" are the archetypal setting for heroic deeds in much Germanic-influenced Western myth, and Tolkien draws heavily upon this canon in all of his fiction.

When the long-suppressed Tookish part of Bilbo's nature is awakened by the challenge Gandalf thrusts upon him, he realizes that he wants "to go and see the great mountains, and hear the pine-trees and the waterfalls, and explore the caves, and wear a sword instead of a walking-stick."[8] Many years later, Frodo (no doubt influenced by Bilbo's old adventure tales) also finds himself restlessly "wondering at times, especially in the autumn, about the wild lands, and strange visions of mountains that he had never seen came into his dreams."[9] But it is not long before both of the Bagginses discover that "adventures are not all pony-rides in May-sunshine,"[10] and it is through the darkness and danger involved in challenging those cruel mountains and dark forests that this wilderness concept infuses Tolkien's adventure tales with its power.

A brief taste of Tolkien's poetry in *The Hobbit* illustrates how he made use of this mythic aspect of wilderness as a dark and forbidding place. The Dwarves sing of their journey to their lost halls "*Far over the misty mountains cold/To dungeons deep and caverns old*" and "*Far over the misty mountains grim / To dungeons deep and caverns dim.*"[11] Similarly, in Beorn's woodland hall the Dwarves begin a song with the gloomy lines

> *The wind was on the withered heath,*
> *but in the forest stirred no leaf:*
> *there shadows lay by night and day,*
> *and dark things silent crept beneath.*[12]

The Wood-elves, merry as they are in their dark forest home, send their barrels downstream to

Leave the halls and caverns deep,
Leave the northern mountains steep,
Where the forest wide and dim
Stoops in shadow grey and grim![13]

This imagery of cold mountains and dark forests seems to serve as a shorthand for the menace of the unknown in wild places.

Still, while the general feeling of this wilderness concept is one of bleak danger, it is not an unmitigated bleakness. This slight ambiguity is also a characteristic of the seemingly grim Anglo-Saxon wilderness that so influenced Tolkien's world and to which this one is directly compared: the wild is dark and perilous, but it is an appropriate setting in which to prove a hero's greatness and can even be beautiful. Roderick Nash goes a bit further, suggesting that this Germanic concept of wilderness has "a twofold emotional tone. On the one hand it is inhospitable, alien, mysterious, and threatening; on the other, beautiful, friendly, and capable of elevating and delighting the beholder."[14] While Nash's friendliness and delight might fit more comfortably into Tolkien's third concept of wilderness, the beauty of most threatening wild places still manages to shine clearly through in Middle-earth.

Marjorie Burns describes the Northern wilderness as a world "of water and rock, of wide sweeps of sea edged by rugged coasts, long, steep-sided valleys (confining and extensive at once), and high dividing mountains that share the crown of the world with vast, desolate uplands."[15] She also points out that this wilderness zone was not a part of the beautiful corner of the planet that lay so close to Tolkien's heart: "England and all of Britain contain green and wooded regions where Tolkienian Elves could appropriately reside; but England lacks true mountains (in the Norse and Alpine sense)."[16] Tolkien did seem to love mountains—he lavishes some of his most dramatic landscape description upon them—but he also respected their power, and portrayed them as both heart-stoppingly beautiful and cruelly dangerous.

Despite England's geologic lack, there is solid biographical material in Tolkien's past to support this love and respect. In a letter to his son Michael, he waxes poetic about the beauty he encountered on a walking tour of the Swiss Alps as a young man, and he explicitly acknowledges the impact the experience had on his writing. He declares himself "delighted" that Michael had

> made the acquaintance of Switzerland, and the very part that I once knew best and which had the deepest effect on me. The hobbit's (Bilbo's) journey from Rivendell to the other side of the Misty Mountains, including the glissade down the slithering stones into the pine woods, is based on my adventures in 1911. . . . We went on foot carrying great packs practically all the way from Interlaken, mainly by mountain paths, to Lauterbrunnen and so to Mürren and eventually to the head of the Lauterbrunnenthal in a wilderness of morains. . . . I left the view of *Jungfrau* with deep regret: eternal snow, etched as it seemed against eternal sunshine, and the *Silberhorn* sharp against dark blue: the *Silvertine* (*Celebdil*) of my dreams.[17]

This textual acknowledgment of the Swiss Alps as a source for the Misty Mountains is reinforced by cues in Tolkien's visual art. Comparing Tolkien's original watercolor of Rivendell to a photograph of the Lauterbrunnenthal makes a striking juxtaposition indeed,[18] and the painting he did for *The Hobbit*'s dust jacket is positively dominated by the energy of jagged mountain peaks: "Mountains march rhythmically across the spread, their snowcaps brightly contrasting with dark lower slopes. Jagged lines like lightning bolts pass across the mountains and pulsate at their feet."[19] Douglas Anderson points out that "as with the Misty Mountains, Tolkien's Lonely Mountain is Alpine in shape and form," and he comments on the similarity between a 1910 photo of the Matterhorn and Tolkien's illustration of the front gate to Smaug's den.[20] Perhaps the profound impact the Swiss landscape had on Tolkien's imagination explains why, despite its decidedly non-English character, the "greater landscape drama" of mountainous terrain is something that all of his heroes find themselves required to face down at one point or another.[21]

Bilbo is the earliest and most obvious example. Despite his starry-eyed expectations, his first experience of a mountain is presented in ominous terms. "Dark and drear it looked, though there were patches of sunlight on its brown sides, and behind its shoulders the tips of snow-peaks gleamed," and the small and quintessentially English hobbit "had never seen a thing that looked so big before."[22] As Bilbo and the Dwarves travel toward and through these foothills of the Misty Mountains, in the description one can hear an echo of the voice of an Englishman encountering alpine terrain for the first time: "They came on unexpected valleys, narrow with steep sides, that opened suddenly at their feet, and they looked down surprised to see trees below them and running water at the bottom. There were gullies that they could almost leap over, but very deep with waterfalls in them. There were dark ravines that one could neither jump over nor climb into."[23] This breathless wonder at landscape extremes is accompanied by a reminder that all of this resplendent beauty can also be deadly; the text goes on to mention bogs, "some of them green pleasant places to look at, with flowers growing bright and tall; but a pony that walked there with a pack on its back would never have come out again."[24] Here, not only does the wilderness demonstrate both beauty and danger, but the beauty actually conceals the danger.

Considering the close relationship to tales like *Beowulf,* one might expect heroes to encounter monsters in such a wilderness, and they are certainly present in *The Hobbit*—but (at least at this early point in the story) the monsters do not represent the true danger of mountainous country. Indeed, while Thorin and company meet with trolls and giants in their journey along "a hard path and a dangerous path, a crooked way and a lonely and a long," these encounters seem to serve as lighter fare, almost jokes, in this children's tale.[25] The giants are portrayed as simply enjoying their thunderous rock-hurling game, and the danger is mostly that one of the Dwarves might "be picked up by some giant and kicked sky-high for a [painfully anachronistic] football."[26] The trolls are presented as downright comic, with their wrangling in their lower-class accents and their shockingly bad manners, which prompt the narrator to almost downplay Bilbo's predicament while observing primly, "Yes, I am afraid trolls do behave like that."[27] Although undoubtedly of similar provenance, the tone of these situations is a far cry from the bloody and deadly peril of Grendel at Heorot.

On close examination, the chief menace of the Misty Mountains in *The Hobbit* lies in the terrain itself. Gandalf gravely informs the company that "it is very necessary to tackle the Misty Mountains by the proper path, or else you will get lost in them, and have to come back and start at the beginning again (if you ever get back at all)."[28] In the same vein, the narrator intones warnings like "there were many paths that led up into those mountains, and many passes over them. But most of the paths were cheats and deceptions and led nowhere or to bad ends; and most of the passes were infested by evil things and dreadful dangers," or sententiously informs the reader that even the best of plans made by the wisest of folk "go astray when you are off on dangerous adventures over the Edge of the Wild," where even Gandalf himself "hardly dared to hope that they would pass without fearful adventure over those great tall mountains with lonely peaks and valleys where no king ruled."[29] Assaults from the cold, the wind, even the rocks themselves must be endured: "it was getting bitter cold up here, and the wind came shrill among the rocks. Boulders, too, at times came galloping down the mountain-sides, let loose by mid-day sun upon the snow, and passed among them (which was lucky), or over their heads (which was alarming)."[30]

These falling boulders are, as many commentators have noted, based on Tolkien's personal experience of mountains in summertime; he describes a specific incident in Switzerland when he and his company

> were strung out in file along a narrow track with a snow-slope on the right going up to the horizon, and on the left a plunge down into a ravine. The summer of that year had melted away much of the snow, and stones and boulders were exposed that (I suppose) were normally covered. The heat of the day continued the melting and we were alarmed to see many of them starting to roll down the slope at gathering speed: anything from the size of oranges to large footballs, and a few much larger. They were whizzing across our path and plunging into the ravine. "Hard pounding," ladies and gentlemen. They started slowly, and then usually held a straight line of descent, but the path was rough and one had also to keep an eye on one's feet. I remember the member of the party just in front of me (an elderly schoolmistress) gave a sudden squeak and jumped forward as a large lump of rock shot between us. About a foot at most from my unmanly knees.[31]

Tolkien knew the dangers of mountainous country, even (perhaps especially) on a pleasant sunny summer day.

When the weather turns foul, the situation is even worse; while the narrator of *The Hobbit* acknowledges that storms in low country can be frightening, he assures his young readers that, in wild and high places of the world, a thunderstorm is downright terrifying: "More terrible still are thunder and lightning in the mountains at night, when storms come up from East and West and make war. The lightning splinters on the peaks, and rocks shiver, and great crashes split the air and go rolling and tumbling into every cave and hollow; and the darkness is filled with overwhelming noise and sudden light."[32] Tolkien's illustration for chapter 4 of *The Hobbit,* entitled "The Mountain-path," captures in visual terms this ominous verbal description of danger embodied in the terrain itself.[33] As if a rain of stones on a sunny day is not bad enough! No monsters are necessary to create a feeling of terrible awe in country like this. It is no wonder that, after being rescued by the Great Eagles, Bilbo is immensely relieved to learn that "at last they were going to escape really and truly from the dreadful mountains,"[34] if only for a short time.

After this escape, however, Tolkien drives his tale inexorably toward another even more perilous mountain, one inhabited by a monster considerably more serious than gamboling giants or squabbling trolls. Bilbo's first glimpse of this high place is quite threatening: "far away, its dark head in a torn cloud, there loomed the Mountain. . . . All alone it rose and looked across the marshes to the forest. The Lonely Mountain! Bilbo had come far and through many adventures to see it, and now he did not like the look of it in the least."[35] As he floats down the river, this mountain "seemed to frown at him and threaten him as it drew ever nearer," and as the days wear on "they could all see the Lonely Mountain towering grim and tall before them."[36] When they finally arrive, the landscape that greets them is quite forbidding:

> The land about them grew bleak and barren. . . . There was little grass, and before long there was neither bush nor tree, and only broken and blackened stumps to speak of ones long vanished. They were come to the Desolation of the Dragon, and they were come at the waning of the year. . . . They went on beyond the end of the southern spur, until lying hidden behind a rock they could look out and see the dark cavernous opening in a great cliff-wall between the arms of the Mountain. Out of it the waters of the Running River sprang; and out of it too there came a steam and a dark smoke. Nothing moved in the waste, save the vapour and the water. . . . The only sound was the sound of the stony water, and every now and again the harsh croak of a bird.[37]

This first look at Smaug's den highlights how the story has made a shift, somewhere; it has begun to feel positively *Beowulfi*an.

The relationship is clear between this grim place and the one where that aged Geatish hero-king "saw a stone arch by the barrow-wall, / and a stream flowing out, its waters afire with angry flames."[38] By the time Smaug goes on to ravage Lake-town and "the lake rippled red as fire beneath the awful beating of his wings," it becomes obvious that the story has mostly shed its light comedic tone.[39] Fiery death and destruction, the defeat of a monster, greed and injustice causing dissension among allies, an ensuing bloody battle: it is in these later chapters of *The Hobbit* that the echoes of *Beowulf* sound most clearly. The wilderness of the children's story has grown up, as have its monsters. When the narrator reminds his readers of the dangers of Bilbo's journey home—"the Wild was still the Wild, and there were many other things in it in those days beside goblins"—it seems a much more foreboding statement than those encountered in the earlier parts of the story.[40]

Many years later, when Frodo finds himself journeying through the same Misty Mountains, the tenor of Tolkien's storytelling has been completely transformed from the children's fare of *The Hobbit,* but the peril of the mountains has not changed significantly. The first view the second generation of young hobbits have of the mountains is described in imagery that is at best inauspicious: "at the left of this high range rose three peaks; the tallest and nearest stood up like a tooth tipped with snow; its great, bare, northern precipice was still largely in the shadow, but where the sunlight slanted upon it, it glowed red."[41] They are no more cheered by their first sight of the terrible mountains than Bilbo himself had been.

The most cruel of these peaks, which would eventually prove an enemy too implacable for even that intrepid company, appears even more unpromising to their frightened eyes: "Caradhras rose before them, a mighty peak, tipped with snow like silver, but with sheer naked sides, dull red as if stained with blood."[42] As they journey closer, the threatening tone of the descriptions never relents:

> The twisting and climbing road had in many places almost disappeared, and was blocked with many fallen stones. The night grew deadly dark under great clouds. A bitter wind swirled among the rocks. By midnight they had climbed to the knees of the great mountains. The narrow path now wound under a sheer wall of cliffs to the left, above which the grim flanks of Caradhras towered up invisible in the gloom; on the right was a gulf of darkness where the land fell suddenly into a deep ravine.[43]

The autobiographical crash of falling stones on a mountain path from Bilbo's story makes an appearance here as well, and this time the dangerous missiles are presented as clear indications that the mountain itself opposes the Fellowship's advance: "They heard eerie noises in the darkness round them. It may have been only a trick of the wind in the cracks and gullies of the rocky wall, but the sounds were those of shrill cries, and wild howls of laughter. Stones began to fall from the mountain-side, whistling over their heads, or crashing on the path beside them. Every now and again they heard a dull rumble, as a great boulder rolled down from hidden heights above."[44]

"Caradhras was called the Cruel," Gimli informs his companions, and the truth of the mountain's reputation becomes clear as the company soldiers on in the face of driving wind and heavy snow.[45] They are finally forced to turn back by the ferocity of a blizzard declared to be the "ill will" of the mountain, which "does not love Elves and Dwarves."[46] After their hard-earned retreat, the mountain sends a final stroke of malice to prevent them from considering another assault upon its mastery: "with a deep rumble there rolled down a fall of stones and slithering snow. The spray of it half blinded the Company as they crouched against the cliff, and when the air cleared again they saw that the path was blocked behind them."[47] The mountain is wholly personalized here, an actor with emotions and agency whose power forces the most intrepid of heroes into a choice that will prove fatal. Cruel Caradhras is the terrain-as-enemy concept fully realized.

Still, for all of the malice and terror in these scenes, Tolkien always manages to remind his readers that the mountains are beautiful as well as deadly. After their disastrous journey through Moria, after the loss of one of the most powerful beings on Middle-earth to a dark terror hiding beneath those cruel mountains, the battered Fellowship stumbles sadly into the daylight. Aragorn grimly informs them that they must go on, even if they "must do without hope," but Gimli begs for a single glimpse of the famed Mirrormere before they go.[48] The imagery of "Kheled-zâram fair and wonderful" is pure, heart-stopping Alpine beauty: "slowly they saw the forms of the encircling mountains mirrored in a profound blue, and the peaks were like plumes of white flame above them; beyond there was a space of sky. There like jewels sunk in the deep shone glinting stars, though sunlight was in the sky above."[49] They must do without hope, perhaps, but not without loveliness. Here, before Frodo and his companions move from the deadly wilderness of the mountains to the Otherworldly wilderness of Lothlórien, they are given a view that, while it may not quite make up for the fatal danger through which they have passed, at least reinforces that even the most dangerous of places can be beautiful.

After the breaking of their Fellowship, the members of the company all go on to encounter more mountains in their disparate journeys, but those mountains (much like the Anglo-Saxon world, which partially inspired them) feel somewhat more representative of the psychological state of the heroes than the fully personalized and implacably unfriendly

Misty Mountains do. Aragorn's dawn glimpse of Gondor's White Mountains is full of the hope of a new day, even to a Ranger weary from days of sleepless pursuit:

> Turning back they saw across the River the far hills kindled. Day leaped into the sky. The red rim of the sun rose over the shoulders of the dark land. Before them in the West the world lay still, formless and grey; but even as they looked, the shadows of night melted, the colours of the waking earth returned: green flowed over the wide meads of Rohan; the white mists shimmered in the water-vales; and far off to the left, thirty leagues or more, blue and purple stood the White Mountains, rising into peaks of jet, tipped with glimmering snows, flushed with the rose of morning.[50]

Caradhras in red twilight is inevitably described in harsh terms of teeth and blood, but the metaphors here are soft and beautiful.

Pippin, too, is struck by the majesty and power of Gondor's mountains and towers, as he approaches the ancient city on the wings of battle: "to his right great mountains reared their heads, ranging from the West to a steep and sudden end, as if in the making of the land the River had burst through a great barrier, carving out a mighty valley to be a land of battle and debate in times to come. And there where the White Mountains of Ered Nimrais came to their end he saw . . . the dark mass of Mount Mindolluin, the deep purple shadows of its high glens, and its tall face whitening in the rising day."[51] Gondor, ancient city of powerful men, besieged but defiant foe of Mordor, hope of the West, center of power at the dawn of the Fourth Age: the White Mountains are certainly a fitting setting for such a grand place, but they are not presented as wilderness. They are, in keeping with the Anglo-Saxon mood of this concept, a backdrop to the boon of civilization.

Merry's journey to Rohan's mountain stronghold at Harrowdale leaves him feeling somewhat more oppressed than hopeful at the sight of the wild mountains around him:

> Away to the right at the head of the great dale the mighty Starkhorn loomed up above its vast buttresses swathed in cloud; but its jagged peak, clothed in everlasting snow, gleamed far above the world, blue-shadowed upon the East, red-stained by the sunset in the West. . . . It was a skyless world, in which his eye, through dim gulfs of shadowy air, saw only evermounting slopes, great walls of stone behind great walls, and

> frowning precipices wreathed with mist. . . . He loved mountains, or he had loved the thought of them marching on the edge of stories brought from far away; but now he was borne down by the insupportable weight of Middle-earth.[52]

As the White Mountains represent an appropriate buttress to the grandeur of Gondor, this landscape matches the spirit of the most Anglo-Saxon of Tolkien's peoples. The Rohirrim, as epitomized by their language,[53] are explicitly described by Legolas as being like to the land itself, "rich and rolling in part, and else hard and stern as the mountains."[54] Both here and later at Helm's Deep, the mountainous wilderness of Rohan is the Germanic place of shelter, a mustering place or a stronghold to which they can retreat and fend off entire legions of enemies.

Frodo and Sam are the ones who eventually encounter the most undiluted of Germanic wasteland wildernesses. If the Misty Mountains are perilous but beautiful and the White Mountains are the stronghold of human greatness, Mordor is a deadly desert, the "fenland" and "mountainous moors" of the Old English concept of wilderness, with no redeeming qualities to mitigate the bleakness.[55] The passage describing what the hobbits encounter before the Black Gate is an oft-quoted one in Tolkien criticism, and for good reason; it capture's Tolkien's vision of a ruined world at its most repulsive:

> Dreadful as the Dead Marshes had been . . . more loathsome far was the country that the crawling day now slowly unveiled to his shrinking eyes. Even to the Mere of Dead Faces some haggard phantom of green spring would come; but here neither spring nor summer would ever come again. Here nothing lived, not even the leprous growths that feed on rottenness. The gasping pools were choked with ash and crawling muds, sickly white and grey, as if the mountains had vomited the filth of their entrails upon the lands about. High mounds of crushed and powdered rock, great cones of earth fire-blasted and poison-stained, stood like an obscene graveyard in endless rows, slowly revealed in the reluctant light.[56]

Dickerson and Evans rightly remark that "it is no wonder that Sam feels sick."[57] These mountains are not beautiful, and they are certainly not majestic. They are the epitome of wasteland. This is how Tolkien envisions a natural world where the engines and evil of modernity reign unopposed, a monument to the "dark labour of its slaves"; it is "a land defiled, diseased beyond all healing—unless the Great Sea should enter in and wash it with oblivion."[58] In Mordor, the beauty of wilderness has been utterly eclipsed, and all that remains is the waste and the danger.

The hobbits, "little squeaking ghosts that wandered among the ash-heaps of the Dark Lord," are turned back by this horror and implacable finality in front of the Black Gate, but—after a brief respite in the forests of Ithilien—their journey on mountain paths to the terrible pass of Cirith Ungol returns them to more *Beowulf* country.[59] They find that the wind-swept mountains there, like Caradhras, "seemed to be trying with their deadly breath to daunt them, to turn them back from the secrets of the high places, or to blow them away into the darkness behind."[60] Their endless climb up Gollum's long stair faintly echoes Beowulf's superhuman swim, and there is a monster truly worthy of the name lurking in the darkness at the end of the long effort. The description of Sam's courage in the wounding of Shelob places him firmly in the company of heroes: "Not the doughtiest soldier of old Gondor, nor the most savage Orc entrapped, had ever thus endured her, or set blade to her beloved flesh."[61] It is all typical saga fare, even if the hobbits are not really typical saga heroes, and the representation of the natural world here is purely Germanic: bleak, hopeless, monster-infested mountainous peril.

It is not only the mountains that are perilous, however. The danger of (and heroism in surviving the onslaught of) immensely powerful natural forces arrayed against humanity has a strong presence in many of Tolkien's forests as well. While Tolkien's second wilderness concept, akin to the Celtic Otherworld, relies heavily on the uncanny magic of wild woodlands, the forbidding dangers of Mirkwood and the Old Forest also belong at least partially in spirit to this grim and hostile first one. Roderick Nash explores in detail the association between Germanic wilderness and woods:

> A more precise meaning of wilderness as forested land is defensible in view of the restriction of the term's etymological roots to the languages of northern Europe. In German, for example, *Wildnis* is a cognate, and *Wildor* signifies wild game. Romance languages, on the other hand, have no single word to express the idea but rely on one of its attributes. Thus in Spanish, wilderness is *immensidad* or *falta de cultura* (lack of cultivation). In French the equivalents are *lieu desert*[62] (deserted place) and *solitude inculte*. Italian uses the vivid *scene di disordine o confusione*. This

> restriction of wilderness to the Teutonic tongues links it to the north of Europe, where uncultivated land was heavily forested. Consequently, the term once had specific reference to the woods. Wild beasts certainly favored them, and the forest, rather than the open field, was the logical place to get lost or confused.[63]

Here are the familiar dark forests of Germanic folklore that form such a large part of the modern Western European cultural foundation; from Little Red Riding Hood, Cinderella, and Sleeping Beauty to Snow White, Rapunzel, and the Frog Prince, Disney's artistic tapestry (and the shape it gives to the mental map of children throughout the Western world) would be bare indeed without the mythic landscapes of Jakob and Wilhelm Grimm. Here is the "unlovely scenery" of Tacitus's bristling woods,[64] the "vast and dangerous reaches of woodland and morass" that so shaped the character of those who dwelt within them.[65] Here is the abode of monsters, the

> secret land they guard,   high wolf-country,
> windy cliffs,   a dangerous way
> twisting through fens. . . .
> . . . .   that fearful lake
> overhung with roots   that sag and clutch
> frost-bound trees   at the water's edge[66]

where the terrible Grendelkin maintain their darksome lair. Tolkien, with his love of Germanic myth and sensitivity to its cultural import, consciously draws on this strong Western archetype of dark, monster-infested forests to create deep mythic resonances in his own work.

Bilbo again serves as the first and clearest example. He certainly must have enjoyed wandering through the woods and fields of the Shire—he had a map hanging in his hall at Bag End "with all his favourite walks marked on it in red ink" after all—but if he ever ventured into the Old Forest near Buckland, it merits no mention in his Red Book.[67] Before his adventure, then, Mr. Baggins would likely have generally experienced woodlands solely within the much more friendly English concept of wilderness. The forested slopes of the Misty Mountains prove a much more serious proposition; in that harsh place Bilbo and the Dwarves follow wooded paths, which become darker and darker as the days go on, and the gloom and silence of the wolf-haunted woods prefigure the even darker places to come. Beorn's "tales of the wild lands on this side of the mountains, and especially of the dark and dangerous . . . terrible forest of Mirkwood" remind the company that "after the mountains it was the worst of the perils they had to pass before they came to the dragon's stronghold."[68] Even considering that he had already come through a great deal of adventure by this point, Bilbo does not really know what he is in for.

He soon finds out. The early glimpses of this "greatest of the forests of the Northern world" are described in terms at least as ominous as those of the mountains: "As soon as it was light they could see the forest coming as it were to meet them, or waiting for them like a black and frowning wall before them. . . . By the afternoon they had reached the eaves of Mirkwood, and were resting almost beneath the great overhanging boughs of its outer trees. Their trunks were huge and gnarled, their branches twisted, their leaves were dark and long. Ivy grew on them and trailed along the ground."[69] At this inauspicious place, much like the mischievous German mountain spirit to which he owes part of his provenance,[70] Gandalf quite inconveniently abandons the company and departs on other business. There is nowhere else for Bilbo and the Dwarves to go but into the darkness. They "turned from the light that lay on the lands outside and plunged into the forest."[71] The description of the entrance to the wood evokes a sense of traveling into a cave or other enclosed space: "The entrance to the path was like a sort of arch leading into a gloomy tunnel made by two great trees that leant together, too old and strangled with ivy and hung with lichen to bear more than a few blackened leaves. The path itself was narrow and wound in and out among the trunks. Soon the light at the gate was like a little bright hole far behind, and the quiet was so deep that their feet seemed to thump along while all the trees leaned over them and listened."[72] The impenetrable darkness of the forest is one of its chief attributes; daytime meant only "a sort of darkened green glimmer," while the night was "pitch dark . . . so black that you really could see nothing," and not even the power of the Elves is able to bring more than the dim light of torches and fires to this dark place.[73]

Indeed, one striking thing about Mirkwood is that, in contrast to the various mountainous wildernesses, there is scant beauty to be found in Tolkien's descriptions of the place. From bright Lothlórien, when the Elves look toward the "fastness of Southern Mirkwood," they see a place of dark power, "clad in a forest of dark fir, where the trees strive one against another and their branches rot and wither," despite the fact that within that forest an Elven realm lies hidden.[74] Given the majesty of Rivendell or Lothlórien, one would naturally assume the halls of the

Elvenking to be beautiful indeed, even allowing for the fact that sylvan Elves were less in power than the Noldor. But those halls are described only in terms relative to Orc-haunts without any of the dazzling poetic artistry of which Tolkien was obviously capable. The reader is told simply that the great cave "was lighter and more wholesome than any goblin-dwelling, and neither so deep nor so dangerous."[75]

The history of Mirkwood is given to readers in the stately narrative of *The Silmarillion:*

> Now of old the name of that forest was Greenwood the Great, and its wide halls and aisles were the haunt of many beasts and of birds of bright song; and there was the realm of King Thranduil under the oak and the beech. But after many years, when well nigh a third of that age of the world had passed, a darkness crept slowly through the wood from the southward, and fear walked there in shadowy glades; fell beasts came hunting, and cruel and evil creatures laid there their snares.
>
> Then the name of the forest was changed and Mirkwood it was called, for the nightshade lay deep there, and few dared to pass through, save only in the north where Thranduil's people still held the evil at bay.[76]

Readers are given here only a few mildly positive images involve spaciousness and birdsong, and even this small bit feels like a later development; the Elvenking is not even named in *The Hobbit.* It is possible that Tolkien's underdeveloped concept of Elves in his children's story was simply not yet strong enough to overcome the full archetypal weight of the Germanic dark forest.

Besides the torches and fires of the Elves, which serve only to lure the travelers from their path, the only other light the company encounters in Mirkwood comes from many pairs of gleaming eyes. These eyes, a "horrible pale bulbous sort of eyes," augment the terror of the forest itself with a creeping fear of its monstrous inhabitants.[77] As mythic monsters in the wilderness go, the giant spiders seem to sit somewhere between the comedy of trolls and the awesome destruction of a dragon. Although Bilbo uses comically insulting verses to infuriate the spiders, the situation of the Dwarves (poisoned, cocooned in sticky webs, hanging like flies from the trees, being squeezed by horrid multieyed many-legged creatures) feels somewhat more serious in tone than it had when they had been simply bagged up by trolls like so much market shopping. The spiders are still considerably less dreadful than Smaug—a single hobbit with a small elf-blade is able to kill half a dozen of them as they try and drag away his portly companion[78]—but they nevertheless manage to inspire a visceral sort of fear in the reader, resonating with the common arachnophobia of the human experience, and invoking the mythic archetypes of large and fearsome creatures hiding in the dark woods at night.

In accordance with his ability to overcome this terror, Bilbo's actions in Mirkwood are what begin to change him from ordinary hobbit into hero. "Somehow the killing of the giant spider, all alone by himself in the dark without the help of the wizard or the Dwarves or of anyone else, made a great difference to Mr. Baggins. He felt a different person, and much fiercer and bolder."[79] Once he has saved the Dwarves, they too see him in a different light, as they "knew only too well that they would soon all have been dead, if it had not been for the hobbit."[80] Here, on an appropriately halfling-sized scale, is a clear reflection of the Germanic idea of heroism: the heroism of a Beowulf or a Sigurd, an accomplishment defined by journeying into the deepest darkness of the wilderness, overcoming its challenges, and vanquishing the monsters that lurk within.

Frodo and his companions must also prove their heroism in dark forests. As befits the more sophisticated tone of *The Lord of The Rings*, however, they face a longer series of dangerous trials than Bilbo did, and those dangers are both more complicated and more overwhelming. They also first encounter this dark woodland wilderness in a place much closer to home. Not an hour's pony ride away from Frodo's house in Crickhollow, Merry leads his friends through a tunnel under the enormous hedge the hobbits of the Buckland had built to keep the Shire safe from the darkness and danger of the Old Forest. The wood is a queer place: "Everything in it is very much more alive, more aware of what is going on, so to speak, than things are in the Shire. And the trees do not like strangers. They watch you. They are usually content merely to watch you, as long as daylight lasts, and don't do much. Occasionally the most unfriendly ones may drop a branch, or stick a root out, or grasp at you with a long trailer."[81]

As the hobbits move into the forest, what they see reinforces these rather inhospitable expectations, echoing Bilbo's experiences in Mirkwood: "Looking back they could see the dark line of the Hedge through the stems of trees that were already thick about them. Looking ahead they could see only tree-trunks of innumerable sizes and shapes: straight or bent, twisted, leaning, squat or slender, smooth or gnarled and branched; and all the stems were green or grey with moss and slimy, shaggy growths."[82]

They pick their way along, leading their ponies around the "many writhing and interlacing roots," and as they proceed "it seemed that the trees became taller, darker, and thicker. There was no sound, except an occasional drip of moisture falling through the still leaves. For the moment there was no whispering or movement among the branches; but they all got an uncomfortable feeling that they were being watched with disapproval, deepening to dislike and even enmity."[83] Here is perhaps a foreshadowing of the hatred of Caradhras; although the Old Forest would not prove as fatal as the Misty Mountains, the wilderness itself is just as much their enemy, and it is portrayed with a similarly alarming amount of malice and agency. Frodo soon comes to regret the fact that "he had ever thought of challenging the menace of the trees."[84] That menace, the malevolence of the forest itself, forces the hobbits from their path and brings them inexorably into the deepest part of the valley of the River Withywindle.

The archetypal monster they encounter in this particular dark mythic forest proves unexpectedly to be of a vegetal rather than animal nature. Old Man Willow is the menace of the whole forest consolidated into "a huge willow-tree, old and hoary. Enormous it looked, its sprawling branches going up like reaching arms with many long-fingered hands, its knotted and twisted trunk gaping in wide fissures that creaked faintly as the boughs moved."[85] Despite Frodo's efforts to resist the sleepy spell and Sam's sturdy hobbit sense in setting a fire against the evil thing to free Merry and Pippin, the terrible old tree proves a foe too great for these as-yet-untried heroes, and they must be rescued by Tom Bombadil (whose power, like that of their arboreal enemy, derives from the land itself).

After a respite, their next adventures take them through another menacing wilderness, that of the Barrow-downs. These hills have a dark reputation, darker even than the Old Forest;[86] although there are some clear Celtic elements in the descriptions of the mist and the mounds and the standing stones, the undead monster lurking at their heart is an Old Norse *draugr* or *haugbúi* straight out of the sagas. Tom Bombadil warns his young guests against tangling with the Northern dangers waiting for them among those perilous green hills: "Don't you go a-meddling with old stone or cold Wights or prying in their houses, unless you be strong folk with hearts that never falter!"[87] Of course the hobbits end up doing exactly that. The Barrow-wight proves to be coldness and darkness in animate form, corpse-like, moaning horribly with "grim, hard, cold words, heartless and miserable. The night was railing against the morning of which it was bereaved, and the cold was cursing the warmth for which it hungered."[88] Although the terror of this ghastly figure first awakens within Frodo the "seed of courage," which would see him through so many subsequent perils, and although he demonstrates more bravery and cleverness than he did when he fell so helplessly under the spell of Old Man Willow, this monster is still too great an enemy for the young hobbits to overcome.[89] They must once again be rescued and escorted safely to Bree.

Beyond Bree, the still rather foolish and helpless hobbits find themselves venturing out into "pathless wilderness" and journeying through lands "empty of all save birds and beasts, unfriendly places deserted by all the races of the world."[90] The vast reaches of Eriador, although more varied than the blackly impenetrable woods of Mirkwood or the Old Forest, are still darkly described: the lands are "wild and pathless; bushes and stunted trees grew in dense patches with wide barren spaces in between. The grass was scanty, coarse, and grey; and the leaves in the thickets were faded and falling. It was a cheerless land, and their journey was slow and gloomy."[91] They spend many days "lost in a sombre country of dark trees winding among the feet of sullen hills," following Strider through bleak wastes and facing down a coordinated attack from the monstrous Black Riders, before they are able to make their way to the Celtic haven of Rivendell at last.[92]

Beyond the Elven Otherworlds of Rivendell and Lothlórien, another forbidding wood awaits some members of the broken Fellowship, a wood as full of enmity toward those who would trespass on its ground as any other wild place in Middle-earth. But in the forest of Fangorn, Tolkien takes the typical details of the Germanic dark forest archetype and cleverly inverts them, prompting the reader to imagine a place where the awesome dark power of the wilderness works for rather than against the heroes compelled to travel through it. Even the monster lurking in Fangorn proves no monster at all—although it is again a personification of the power of wilderness—but a powerful menace directed at the same evils threatening the heroes because those evils also threaten the forest itself.

When Merry and Pippin flee from their Orc captors, they encounter a forest steeped in imagery of darkness: "the dark edge of the forest loomed up straight before them. Night seemed to have taken refuge under its great trees, creeping away from the coming Dawn."[93] Later Aragorn, Legolas, and Gimli pause in their pursuit to build a fire under the eaves of Fangorn, and "suddenly the dark and unknown forest, so near at hand, made itself felt as a great brooding presence, full of secret purpose."[94] If anyone could be expected to approach wooded wilderness with equanimity, it should be a sylvan Elf and a Ranger, but Legolas and Aragorn have a serious discussion about the dangers of the brooding darkness before them. It is very old, "as old as the forest by the Barrow-downs, and it is far greater. Elrond says that the two are akin, the last strongholds of the mighty woods of the Elder Days. . . . Yet Fangorn holds some secret of its own."[95] Considering the hardships and hazards they have endured at the hands of wilderness powers thus far in the tale, it is no wonder that they expect similar threats to be lurking in this dark wood.

As they move into the forest, however, the sinister quality of its secret darkness gradually seems to shift somehow. Legolas senses that "it is not evil, or what evil is in it is far away. I catch only the faintest echoes of dark places where the hearts of the trees are black."[96] In Pippin's earlier observation, Fangorn "does not look or feel at all like Bilbo's description of Mirkwood. That was all dark and black, and the home of dark black things. This is just dim, and frightfully tree-ish."[97] To support his inversion of the Germanic dark forest archetype, Tolkien plays a bit with perspective here; when Gimli remarks that he "thought Fangorn was dangerous," Gandalf reminds him that, by their enemies, all powerful beings are considered dangerous: "'Dangerous!' cried Gandalf. 'And so am I, very dangerous: more dangerous than anything you will ever meet, unless you are brought alive before the seat of the Dark Lord. And Aragorn is dangerous, and Legolas is dangerous. You are beset with dangers, Gimli son of Glóin; for you are dangerous yourself, in your own fashion. Certainly the forest of Fangorn is perilous—not least to those that are too ready with their axes; and Fangorn himself, he is perilous too.'"[98] No less a personage than the Lord Celeborn had warned the travelers not to "risk becoming entangled in the Forest of Fangorn," but when the hobbits report this, Treebeard himself points out that he "might have said much the same, if you had been going the other way. Do not risk getting entangled in the woods of *Laurelindórenan!*"[99] Here the old Ent is clearly trying to draw a parallel between the two places, but the reader was given no hint of darkness as the characters approached and entered bright and golden Lothlórien. The dark trees of Fangorn, however, daunt even the bravest—and against enemies wielding ax and fire the trees themselves prove to be quite fatal.

Later in the story, a looming forest appears suddenly on the banks of the Deeping-coomb, where "great trees, bare and silent, stood, rank on rank, with tangled bough and hoary head; their twisted roots were buried in the long green grass. Darkness was under them."[100] Entire hosts of Orcs, fleeing onslaughts from Théoden and Aragorn on one side and Gandalf and Erkenbrand on the other, are forced unwillingly into that black wood, where "wailing they passed under the waiting shadow of the trees; and from that shadow none ever came again."[101] When Gandalf and Théoden and company approach the wood the next day, they are faced with as black a Germanic forest wilderness as any thus far encountered in Middle-earth, full of a "great wrath" so strong it throbs in Legolas's ears: "The trees were grey and menacing, and a shadow or a mist was about them. The ends of their long sweeping boughs hung down like searching fingers, their roots stood up from the ground like the limbs of strange monsters, and dark caverns opened beneath them. . . . On either side the great aisles of the wood were already wrapped in dusk, stretching away into impenetrable shadows; and there they heard the creaking and groaning of boughs, and far cries, and a rumour of wordless voices, murmuring angrily."[102] Gandalf leads them confidently forward, and they pass beneath an "arched gate under mighty boughs" and ride into the darkness.[103] When Legolas discerns that the trees "do not belong here" but have come "from the deep dales of Fangorn," Gimli shudders and declares that to be "the most perilous wood in Middle-earth."[104] Perilous, indeed—but only the servants of the Enemy truly suffer that peril.

Fangorn, like Mirkwood, is never favored with the stunning spectacles of poetic descriptions Tolkien employs elsewhere, but unlike in Mirkwood there do appear some moments of quiet pleasantness. Where Merry and Pippin first meet Treebeard, on a rocky hill rising out of the forest to reach for the sunshine, the imagery of darkness shifts into something deep and handsome: "where all had looked so shabby and grey before, the wood now gleamed with rich browns, and with the smooth black-greys of bark like polished leather. The boles of the trees glowed with a soft green like young grass: early spring or a fleeting vision of it was about them."[105] Treebeard's home at Wellinghall, although in a "steep dark land" at the "feet of the mountains" near the "green roots of tall Methedras," is washed in lovely gloaming imagery: on a "long slope, clad with grass, now grey in the twilight" the hobbits see that "stars were shining already in lakes between shores of cloud," and the entrance to the hall is guarded by evergreen trees whose leaves were "dark and polished, and gleamed in the twilight."[106] Still, in contrast to the singing golden beauty of Lothlórien, Fangorn forest always retains its dark wild character, full of "thickets of birch and rowan, and beyond them dark climbing pinewoods" and "deep groves, where the trees were larger, taller, and thicker than any that the hobbits had ever seen before" where they can feel the dark "sense of stifling which they had noticed when they first ventured into Fangorn."[107] Fangorn may be beautiful, but it is beautiful in the ways that the mountains are beautiful, and like them it is a beauty that is paired with deadly peril.

In some places Fangorn's perilous beauty demonstrates a good deal of overlap with the Celtic concept of wilderness, but the Germanic flavor to the darkness of the forest is just as strong. Cold, harsh, Northern streams of influence run through it, from the black menace of the angry Huorns to the hopeless doom that echoes in the pounding of the song accompanying the last march of the Ents:

To Isengard! Though Isengard be ringed and barred with doors of stone;
Though Isengard be strong and hard, as cold as stone and bare as bone,
We go, we go, we go to war, to hew the stone and break the door;
For bole and bough are burning now, the furnace roars—we go to war!
To land of gloom with tramp of doom, with roll of drum, we come, we come;
To Isengard with doom we come!
With doom we come, with doom we come![108]

"Of course, it is likely enough, my friends . . . that we are going to our doom," Treebeard rumbles, but he and his fellow Ents march on nevertheless, as grimly determined as the *einherjar* riding behind Odin to the last great battle that will destroy the world.[109]

This echo of Ragnarök leads into the last piece of Tolkien's Germanic wilderness concept to be examined here: the presence of a group of people valorous enough, and stalwart enough, to continually expose themselves to all the darkness and danger of the threatening Wild. Tolkien's work has given many gifts to the modern mythic landscape, but one of the most powerful and interesting is embodied in the Ranger archetype.[110] The word *ranger* certainly appears before Tolkien; the *OED* cites its use for a forester or gamekeeper in the fourteenth century, and notes a Spenserian line that (with modernized spelling) could be inserted in Tolkien's legendarium unchanged.[111] There are other clear predecessors, from the Yeoman of Chaucer to Robin Hood to James Fenimore Cooper's Natty Bumppo, but it was Tolkien who gathered the various pieces of the character archetype together and presented it in a compelling myth for modern people. Because of him, the concept of grim and solitary

Rangers hunting monsters in the wilderness has now joined other ideas flowing in currents from ancient stories—tall and beautiful Elves with bows, gold-greedy Dwarves, and typical parties of multiracial adventurers journeying together are other examples—which have been gathered and shaped by Tolkien into what have become mythic tropes in today's fantasy fiction and role-playing games.

The most central attribute of the Rangers, and the reason they are important in the context of this study, is the fact that they are a wandering people who make their home in the wilderness. As the narrator of *The Lord of the Rings* explains,

> In those days no other Men had settled dwellings so far west, or within a hundred leagues of the Shire. But in the wild lands beyond Bree there were mysterious wanderers. The Bree-folk called them Rangers, and knew nothing of their origin. They were taller and darker than the Men of Bree and were believed to have strange powers of sight and hearing, and to understand the languages of beasts and birds. They roamed at will southwards, and eastwards even as far as the Misty Mountains; but they were now few and rarely seen.[112]

Their association with wilderness makes the Rangers highly suspect to people who live within the borders of civilization. The fat old innkeeper Barliman Butterbur, who had never left Bree and "wouldn't do that for any money," warns the hobbits against the "strange-looking weather-beaten man"[113] asking to accompany them. Steady and sturdy Samwise voices a similar mistrust, arguing that the stranger "comes out of the Wild, and I never heard no good of such folk."[114] Much is made of Strider's uncouth appearance, and Tolkien works hard to cast doubt upon his character in order to heighten the tension of Frodo's situation.

Wiser beings in Middle-earth know better, however. Although the information is not especially noted by four young hobbits still frightened by their experience in the lair of the Barrow-wight, Tom Bombadil mentions the Rangers: "Few now remember them . . . yet still some go wandering, sons of forgotten kings walking in loneliness, guarding from evil things folk that are heedless."[115] Gandalf, of course, knows the truth; he disabuses Frodo of the notion that Strider is "only a Ranger," and explains their high lineage: "that is just what the Rangers are: the last remnant in the North of the great people, the Men of the West."[116] As the story progresses, Tolkien gives his readers many hints that—despite the way he introduced them in

Bree—these mysterious and high-born folk are to be respected rather than denigrated for their deep association with wild places.

Aragorn's long declamation to Boromir at the Council of Elrond makes clear that it is not just scenery and solitude that draw the Rangers into the wilderness; they sojourn there to hunt the monstrous inhabitants of wild places and protect the borders of civilized lands: "Lonely men are we, Rangers of the wild, hunters—but hunters ever of the servants of the Enemy; for they are found in many places, not in Mordor only. . . . But when dark things come from the houseless hills, or creep from sunless woods, they fly from us."[117]

Other Rangers besides the Dúnedain also roam Middle-earth, protecting their civilized countries from the dangerous inhabitants of the wildernesses outside their borders. Faramir's company, a group who identify themselves to Sam and Frodo as "Rangers of Ithilien," are described as "forayers, who crossed the Anduin secretly . . . to harry the Orcs and other enemies that roamed" in the wilderness around Gondor.[118] Also, although they are not given the name of Rangers, in Beleriand during the First Age the march-wardens of the Elven kingdom of Doriath perform a similar service: "Then Beleg Strongbow, chief of the march-wardens of Thingol, brought great strength of the Sindar armed with axes into Brethil; and issuing from the deeps of the forest . . . took an Orc legion at unawares and destroyed it. Thereafter the black tide out of the North was stemmed in that region."[119]

Several hundred years later this same Beleg, who "dwelt ever on the marches of Doriath" and was "the greatest woodsman of those days," would become the boon companion of the ill-starred but formidable Elf-friend Túrin Turambar.[120] Túrin, along with the other march-wardens, "waged unceasing war upon the Orcs and all servants and creatures of Morgoth," and his many years in the wilderness gave him the weather-beaten look so characteristic of Rangers: "he cared no longer for his looks or his attire, but his hair was unkempt, and his mail covered with a grey cloak stained with the weather."[121] These two, mighty Elf and hard-handed man, earned great renown in their battles with the creatures of the Enemy: "One only was mightier in arms among the march-wardens of Thingol at that time than Túrin, and that was Beleg Strongbow; and Beleg and Túrin were companions in every peril, and walked far and wide in the wild woods together."[122] The wilderness of the march-wardens and Rangers is a wilderness of monsters, dark and dangerous, and they are heroic people indeed who live in that wild place.

Naturally, as befits wilderness-dwellers and monster-hunters, a singular defining characteristic of the Rangers is their impressive fortitude. Anyone short of an ultramarathoner grows weary just reading about the pursuit of Merry and Pippin's Orc captors across Rohan. However, when Aragorn admits to being "weary as I have seldom been before, weary as no Ranger should be with a clear trail to follow," he seems to take for granted that he should have been able to basically sprint more than a hundred miles on foot with scant rest without ill effect, and attributes his fatigue instead to "some will that lends speed to our foes and sets an unseen barrier before us: a weariness that is in the heart more than in the limb."[123] Later, after riding hard through the night, at dawn in a high chamber of the Hornburg Aragorn dares and wins a battle of wills with the Dark Lord himself over the prize of the Palantír of Orthanc. It requires this supernatural battle to finally take its toll on the seemingly inexhaustible man; afterwards his grim face makes him look like "one who has laboured in sleepless pain for many nights," and he admits that while he judged that he "had both the right and the strength" to use the stone, his strength proved "enough—barely," as it had been "a bitter struggle, and the weariness is slow to pass."[124] "Does he feel no fear?" wonders Gimli, as Aragorn leads them all unflinching through the terror-haunted darkness of the Paths of the Dead.[125]

Singular, superhuman heroes like this are not uncommon in Germanic myth—Beowulf could certainly stand without embarrassment in Aragorn's company, as could Sigurd or even Gawain—but it is not only Aragorn but all of the Rangers who demonstrate this tenacious valor. The arrival of the Grey Company in Rohan prompts Théoden to remark that "thirty such knights will be a strength that cannot be counted by heads."[126] Gimli observes that "stout men and lordly they are, and the Riders of Rohan look almost as boys beside them; for they are grim men of face, worn like weathered rocks for the most part, even as Aragorn himself; and they are silent."[127] Éowyn criticizes Aragorn's "madness" in wasting the valor of his company on the Paths of the Dead: "here are men of renown and prowess, whom you should not take into the shadows, but should lead to war, where men are needed."[128] All of this soldierly praise is interesting, considering that the company demonstrates little of the glitter or grandeur typical of military units:

> A little apart the Rangers sat, silent, in an ordered company, armed with spear and bow and sword. They were clad in cloaks of dark grey, and their

> hoods were cast now over helm and head. Their horses were strong and of proud bearing, but rough-haired. . . . There was no gleam of stone or gold, nor any fair thing in all their gear and harness; nor did their riders bear any badge or token, save only that each cloak was pinned upon the left shoulder by a brooch of silver shaped like a rayed star.[129]

These grim, silent, and strong warriors may not be much to look at, but Tolkien makes it very clear that they are heroic indeed, especially when they proceed on a path so dark even the valiant Théoden trembles to think of it.

The entire affair of the Paths of the Dead, with its courageous confrontation of undead terrors and its unstoppable phantom army, is among the most purely Germanic episodes in the Middle-earth legendarium, as pure as Túrin's Sigurd-inspired slaying of Glaurung or Bilbo's theft of a golden cup from a dragon's hoard. The grim troop rides at dawn, following Aragorn into darkness "under the gloom of trees that not even Legolas could long endure," knowing they are riding to their deaths.[130] When they reach a "sheer wall of rock" where a "Dark Door gaped before them like the mouth of night," they pause; "this is an evil door," remarks one of them, "and my death lies beyond it. I will dare to pass it nonetheless."[131] The wilderness imagery here is as bleak as can be, and there is not a saga hero worth the name who did not utter similar words. The Rangers proceed through a black passage, which Tolkien's prosecraft continues to wrap in the deepest terror of creeping death and undeath.

In the dark vale beyond the cave there is little time for respite; the Grey Company follows steadfastly as Aragorn leads them "upon the journey of greatest haste and weariness that any among them had known, save he alone, and only his will held them to go on. No other mortal Men could have endured it, none but the Dúnedain of the North."[132] The result of all this bitter courage, an army of oathbreaking undead, which Aragorn uses to defeat the Corsairs of Umbar so he can lift the siege of Gondor, also powerfully echoes Northern European traditions of ghostly warriors, from the dreadful howling hosts of Jakob Grimm's *Wilde Jagd* to the black-clad wraiths who slaughtered Romans by the legion in the dark forests of Central Europe,[133] and it establishes Aragorn and his dour-handed kinsmen as the mightiest heroes of their age.

Ultimately, the wilderness of the Rangers is the Germanic concept of wilderness. These "mysterious vagabonds," a people "unused to cities and houses of stone," have the strength, courage, fortitude, woodcraft, and general endurance to travel in all of the dark and dangerous wild places, far away from the light of civilization's golden halls.[134] They sojourn alone from the highest peaks of the cruel Misty Mountains to the blackest depths of Mirkwood and beyond. They do battle with evil monsters beyond the borders of civilized countries. They are sterling examples of what Tolkien himself referred to as "Northern courage," the "creed of unyielding will," which he considered "the great contribution of early Northern literature."[135] This is the courage of the Rangers: ancient courage, heroic courage, the courage of Beowulf facing the fatal dragon or Gawain bending unflinchingly beneath the raised ax of Bertilak. It is the kind of courage Tom Shippey has in mind when he observes that "few modern readers of *Beowulf*, or the *Elder Edda*, or the Icelandic 'family sagas', can escape a certain feeling of inadequacy as they contemplate whole sequences of characters who appear, in a casual and quite lifelike way, not to know what fear is."[136] The same can certainly be said of Aragorn and company, and—unlike the hobbits, who are much closer to modern readers in temperament, and whose undeniably great courage is generally of a more modern sort—the Rangers carry within their mythical inheritance all of the darkness and danger of the Germanic concept of wilderness.

Many Tolkien scholars have noted that this concept is one of the strongest flows running through Tolkien's work. Marjorie Burns lists many occasions where Tolkien's characters must pass various barriers such as bridges, gates, or doorways, and she argues that almost always "darkness, intensified danger, and confrontation with actual or symbolic death lie on the other side. Like the Norse gods on their heroic or shamanistic quests (where rushing water, vast forests, towering mountains, massive doorways, or guardian figures intercede before they reach their challengers), Tolkien's heroes must overcome similar obstacles, similar impediments, before confronting their own versions of risk and enmity in highly eddic forms."[137]

Similarly, although they do not comment on any Germanic provenance, Dickerson and Evans observe a hostility in Tolkien's work that, by the time of the Third Age, has "hardened into something like a general environmental principle according to which Men and other races are alienated from the wild regions of the landscape."[138] They go on to question why, "considering Tolkien's love of trees," he would go to such lengths to "paint such a dark and even evil picture of Mirkwood and the Old Forest," and they conclude that the presence of this dangerous wilderness concept serves largely narrative purposes: "we must remember that Tolkien above all wanted to tell a good story, and having these characters pass through a frightening and often hostile woods makes for a dramatic atmosphere."[139] This humans-versus-nature narrative is certainly older than Germanic myth—it goes all the way back to the dawn of agriculture—but it is generally true that the "howling wilderness" stories that are current in Western culture today have detoured through Northern Europe on their journey from prehistory. With its roots drinking so deeply from the stream of Germanic myth and literature, it is no wonder that Tolkien's work includes such a cold and unforgiving concept of wilderness.

But, just as Tolkien's influence stream flows largely but not completely from the high mountains of Teutonic lore, the wilderness in his work is not entirely the grim and perilous darkness of this Anglo-Saxon heritage. There are many places in Middle-earth—some of them the very same places already mentioned—that demonstrate a different wilderness idea, one based on another stream of cultural influence. When the Anglo-Saxons left the boundless forested mountains of Europe behind them, they encountered a different wilderness concept in the misty landscape of the Irish Sea zone: the uncanny, beautiful-but-dangerous, and thoroughly enrapturing wilderness of the Celtic Otherworld.

CHAPTER FIVE

Elves in the Forest

All of Tolkien's wilderness concepts draw heavily on medieval ideas. Where the first concept was one of brutal opposition, relying on ideas of separation and struggle, the second is less harsh and more subtle, less grim and more uncanny. There is in this wilderness less cold blackness and more golden green loveliness. Instead of the abrupt reality of mountain passes or the black shadows of dark forests, this natural world is characterized less by a lack of human civilization than by the presence of something unseen and mysterious overlaid upon the normal human plane of existence, where "immortal realms interlaced with the everyday world of physical experience and natural topography" are present in the wild places of forest and fen.[1] This is not to say that overall the wilderness of this second concept is necessarily any less dangerous or any more beautiful—it is just that, as Tolkien's heroes move through this second type of carefully crafted wild lands, the beauty is foregrounded against the peril instead of the reverse.

Tolkien himself refers to the influence of "more inquisitive and less severe Celtic learning" on the later English inheritors of *Beowulf*'s bleak Northern cultural atmosphere.[2] Marjorie Burns notes that this difference in mindset relies at least partially on the geography of the Irish Sea zone: "Britain's weather, seasons, and topographical formations have always been less hostile to human endeavour than what the Scandinavians knew. Ups and downs are less extreme in the British Isles. . . . Britain's Celts were not in a position to experience elemental nature and lonely, uncivilized space to the extent the Norsemen did. There were fewer inaccessible regions and therefore fewer places that could be thought of as inevitably belonging to either monsters or gods."[3]

Alfred K. Siewers (whose detailed examination both of Celtic overlay landscapes and Tolkien's use of these traditions has been important in shaping this study) notes how this difference in landscape influences how humans conceived of themselves in relation to the larger powers of the universe: "the Irish *síde* (paralleled in Welsh notions of the Otherworld *gorsedd*), unlike the Anglo-Saxon mead hall, arguably externalized rather than internalized cosmic connections with dynamic larger realities."[4] This externalization generally means that, in a Celtic-influenced idea of wilderness, magic and mystery and power are presented more as attributes of a place rather than of the hero daring to travel through it. Siewers also argues elsewhere that Tolkien's overlay landscape involves a sense in which "forests, rivers, mountains, and animals become characters, not really anthropomorphized, but representing powers larger than or beyond the human, a cosmic poly-centered focus for the narrative."[5] The Germanic wilderness is a place of black darkness into which heroes bring light from the golden halls of civilization; in contrast, light and wonder—as well as a mysteriously powerful landscape with agency of its own—are waiting for the hero brave enough to journey into the uncanny Celtic wilds.

This Celtic wilderness generally manifests in Tolkien's legendarium as Otherworldly forest retreats, characterized by dazzling natural beauty, the presence of hidden and mysterious powers, and a dreamlike alterity in the flow of time. Siewers observes that "the woods of Middle-earth themselves provide an example of a specific analogy with early Celtic traditions," and it seems that Tolkien was happy to bring these traditions into his story to stand alongside (and sometimes even within) the grim Germanic woodlands already there.[6] Most obviously, as Marjorie Burns points out, "in Tolkien's stories the closest parallels to the Celtic Otherworld are Rivendell and Lothlórien," but she also notes the presence of other "pockets of Celticness . . . enclaves of Elven enchantment within a harsh and Nordic expanse."[7] There are several of these Celtic enclaves where the bleakness of the Germanic wilderness lessens; in these places the presence of Otherworldly creatures (usually but not exclusively Elves) thins the boundaries between worlds, and eventually causes the heroes to move into a place of bright and mysterious powers they do not fully understand.

. . .

An early example of these Celtic retreats appears in *The Hobbit*, hidden within the blackness of Mirkwood. Although Mirkwood is a quintessentially Germanic dark forest, "all dark and black, and the home of dark black things," and although the harsh Nordic character of it seems to ultimately overshadow Tolkien's still-developing conception of the powers of his later Elves, an unmistakable glimmer of the uncanny Celtic otherworld still manages to peek through in the woodland realm of the Elvenking.[8]

The punctilious narrator observes that, had the company "considered the meaning of the hunt and the white deer that had appeared on their path"[9] when they crossed the enchanted stream, they might have been able to guess the import of the "disquieting laughter" and "singing in the distance" they hear in the darkness, but sadly their Celtic/Elvish lore is lacking:[10] "the laughter was the laughter of fair voices not of goblins, and the singing was beautiful, but it sounded eerie and strange, and they were not comforted, rather they hurried on from those parts with what strength they had left."[11] As the days of darkness wear on, the weary and hungry travelers, whose food was many days past gone, are eventually enticed off their path by a series of wondrous mirages of firelight and feasting and song: "The feast that they now saw was greater and more magnificent than before; and at the head of a long line of feasters sat a woodland king with a crown of leaves upon his golden hair. . . . The elvish folk were passing bowls from hand to hand and across the fires, and some were harping and many were singing. Their gleaming hair was twined with flowers; green and white gems glinted on their collars and their belts; and their faces and their songs were filled with mirth. Loud and clear and fair were those songs."[12]

When Bilbo and the Dwarves intrude onto these circles, however, the overlay landscape vanishes: darkness falls, the beautiful bright people disappear, the unlucky individual foolish enough to step into the light is thrown into a magical slumber of bewitching dreams, and the rest are surrounded once again by the black menace of the Germanic forest.

Fleeing from the eight-legged monsters hiding in the darkness, Bilbo and the Dwarves come upon "the edge of a ring where elf-fires had been," and they find that "some good magic lingered in such spots, which the spiders did not like" and "the light was greener, and the boughs less thick and threatening."[13] The Elves are described as a woodland people who "mostly lived and hunted in the open woods, and had houses or huts on the ground and in the branches. The beeches were their favourite trees."[14] It is hard to reconcile this imagery of openness and safe houses, what Burns calls the "unfettered, open-air quality" of the Elven homeland, with the endless black darkness of Mirkwood.[15] This dichotomy makes the realm of the Elvenking a very striking example of "the power of the Otherworld in shaping time and space in relation to landscape"; the "real" world of the dangerous and spider-infested forest wilderness and the Otherworld of the uncanny green woods are at almost complete odds, and yet occupy the same physical space.[16]

In *The Lord of the Rings,* this same sort of Elven overlay landscape appears even within the borders of the prosaic landscape of the Shire. Threatened by the dark shadow of a Black Rider, Frodo is saved from an evil compulsion when, at just the right moment, "there came a sound like mingled song and laughter. Clear voices rose and fell in the starlit air."[17] As Siewers notes, "the music and otherworldly light of the Elves echo Celtic otherworldly tales,"[18] and the unearthly light and Celtic flavor of these High Elves is unmistakable: "they passed slowly, and the hobbits could see the starlight glimmering on their hair and in their eyes. They bore no lights, yet as they walked a shimmer, like the light of the moon above the rim of the hills before it rises, seemed to fall about their feet."[19] Unlike the Elves of Mirkwood, these do not vanish but permit the hobbits to join them in the strange world, which overlays the landscape wherever they walk.

The woods through which they journey are described much as ordinary woods might be, as "wooded slopes" leading to "a shoulder of the hills that stood out into the lower land of the river-valley."[20] When they stop walking, however, the small adventurers fall into a strange sleep, and awaken in a clearing that echoes strongly the bright circles of firelight described in *The Hobbit.* The imagery shifts from the ordinary to the extraordinary, with trees morphing into a pillared hall and magic lights of gold and silver: "There the green floor ran on into the wood, and formed a wide space like a hall, roofed by the boughs of trees. Their great trunks ran like pillars down each side. In the middle there was a wood-fire blazing, and upon the tree-pillars torches with lights of gold and silver were burning steadily. The Elves sat round the fire upon the grass or upon the sawn rings of old trunks. Some went to and fro bearing cups and pouring drink; others brought food on heaped plates and dishes."[21]

The impact of the scene on the hobbits is given in the beautiful dreamtime of a typical Celtic Otherworld; Pippin "afterwards recalled little of either food or drink, for his mind was filled with the light upon the elf-faces, and the sound of voices so various and so beautiful that he felt in a waking dream. But he remembered that there was bread, surpassing the savour of a fair white loaf to one who is starving; and fruits sweet as wildberries and richer than the tended fruits of gardens; he drained a cup that was filled with a fragrant draught, cool as a clear fountain, golden as a summer afternoon."[22]

After the magical night, Frodo wakes refreshed, in "a bower made by a living tree with branches laced and drooping to the ground; his bed was of fern and grass, deep and soft and strangely fragrant. The sun was shining through the fluttering leaves, which were still green upon the tree."[23] Unlike in the earlier and more Germanic work of *The Hobbit*, where the description of the Elves and their habitations was somewhat restrained, it seems that Tolkien feels more free to demonstrate the virtuosity of his prosecraft in his later work, where the ravishing natural beauty of his concept of Celtic wilderness comes into its own.

This same experience of overlay landscape as Elves journey through the Shire is repeated at the very end of the tale, on the last journey of the Ring-bearers to the Grey Havens: "though they rode through the midst of the Shire all the evening and all the night, none saw them pass, save the wild creatures; or here and there some wanderer in the dark who saw a swift shimmer under the trees, or a light and shadow flowing through the grass as the Moon went westward."[24] The ephemeral experience with these Otherworldly companies is indeed a "pocket of Celticness," situated in the liminal area between the friendly woods of the Shire and more threatening places such as the Old Forest.

That dangerous and Germanic wood on the edge of the Shire has its own otherworldly flavor, and on its distant edge the hobbits encounter a place imbued with a magic as uncanny as that of the Elves—but also somehow more mundane. Between the peril of Old Man Willow in the Old Forest and the cold deathly danger of the Barrow-downs, they discover the magical country of the enigmatic Tom Bombadil. One obvious parallel between Tom and the Elves is the fact that his life seems to be one continuous merry song: "*Hey dol! merry dol! ring a dong dillo! / Ring a dong! hop along! fal lal the willow! / Tom Bom, jolly Tom, Tom Bombadillo!*"[25] The feel of this bubbling music is much closer to that of the light-hearted songs of the Rivendell Elves in *The Hobbit*, with their "*O! tril-lil-lil-lolly / the valley is jolly, / ha! ha!*"[26] than it does to the stately staves of Gildor Inglorion and his companions:

O Elbereth! Gilthoniel!
We still remember, we who dwell
In this far land beneath the trees,
Thy starlight on the Western Seas.[27]

While both groups are purportedly denizens of Imladris, the difference between them (especially as reflected in their poetry) is striking. It is almost as though, after the Elves developed from their somewhat diminutive origins in *The Hobbit* to the solemn and wise loremasters they became in *The Lord of the Rings*, Tolkien felt something was missing, and he called up one of his oldest creations (Tom Bombadil significantly predates even *The Hobbit*) to provide it.

Bombadil is a mysterious character who presents perennial and irresistible challenges to the Tolkien scholar. He is a composite mythic power, a mysterious riddle posed to his readers by the wily Professor: "even in a mythical Age there must be some enigmas," he wrote in a letter, "Tom Bombadil is one (intentionally)."[28] This odd, multifaceted personification of nature[29] is very powerful indeed; he has only to hold up a hand to stop the hobbits in their tracks "as if they had been struck stiff,"[30] and with his songs and silliness he vanquishes, with seemingly very little effort, the powerful monsters hiding in the harsh Northern wildernesses adjacent to the distinctly non-Northern place he calls home. Consider the forest through which the hobbits journey after they have been rescued from Old Man Willow: "Great shadows fell across them; trunks and branches of trees hung dark and threatening over the path. White mists began to rise and curl on the surface of the river and stray about the roots of the trees upon its borders. Out of the very ground at their feet a shadowy steam arose and mingled with the swiftly falling dusk."[31]

All this "darkling wood" imagery is somewhat similar to the Germanic idea, but here the tone relies more on mist and shadow than stifling blackness. As they continue along the path things get more frightening and uncanny: "Strange furtive noises ran among the bushes and reeds on either side of them; and if they looked up to the pale sky, they caught sight of queer gnarled and knobbly faces that gloomed dark against the twilight, and leered down at them from the high bank and the edges of the wood. They began to feel that all this country was unreal, and that they were stumbling through an ominous dream that led to no awakening."[32]

Strange faces in the twilight are undoubtedly as frightening as gleaming eyes in the blackness, and Tolkien certainly makes the reader feel that this is a perilous place. But the "perception of danger" in this kind of landscape is "mild, more a feeling of intensifying eeriness and isolation, more a sense of Celtic uncanniness, than a threat of actual harm."[33] It is a peril much closer in tone to the mound of Gorsedd Arberth than the dreadful mere of the Grendelkin. Twilight, unreality, dreams—the hobbits are in an Otherworldly wilderness where a musical, whimsical, powerful being is the Master, and as it turns out, the home of Tom Bombadil serves beautifully as a place of bright respite amid the darkness of their adventures.

There are other brief examples of these Otherworldly "pockets of Celticness" in *The Lord of the Rings.* At Derndingle, the pleasant dell in Fangorn where the Entmoot is held, there is a "little glittering fountain" from which Merry and Pippin drink "a clean, cold, sharp draught" and rest a while in what "seemed a very strange and remote place, outside their world, and far from everything that had ever happened to them."[34] The retreat of Faramir's company at the "Window of the Sunset, Henneth Annûn, fairest of all the falls of Ithilien" is described in stunningly beautiful imagery, which again shows off Tolkien's metaphoric virtuosity: "But in front a thin veil of water was hung. . . . It faced westward. The level shafts of the setting sun behind beat upon it, and the red light was broken into many flickering beams of ever-changing colour. It was as if they stood at the window of some elven-tower, curtained with threaded jewels of silver and gold, and ruby, sapphire and amethyst, all kindled with an unconsuming fire."[35] Later, under the bright light of the silver moon, this unearthly curtain of water becomes "a dazzling veil of silk and pearls and silver thread: melting icicles of moonlight."[36] These places and others, washed in water and light, serve as welcome havens within the Nordic expanse through which the various groups of hobbits find themselves traveling.

One interesting characteristic of these pockets of Celticness is that, though they are not all peopled by Elves, like Henneth Annûn they are almost always described in Elven terms. There is no doubt that the lands of the Elves, those quintessentially "dangerously beautiful and typically Celtic" peoples, demonstrate most completely the Celtic idea of wilderness in Middle-earth.[37] In *The Silmarillion* readers are given many examples of often hidden and always Otherworldly Elven wilderness realms in the First and Second Ages: Doriath protected by the quasi-divine magic of the girdle of Melian, the vaulted domes of underground Nargothrond, the hidden mountain fastness of Gondolin. The secluded land of mysterious Elven power is an idea that clearly lay very close to Tolkien's heart. But in wilderness terms these places are similar enough to each other, and share enough typical characteristics with the Elven wildernesses described in the Third Age, that to examine them all in detail would be repetitive; as Dickerson and Evans observe, "the many dissimilarities among the various Elvish kingdoms are outweighed by their similarities."[38] The rest of this chapter will therefore focus on the two Elven realms given the most detailed descriptions and fullest consideration in *The Hobbit* and *The Lord of the Rings*, the places safeguarded by the power of the uncorrupted Great Rings and ruled over by the highest of the High Elves of Middle-earth: Rivendell and Lothlórien.

The "fair valley of Rivendell where Elrond lives in the Last Homely House" first appears in *The Hobbit* as a brief place of respite between the dangers of trolls in the hills and goblins in the mountains.[39] It is the quintessential "pocket of Celticness," hidden in a deep cleft amid all the dangers of the Misty Mountains. Burns observes that "to enter Rivendell is to leave, for a time, the uplands' bleak, mountainous, northerly terrain," and—whether coming or going—the approach to this valley is always described in a way that highlights its separateness, its distinctness from the stark Germanic wilderness surrounding it.[40]

On the first approach, readers of *The Hobbit* are informed that "it was not so easy as it sounds to find the Last Homely House west of the Mountains," but when Gandalf finally spots the path "at the edge of a steep fall in the ground," the Dwarven company follows him on what is clearly a passage into a different and somewhat dreamlike wilderness world:[41]

> They saw a valley far below. They could hear the voice of hurrying water in a rocky bed at the bottom; the scent of trees was in the air; and there was a light on the valley-side across the water.
>
> Bilbo never forgot the way they slithered and slipped in the dusk down the steep zig-zag path into the secret valley of Rivendell. The air grew warmer as they got lower, and the smell of the pine-trees made him drowsy. . . . Their spirits rose as they went down and down. The trees changed to beech and oak, and there was a comfortable feeling in the twilight.[42]

When Frodo and his companions make this same journey, pursued by Black Riders, the imagery of separation is even sharper, with an even deeper contrast between the dangerous darkness of the Germanic wilderness and the bright lights of the Celtic one:

> They came to a place where the Road went suddenly under the dark shadow of tall pine-trees, and then plunged into a deep cutting with steep moist walls of red stone. . . . All at once, as if through a gate of light, the Road ran out again from the end of the tunnel into the open. There at the bottom of a sharp incline they saw before them a long flat mile, and beyond that the Ford of Rivendell. On the further side was a steep brown bank, threaded by a winding path; and behind that the tall mountains climbed, shoulder above shoulder, and peak beyond peak, into the fading sky.[43]

While the only battle Bilbo had to contend with was the challenge of finding the place and making his way down the treacherous path, Frodo and his friends find that the ford is held against them. They must fight and flee their way across this transition between dark danger and bright haven, and it eventually requires the power of the very landscape itself to save the day: "Dimly Frodo saw the river below him rise, and down along its course there came a plumed cavalry of waves. . . . He half fancied that he saw amid the water white riders upon white horses with frothing manes."[44] The appearance of these mysterious whitewater horses to overpower the enemies of the company is a strong Celtic allusion. Siewers points out how "the rising up of the waters at the boundary of Rivendell upon the approach of the Black Riders parallels the rivers defending Ulster in the *Táin*," and the incident also reinforces the idea of Rivendell as existing beyond a distinct border, part of another world.[45]

This clear demarcation is visible on the successful heroes' return trips to Rivendell in both books as well, although in the text there is much less landscape description and much more cheer and song involved. As Bilbo and Gandalf ride down the steep path from the "brink of the valley of Rivendell," Bilbo hears "the elves still singing in the trees, as if they had not stopped since he left; and as soon as the riders came down into the lower glades of the wood they burst into a song of much the same kind as before."[46] Frodo, traveling with the master of Rivendell himself, experiences another abrupt transition from one wilderness concept to the other: "At last one evening they came over the high moors, suddenly as to travellers it always seemed, to the brink of the deep valley of Rivendell and saw far below the lamps shining in Elrond's house. And they went down and crossed the bridge and came to the doors, and all the house was filled with light and song for joy at Elrond's homecoming."[47] Here the picture of distinction between Germanic mountains and Celtic haven is drawn more with imagery of song than of light, but the term *brink*, used in both texts, has connotations of extreme edges or crucial moments that underline the clear boundary between the worlds.

Departure from Rivendell also requires crossing a border, a transition between the dreamlike Otherworld inside and the stern reality of the normal, more Germanic world beyond. In *The Hobbit*, the description of Bilbo's outbound departure emphasizes the refreshment, healing, and timeless pleasures of the haven in contrast to the darkness and danger of the road leading away from it. When the Dwarven company begins the next phase of their journey to the Lonely Mountain, they do so in an environment of pleasant happiness and summer joy: "The next morning was a midsummer's morning as fair and fresh as could be dreamed: blue sky and never a cloud, and the sun dancing on the water. Now they rode away amid songs of farewell and good speed, with their hearts ready for more adventure, and with a knowledge of the road they must follow over the Misty Mountains to the land beyond."[48]

When Bilbo and Gandalf depart Rivendell for the Shire on their return journey in *The Hobbit*, they leave behind "many a merry jest and dance, early and late, with the elves of the valley" and are immediately faced with the reality of unpleasant weather outside the uncanny beauty of the magical place: "even as they left the valley the sky darkened in the West before them, and wind and rain came up to meet them. 'Merry is May-time!' said Bilbo, as the rain beat into his face. 'But our back is to legends and we are coming home.'"[49] The feeling of this departing transition is less bright and celebratory than the first.

This trend of increasing solemnity continues in *The Lord of the Rings*. The circumstances of the midwinter departure of the Nine Walkers from Rivendell on the first leg of the journey to Mount Doom are described quite differently from those of the Dwarves' midsummer jaunt: "It was a cold grey day near the end of December. The East Wind was streaming through the bare branches of the trees, and seething in the dark pines on the hills. Ragged clouds were hurrying overhead, dark and low. As the cheerless shadows of the early evening began to fall the Company made ready to set out."[50]

There is no jesting or merriness remaining in Tolkien's prose, as he so carefully crafts the image of this solemn passage from magical safety into terrible danger. There is only the sudden call of Boromir's horn, the moody reflections on provisions and preparations, the somber speech of Elrond. The entire scene is one of fateful doom: "There was no laughter, and no song or music. . . . They crossed the bridge and wound slowly up the long steep paths that led out of the cloven vale of Rivendell; and they came at length to the high moor where the wind hissed through the heather. Then with one glance at the Last Homely House twinkling below them they strode away far into the night."[51]

Frodo's last departure from Rivendell is not directly described in the text, but he does experience an uncanny bout of mysterious pain in his shoulder to mark the Otherworldly transition at the ford. Whereas travelers coming into Rivendell can always expect song and joy and welcome, as the story matures the heroes' departures from Elrond's magical refuge become more and more sober affairs.

Much of this increasing gravity can be attributed to the difference in tone of Tolkien's two works, so separated in time and purpose and scope; in a way, his conception of Rivendell matured alongside that of the Elves who dwell there. There is a core of mysterious power at the center of all Tolkien's Celtic wilderness places: Thranduil on the edges of Mirkwood, Tom Bombadil in his lovely river country, the powerful old Ent Treebeard striding through the darkness of Fangorn forest. Rivendell is no exception, but the shape and might of its hidden power changes over time as Tolkien's mythos develops. In *The Hobbit*, readers are told of the Last Homely House that "the master of the house was an elf-friend—one of those people whose fathers came into the strange stories before the beginning of History. . . . In those days of our tale there were still some people who had both elves and heroes of the North for ancestors, and Elrond the master of the house was their chief."[52]

This early Elrond certainly is presented as a loremaster; he "knew all about runes of every kind" and discovers the moon-letters on Thorin's map.[53] But Tolkien admits that Elrond's inclusion in *The Hobbit* was actually a "fortunate accident, due to the difficulty of constantly inventing good names for new characters. I gave him the name Elrond casually, but as this came from the mythology . . . I made him half-elven.[54] Only in *The Lord* was he identified with the son of Eärendel, and so the great-grandson of Lúthien and Beren, a great power and a Ringholder."[55]

As his mythology expanded into his published works and Tolkien decided to associate the mere "elf-friend" of *The Hobbit* with the "great power" of *The Lord of the Rings*, he went back and reworked his concepts, explaining to his publisher that in *The Hobbit* Elrond was actually "an important character, though his reverence, high powers, and lineage are toned down and not revealed in full."[56] In the later work, Rivendell develops into a redoubtable stronghold, a bastion of resistance against the Dark Lord, where lived "some of his chief foes: the Elven-wise, lords of the Eldar from beyond the furthest seas."[57] Gandalf reassures Frodo that "indeed there is a power in Rivendell to withstand the might of Mordor, for a while."[58] But, although its mystery and power are enhanced by the increasing majesty of its master as the story develops, Rivendell is itself true from the outset to a very specific concept of place demonstrative of Tolkien's Celtic wilderness idea: a hidden and Otherworldly refuge in the mountains where the heroes find rest and strength.

As with most of Tolkien's wilderness areas, Rivendell is characterized by stunning natural beauty, but it is the beauty of the Celtic Otherworld, full of mist and light and birdsong. In *The Lord of the Rings,* where Tolkien provides a much fuller description of the landscape than he did in *The Hobbit,* the beauty of Imladris comes into its own. A healed and refreshed Frodo meets his friends in the evening in "a high garden above the steep bank of the river. . . . Shadows had fallen in the valley below, but there was still a light on the faces of the mountains far above. The air was warm. The sound of running and falling water was loud, and the evening was filled with a faint scent of trees and flowers, as if summer still lingered in Elrond's gardens."[59]

The next morning, Frodo walks "along the terraces above the loud-flowing Bruinen" and watches "the pale, cool sun rise above the far mountains, and shine down, slanting through the thin silver mist; the dew upon the yellow leaves was glimmering, and the woven nets of gossamer twinkled on every bush."[60] Sam gazes up "with wonder in his eyes at the great heights in the East. The snow was white upon their peaks."[61] At the call of a "single clear bell" they move to a beautiful porch, where "the light of the clear autumn morning was now glowing in the valley. The noise of bubbling waters came up from the foaming river-bed. Birds were singing, and a wholesome peace lay on the land"; in this peaceful place "the rumours of the darkness growing in the world outside, already seemed only the memories of a troubled dream."[62] The cumulative effect of all of this glittering description is to build in the reader's mind an idea of a certain kind of magic, the magic inherent in beautiful natural places, as well as that of comfortable havens established in their midst and drawing on their power.

This is a sort of wilderness magic that refreshes rather than threatens, and its beauty is both cause and effect of the hidden power establishing the place as "a refuge for the weary and the oppressed, and a treasury of good counsel and wise lore."[63] Bilbo in *The Hobbit* finds Elrond's house a special place, one completely "perfect, whether you liked food, or sleep, or work, or storytelling, or singing, or just sitting and thinking best, or a pleasant mixture of them all. Evil things did not come into that valley."[64] Similarly, Frodo and his friends find that, after their terrible experiences with the Black Riders, "merely to be there was a cure for weariness, fear, and sadness."[65] But in the earlier work, Rivendell is one of many similar places of respite in the long traveler's adventure of the tale, a place where Gandalf simply hopes to find "rest in reasonable safety," and it receives considerably less descriptive and conceptual attention than many other places, such as Beorn's grand Anglo-Saxon mead hall.[66] Once it reaches its full maturity in *The Lord of the Rings*, however, Rivendell becomes a full-blown overlay landscape of dreamy timelessness and overwhelming beauty.

Frodo finds himself utterly spellbound by "the beauty of the melodies and of the interwoven words in elven-tongues" in the Hall of Fire:

> Almost it seemed that the words took shape, and visions of far lands and bright things that he had never yet imagined opened out before him; and the firelit hall became like a golden mist above seas of foam that sighed upon the margins of the world. Then the enchantment became more and more dreamlike, until he felt that an endless river of swelling gold and silver was flowing over him, too multitudinous for its pattern to be comprehended; it became part of the throbbing air about him, and it drenched and drowned him. Swiftly he sank under its shining weight into a deep realm of sleep.[67]

Mist, enchantment, lights of gold and silver, watery imagery of drenching and drowning—this dreamy sojourn moves through as pure a Celtic landscape as anything appearing in the *Mabinogion* or the *Táin Bó Cúailnge*, and Manawydan, Oisín, or Thomas the Rhymer would likely feel right at home. Bilbo often remarks on the timelessness of the place; he observes to Frodo that "time doesn't seem to pass here: it just is. A remarkable place altogether," and he later responds to a question about a length of time with "Oh, I don't know. I can't count days in Rivendell."[68] Despite the terrible peril of their upcoming journey, the hobbits discover that nothing can overcome the time-shifting power that keeps the house of Elrond suspended in an endless present moment: "such was the virtue of the land of Rivendell that soon all fear and anxiety was lifted from their minds. The future, good or ill, was not forgotten, but ceased to have any power over the present."[69] Time does not flow in normal ways in magical Rivendell, and this is one of the clearest indications of its Celtic Otherworldly provenance.

Natural beauty, hidden power, timelessness—even in its earliest conception, Rivendell demonstrates at least a glimpse of all these very Celtic ideas of the wilderness. But, as Tolkien's concept of the High Elves developed from the near-Victorian silliness of *The Hobbit* to the stately grandeur of his later tales, the sense of timeless separation and great, mysterious power of the Elven realms grew into something far beyond its original scope. Tolkien himself noted, as he was drafting the last chapters of *The Lord of the Rings*, that by the end everything had become "much larger and loftier" in the process of creation.[70] This means that, to fully appreciate the epitome of Tolkien's second concept of wilderness, readers must visit a place that does not appear in *The Hobbit* at all and receives only the briefest of mentions in *The Silmarillion*, where "the bliss and beauty of the Elves remained still undiminished while that Age endured . . . the hidden land between Celebrant and Anduin, where the trees bore flowers of gold and no Orc or evil thing dared ever come":[71] the magical golden wood of Lothlórien.

The hidden kingdom, which Aragorn calls "the heart of Elvendom on earth," is Tolkien's most beautiful, most uncanny, most Celtic wilderness place.[72] There is an early hint of supernatural peril about it; when Aragorn bids the company to follow him beneath the trees, Boromir—that most manly of Men—is "irresolute" and questions their path: "And now we must enter the Golden Wood, you say. But of that perilous land we have heard in Gondor, and it is said that few come out who once go in; and of that few none have escaped unscathed."[73] Aragorn admits there is a certain danger—"Say not unscathed, but if you say unchanged, then maybe you will speak the truth"—but sternly admonishes the proud man that "lore wanes in Gondor" if, "in the city of those who once were wise they now speak evil of Lothlórien."[74] Boromir acquiesces, with a last warning that "it is perilous," and Aragorn agrees: "Perilous indeed . . . fair and perilous; but only evil need fear it,[75] or those who bring some evil with them."[76] No reader, having witnessed Boromir's steady courage in battle in the mines of Moria, would truly expect that stout warrior to fear any physical danger. But this peril is that of the Celtic Otherworld, whose dangers are "consistently more suggestive of magical risk than they are of physical harm."[77] Although Tolkien seems to make at least a half-hearted attempt to cast a shadow of doubt over this Otherworldly place, it quickly becomes clear that this particular conversation says much more about the character of Boromir than the character of Lothlórien.

This enchanted forest is certainly a place that lay very close to Tolkien's heart. For one thing, it is the recipient of the most lavish attention from Tolkien's masterful prosecraft; Dickerson and Evans note that "of the three Elvish realms described in *The Hobbit* and *The Lord of the Rings*, Lothlórien is painted in the most vivid detail," and they also observe how "the narrative passages in *The Lord of the Rings* that describe the beauties of Lothlórien reveal the artistic eye with which Tolkien viewed these imaginary scenes."[78] The thick and layered descriptions of the gorgeous Golden Wood do serve to remind the reader that Tolkien was a skilled visual artist as well as a writer. They also demonstrate how, for Tolkien, the natural world is the source of the most exquisite aesthetic pleasure, the pinnacle of true beauty.

When Aragorn first points out to the sad and weary company where he plans to lead them on their flight from disaster in Moria, their eyes follow a stream "leaping down to the trough of the valley, and then running on and away into the lower lands, until it was lost in a golden haze."[79] This "golden haze" is a constant feature of the visual landscape throughout the next three full chapters due to the presence of *mallorn* trees, a species invented by Tolkien. Legolas positively gushes about these magical trees: "That is the fairest of all the dwellings of my people. There are no trees like the trees of that land. For in the autumn their leaves fall not, but turn to gold. Not till the spring comes and the new green opens do they fall, and then the boughs are laden with yellow flowers; and the floor of the wood is golden, and golden is the roof, and its pillars are of silver, for the bark of the trees is smooth and grey."[80]

Dickerson and Evans note that Legolas has at this point personally never seen the great *mellyrn*, but they are "so important in Elvish lore that he knows them through legend."[81] Later he shares with his companions further "tales of Lothlórien that the Elves of Mirkwood still kept in their hearts, of sunlight and starlight upon the meadows by the Great River before the world was grey," and he explains that the Elves of this land "dwell in the trees. . . . Therefore they are called the Galadhrim, the Tree-people.

Deep in their forest the trees are very great."[82] These fantastic trees are the defining attribute and crowning glory of the Golden Wood.

For readers aware of Tolkien's underlying mythology, the gold and silver of the *mellyrn,* like the gold and silver lamps encountered by the hobbits on their dreamlike feast with Gildor Inglorion, draw upon "an aesthetic system running through the whole of the Middle-earth canon, one that connects trees, green leaves, and the beauty of the environment with Elves and golden and silver light."[83] This aesthetic ultimately recalls the light of the original Two Trees of Valinor, silver Telperion and golden Laurelin, created by the Vala Yavanna to light that blessed land:

> The one [Telperion] had leaves of dark green that beneath were as shining silver, and from each of his countless flowers a dew of silver light was ever falling, and the earth beneath was dappled with the shadow of his fluttering leaves. The other [Laurelin] bore leaves of a young green like the new-opened beech; their edges were of glittering gold. Flowers swung upon her branches in clusters of yellow flame, formed each to a glowing horn that spilled a golden rain upon the ground; and from the blossom of that tree there came forth warmth and a great light.[84]

The importance of arboreal beauty to Tolkien's entire world view is thus established from the very beginning—light though they may the entirety of Arda, even the sun and the moon are only diminished replicas of this glory, small things coaxed by Yavanna from the lifeless stems of Telperion and Laurelin after Melkor and Ungoliant destroyed them and cast Valinor into darkness. It is quite fitting that Lothlórien, the bright and enchanted land of gold and silver trees, is ruled by Galadriel, the only remaining descendant in Middle-earth of the high kings of the Noldor who had lived in Valinor and seen the light of the Trees.[85]

The *mellyrn* themselves are but reflections of reflections of that original glory, and yet they are given in the text to be among the most beautiful things still remaining in Middle-earth. Frodo and company first come to the eaves of the magical wood at night, and the trees greet them with whispers: "The night-wind blew chill up the valley to meet them. Before them a wide grey shadow loomed, and they heard an endless rustle of leaves like poplars in the breeze. . . . Under the night the trees stood tall before them, arched over the road and stream that ran suddenly beneath their spreading boughs. In the dim light of the stars their stems were grey, and their quivering leaves a hint of fallow gold."[86]

Here, even in the darkness, the trees' golden visual quality makes itself known. "Alas that it is winter!" laments Legolas, but when dawn comes, the gilded beauty is enough to change the hobbits' perception of the seasons: "Day came pale from the East. As the light grew it filtered through the yellow leaves of the mallorn, and it seemed to the hobbits that the early sun of a cool summer's morning was shining. Pale-blue sky peeped among the moving branches."[87] In this mysterious time-shifting dawn sunlight they are treated to a vision of "all the valley of the Silverlode lying like a sea of fallow gold tossing gently in the breeze."[88] Tolkien seems to have been fond of the phrase "fallow gold"; in a letter to his son Christopher, he describes a vision of autumn trees in a "green and leafy October-end" in a passage that could easily be inserted into his fiction: "at no time do birches look so beautiful: their skin snow-white in the pale yellow sun, and their remaining leaves shining fallow-gold."[89] The same unusual expression appears twice in ten pages in the Lothlórien chapter of *The Lord of the Rings*, clearly illustrating the debt owed to Tolkien's love of autumnal birches by the aptly named Golden Wood.

Once his characters find themselves fully within that wood, the Otherworldly landscape they experience is given some of the most flowery description in the entire legendarium. Even while traveling blindfolded, before there is any visual imagery to work with, Frodo obviously feels himself to be walking in pleasant beauty: "He could smell the trees and the trodden grass. He could hear many different notes in the rustle of the leaves overhead, the river murmuring away on his right, and the thin clear voices of birds high in the sky. He felt the sun upon his face and hands when they passed through an open glade."[90] Then, once the blindfold comes off, the enchanted landscape comes into its visually stunning own:

> They were standing in an open space. To the left stood a great mound, covered with a sward of grass as green as Springtime in the Elder Days. Upon it, as a double crown, grew two circles of trees: the outer had bark of snowy white, and were leafless but beautiful in their shapely nakedness; the inner were mallorn-trees of great height, still arrayed in pale gold. . . . At the feet of the trees, and all about the green hillsides the grass was studded with small golden flowers shaped like stars. Among them, nodding on slender stalks, were other flowers, white and palest green: they glimmered as a mist amid the rich hue of the grass. Over all the sky was blue, and the sun of afternoon glowed upon the hill and cast long green shadows beneath the trees.[91]

Frodo is utterly enthralled by this view. In the sentences exploring his reaction to the beauty of this mound of Cerin Amroth,[92] readers are treated to a visual feast of color and light, in one of Tolkien's most-quoted passages:

> It seemed to him that he had stepped through a high window that looked on a vanished world. A light was upon it for which his language had no name. All that he saw was shapely, but the shapes seemed at once clear cut, as if they had been first conceived and drawn at the uncovering of his eyes, and ancient as if they had endured for ever. He saw no colour but those he knew, gold and white and blue and green, but they were fresh and poignant, as if he had at that moment first perceived them and made for them names new and wonderful. In winter here no heart could mourn for summer or for spring.[93]

The personal meaning for Tolkien of this particularly beautiful place shines clearly through in these radiant lines. As he explained in a letter, "I came eventually and by slow degrees to write *The Lord of the Rings* to satisfy myself. . . . Certain features of it, and especially certain places, still move me very powerfully. The heart remains in the description of Cerin Amroth."[94] Readers cannot help but be moved themselves—and at this point the characters have not yet entered the great tree-city itself.

To do that, they must first circle a deep fosse surrounding a "green wall encircling a green hill thronged with mallorn-trees," which "stood up in the twilight like living towers. In their many-tiered branches and amid their ever-moving leaves countless lights were gleaming, green and gold and silver."[95] It is a long way, and the description of this journey adds more layers of mysterious song and silver light and majestic trees to the sense of surrealism permeating this uncanny woodland wilderness:

> Far away up on the hill they could hear the sound of singing falling from on high like soft rain upon leaves.
>
> They went along many paths and climbed many stairs, until they came to the high places and saw before them amid a wide lawn a fountain shimmering. It was lit by silver lamps that swung from the boughs of trees, and it fell into a basin of silver, from which a white stream spilled. Upon the south side of the lawn there stood the mightiest of all the trees; its great smooth bole gleamed like grey silk, and up it towered, until its first branches, far above, opened their huge limbs under shadowy clouds of leaves.[96]

The cumulative effect of all of this layered and luminous prosody is a strong sense of magic manifested as natural beauty. This sense is one of the main characteristics of Tolkien's Celtic wilderness concept, and it is most clearly and completely embodied here, in the dreamlike glades of Lothlórien.

If the wilderness attribute of natural beauty finds its greatest expression in the Golden Wood, so also does the concept of a hidden and magical wilderness power. The heroes glimpse only brief hints of enchantment in the various uncanny retreats discussed above, and while Rivendell certainly demonstrates this sense of hidden virtue, even at its most Otherworldly it still manages to retain its characterization as a Homely House, a haven, a place for weary travelers to rest. Rivendell is a place that, while separated from its mountainous surroundings by the uncanny barrier of its hidden power, is nevertheless reasonably accessible to good people in search of shelter or wise counsel. In contrast, Lothlórien is much more fenced off from normal reality, and the sense of something hidden yet vastly powerful permeates every moment of the characters' experience.

Before they even enter the wood, Legolas explicitly informs his companions that "there is a secret power here that holds evil from the land."[97] When Sam's blindfold is removed and he gazes upon Cerin Amroth, he remarks that it is "more Elvish than anything I ever heard tell of. I feel as if I was *inside* a song," and a smiling Haldir assures him that what he feels is "the power of the Lady of the Galadhrim."[98] Later, Sam—although he still clearly senses the presence of something vastly powerful—protests in his pragmatic way that "nothing seems to be going on, and nobody seems to want it to. If there's any magic about, it's right down deep, where I can't lay my hands on it," and he actually complains that the magic is there but "you can't see nobody working it. . . . I'd dearly love to see some Elf-magic, Mr. Frodo!"[99] His wish is ultimately granted by the wielder of the hidden power herself. After they look in her mirror, Galadriel admonishes the hobbits: "do not think that only by singing amid the trees, nor even by the slender arrows of elven-bows, is this land of Lothlórien maintained and defended against its Enemy."[100] The hidden power in Lothlórien provides unassailable protection to its uncannily beautiful forest wilderness even to the very end of the War of the Ring: "Three times Lórien had been assailed from Dol Guldur, but besides the valour of the elven people of that land, the power that dwelt there was too great for any to overcome, unless Sauron had come there himself. Though grievous harm was done to the fair woods on the borders, the assaults were driven back; and when the Shadow passed, Celeborn came forth and led the host of Lórien over Anduin in many boats. They took Dol Guldur, and Galadriel threw down its walls and laid bare its pits, and the forest was cleansed."[101] This power, formed from a joining of the great ring with its wielder, the "mightiest and fairest of all the Elves that remained in Middle-earth," is greater than others in the same way that the *mellyrn* are greater than other trees; its presence reinforces the status of the Otherworldly woodland of Lothlórien as the greatest of its kind in Middle-earth.[102]

The third attribute demonstrated by all places that fit into Tolkien's Celtic wilderness concept, that of a dreamlike timelessness, is likewise characterized most strongly in Lothlórien. Considering the first half of the phrase "dreamlike timelessness," there is no doubt that the wood is presented in oneiric terms; even its name has a connection to dreams. In the early cosmogonic legends of *The Silmarillion*, readers are told of a Vala known as Irmo, "the master of visions and dreams," and they learn that "in Lórien are his gardens in the land of the Valar, and they are the fairest of all places in the world."[103] The Maia Melian "dwelt long in Lórien, tending the trees that flower in the gardens of Irmo" before she came to Middle-earth and wed King Thingol of Doriath.[104] After that, for unnumbered years in the First and Second Ages, Galadriel dwelt in Doriath out of love for her husband Celeborn, who was a kinsman of Thingol; there she "abode with Melian, and of her learned great lore and wisdom concerning Middle-earth."[105]

All of this complex mythological history was not available to readers when *The Lord of the Rings* was first published, of course, but it is hinted at in Treebeard's rumbling ruminations on the deeper meanings of the many changes in the name of the Golden Wood over the years, when he translates Lothlórien as "Dreamflower."[106] While there is no explicit confirmation that Galadriel herself visited the gardens of Irmo during her time in Valinor, she certainly could have done; in a surviving textual note Tolkien seems to specify that the name at least is an intentional echo of that "place of rest and shadowy trees and fountains, a retreat from cares and griefs," musing that "the resemblance cannot be accidental. She [Galadriel] had endeavoured to make Lórien a refuge and an island of peace and beauty, a memorial of ancient days, but was now filled with regret and misgiving, knowing that the golden dream was hastening to a grey awakening."[107] By the Third Age, the wood of Lothlórien is undeniably a place of dreams. Sam's vision in Galadriel's mirror is explicitly described as "like a dream."[108] While Gimli notes that for Elves "memory is more like to the waking world than to a dream," he assures Legolas that it is "not so for Dwarves" and deeply regrets the awakening to a colorless world that accompanies his parting from the Lady of the Golden Wood.[109] As dreams go, ultimately Lórien is a melancholy one, and neither the characters nor the reader is able to escape the sadness that permeates its beauty and majesty unscathed.

If the Golden Wood is a more dreamlike place than anywhere else in Middle-earth, it is also a more timeless one. Verlyn Flieger examines in detail the many aspects of time as experienced by the characters in the Golden Wood, and she observes that "every carefully wrought phrase suggests that Lórien is a refuge from linear time, an island where the past still somehow exists in the present."[110] Marjorie Burns notes that "like the Celtic realms of the Tuatha Dé Danann, this is a realm where time moves differently, a realm less bound by the strictures of what is occurring now. In Lothlórien, the past maintains a presence and the future is not fully obscured."[111] Tolkien's text itself explains that "in Rivendell there was memory of ancient things; in Lórien the ancient things still lived on in the waking world,"[112] and explicitly uses the phrase "timeless land" in a passage that highlights the time-shifting magic of the place: "Though he walked and breathed, and about him living leaves and flowers were stirred by the same cool wind as fanned his face, Frodo felt that he was in a timeless land that did not fade or change or fall into forgetfulness. When he had gone and passed again into the outer world, still Frodo the wanderer from the Shire would walk there, upon the grass among *elanor* and *niphredil* in fair Lothlórien."[113]

Here, not only does time cease to flow in the present, it also reaches ahead to claim a place in future memory. This timeless land also has great power to call forward the past; on Cerin Amroth, Frodo finds Aragorn lost in a long-ago time, "wrapped in some fair memory," and he watches in wonder as "the grim years were removed from the face of Aragorn, and he seemed clothed in white, a young lord tall and fair; and he spoke words in the Elvish tongue to one whom Frodo could not see."[114] In the same way that the hobbits found that merely being present in Rivendell was a cure for their psychological ills, Legolas admits to Celeborn that, despite their devastating loss in Moria, the travelers "almost forgot our grief for a time, as we walked in gladness on the fair paths of Lórien."[115] An Otherworldly sense of an eternal present permeates the company's entire sojourn in the Golden Wood: "They remained some days in Lothlórien, so far as they could tell or remember. All the while that they dwelt there the sun shone clear, save for a gentle rain that fell at times, and passed away leaving all things fresh and clean. The air was cool and soft, as if it were early spring, yet they felt about them the deep and thoughtful quiet of winter. It seemed to them that they did little but eat and drink and rest, and walk among the trees; and it was enough."[116] Throughout the legendarium these Celtic enclaves have a certain air of timelessness about them, but in Lórien—as Sam discovers later, "counting on his fingers" to try and reconcile his memories with the reality of the moon—time itself stops its running, bows down, and waits upon the whim of the Lady.[117]

The protracted departure of the company from Lothlórien highlights in one final elaboration the beauty, power, and timelessness of the Golden Wood. The landscape is shifted around the characters in stages, beginning in a place deep within the overlay landscape where they are informed by the Lord of the Wood that they must "harden their hearts to leave this land."[118] They linger for a while in the liminal space where the worlds overlap, dining on a "long lawn of shining grass, studded with golden *elanor* that glinted in the sun. The lawn ran out into a narrow tongue between bright margins: on the right and west the Silverlode flowed glittering; on the left and east the Great River rolled its broad waters, deep and dark," and there Frodo first perceives the eventual fading of Galadriel, "present and yet remote, a living vision of that which has already been left far behind by the flowing streams of Time."[119] Finally they mount their boats and commit themselves to the river, and their perspective flips again in one final shift: "Lórien was slipping backward, like a bright ship masted with enchanted trees, sailing on to forgotten shores, while they sat helpless upon the margin of the grey and leafless world."[120] With the haunting strains of Galadriel's painfully melancholic farewell in their ears, they emerge fully into the normal world with deep regret and many tears. Tolkien once more brings to bear his descriptive artistry on the now-colorless landscape:

> Bare woods stalked along either bank. . . . The breeze died away and the River flowed without a sound. No voice of bird broke the silence. The sun grew misty as the day grew old, until it gleamed in a pale sky like a high white pearl. Then it faded into the West, and dusk came early, followed by a grey and starless night. Far into the dark quiet hours they floated on, guiding their boats under the overhanging shadows of the western

> woods. Great trees passed by like ghosts, thrusting their twisted thirsty roots through the mist down into the water. It was dreary and cold.[121]

All this imagery of grey silence serves well to underline how the company has left the embrace of Middle-earth's greatest Celtic haven; now they must return to, and fight to survive, the bleak dangers of the surrounding Germanic wilderness.

If the harsh and hostile Germanic concept of wilderness provides the drama and danger for Tolkien's legendarium, the beautiful and uncanny Celtic wilderness places hidden within it allow his characters—at least those deemed worthy to face the not-insignificant peril—space for relief and recuperation. The power of these places runs along a spectrum, from the Elvenking's domain overlaying the blackness of Mirkwood to the green and golden radiance of inviolable Lothlórien, and its richness and beauty fills an area in the reader's mental map significantly larger than the amount of land it occupies in Middle-earth. Marjorie Burns opines that the "expanse of less restrictive time (plus Elven longevity) . . . largely allows Tolkien's Celtic enclaves to compete with the heftier weight and broader mass of his more Nordic regions and worlds," but this timeless quality is only part of the equation.[122] The sheer mass of carefully crafted words piled upon the natural beauty and the hidden powers within the timeless lands highlights how important the entire concept of enchanted woodlands truly was to Tolkien.

There is a symbolically evocative exchange in *The Lord of the Rings* that, although it takes place within the boundaries of the supremely Anglo-Saxon country of Rohan, seems to capture the way the Germanic and Celtic ideas mingle in Tolkien's conception of wilderness. It is a short snippet of dialogue, a question from a rider of Rohan and Aragorn's answer:

> "Do we walk in legends or on the green earth in the daylight?"
>
> "A man may do both," said Aragorn. "For not we but those who come after will make the legends of our time. The green earth, say you? That is a mighty matter of legend, though you tread it under the light of day!"[123]

The time-shifting perspective here is easy to overlook, as is the clear allusion to an overlay landscape, but both are noteworthy. Here Aragorn—as grimly courageous a Norse hero-king as ever drew a sword—expresses an awareness of landscape in a very Celtic way. His status as a hero of great renown may rely on his unflinching willingness to face the dangers of the Germanic wilderness, but he also proves himself worthy of (and inextricably bound up with) the Celtic powers that permeate the woodland wilderness of the Elves.

Clearly both of these wilderness concepts are important in shaping one of Tolkien's greatest heroes, and therefore objectively important in Middle-earth. The places embodying these wilderness concepts are fully realized and valuable in and of themselves, whatever they may mean to the human-like characters moving through them. Whether challenging the heroes like the Misty Mountains or protecting them like Rivendell or Lórien, or whether indifferent to the requirement to do either of those things like the wild lands of Eriador, the considerable natural power in the landscape is represented as utterly beyond human capacity and understanding. As Dickerson and Evans observe, in many places "woods and forests—often wild, untamed, and trackless—serve as a potent image for the primordial value of the natural order, irrespective of and sometimes inimical to the self-centered concerns of Elves, Men, and other beings."[124]

All of these ideas fit fairly well into the connotations of the modern English word *wilderness*, but beautiful harshness and uncanny beauty do not quite exhaust Tolkien's imagination of wild places in his great story. As Susan Jeffers notes, "Lothlórien and Rivendell are places apart in space and time. There is virtue in this difference . . . but it is a difference and a separation nonetheless."[125] There is in Middle-earth a third concept, somewhat but not completely a semiwild amalgam of the first two, where this difference and separation between wilderness and the realm of human activities is less clearly defined. This concept is less overwhelming in its power but in the end perhaps more relevant to the everyday lives of his modern readers; whereas not everyone who reads *The Lord of the Rings* can claim personal experience of Germanic or Celtic wildernesses, nearly everyone can relate in some way to the generally orderly and yet still untamed wild lands within the borders of the Shire.

CHAPTER SIX

Hobbits in the Shire

Tolkien's third concept of wilderness does not sit as comfortably within the modern idea of the word as his first or second ones do. Still, there are wild places in Middle-earth, as well as in the real world it reflects, which do not quite fit into the Germanic and Celtic molds. These places demonstrate neither the unforgiving harshness of the Misty Mountains or Mordor nor the magical Otherworldliness of Rivendell or Lothlórien, but they nevertheless draw on the wildness inherent in the natural world as it exists in the English cultural imagination.

England's pleasant greenwoods can be seen as a loose blend of the sheltering aspect of Germanic woodlands with the overlay landscape of Celtic ones, perhaps colored with a heavy dose of English Romantic nostalgia. Simon Schama describes in detail how medieval wild landscapes shifted in concept away from "Dante's selva oscura, the darkling forest where one lost oneself at the entrance to hell," akin to the grim fens of Old English poetry, and toward the famous "sylvan habitat of Merrie England: there it is forever green, always summer. The nightingales sing, the ale is heady, and masters and men are brought together in fellowship."[1] Roderick Nash directly links a general shift in emotional response to wilderness from fear and hatred to appreciation with the "flowering of Romanticism in the eighteenth and early nineteenth centuries," when he notes that "wild country lost much of is repulsiveness. It was not that wilderness was any less solitary, mysterious, and chaotic, but rather . . . these qualities were coveted."[2] The hobbitish idea of wilderness, like the

Shire itself, draws heavily upon both the Romantic pastoral and the related ideology of Merrie England, which was so much a part of the popular consciousness in Victorian and Edwardian times.[3]

This concept of Merrie England deserves a bit of examination. The first recorded use of the term is in 1522, when a certain Dr. John Caius is found urging his readers "to live quietly, friendly and merrily one with another, as men were wont to do in the old world, when this country was called merry England."[4] Here in the early sixteenth century the concept is already a nostalgic one, and Caius was writing a solid decade before Henry VIII initiated the cultural and religious upheaval that characterized his Reformation. Elizabeth I, "an extremely conservative kind of Protestant, with a taste for ritual and decoration," navigated as best she could the delicate balance between the puritanical strains of English Protestantism and the burgeoning nostalgia for traditional celebrations, but the "seasonal ceremonies and pastimes" so carefully chronicled by historians nevertheless "underwent a considerable decline" during her reign.[5] There is general agreement that "it was in defence of such pastimes against their puritan critics that the myth of Merry England finally emerged" in the late Elizabethan period.[6] However, its power became all the greater in the English imagination once the dour Protestant Parliament beheaded the king and canceled even Christmas.

Over the next few centuries, the attraction of this Arcadian myth only continued to strengthen. As historian Keith Thomas notes, each era situated its "nostalgic image of the village green with its maypole and dancing, its curds and cream, cheesecake and syllabub" in a vision of the relatively recent but rapidly receding past: for the Elizabethans, it was the time before the Reformation; for the Stuarts the reign of the Virgin Queen; for the Hanoverians the age of Queen Anne.[7] By mid-Victorian times, "the past invoked by the demure revivals of maypoles and rush-bearing was too vague to be capable of any precise chronological location. But the attributes of Merry England were constant: a contented, revelling peasantry and a hierarchical order in which each one happily accepted his place and where the feast in the baronial hall symbolized the ideal social relationship."[8]

Folklorist Roy Judge notes that the entire idea is really "a world that has never actually existed, a visionary, mythical landscape" that carries the idea of "a pleasant or delightful country, one which was prosperous or fertile," but Merrie England was more than just a pastoral vision of classical Arcadia.[9] It was an idealized picture of a reality "shaped by the historical circumstances of post-Reformation England," an "amalgam in which real social facts jostled together with the images of literary convention and the inherent nostalgia of social criticism" that continues to exert a powerful influence on the Anglophone imagination even today.[10]

Tolkien's work plays no small part in that influence. In explicitly describing the Shire as "more or less a Warwickshire village of about the period of the Diamond Jubilee," he places it squarely inside the idealized Victorian concept of rural England.[11] When he opens his tale of an eccentric bachelor living in a hole in the ground by recalling a time "one morning long ago in the quiet of the world, when there was less noise and more green, and the hobbits were still numerous and prosperous,"[12] he reflects almost exactly psychologist Oded Heilbronner's observation that "in the Victorian era there was a great deal of nostalgia. . . . In that time of rapid industrialization and developing technology, many people visualized a tranquil and dreamlike England, rural and romantic, characterized by goodhearted, slow, somewhat alienated types, who were distinctive and lovable but strange."[13] Joseph Pearce's *Merrie England: A Journey Through the Shire* perfectly captures (with a peculiar innocence and evident lack of irony) Tolkien's fundamental position in this relentlessly nostalgic ideology:

> England is eternally greater than those who happen to be wandering around today on the geographical stage on which the drama of England is being performed. Most people walking around on the stage today have no idea what England is or who they themselves are. . . . They are relatively insubstantial. They are certainly less real as Englishmen than Alfred the Great, Bede the Venerable, St. Edward the Confessor, Chaucer, St. Thomas More, the hundreds of English martyrs, Shakespeare, Austen, Newman, or Tolkien. All of these people *are* England. Please note: They *are* England.[14]

Pearce's book has almost nothing to do specifically with Tolkien's work—it is a sort of spiritual travelogue through and paean to an idealized England—but its title and theme handily demonstrate how Tolkien's pastoral idyll has become an unquestioned cultural touchstone inextricably linked to the Arcadian Merrie England ideology.

The Englishness of the hobbits is generally taken as a given in Tolkien criticism. Tom Shippey says of hobbits that "they are very specifically English," noting that Tolkien "makes the whole history of the Shire correspond point for point with the history of early England."[15] He goes on to narrow their Englishness to a specific period: "Bilbo is . . . defined from the start by time, class, and culture. He is English; middle class; and roughly Victorian to Edwardian. Hobbits in general . . . prove to be all these things even more definitely than Bilbo, except that some of them will be working class."[16] Verlyn Flieger asserts plainly that "Hobbiton is modeled on a pre-industrial rural English village like the one where Tolkien spent his happiest years of childhood."[17] Marjorie Burns states that hobbits are "the most able, persistent, and appealing representatives of England," and that "where they go, England is carried along."[18] All of this critical agreement is based on the fact that Tolkien himself is both explicit and emphatic in his personal association with hobbits, the Shire, and England. In a letter (in which he grumbles that he does not "like giving 'facts' about myself," but then goes on to do so) he lays things out quite clearly:

> I was born in 1892 and lived for my early years in "the Shire" in a premechanical age. . . . I am in fact a *Hobbit* (in all but size). I like gardens, trees and unmechanized farmlands; I smoke a pipe, and like good plain food (unrefrigerated), but detest French cooking; I like, and even dare to wear in these dull days, ornamental waistcoats. I am fond of mushrooms (out of a field); have a very simple sense of humour (which even my appreciative critics find tiresome); I go to bed late and get up late (when possible). I do not travel much.[19]

A deep association between hobbits and a somewhat idealized Englishness is obvious here, and it provides a solid starting point from which to begin teasing out the complexities of the relationships between Tolkien's hobbits and the wild natural world.

Simon Schama explores English landscape ideas at several points in his expansive book *Landscape and Memory*. He observes how the sylvan habitat of Merrie England "became the forest of English fellowship where English class magically dissolved into the moss."[20] But he also argues that, while it is true that "the forest as the opposite of court, town, and village—the sylvan remnant of arcady, or what Shakespeare called the 'golden world'—was an idea that would lodge tenaciously in the poetic and the pious imagination," it is also true that "in England the reality was different."[21] In contrast to the deep Continental forests (or even the lands afforested by the Continental conqueror of 1066), by medieval times the numerous areas of woodland accessible to common Englishmen were at most semiwild:

> Even the broadest forests were laced with cart tracks, footpaths, and trails . . . It was mapped by distinctive landmarks: rocky outcrops wrapped in liverwort; ancient lightning-blasted trees; trunks and roots fallen and decayed into shapes suggestive enough to earn nicknames. . . . In contrast to the most ancient forests of Germany and Poland and to the conifer woods of the Scottish Highlands and the oak forests of the English aristocratic estates . . . these ancient woodlands seem thinner and almost patchy, with swathes of grassy meadow and wild flowers blooming between pollarded and truncated broadleaf trees. The exact opposite of what is now considered to be the ideal norm of a forest habitat—the untended wilderness—they have light and space and variety: a working room for an authentic woodland culture.[22]

These English woodlands, while rather wild and unruly, "a landscape in which town dwellers might become quickly disoriented," are not *too* wild—and they do seem very much like the sort of place hobbits would enjoy.[23]

In the texts of the Middle-earth legendarium, hobbits are characterized as an agrarian people living archetypically close to the land. They are lovers of order and plenty who raise the enjoyment of simple and plentiful food and drink to the level of art. There are ponderously heavy echoes of Merrie England here, with its contented peasantry and unquestioned hierarchical order. Readers are told from the very beginning of *The Lord of the Rings* that hobbits are "an unobtrusive but very ancient people" who "love peace and quiet and good tilled earth: a well-ordered and well-farmed countryside was their favourite haunt."[24] When the first hobbit settlers entered the area that would eventually become the Shire, they found that "the land was rich and kindly, and though it had long been deserted when they [hobbits] entered it, it had before been well tilled, and there the king had once had many farms, cornlands, vineyards, and woods."[25] This last word gives a subtle clue to the heart of Tolkien's third concept of wilderness; significantly, even before they came to the Shire, the well-ordered countryside of the hobbits included areas given over to the disorderly reign of at least partially wild woodlands in the English mode. These forested areas are certainly tame by more ancient wilderness standards—they are neither black and perilous like Mirkwood nor green and perilous like the Golden Wood—but they are woods nonetheless, specifically the exact sort of English woods that Schama discusses. It is in the hobbits' attitudes toward them where a glimpse of Tolkien's non-Germanic and non-Celtic wilderness concept begins to appear.

On close examination, their love of comfort notwithstanding, hobbits are presented as a people who often travel in and quite enjoy the woods. Tolkien mentions several times that "hobbits can move quietly in woods, absolutely quietly," and even that they "take a pride in it,"[26] and he makes clear that their ability to vanish so completely is not a magic ability but rather one due to "a professional skill that heredity and practice, and a close friendship with the earth, have rendered inimitable by bigger and clumsier races."[27] Even with a hereditary head start, the development of such a skill would still obviously require long exposure to, and practice moving through, natural areas. Frodo and his friends possess this skill: "they went in single file along hedgerows and the borders of coppices, and night fell dark about them. . . . Since they were all hobbits, and were trying to be silent, they made no noise that even hobbits would hear. Even the wild things in the fields and woods hardly noticed their passing."[28] Walking appears to be a common pursuit in the Shire, at least among Bilbo and Frodo and their friends; Bilbo's map "with all his favourite walks marked on it in red ink"[29] indicates his enjoyment of the pastime, Frodo's offhand comment to Pippin and Sam that "we all like walking in the dark" clearly indicates that they have done so more than once before, and Sam's belief that "he had once seen an Elf in the woods"[30] obviously requires him to have been in the woods himself at the time.

A seemingly unimportant exchange between Frodo and Gandalf in Rivendell provides a good insight into this hobbitish delight in woodlands; when Frodo says that "most of all I should like to go walking today and explore the valley. I should like to get into those pine-woods up there,"[31] it is not because he wants or expects to test his heroism against implacable natural powers, or find adventure in a timeless dreamlike Otherworld. It is also not only because he wants to experience the beauty of green and growing things, since he could do that in perfect comfort with a wander through Elrond's well-tended gardens, in the midst of which the conversation takes place. It is simply because he finds walking through beautiful woodlands a pleasant thing to do.

It could be argued that Frodo is unusual for a hobbit—Tolkien explicitly states in an aside that the Bagginses "were as bachelors very exceptional, as they were also in many other ways"—and, even though he enjoys "tramping over the Shire" with his friends, "more often he wandered by himself, and to the amazement of sensible folk he was sometimes seen far from home walking in the hills and woods under the starlight."[32] But, whether Frodo's indicated exceptionalism derives from his desire to wander by himself, or to wander far from home, or just from the queerness of Bagginses in general, it would seem that the tramping itself is not all that unusual. When Gandalf growls at Pippin in Moria, scolding that "this is a serious journey, not a hobbit walking-party," he presupposes the existence of (and presumably the silliness expected from) hobbit walking-parties.[33]

There is certainly a place for seemingly disordered woods within the ordered district of the Shire. Christopher Tolkien's published map of "A Part of the Shire" shows several areas covered in meticulously drawn clusters of trees: Bindbole Wood in the North Farthing, the Green Hill Country and the Woody End in the East Farthing, and of course the great Old Forest fenced out by the hedge surrounding Buckland.[34] By examining the way hobbits interact with these various wooded places on the map, it is possible to see how Tolkien's third idea of wilderness, although less dramatically forceful than the other two, is still quite important in his overall vision of the ideal relationship between humans and the natural world.

Considering how richly Tolkien embroiders his landscape description in his later work, it is interesting that Bilbo's home country is given only the sparsest of depictions in the text of *The Hobbit;* indeed, it is not even given a name.[35] When Thorin and company leave the Green Dragon Inn in Bywater, their journey begins with pleasant travel through "hobbit-lands, a wide respectable country inhabited by decent folk, with good roads, an inn or two, and now and then a dwarf or a farmer ambling by on business," but the text notes nothing more of the landscape until the "dreary hills, rising higher and higher, dark with trees" of the gloomy Lone-lands.[36] On the return journey, Bilbo and Gandalf travel in the space of a single paragraph from the burial place of the troll-gold to "the country where Bilbo had been born and bred, where the shapes of the land and of the trees were as well known to him as his hands and toes."[37] Other than a brief mention of "the wood beyond The Water," for a detailed picture of the woods of the Shire—or indeed of any other natural elements there—readers must look to *The Lord of the Rings.*[38]

Thankfully, there is plenty of landscape description to work with in Tolkien's later work. Once all of the rambling birthday parties and back-story are out of the way, Frodo and his friends begin their adventurous journey with a walk through the uncultivated areas of the Shire on their way to Frodo's purported new home at Crickhollow. After passing quietly over the fields of Hobbiton and Tookland, they enter the Green Hill Country and find the road to Woodhall, which "climbed away from the main road in the Water-valley, and wound over the skirts of the Green Hills towards Woody End, a wild corner of the Eastfarthing."[39] Sam knows the land well in this area, and he directs them to the perfect camping spot. To readers familiar with the bleakly Germanic wilds of *The Hobbit*, the woods of this "wild corner" of the Shire are remarkable for their friendliness:

> The night was clear, cool, and starry, but smoke-like wisps of mist were creeping up the hill-sides. . . . Thinclad birches, swaying in a light wind above their heads, made a black net against the pale sky. . . . Just over the top of the hill they came on the patch of fir-wood. Leaving the road they went into the deep resin-scented darkness of the trees, and gathered dead sticks and cones to make a fire. Soon they had a merry crackle of flame at the foot of a large fir-tree and they sat round it for a while, until they began to nod. Then, each in an angle of the great tree's roots, they curled up in their cloaks and blankets, and were soon fast asleep. They set no watch; even Frodo feared no danger yet, for they were still in the heart of the Shire.[40]

Although there is some commentary in the text on how this activity is unusual for hobbits,[41] and although there is some good-natured grumbling about stiffness when they all wake up, it is all presented as the sort of pleasure holiday familiar to anyone who has ever gone on a camping trip.

That morning Frodo walks off "to the edge of the wood," where he is treated to the sort of lyrically described view that rewards recreational wilderness visitors everywhere: "away eastward the sun was rising red out of the mists that lay thick on the world. Touched with gold and red the autumn trees seemed to be sailing rootless in a shadowy sea."[42] The next day they make their way through "lower lands dotted with small clumps of trees that melted away in the distance to a brown woodland haze."[43] It is not until the second afternoon, as they follow the road through "grassland sprinkled with tall trees, outliers of the approaching woods," that the first hint of danger appears in the form of a Black Rider.[44] Even that first incident is given in what initially feel like only vaguely threatening terms, and the hobbits continue, with more concern than real fear, on a lane "winding through a wood of ancient oak-trees on its way to Woodhall."[45] There they stop and take a rest in "the huge hulk of a tree: it was still alive and had leaves on the small branches that it had put out round the broken stumps of its long-fallen limbs; but it was hollow, and could be entered by a great crack on the side away from the road."[46] It is not until after the second appearance of the Black Rider, which is driven off by the High Elves as they bring their overlay landscape with them into this wild corner of the Shire, that Frodo experiences a significant sense that "the bright morning—treacherously bright . . . had not banished the fear of pursuit."[47] Until this point, the entire adventure has been characterized as a hobbit walking-party as light-minded as Gandalf could imagine.

As the pressure of dark and mysterious pursuit increases, however, they begin to move through a landscape that becomes, if not completely perilous, at least less pleasant in its descriptions. When Frodo decides they should stay off the road, Pippin complains that "short cuts make long delays. . . . The country is rough round here, and there are bogs and all kinds of difficulties down in the Marish—I know the land in these parts. And if you are worrying about Black Riders, I can't see that it is any worse meeting them on a road than in a wood or a field."[48] Frodo disagrees, invoking the spirit of the Old English idea of shelter in woodlands: "It is less easy to find people in the woods and fields."[49] At his insistence, they begin to "toil through bog and briar," and after they have "scrambled down a steep green bank and plunged into the thick trees below" on a course they hoped would "cut slanting through the woods that clustered along the eastern side of the hills," they discover that the going is much less friendly indeed:[50] "the thicket was closer and more tangled than it had appeared. There were no paths in the undergrowth, and they did not get on very fast. When they had struggled to the bottom of the bank, they found a stream running down from the hills behind in a deeply dug bed with steep slippery sides overhung with brambles. Most inconveniently it cut across the line they had chosen. They could not jump over it, nor indeed get across it at all without getting wet, scratched, and muddy."[51]

Just at that moment, danger presses down on them in the form of the Black Rider on their heels, and fear pushes them deeper into the shelter of the wild woods: "Frodo led the way, and plunged quickly into the thick bushes beside the stream. . . . Going on was not altogether easy. They had packs to carry, and the bushes and brambles were reluctant to let them through. They were cut off from the wind by the ridge behind, and the air was still and stuffy. When they forced their way at last into more open ground, they were hot and tired and very scratched, and they were also no longer certain of the direction in which they were going."[52]

When Pippin gets his bearings again, he tries to get them back on course just as the expected gloomy weather arrives: "They waded the stream, and hurried over a wide open space, rush-grown and treeless, on the further side. Beyond that they came again to a belt of trees: tall oaks, for the most part, with here and there an elm tree or an ash. The ground was fairly level, and there was little undergrowth; but the trees were too close for them to see far ahead. The leaves blew upwards in sudden gusts of wind, and spots of rain began to fall from the overcast sky. Then the wind died away and the rain came streaming down."[53] The hobbit walking-party has definitely wandered into less cheerful country at this point.

Still, their dismay proves short-lived. By that afternoon—once the rain has passed and they have enjoyed some of the clear honeyed drink of the Elves—they are singing again, a song of the joys of walking and tall trees:

Ho! Ho! Ho! to the bottle I go
To heal my heart and drown my woe.
Rain may fall and wind may blow,
And many miles be still to go,
But under a tall tree I will lie,
And let the clouds go sailing by.[54]

This bout of merriment is eventually cut short when "a long-drawn wail came down the wind, like the cry of some evil and lonely creature. It rose and fell, and ended on a high piercing note. . . . It was answered by another cry, fainter and further off, but no less chilling to the blood."[55] The monster-fear put into them here marks a partial transition of the land around them into more Germanic country. By the time the wood comes "to a sudden end," they are all approaching their journey quite seriously: "creeping cautiously out from the edge of the trees, they set off across the open as quickly as they could," and they find themselves "afraid, away from the shelter of the wood."[56] Again, however, the detour into a more dangerous landscape is brief. They soon find themselves back again in their own familiar English countryside: "The sun escaping from the breaking clouds, as it sank towards the hills they had left, was now shining brightly again. Their fear left them, though they still felt uneasy. But the land became steadily more tame and well-ordered. Soon they came into well-tended fields and meadows: there were hedges and gates and dikes for drainage. Everything seemed quiet and peaceful, just an ordinary corner of the Shire. Their spirits rose with every step."[57] By the time they stumble over the lane to Farmer Maggot's, "the Black Riders began to seem like phantoms of the woods now left far behind" and they go on to find hobbitish hospitality (and mushrooms) within the friendly walls of his farmhouse.[58]

Some interesting points come out of an examination of this particular hobbit walking-party, which passes from the "gate in the lane beyond the meadows" of Hobbiton, through a wild corner of the Shire, and then into the Marish and "the thatched roofs of a large house and farm-buildings peeping out among the trees" of Farmer Maggot's farm at Bamfurlong.[59] The land through which they pass is unruly enough that Pippin's excuse "we lost our way in the woods, back near Woodhall, trying to take a short cut to the Ferry" is accepted by Maggot without question.[60] However, it is not so unruly that the hobbits even remotely consider the possibility of encountering real danger; they never seem concerned about (or even mention) meeting any typical wilderness perils such as bears, wolves, or two-legged beasts such as outlaws or robbers (never mind giant spiders, trolls, or dragons).

In *The Hobbit* readers are told "there were no wolves living near Mr. Baggins' hole at home," and the narrator is compelled to explain Bilbo's familiarity with the sound of wolf howls with the tidbit that "one of his elder cousins (on the Took side), who had been a great traveller, used to imitate it to frighten him."[61] Several times in *The Lord of the Rings* readers hear of an old incident when "white wolves invaded the Shire over the frozen Brandywine," but its singularity, and the fact that it was considered an invasion, seems to imply that—like all English forests after about the turn of the first millennium—there are no ravenous beasts to be encountered in the woods of the Shire.[62] Generally the most inconvenience they expect from their sojourn involves unpleasant weather and the possibility of getting lost. Frodo's complaint to Gildor captures this sentiment clearly: "I knew that danger lay ahead, of course; but I did not expect to meet it in our own Shire. Can't a hobbit walk from the Water to the River in peace?"[63] The threatening presence of the Black Rider is completely out of everyone's expectations, from the Gaffer to the Elves to Farmer Maggot, and the unexpected press of its danger on the pleasant semiwild woodlands of the Shire is one of the main engines driving the action of these early chapters.

At the end of *The Lord of the Rings*, the woods of the Shire are again important to the story, this time as victims of the many evils inflicted by Saruman on the hobbits' green and pleasant land. The first hint that all is not well in the woods comes from Barliman Butterbur, who informs the returning hobbits that some men who had caused "bad trouble" in Bree had been turned out of the town and "gone for robbers and live outside, hiding in the woods beyond Archet, and out in the wilds north-away."[64]

He goes on to observe darkly that "there's been worse than robbers about. Wolves were howling round the fences last winter. And there's dark shapes in the woods, dreadful things that it makes the blood run cold to think of."[65] Of course, Bree is outside the Shire, and the appearance of dark things in the woods is more tied to the fact that "the Rangers have all gone away" than to events over the Brandywine River.[66] But even if all of these developments cannot be blamed on Saruman, they are to Butterbur's mind unexpected and undesirable ones, indicating that this town where hobbits live in peace with the Big People shares with the Shire similar ideas of what proper woodlands should be like.

Later, as Frodo and his friends set off from the Brandywine Bridge toward Hobbiton, they notice that "there seemed an unusual amount of burning going on, and smoke rose from many points round about. A great cloud of it was going up far away in the direction of the Woody End."[67] Then, in what the text plaintively describes as "one of the saddest hours in their lives," they make the trip to Bag End to see the full horror of Saruman's "little mischief in a mean way."[68] While the only specific mention of the semiwild woodlands is the damage implied by the smoke in the Woody End, the text does state explicitly that, of the many examples of devastation, "the trees were the worst loss and damage . . . they had been cut down recklessly far and wide over the Shire."[69] Part of the healing necessary is the restoration of the woodlands. Sam's efforts are explicitly referred to as "forestry work," while "the task of hunting out the last remnant of the ruffians was left to Merry and Pippin, and it was soon done. . . . Before the Year's End the few survivors were rounded up in the woods, and those that surrendered were shown to the borders."[70] For the Shire to be considered "scoured," rebuilding houses is not enough; it is also necessary to return its woods to their proper, pleasant, and robber-free state.

The Old Forest surrounding Buckland certainly fits solidly within the "darkling wood" idea of Germanic fairy tales, and parts of it also mingle with the Celtic overlay landscape of Tom Bombadil's magic country, but its position just on the edge of hobbit lands allows it to brush up against this English concept as well. While his perspective is admittedly a much higher and more sophisticated one than that of the hobbits, Elrond speaks of the place fondly: "of the Old Forest many tales have been told: all that now remains is but an outlier of its northern march. Time was when a squirrel could go from tree to tree from what is now the Shire to Dunland west of Isengard. In those lands I journeyed once, and many things wild and strange I knew."[71] Dickerson and Evans note that, in this statement, Elrond is making "an explicit connection between forests and wildness" and suggesting that "things 'wild and strange' are worth knowing and that tales about them are worth telling—in short, that wilderness is valuable."[72]

There is no doubt that the adventurous hobbits of Buckland, who "live on the wrong side of the Brandywine River, and right agin the Old Forest" in what the text describes as "a sort of colony from the Shire," would agree with such sentiments.[73] As "most of the folk of the old Shire regarded the Bucklanders as peculiar, half foreigners as it were," it is probably to be expected that their attitude toward woods might be a bit different than that of those who live in the Shire proper, but both their attitude and the Forest itself appear to differ more in degree than kind.[74] Since the burrows and holes of the warren that is Brandy Hall, as well as the bustling village of Bucklebury behind it, had been established beyond the protection of the Brandywine river, over the years the Brandybucks had created their own barrier to the East: "on that side they had built a hedge: the High Hay. It had been planted many generations ago, and was now thick and tall, for it was constantly tended. It ran all the way from Brandywine Bridge, in a big loop curving away from the river, to Haysend (where the Withywindle flowed out of the Forest into the Brandywine): well over twenty miles from end to end. But, of course, it was not a complete protection. The Forest drew close to the hedge in many places."[75] The implication here seems to be that the protection was erected against the menace of the Forest, and this may be so—but the text also goes on to mention that "the Bucklanders kept their doors locked after dark, and that also was not usual in the Shire," and it is hard to imagine the hobbits fearing burglary or home invasions from trees.[76]

It is somewhat unclear whether the Old Forest harbors anything dangerous under its dark boughs besides its brooding and black-hearted trees. The white wolves mentioned above are described as having "come ravening out of the North in bitter white winters," not from the Old Forest to the east.[77] Merry explicitly dismisses "the old bogey-stories Fatty's nurses used to tell him, about goblins and wolves and things of that sort," and only mentions rumors he's heard of "various queer things living deep in the Forest, and on the far side."[78] When Fatty raises the alarm after the Black Riders come to Crickhollow, the Bucklanders assume, wrongly, that the enemies are "some strange invasion from the Old Forest."[79] The lore the hobbits learn from Tom Bombadil is also uncertain; in his "tales of bees and flowers, the ways of trees, and the strange creatures of the Forest, about the evil things and good things, things friendly and things unfriendly, cruel things and kind things, and secrets hidden under brambles," there are no indications one way or another regarding the presence of dangerous wild animals.[80] While objectively inconclusive, however, the real danger in the Old Forest is always presented as coming from the trees and their "hatred of things that go free upon the earth," not from any ravenous beasts or monsters lurking within.[81]

A lack of dangerous predators is certainly characteristic of English forests, and the fact that the Old Forest seems to share in that lack may help to explain why, after erecting the High Hay at such great trouble and expense, the Brandybucks went ahead and burrowed beneath it, creating a deep path with "walls of brick at the sides," which "arched over and formed a tunnel that dived deep under the Hedge and came out in the hollow on the other side."[82] Although homebodies like Fatty Bolger would never consider such a thing, there are some intrepid hobbits who occasionally and intentionally go into the Old Forest, evidently seeking pleasure in a bit of woodland adventure. Merry speaks of rumors that Farmer Maggot "used to go into the Old Forest at one time, and he has the reputation of knowing a good many strange things," and when the non-Brandybuck Fatty wails that "People don't go in there," he disagrees: "Oh yes they do! . . . The Brandybucks go in—occasionally when the fit takes them. We have a private entrance. Frodo went in once, long ago. I have been in several times: usually in daylight, of course, when the trees are sleepy and fairly quiet."[83] Frodo (who is actually considered to be "more than half a Brandybuck" by some old gossips in the Shire), certainly thinks that—compared to the serious fear put into him by the Black Riders—he is taking a much less dangerous path by choosing to go into the Old Forest: "if there are no worse things ahead than the Old Forest, I shall be lucky."[84] When taken, this decision does not feel like the sort of grim choices between great dangers with which someone like Aragorn is often portrayed as wrestling. Even if their shortcut through the Old Forest does end up being every bit as perilously Germanic as Fatty Bolger could imagine, and even if there does turn out to be uncanny Celtic weirdness waiting for them on its far side, there are nevertheless strong elements of the Forest (not to mention at least some hobbits' attitudes toward it) that fit into the pleasant English concept of wilderness.

This less perilous, less uncanny wilderness concept also makes a few appearances at other places in *The Lord of the Rings*. When the hobbits leave Bree with Strider, they venture into pathless Eriador. In a later edition of

The Hobbit, published after *The Lord of the Rings* was finished, Tolkien renamed this area the "Lone-lands" and described it as a gloomy place where "there were no people left, no inns, and the roads grew steadily worse."[85] Douglas Anderson notes that the change in the earlier work involves a fairly subtle linguistic hook into the later one: "In introducing the name Lone-lands into the 1966 edition of *The Hobbit,* Tolkien was providing a linguistic equivalent of the Sindarin Elvish name Eriador (wilderness), which in *The Lord of the Rings* refers to the vast lands between the Blue Mountains to the west and the Misty Mountains to the east. The Shire, where the Hobbits dwell, lies near its center."[86] Interestingly, this minor retcon places the Shire quite literally in the center of the wilderness.

As mentioned briefly in chapter 4, overall the passage through these pathless lands is dangerous, gloomy, and unpleasant, but at the beginning of their journey through the Bree-lands readers can glimpse in the description of the landscape the hobbits' more friendly and familiar concept of woodlands: "Walking was not unpleasant. Indeed, if it had not been for the disturbing events of the night before, they would have enjoyed this part of the journey better than any up to that time. The sun was shining, clear but not too hot. The woods in the valley were still leafy and full of colour, and seemed peaceful and wholesome. Strider guided them confidently among the many crossing paths."[87] There is no real sense of danger at this point: "they saw no sign and heard no sound of any other living thing all that day: neither two-footed, except birds; nor four-footed, except one fox and a few squirrels."[88] They are still in the Chetwood, only just beyond the edges of that map of "A Part of the Shire." It is a solid three days before they really make their way out of the English-feeling wilderness: "The next day they began to steer a steady course eastwards; and still all was quiet and peaceful. On the third day out from Bree they came out of the Chetwood. The land had been falling steadily, ever since they turned aside from the Road, and they now entered a wide flat expanse of country, much more difficult to manage. They were far beyond the borders of the Bree-land, out in the pathless wilderness, and drawing near to the Midgewater Marshes."[89] These marshes, "bewildering and treacherous," with "no permanent trail even for Rangers to find through their shifting quagmires" are the first real indication that they have moved past the liminal spaces on the edge of the Shire into more Germanic territory.[90]

Another area of Middle-earth that reflects the English concept of wilderness is the forest of Ithilien. Embedded within a bleakly Germanic wilderness, the former garden of Gondor, a "fair country of climbing woods and swift-falling streams," provides a welcome respite for Frodo, Sam, and Gollum as they flee the horror and blasted desolation they so famously encounter in front of the Black Gate.[91] As the three dispirited travelers pass out of the line of sight of the Eye and into a land "less barren and ruinous," they encounter "slopes covered with sombre trees like dark clouds," surrounded by "a tumbled heathland, grown with ling and broom and cornel, and other shrubs that they did not know. Here and there they saw knots of tall pine-trees."[92] Tolkien then goes on to make the comparison between the Shire and Ithilien quite explicit: "the hearts of the hobbits rose again a little in spite of weariness: the air was fresh and fragrant, and it reminded them of the uplands of the Northfarthing far away."[93] As they pass further into this fair land, Tolkien's rich prose shifts from the disgust and horror evoked by the desolation of Mordor, and begins to paint a picture of a green land rich with trees: "All about them were small woods of resinous trees, fir and cedar and cypress, and other kinds unknown in the Shire, with wide glades among them; and everywhere there was a wealth of sweet-smelling herbs and shrubs. . . . Here Spring was already busy about them: fronds pierced moss and mould, larches were green-fingered, small flowers were opening in the turf, birds were singing. Ithilien, the garden of Gondor now desolate kept still a dishevelled dryad loveliness."[94]

The long descriptive passage continues. In a huge chunk of a paragraph (which incidentally serves as solid evidence for any critic seeking to argue that Tolkien occasionally gets a little carried away with his landscape description), readers are treated to a veritable catalog of botanical delights:

> Many great trees grew there, planted long ago, falling into untended age amid a riot of careless descendants; and groves and thickets there were of tamarisk and pungent terebinth, of olive and of bay; and there were junipers and myrtles; and thymes that grew in bushes, or with their woody creeping stems mantled in deep tapestries the hidden stones; sages of many kinds putting forth blue flowers, or red, or pale green; and marjorams and new-sprouting parsleys, and many herbs of forms and scents beyond the garden-lore of Sam. The grots and rocky walls were already starred with saxifrages and stonecrops. Primeroles and anemones were awake in the filbert-brakes; and asphodel and many lily-flowers nodded their half-opened heads in the grass: deep green grass beside the pools, where falling streams halted in cool hollows on their journey down to Anduin.[95]

Sam passes through this gardener's paradise, "smelling and touching the unfamiliar plants and trees, forgetful for the moment of Mordor," and the companions rest during the bright, warm day in "a deep brown bed of last year's fern" crowned by "a thicket of dark-leaved bay-trees climbing up a steep bank that was crowned with old cedars."[96] Tom Shippey discusses how this whole scene is "a little cluster of anachronisms," from the use of words like *coneys* and *taters* to Sam's yearning for fried fish and chips, and he observes wryly that "not much would be *less* distinctively Old English."[97] The landscape of Ithilien is just as distant from the Germanic idea of wilderness as the colloquial language is from the sonorous tones of *Beowulf*, and Sam's rabbit-and-herb stew puts the finishing touches on this strangely homelike wilderness interlude.

None of this should be taken to imply that Eriador and Ithilien are not dangerous places. Without Strider's woodcraft and bravery, the Ring would have been taken at Weathertop. Sam may lose himself in botanical beauty in the disheveled garden of Ithilien, but he is brought back quickly to the dangers of the real world when he comes across a circle of burned bones.[98] Only the appearance of Faramir and his men saves the Ringbearer from getting caught in the center of a bloody ambush as an army of the enemy moves up through the woods from the south. But, just as Mirkwood can fit into both the first and second of Tolkien's wilderness concepts depending on the flow of the story and the way he chooses to describe the landscape, these dangerous areas outside the Shire are described in terms that link them to the third. Wild places can be bleak, they can be uncanny—and they can also be pleasant places to pass through on a beautiful day with the sun high and clouds scudding on a fragrant breeze through a beautiful blue sky. The idea of wilderness as a friendly place, a destination for relaxation and recreation, is a concept that would likely seem incomprehensible to the authors of Tolkien's medieval sources, but it is one that resonates strongly with many people in the world today.

In a 1944 letter to his son Christopher, who at the time was serving abroad in the Royal Air Force, Tolkien writes of what could be described as a yearning for the English concept of wilderness: "I have the autumn wanderlust upon me, and would fain be off with a knapsack on my back and no particular destination, other than a series of quiet inns. One of the too long delayed delights we must promise ourselves, when it pleases God to release us and reunite us, is just such a perambulation, together, preferably in mountainous country, not too far from the sea, where the scars of war, felled woods and bulldozed fields, are not too plain to see."[99] Tolkien refers to himself elsewhere as "very untravelled," and his insistence that "I do not travel much" is quoted above.[100] The yearning described in this letter, therefore, is arguably not for the sort of travel undertaken with a "real tug of desire to go and 'see places,'" but rather a desire to walk leisurely with no particular destination through beautiful country, country that is presumably only semiwild (as he clearly hopes to enjoy the comforts of quiet inns).[101]

Such leisurely walking was undoubtedly important to Tolkien throughout his entire life. From his early experiences as a child "walking through the river-meadows up the hill" to be enchanted by a view of Mosely Grammar School "illuminated with fairy-lights for Queen Victoria's Diamond Jubilee," to a day very near the end of his life when he decided to ignore his work and instead take his secretary on a long walk through the Oxford Botanic Garden and through the river willows in order "to see all his favourite trees," he seems to have often found inspiration, respite, and solace in the English countryside.[102] During his college years, he spent one summer vacation walking in Berkshire and Buckinghamshire[103] and another exploring the "open country" of the Lizard Peninsula in Cornwall on paths that "twisted and wiggled and wobbled and upped and downed until dusk."[104] While a professor at Oxford, he strolled endlessly along Addison's Walk at Magdalen College in conversation with C. S. Lewis, once quite famously discussing the purpose of myth and the truth of Christianity.[105] He also occasionally accompanied the other Inklings on various walking holidays through beautifully hilly and semiwild areas of southern England, including the Quantock Hills in Somerset with C. S. Lewis and Owen Barfield[106] and the Malvern Hills with the Lewis brothers[107] and George Sayer.[108] Mild outdoor adventures such as these were clearly an important part of the way Tolkien experienced his beloved England, and glimpses of them gleam through in his presentation of the natural world of Middle-earth.

It is interesting to note how Tolkien bequeaths a similar predilection for leisurely walking, and indeed even a characteristic autumn wanderlust, to his wandering hobbit hero in *The Lord of the Rings.* The young Frodo finds himself "wondering at times, especially in the autumn, about the wild lands," and he specifically chooses to wait to leave the Shire until after summer passes because "when autumn came, he knew that part at least of his heart would think more kindly of journeying, as it always did at that season."[109] Perhaps the pleasures of autumn walking holidays are not a universally English concept, but they are certainly a Tolkienian one, and they rely on the existence of a concept of wilderness that, while wild, is not too wild; requires some discomfort, but not too much; provides some adventure, but no real danger.

Even set against the dramatic impact of an ostensibly more exciting Germanic or Celtic wilderness, this in-between concept has a curiously strong draw and remarkable staying power. Tom Shippey notes how, both in *The Hobbit* and *The Lord of the Rings,* Tolkien "found the transit from familiar Shire to archaic Wilderland an inhibiting one."[110] In his opinion, "*The Hobbit* does not quite take off till Bilbo finds the ring."[111] He also points out how "Frodo has to be dug out of no less than five 'Homely Houses' before his quest is properly launched," and argues that, at this early point in the tale, "there is a sense that the zest of the story goes not into the dangers but the recoveries—hot baths at Crickhollow, song and dancing at Bree, Goldberry's water that seems like wine, and Butterbur's 'small and cosy room' with its 'hot soup, cold meats, a blackberry tart, new loaves, slab of butter, and half a ripe cheese'.... Meanwhile the Black Riders, for all their snuffling and deadly cries, are not the menace they later become."[112] Shippey attributes this apparent reluctance to shift out of familiar-feeling places to a characteristic foible of Tolkien's creative process, but when considered in the context of the wilderness concepts under discussion here, it also underlines the ability of the seemingly less dramatic English landscape to fully capture the imagination of both writer and reader.

There is also a parallel between the function of this wilderness concept and the function that the hobbits serve in Tolkien's narrative craft. They are, as many critics have noted, anachronisms in the ancient, heroic world of the legendarium. Tom Shippey's analysis reflects the general critical agreement:

> Hobbits are, and always remain, highly *anachronistic* in the ancient world of Middle-earth. That indeed is their main function.... In setting a work in some distant time, an author may well find that the gap between that time and the reader's modern awareness is too wide to be easily bridged; and accordingly a figure essentially modern in attitudes and sentiment is imported into the historical world, to guide the reader's reactions, to help the reader feel "what it would be like" to be there.[113]

In the mind of a twentieth- or twenty-first-century reader, the grim and determined courage of an Aragorn or the ancient unknowable wisdom and magic of a Galadriel can be thrilling, admirable, and aesthetically arresting. However, for people whose own personal experiences do not necessarily include leading armies of undead or throwing down the walls and clearing the black pits of evil sorcerers (or even the real-world equivalents that might come from such things as military combat or a law-enforcement background), a lifelong education founded on the irony and disillusionment of contemporary literature can sometimes make it difficult to enter fully into identification with them.

The same can be said of the hobbit landscape characterizing this third concept of wilderness. Tolkien says explicitly that, in his mind, hobbits "lived on the borders of The Wild, and were mostly unaware of it."[114] People who do not live in areas where alpine terrain is accessible are likely to lack the personal experience that could deepen their response to the descriptions of the Misty Mountains in the text. However, anyone who has at least some passing acquaintance with the sort of semiwild woodlands to be encountered in the Shire will react to them in the same way they react to the hobbits who live there: as mediators, as familiar starting points just on the outside of their own lands, which can serve as jumping-off points to the more fantastic and more exciting people and places to come.

Bilbo is once again the main example. His bourgeois sensibilities give him an inescapably anachronistic perspective on the ancient Germanic and Celtic mythological ideas that so animate *The Hobbit*. In a sense, Tolkien "wanted finally to bridge the gap between the ancient world and the modern one," and the beautifully developed landscape into which his unsuspecting readers follow the slightly comic hobbit serves as "the world of fairy-tale and of the ancient Northern imagination which lay behind fairy-tale, rendered accessible to the contemporary reader."[115] Much critical attention is placed on the mediation between the readers and the human (and larger-than-human) heroic characters involved in this fairy-tale world, but Bilbo's perspective is also used to help readers navigate the shift between different concepts of wilderness. Shippey highlights a scene near the end of *The Hobbit*, which, as opposed to what he calls "the last scene of chaos and tidying-up," he considers the true ending of the work, characterized as a "regretful farewell to the Wild . . . as archaic Took cedes to Edwardian Baggins":[116]

> they came to that high point at morning, and looking backward they saw a white sun shining over the outstretched lands. There behind lay Mirkwood, blue in the distance, and darkly green at the nearer edge even in the spring. There far away was the Lonely Mountain on the edge of eyesight. On its highest peak snow yet unmelted was gleaming pale.

> "So comes snow after fire, and even dragons have their ending!" said Bilbo, and he turned his back on his adventure."[117]

Bilbo returns quite gratefully to his life in the idealized Merrie England of the Shire, but he is no longer completely able to escape the draw of other concepts of wilderness. Near the end of his life, in a Middle-earth much more developed than that of his earlier adventures, he distinguishes between the wilderness to be found in the Shire and that of other concepts in a somewhat plaintive confession to Gandalf; "I want to see the wild country again before I die, and the Mountains," he muses, even as he recognizes that Frodo "is still in love with the Shire, with woods and fields and little rivers."[118] Frodo and his friends go on to follow, sometimes quite literally, in Bilbo's footsteps; they learn the same lessons, discover the same attractions of other ideas of wilderness, and serve the same mediating function in the much grander tale of *The Lord of the Rings*—but, nevertheless (to paraphrase Burns) where they go, Merrie England goes also.

In the end, even if the nostalgic idea of Merrie England is as legendary a place as the mere of the Grendelkin or the magical hills of Tír na nÓg, it is a legend much closer in the flow of the mythic river to the sensibilities of Tolkien's readers today. The wilderness concept based on this idealized Englishness admittedly does not sit quite as comfortably as the other two inside the fences placed around the modern idea of wilderness by the writers and philosophers interested in defining that sort of thing. But Tolkien seems to accord wilderness status more freely than they; when he writes to his son that "the garden is its usual wilderness self, all deep green again, and still with abundant roses," the "wilderness" he mentions is much closer to wildness in the Thoreauvian sense than to any purist ideas of vast landscapes untrammeled by human existence.[119]

As mentioned at the outset, there is a difference between wildness and wilderness, and it is the former and not the latter that Thoreau puts forth as the salvation of the world. Tolkien's use of this subtle but powerful concept serves to make his vast archaic creation more accessible to readers who might not have the education or inclination to wade through the challenges of a *Beowulf* or a *Mabinogion*, and it is easily as important as the other two in defining what he considers the ideal relationship between his ambulant characters and the crucial central character in the legendarium that is Middle-earth itself.

. . .

The universe is not a place of exclusive absolutes. It is beautiful and ugly. It is vulgar and sublime. It is characterized by glory and danger and mud and blood and terror and joy and the entire spectrum of material existence, and is in ultimate reality more than the sum of all of these (and of all possible other) parts. When humans tell themselves stories about the natural world in order to understand their place in it, those stories reflect this deep ambiguity; the landscapes of tales can be friendly or hostile, bright and beautiful or dark and forbidding, and frequently—in the best tales, at least—they manage to be all of these at the same time.

Tolkien's stories are no exception to this rule. The presence of his three distinct wilderness concepts demonstrates how this ambiguity characterizes even literature that is not explicitly concerned with wilderness or the natural world. The great menace of Caradhras is balanced in the Germanic wilds of the Misty Mountains with the heart-stopping beauty of Kheled-zâram. The feast and light and song of the Elvenking shine amid the blackness of Mirkwood. The physically strong but ultimately spiritually weak hero Boromir first encounters his fatal doom within the stunning vision of uncanny Celtic Lothlórien. And even the thoroughly English Bilbo eventually finds himself longing to escape the quiet pleasantness of the Shire and the narrow-minded parochialism that infects its inhabitants. Like the mythic and cultural terrain that partially inspired them, each of these landscapes is both beautiful and deadly, both desirable and dangerous—and they all have something to teach the varied group of heroes who journey through their fully presented realms.

In some ways it is the interaction between and even the mingling of these concepts that highlights their presence and importance. Marjorie Burns observes how Tolkien uses Bilbo's story in *The Hobbit* to explore the layers lurking beneath the surface of his quintessentially English world: "What Bilbo has acquired (or rediscovered within himself) is an Englishman's northern roots. He has gained an Anglo-Saxon self-reliance and a Norseman's sense of will, and all of this is kept from excess by a Celtic sensitivity, by a love of earth, of poetry, and of simple song and cheer."[120] In *The Lord of the Rings,* the whole mysterious Bombadil sequence can be viewed as a clever amalgamation of all three wilderness concepts into a single episode; in a sense, the young hobbits' English preconceptions of wilderness get them into trouble, and it takes a positive personalization of the uncanny Celtic wilderness to save them from two separate threatening personalizations of the dangerous Germanic wilderness. When the young heroes reenter the familiar and friendly wilderness of the Bree-lands, they are a bit wiser, a bit more wary, and more prepared than they were before to truly begin their long and varied adventures. The interconnection between all these different concepts is one of the things that makes journeying through the natural world of *The Lord of the Rings* such a rich experience.

Of course, Tolkien does not explore in detail every thread woven into the cloth of the modern concept of wilderness. The idea of peace in desert solitude is notably absent, as is the lush tropical beauty of jungle wildernesses, or the long stretches of palm-studded golden beaches that often feature in tales of uninhabited places in other parts of the world. But he is not blind to the value of such places. In a letter, he acknowledges that beauty can be found even in what other people might consider wasteland:

> Much though I love and admire little lanes and hedges and rustling trees and the soft rolling contours of a rich champaign, the thing that stirs me most and comes nearest to heart's satisfaction for me is space, and I would be willing to barter barrenness for it; indeed I think I like barrenness itself, whenever I have seen it. My heart still lingers among the high stony wastes among the morains and mountain wreckage, silent in spite of the sound of thin chill water. Intellectually and aesthetically, of course; man cannot live on stone and sand, but I at any rate cannot live on bread alone; and if there was not bare rock and pathless sand and the unharvested sea, I should grow to hate all green things as a fungoid growth.[121]

It is clear from all of his writings that Tolkien esteems green and growing things very highly indeed, so this last statement places some powerful weight behind the idea that wilderness and wild lands of all kinds are something to be accorded the highest of value.

Tolkien demonstrates this value most clearly in his careful construction of Middle-earth's natural world. Alfred Siewers observes that "the blessed lands beyond the sea, the Elven realms of Rivendell and Lothlórien, the Old Forest and Fangorn, and many descriptions of place throughout *The Lord of the Rings*, all reflect a similarly dynamic and relatively non-objectified sense of place."[122] If it is true that Patrick Curry's original assertion about Middle-earth as "a character in its own right" has become somewhat of a critical commonplace,[123] Siewers's observation here highlights a good reason why; Tolkien's landscapes are so dynamic, so alive, so complete in themselves, that they have agency and worth and a fully developed reality. They are as varied and complex as characters as the humans, Elves, hobbits, Ents, and even foxes moving through them. Like the real-world wild places on which it is based, "the wilderness of Middle-earth is vast, it is forbidding, and it is sometimes dangerous, but it is also beautiful," and the power of that beauty forms a large part of the mythic force wielded by the whole of the tale.[124]

That mythic force has proven over the years more than strong enough to make Tolkien's work a worldwide phenomenon. Whether they hate him or love him, praise or revile him, there are none operating within the boundaries of speculative fiction today who can ignore him, and few even outside those boundaries who have not at least heard of him. And, although Tolkien died in 1972, the power of Middle-earth to influence the mythic imagination of countless readers has only continued to grow since the end of the twentieth century. Examining how Tolkien's wilderness concepts interact with the foundational ideas of modern wilderness philosophy, discussing how Middle-earth's landscapes appear in New Media adaptations, and considering how their power might be harnessed to reshape some of the modern destructive environmental stories will be the aim of part III.

PART III
THE WILDERNESS OF MYTH

The Elder Days are gone. The Middle Days are passing.
The Younger Days are beginning.
(Saruman to Gandalf)
—Tolkien, *Lord*, 259

The Younger Days

When approaching the continuing evolution of Middle-earth and its concepts of wilderness in the Western cultural consciousness, it is important to remember that the river of influence does not stop with Professor Tolkien. The earlier works that shaped his thinking are still strongly present in that cultural flow, and are themselves enriched through interaction with his later ones; those readers who find enjoyment and mythic instruction in the tales of Middle-earth are also likely to find them in Tolkien's more important sources,[1] and to find their experience of those sources to be deeply enhanced by their familiarity with Middle-earth. But, just as the nameless *Gawain* poet's reworking of old material in the creation of a new and unique work of art has mingled since its inception with many other flows to form the modern concept of the Arthurian cycle, it is Tolkien's own work—both in blending with admirable skill the various streams of the works that influenced him, and in adding something new and powerful from the depths of his own imagination—that constitutes his greatest influence. The Middle-earth legendarium serves as the main wellspring of a vast and immensely strong current in Western culture, which can generally be grouped under the broad and nonspecific heading of "fantasy."

For those who love fantasy literature, who grew up in a cultural landscape that includes elegant Elves or irascible Dwarves or swords-and-sorcery epics as a matter of course, it is easy to forget that these tropes were not present in the broad popular mindset of the Western world at the turn of the twentieth century. Educated people studied the classics and other great works like *Beowulf* or Shakespeare, of course, but for general readers the exposure to such imaginative tales was limited to a narrow and time-restricted part of their lives. There were the thickly ornamented works of Lord Dunsany or the goblins of George MacDonald, but theirs was a fairly niche market; neither achieved the mass appeal enjoyed by spy novels or detective stories or even the genre of Gothic horror so popular in the nineteenth century. The many collections of fairy tales and folktales came close, as did the smattering of Victorian children's literature of the *Peter Pan* or *Alice* variety, but readers of such things were expected to grow out of them eventually and replace them with more mature amusements. Tolkien was arguably the first to successfully bring the literature of the fantastic to a wide and nonspecialist adult audience.

Today fantasy (often grouped with science fiction and sometimes horror under the broader umbrella of "speculative fiction") is a multibillion-dollar entertainment industry. From television to films, from tabletop games to the latest high-resolution gaming consoles, Tolkien-style high fantasy is ubiquitous in Western culture. The number of people who actively participate in the various fantasy fandoms is still admittedly a minority subset of the overall population, but it is a growing minority, and the emotional commitment of that audience to the mythic power of Tolkien and his inheritors is remarkably strong. The very existence in the mainstream consciousness of various fandom tropes—people to be ridiculed because they wear pointy ears to conventions or write poetry in elvish, or really anyone who demonstrates story-inspired "irrational" behavior outside of that sanctioned by the myths surrounding professional sports cultures—is a testament to the power of those stories. This power has proven that it is able to change people's behavior in profound ways.

The behavior shaped by the Zeitgeist of the twenty-first century, however, is not the same as that which was current during Tolkien's lifetime. The Middle-earth legendarium is one of the most timeless and powerful myths extant today, but even its most ancient and enduring ideas mean different things to contemporary fans than they did to Tolkien's twentieth-century readers, and differ significantly again from what they meant to him when he conceived them out of his Edwardian mind. As an example, consider the whole emotional experience surrounding his idealization of the Shire, which can be attributed to his memory of (and longing for) the lost idyllic rural landscape of his childhood. Such memories are certainly universal to the shared human tendency toward nostalgia, but at the same time they are extremely specific to the village (and even to individual buildings such as the old mill) of Sarehole in Warwickshire. Both this universality and this specificity contribute to the staying power of his modern myth.[2]

There will always be a certain amount of distance between the mindset of an old story and that of readers of another time encountering that story. It is arguably the ability to manage that difference that makes or breaks a myth's effectiveness in a different culture or era; only those myths able to successfully bridge that gap will retain their original power to influence beliefs and behavior in different times and places. The chapters in part III will examine that gap, as well as its implications on the modern destructive stories about the natural world, from three different perspectives: the powerful resonance between Tolkien's wilderness ideas and influential ones in current wilderness philosophy; how Tolkien's wilderness story has evolved through its various New Media incarnations; and the ways that a particularly Tolkienian brand of courage embodied in representatives of his three wilderness concepts might inspire better stories and better action in today's debates over the value of wildness and wilderness.

CHAPTER SEVEN

Tolkien and American Wilderness Philosophy

The contemporary English word *wilderness* is a slippery one. On the surface it seems clear enough, but under even the gentlest of examination it shifts into a mutable concept encompassing many conflicting ideas: a desolate wasteland and a place to meet God, a dangerous abode of monsters and a haven of breathtaking beauty, a place to be shunned as dehumanizing, and a place to be sought out in order to learn what it really means to be human. To medieval Britons, it still harbored a supernatural power far beyond anything humanity could muster. After the Renaissance-inspired Scientific Revolution of the eighteenth century and the Enlightenment-inspired Industrial Revolution of the nineteenth, however, the human animal's sense of control over its environment expanded dramatically. Now, nearly two centuries into the breathtaking destruction wrought by that expansion, an important postmodern general trend of connotation has begun to develop. Wilderness, despite its many ambiguities, is slowly shifting from something to be destroyed into something to be protected.

This transition is hardly comprehensive or complete. To the extent that wilderness has recently been accorded value beyond the economic (or even the aesthetic), the actual safeguarding of such value is still limited to a tiny portion of the landscape, and even such limited protection is often resented and underenforced. Oelschlaeger argues that "the so-called *progressive conservation movement* was philosophically grounded in modernism. Wild nature was conceived as little more than a stockpile of raw materials of no intrinsic value; only through the productive enterprise—the humanizing of the wilderness—did nature gain value."[1]

In a story about stockpiles and materials, wilderness is at best a place where the natural resources have not yet begun to be extracted. Anyone who doubts that this modernist story is still the dominant one in the Western world today need only visit the vast old-growth logging operations of British Columbia and the US Pacific Northwest, or smell the smoke of the burning Amazon rainforests being destroyed to clear land for cattle and palm oil plantations.

But wilderness is also becoming attached to different stories, stories of spiritual and ethical value, of preservation and conservation, even of scientific bulwarks against climate change. While such story shifts are slow and halting, and often find themselves blown backwards by the fickle winds of political power, they nevertheless represent a perceptible trend. Tolkien's environmental and wilderness themes can be seen as emerging at the time this trend was only just beginning to develop in response to the growing realization that industrialization was not an unmitigated good. Leslie Ellen Jones notes that "Prior to the burgeoning pollution of the Industrial Revolution, nature was humankind's enemy; it was more powerful than we are. The necessity for the natural world to go out of its way to overthrow a threat from humankind, rather than simply swatting it like a fly (or absent-mindedly burying it under floods, lava flows, landslides, earthquakes, and blizzards) is the sort of thing that would only occur to the kind of person who had to live in the grime and noise of turn-of-the-century Birmingham after the rural heaven of Sarehole Mill."[2]

Tolkien, although "writing prior to the advent of any 'organised' green agenda, before the literary birth of words such as ecotheology or ecocriticism," still presents in his fiction an ecological world view "surprisingly developed in terms of its consonance with much of what we now understand as environmentalism."[3] That consonance, rather than any conscious or unconscious direct relationship, is what links Tolkien's thought to the modern environmental movement. It also provides some hints as to how the mythical power of Tolkien's legendarium might be harnessed to support and accelerate positive change in today's wilderness stories.

In an intellectual history framework, what change has already occurred relies heavily on a school of thought loosely known as American Wilderness Philosophy. A continuum of late nineteenth- and early twentieth-century American thinkers, from Ralph Waldo Emerson to Aldo Leopold and beyond, has slowly established the idea in the modern Western consciousness of wilderness as a valuable resource. This idea eventually made its way into United States public policy, first with the establishment of national parks, and then later with the passage of the famous Wilderness Act of 1964. While the assertion that such concepts are "America's gift to the world" or "America's best idea" has been repeated to the point of triteness, it does include a grain of truth. This concept, which has expanded into the world's mental map along with the rest of the American cultural juggernaut, grew out of the American experience of endless expansion into a wild frontier followed by the sober discovery that said frontier was not actually endless.

It is true that the idea of wilderness as something valuable, or that places of great wildness are worth preserving, long predated the American cultural consciousness. In medieval Britain the very word *forest* served as "a juridical term referring to land that had been placed off limits by a royal decree. . . . Once a region had been 'afforested' . . . it could not be cultivated exploited, or encroached upon. It lay outside the public domain, reserved for the king's pleasure and recreation."[4] The *wyldrenesse of wyrale* through which Gawain wandered on his search for the Green Knight was just such an afforested area. But this medieval idea of wilderness recreation was a muscular, Germanic one; kings pursued blood sports like hunting and shooting, and employed people (who incidentally would come to be called rangers) to keep poaching commoners away from their royal lands and deer. The American innovation, therefore, was to extend rather than originate the idea. In this new conception, everyone had a right to pleasure and recreation on wild lands, and it was the beauty of the lands themselves (as opposed to the pursuit and defeat of creatures within them) that was the basis of such recreation.

It is also true that Tolkien himself does not come across as particularly fond of the United States, at least in the abstract. In a letter to his son Christopher he laments the introduction of "American sanitation, morale-pep, feminism, and mass production" throughout the world and warns of a spreading "Americo-cosmopolitanism," which he says he finds "very terrifying."[5] There is no evidence to indicate Tolkien ever read Thoreau or Muir or Leopold or even European writers such as the Norwegian deep ecology crusader Arne Naess. But the influence of American wilderness literature on the Anglophone mythic imagination of the nineteenth and twentieth centuries was strong and Tolkien did not escape it. Ruminating on the children's books he enjoyed as a child, he dismisses blander fare such as *Alice* and *Treasure Island* and explains that "Red Indians were better: there were bows and arrows (I had and have a wholly unsatisfied desire to shoot well with a bow),[6] and strange languages, and glimpses of an archaic mode of life, and, above all, forests in such stories."[7] These childhood impressions seem to color his complaints about the "horrors of the American scene" at the end of his life, when he muses that Americans "arise in an entirely different mental climate and soil, polluted and impoverished to a degree only paralleled by the lunatic destruction of the physical lands which Americans inhabit."[8] This last sentiment clearly echoes the laments of American wilderness writers as far back as the turn of the nineteenth century.

Especially useful in examining the resonance between Tolkien's ideas and those of the American wilderness philosophers is Susan Jeffers's analysis of the communities formed between humans (or human analogues like Elves or hobbits) and their environments in Tolkien's work. Jeffers notes that, as human beings, "we understand the environment portrayed in a text based on our understanding of our actual lived environments."[9] The conceptual model from which Tolkien's concepts of wilderness arose is deeply rooted in the medieval English experience, which itself grew out of the medieval Germanic and Celtic cultural streams. Considering that one of the major mythological rivers that flowed into the New World originated in Britain, it is not surprising to find significant parallels between the English lived environment and the one that would eventually produce the canon of American Wilderness Philosophy.

The Germanic and English concepts of wilderness in Tolkien's work translate fairly directly into the American intellectual setting, and a scholar attuned to the more subtle elements of Celtic influence can spot them if she looks hard enough. But the first English settlers in the New World wandered off the mythological path leading from works such as *Beowulf* and the *Mabinogion* to Tolkien long before either of those works was present in the intellectual constellation of educated people.[10] This divergence means that such influences, while present, are less explicitly tied in the American experience to the ethnic and cultural European groups implied by the terms *Germanic, Celtic,* and *English.* Still, there are many conceptual extensions of the ideas, both in the context of the archaic, Romantic, and pastoral ecocritical tropes they embody, as well as in the harsh, uncanny, or friendly characteristics demonstrated by these different sorts of wildernesses, that demonstrate much of the same progression through American intellectual history as they did through that of Tolkien's England.

. . .

The original wilderness of the American colonies was a real-world embodiment of the first concept Tolkien drew on in his fiction, the Germanic place of danger and heroism and monsters in the dark woods. The earliest Western explorers in North America found a place utterly unlike the heavily settled and well-trodden paths of the Old World. Here in real life was the Mirkwood of their myths, a place that their ancestors wrote about but which had largely disappeared from the landscape of seventeenth-century Western Europe. Roderick Nash points out that "the transatlantic journey and subsequent western advances stripped away centuries. Successive waves of frontiersmen had to contend with wilderness as uncontrolled and terrifying as that which primitive man confronted.... For the first Americans, as for medieval Europeans, the forest's darkness hid savage men, wild beasts, and still stranger creatures of the imagination."[11] It was not that there were no places of wildness in the Old World, of course. There were, and they still held great mythic power over the Western cultural imagination; in the seventeenth and eighteenth centuries the Age of Enlightenment was only just beginning to wear away at humanity's more ancient conceptions of the natural world. But the scope of America's wilderness was just so vast. "For Europeans wild country was a single peak or heath, an island of uninhabited land surrounded by settlement. They at least knew its character and extent. But the seemingly boundless wilderness of the New World was something else. In the face of this vast blankness, courage failed and imagination multiplied fears."[12] It is no wonder, then, that the early Western national myth in North America was a grimly Germanic one, describing small points of light amid the vast wild darkness. Set against the harsh truth of life on the eastern edge of an unknown continent, the colonists found powerful relevance in the "long Western tradition of imagining wild country as a moral vacuum, a cursed and chaotic wasteland," and these attitudes were only reinforced by the mythos of heroism and strength needed to survive this wilderness condition.[13]

Environmental philosophers J. Baird Callicott and Michael P. Nelson note that "the originally colonial and eventually postcolonial received concept of wilderness is first and foremost an artifact of the sharp dichotomy, in Puritan thinking, between humanity on one hand... and nature, on the other."[14] This dichotomy is a constant presence in colonial American writings. Plymouth Governor William Bradford (while not technically a Puritan) shared a similar attitude with Massachusetts Bay

Governor (and actual Puritan) John Winthrop toward the "hideous and desolate wilderness, full of wild beasts and wild men" where the early colonists were trying to establish a life for themselves.[15] John Winthrop's famous 1630 "citty [*sic*] upon a hill,"[16] while a direct biblical reference from a man who could not have known *Beowulf*, nevertheless grows out of the same cultural soil as the Anglo-Saxon concept that "the human race lives precariously, with only brief moments of respite in places of refuge like the hall, which is surrounded on all sides—besieged even—by the forces of the natural world."[17] This shining city can be seen as a parallel to Hrothgar's hall at Heorot: "Majesty lodged there, its light shone over many lands."[18] More than two centuries after the Puritans landed at Plymouth, well after the American wilderness myth began its transformation into something close to a completely opposing idea, this idea continues to appear in the rhetoric of those seeking to champion their beliefs about what America could mean to the world.

Winthrop's famous mythic image has been harnessed over the years in order to advance the related myth of American exceptionalism. That particular story has been accused (and not without good reason) of creating many problems around the world, not to mention accelerating the destruction and degradation of wild lands in the United States. But it is interesting to consider that the Middle-earth legendarium includes another version of Winthrop's concept. Closer in spirit and ideal than *Beowulf*, and a bit more useful than America's problematic ideological superiority complex, this version demonstrates how the Germanic idea can serve as a positive rather than negative example of the relationship between humankind and the natural world. While Edoras and the golden hall of Meduseld are a letter-perfect calque on the Anglo-Saxon poem, and probably reflect what Tolkien considered the earliest and purest form of the idea, in Middle-earth the country they represent is peopled with a more primitive folk, "wise but unlearned, writing no books but singing many songs, after the manner of the children of Men before the Dark Years."[19] The pinnacle of Tolkien's human civilization at the end of the Third Age and beginning of the Fourth does not stand in Rohan. It lies instead where the people of greatest wisdom and learning and nobility reside, a beleaguered but still powerful country, whose capital is a literal shining city on a hill in the purest Winthropian mode: the realm of Gondor.[20]

Tolkien describes the scene when Pippin first encounters the White City of Minas Tirith gleaming upon its grand hill in words the likes of which any Puritan preacher could be proud:

> Even as Pippin gazed in wonder the walls passed from looming grey to white, blushing faintly in the dawn; and suddenly the sun climbed over the eastern shadow and sent forth a shaft that smote the face of the City. Then Pippin cried aloud, for the Tower of Ecthelion, standing high within the topmost wall, shone out against the sky, glimmering like a spike of pearl and silver, tall and fair and shapely, and its pinnacle glittered as if it were wrought of crystals; and white banners broke and fluttered from the battlements in the morning breeze, and high and far he heard a clear ringing as of silver trumpets.[21]

It is striking to set this imagery next to that of US President Ronald Reagan in his 1989 farewell address as he consciously and intentionally evokes John Winthrop's image:

> I've spoken of the shining city all my political life, but I don't know if I ever quite communicated what I saw when I said it. But in my mind it was a tall, proud city built on rocks stronger than oceans, wind-swept, God-blessed, and teeming with people of all kinds living in harmony and peace; a city with free ports that hummed with commerce and creativity. And if there had to be city walls, the walls had doors and the doors were open to anyone with the will and the heart to get here.... After 200 years, two centuries, she still stands strong and true on the granite ridge, and her glow has held steady no matter what storm.[22]

The emotional resonance between these two passages is clear. This is of course not to argue that there is any direct relationship between the words of these two men; it is more to note that they both are tapping into the same deep spring at the origin of their shared Germanic-influenced, biblically oriented, and British-founded Western culture. The waters in this spring are archaic, traditional, and heroic ones, to be sure, and such imagery represents ideals of values and behavior that in both contexts are in truth rarely achieved, but its mythic power is undeniable. The position of Gondor in the cultural map of Middle-earth is not dissimilar to that which US presidents from Kennedy to Obama have sought to champion for their own country.

Susan Jeffers describes the people of Gondor as relating to their natural world in a "power from" manner, which she suggests occupies a middle ground between the ideal "power with" relationship of the Ents, Elves, and hobbits and the destructive "power over" attitude of villains like the

Orcs, Saruman, and Sauron.[23] This situates Tolkien's great human city in a "liminal space between a relationship based on community and one based on oppression" whose inhabitants "demonstrate both how people can improve their relationship with their places and how people can erode this connection."[24] In one sense this is a typically Germanic, Anglo-Saxon idea; when Jeffers says "the people of Gondor connect to their surroundings and the individual elements in these surroundings at a symbolic level. They use their environment to define themselves, even if it means first shaping that environment to properly reflect that self-definition," she is elucidating an idea that goes all the way back to the psychologically mutable wild landscape of *Beowulf*.[25] But unlike Hrothgar's Spear-Danes, who need a hero to come in and destroy the monstrous symbol of wild nature plaguing them, the salvation of Gondor is tied instead to the reestablishment of a healthy relationship with nature as symbolized by the restoration of a living, thriving White Tree to its place of honor in the center of the city. Jeffers argues that this symbol implies a capacity for growth, which is not shared by the childless Ents or the fading Elves; while the "power with" relationship of those groups might be the ideal, the hope that Gondor represents at the end of the story speaks to a possibility for "the people of Gondor to reconnect to their place and develop into even better people."[26] This is an idea about the relationship between humankind and the natural world that is quite unlike anything in *Beowulf*.

The United States also has a similar and strong "power from" current in its mythological makeup. In Jeffers's construction, this kind of relationship is generally one where "person and place are pulled together in a dialectic, as people use their environment to define themselves—both as what they are and as what they are not."[27] It is easy to see such a relationship in the American cultural stream; the presence of a harsh, Germanic wilderness was the defining characteristic of the American place from its earliest conception, and the interactions between people and that wilderness lie at the core of the nascent American self-image. Other countries could boast equally breathtaking natural beauty, of course, and Roderick Nash comments on how "an attribute unique to nature in the New World had to be found" to distinguish the American landscape; he concludes that "the search led to the wilderness. In the early nineteenth century American nationalists began to understand that it was in the wildness of its nature that their country was unmatched."[28] From the vast fortunes made trading beaver pelts to the thick terrain perfect for patiently defensive guerrilla warfare tactics in war against Britain, the power of American culture from its earliest days came from the unique wildness of its landscape.

Unfortunately, there are also many perspectives in which American history veers deeply into the brutally destructive territory of Jeffers's "power over" concept. The dark side of early America is dark indeed (and not only in the Germanic wilderness sense). Considering William Bradford's famous thundering about hideousness and desolation quoted above, it is painfully ironic to read in his writings about his settlers coming upon "a good quantity of clear ground where the Indians had formerly set corn, and some of their graves" and later "two of their houses covered with mats" with "more of their corn and of their beans of various colours," which were "brought away" as "seed to plant them corn the next year, or else they might have starved."[29] These are unquestionably not the elements of an unsettled wilderness.

In fact, entire human civilizations flourished on the North American continent well before the late fifteenth century, civilizations that variously boasted impressive urban centers (Aztec), a logosyllabic script paired with sophisticated mathematics (Maya), and even an extensive federal system of representative government (Iroquois). The myths defining the relationship between humanity and the natural world in those civilizations were very different from the tales carried aboard the ships from Western Europe. These unfortunate native inhabitants were placed by the European invaders quite firmly on the nonhuman side of the human-nature dichotomy, and their mythological influence on the American story would not take root until well after their physical presence had largely been wiped away.

But this sad truth does not invalidate the comparison to Gondor. That kingdom is hardly presented by Tolkien as a perfect one; it was founded by the survivors of a country every bit as guilty of hubris and destructive pride as the United States, and in the last days of the Third Age the beleaguered state of the once-great realm is represented by the moral failure of Boromir and the haughty, destructive madness of his father Denethor. Importantly, however, at the end of *The Lord of the Rings* Gondor is renewed. Its final state is a positive example of an ideal human country, a model of good government, symbolized no longer by an unhinged steward and a dead tree but by its heroic, noble, and beloved king.

Aragorn serves as a good example of the kind of resonance that can be found between this Middle-earth superpower and the national mythos of colonial America. While he is a king who (somewhat contrary to the American ideal) derives his right to rule from his noble bloodline,[30] his strength and nobility are depicted in terms that draw heavily on the "brave man skilled in woodcraft" hero archetype of the English tradition, flavored with a dash of the way that archetype developed in the colonies. There is a distinct frontiersman undercurrent in Aragorn's attributes and actions as Strider the Ranger, mediated through Tolkien's admitted childhood fondness for "Red Indian" tales. Aragorn could stand quite proudly in the company of Beowulf or Gawain, yes, but it is also satisfying to imagine him swapping tales over a flagon with the likes of Natty Bumppo or the mythologized folk-hero version of Daniel Boone. Were these individuals to consider the matter, it seems likely that they would all agree on what a healthy relationship between humans and the natural world looks like—and that none of them would consider factory farming or clear-cutting forests a positive development, even if they did champion the advancement of civilization into the wilderness. In colonial and early America, the ideal end result of such advancement looked much more like the Shire than Mordor.

The entire incident of the "primitive" Drúedan living in the great forest on the borders of Rohan provides an interesting ethical window into Tolkien's value judgments in the context of colonial American cultural ideas. "Wild Men are wild, free, but not children," Ghân-buri-Ghân admonishes the somewhat patronizing king of Rohan in a dialect disturbingly reminiscent of the stereotypical "how now, heap big wampum, paleface" tropes of Tonto Talk; his tribe eventually aids the Rohirrim with the express purpose of securing a world where "Wild Men can go back to sleep in the wild woods."[31] On Aragorn's return journey through that border country accompanying Théoden's funeral procession, he performs an act as king, which is easy to view as Tolkien's take on the ethical way to deal with a place's aboriginal inhabitants:

> Without haste and at peace they passed into Anórien, and they came to the Grey Wood under Amon Dîn; and there they heard a sound as of drums beating in the hills, though no living thing could be seen. Then Aragorn let the trumpets be blown; and heralds cried:
>
> "Behold, the King Elessar is come! The Forest of Drúadan he gives to Ghân-buri-Ghân and to his folk, to be their own for ever; and hereafter let no man enter it without their leave!"
>
> Then the drums rolled loudly, and were silent.[32]

Today's bitter hindsight regarding how often the same promise was made and later broken by the United States government in its dealings with various native tribes unfortunately makes such a declaration ring superficial and false, especially to an American reader, but it is unlikely that Tolkien intended this incident to be in any way ironic.

Considering the time period and prevailing attitudes of Tolkien's Edwardian upbringing, this neat resolution is no more romanticized than his idealized English village of the Shire. Was the land Aragorn's to give? Of course not, and today's critics can justifiably condemn the episode as patronizing, derivative, even racist. But Aragorn also makes—and keeps himself—the same promise to the distinctly English inhabitants of the Shire. Tolkien was obviously not writing from the perspective of postmodern multicultural multiplicity. But he undoubtedly would have deplored the breaking of the American government's promises to the Native Americans as much as he deplored the wide-scale destruction of the American wilderness. Whether or not they were always honored in the Primary World of history, the ethics Tolkien presents here in his Secondary World are absolutely clear: those living close to the land (regardless of their level of "civilization") should be left alone, good government is represented by a cooperative rather than destructive relationship with the natural world, and both the courage to face the harsh wilderness and the sensitivity to appreciate its beauty are required to make a good king.

The fact that Tolkien found such characters and themes interesting enough to include in his otherwise High Medieval and very traditionally English tale highlights both the presence in Western popular culture of the myth of the American frontier, as well as the associated ethical beliefs about right action he so carefully wove into his works. But, just as wilderness in Middle-earth proves to be a multivaried concept, wild places in America were not only perceived as something harsh and Germanic. As the United States marched its way west over the vast continent, the way that the country viewed itself and its environment changed in ways that would later prove critical to the development of the wilderness philosophy that would eventually influence the world.

It was not long in mythological time before the lands and cities of the eastern seaboard of the United States began to resemble more and more the thickly settled landscape of Europe, but the vastness of the new continent meant that America had something Europe did not: a frontier. This ever-advancing line between the light of civilization and the wild dark lands beyond stretched continually out to the west, providing more than a century of cultural influence and mythic instruction for the muscular young country as it sought to establish its place in the world. The lands beyond the frontier were threatening in their wildness, an enemy of great power and danger. But as the frontier advanced, the place of wilderness in the American mythic imagination began to undergo a slow metamorphosis: the primary image shifted away from one of howling desolation toward one of virgin land awaiting transformation. This is a subtle change, but it is a change. "The metaphor of virginity played a crucial role in the environmental reconception of wilderness in positive terms," argues Val Plumwood; wild lands as "an object of conquest, as a primitive, disordered, or empty space ready to receive the imprint of a masculinist civilization" are conceptually different than those in the pure Anglo-Saxon tradition, which represent only the danger of an unknown natural force so powerful that humans could only hope to build themselves protected islands of light in a great sea of darkness.[33] The measure of Beowulf's heroism was demonstrated in killing Grendel's mother, not in transforming her.

Roderick Nash identifies the burgeoning European Romantic movement as a significant early influence on this American shift. He points out that "the literary gentleman wielding a pen, not the pioneer with his axe, made the first gestures of resistance against the strong currents of antipathy" between humans and the wilderness.[34] In the context of city-dwelling artists seeking the sublimity of God in nature and idolizing Rousseau's noble primitivism, it makes sense that the mysterious New World, "with its abundance of pathless forests and savages," would prove intriguing to the Romantic imagination.[35] It was this imagination, perhaps, that prompted the "literati of the major Eastern cities to make periodic excursions into the wilds, collect 'impressions,' and return to their desks to write descriptive essays which dripped love of scenery and solitude in the grand Romantic manner."[36] It was this imagination that "softened the opinions of those for whom the necessity of battling wild country might otherwise have produced unmitigated hostility," and in the end this imagination managed to clear away "enough of the old assumptions to permit a favorable attitude toward wilderness without entirely eliminating the instinctive fear and hostility a wilderness condition had produced."[37] This sublimity tinged with fear came to be characteristic of the Western intellectual Zeitgeist of the mid-to-late nineteenth century, and literary engagement with their excess of wildness perhaps allowed educated Americans to feel that they too could participate in high (read: sophisticated European) culture.

European influence can only go so far in explaining the American experience, however, a truth that can be easily demonstrated by considering the example of Ralph Waldo Emerson. That great transcendentalist carefully studied the German Romantics (he owned a fifty-five-volume set of the collected works of Johann Wolfgang von Goethe) and idolized the English poets of the Romantic tradition so much that he embarked on a transatlantic trip because, as he said himself, his "narrow and desultory reading had inspired the wish to see the faces of three or four writers."[38] While in Great Britain in 1833 he called on Samuel Taylor Coleridge in London, wandered the paths of the Lake District with William Wordsworth, and spent time in the Scottish Highlands with Thomas Carlyle, with whom he would go on to maintain a lifelong friendship and correspondence. Considering his foundational position in American letters, Emerson as a conduit for European Romantic ideas would seem to be clearly established—and yet, when he returned home and began his own career, he famously declared America's literary independence: "Perhaps the time is already come . . . when the sluggard intellect of this continent will look from under its iron lids, and fill the postponed expectation of the world with something better than the exertions of mechanical skill. Our day of dependence, our long apprenticeship to the learning of other lands, draws to a close. The millions that around us are rushing into life, cannot always be fed on the sere remains of foreign harvests."[39] Emerson does not deny the existence of America's "long apprenticeship" to European culture, but he is encouraging American thinkers to nourish their people with stories grown out of their own soil, wilder than that of Europe. "The nervous, rocky West is intruding a new and continental element into the national mind," he wrote later, "and we shall yet have an American genius."[40] Via Emerson and his transcendentalist celebration of the power of nature, American cultural independence was from its beginnings intimately intertwined with ideas of wilderness and the frontier.

As the frontier came to an end, however, Americans began to realize that something important, something that defined them, was passing away. The historian Frederick Jackson Turner, who explicitly acknowledged the powerful influence of Emerson on his own thinking, famously noted that "it is with a shock that the people of the United States are coming to realize that the fundamental forces which have shaped their society up to the present are disappearing."[41] Turner's frontier hypothesis, and the somewhat idealized concept of wilderness that went along with it, still retains its position as one of the most cherished stories of the American mytho-historical canon[42]—as late as 1987, nearly a full century after the frontier was officially closed, William Cronon remarks on how Turner's thesis "expresses some of the deepest myths and longings many Americans still feel about their national experience."[43] The vanishing of the frontier necessarily implied, almost by definition, that the wilderness that characterized it was also disappearing. That fact would set the stage for the next important shift in American ideas about wilderness, away from something to be transformed and toward something to be protected.

Emerson's influence can be detected in this intellectual development as well. His impact on Henry David Thoreau was as deep and enduring as Thoreau's own impact on the generations of environmentalists who followed in his footsteps would be. Here at the point where the American wilderness conservation movement first emerges into the sunlight, it becomes easy to see how Tolkien's work—standing squarely inside the antimodernist neo-Romantic movement of the late nineteenth and early twentieth centuries—drew heavily on some of the same mythic springs as the first American wilderness philosophers. Oelschlaeger, following Nash, notes how wild nature had come to be "idealized as an oasis free of the ills of civilization" and the overall Romantic attitude of the time was "characteristically one of intense personal involvement with and aesthetic response to nature."[44] All of this feels very familiar indeed to readers of *The Hobbit* and *The Lord of the Rings*, and deep resonances with Tolkien's wilderness ethics can be found in pretty much any nineteenth-century American nature philosopher (Emerson and Thoreau themselves not least among them). But in lyricism of prose, capacity for vast amounts of natural detail, and overall willingness to accord other parts of the universe equality with humanity, one of the most Tolkienian of this group is undoubtedly naturalist, philosopher, and champion of wilderness preservation par excellence John Muir.

The details of Muir's personal biography make him seem a bit like a real-life example of the indefatigably hardy Dúnedain. By the end of the nineteenth century, he had walked a thousand miles from Kentucky to the Gulf of Mexico, become intimately familiar with every peak and lake and mountain pass in the Sierra Nevada mountains in California, and even ventured on foot and kayak into the glacier-draped wilderness of southeast Alaska. The often hair-raising tales he relates in his many travel writings establish him as the quintessential mountaineer, with endurance, strength, and mental toughness to match any man of Westernesse. But despite his undeniably Germanic-hero Ranger-like qualities, the ideas in Muir's writings echo more strongly and clearly Tolkien's second, Celtic-influenced, uncanny but beautiful concept of wilderness.

In reading Muir's work, there are places—indeed quite a large number of places—where the writing feels positively Tolkienian. Both men delighted in the smallest details of natural things, and both men believed in the beauty of the natural world and its ability to heal the damaged human soul. A good initial example can be found in Muir's discussion of the Sugar Pine in *The Mountains of California*, where he could with zero editing be describing the golden *mellyrn* of Lothlórien: "the majestic crowns, approaching each other in bold curves, make a glorious canopy through which the tempered sunbeams pour, silvering the needles, and gilding the massive boles, and flowery, park-like ground, into a scene of enchantment."[45] While there is no evidence indicating Tolkien was familiar with Muir's work, it is difficult to read without coming away with the impression that he would have enjoyed it.

In Susan Jeffers's analysis, the most positive example of how humans relate to the natural world in Tolkien's work is what she calls a "power with" relationship, demonstrated by the ways that Ents, Elves, and hobbits inhabit and interact with their places. Of these three examples, the manifestation of the hobbits' relationship fits more neatly into Tolkien's third concept of wilderness. But the Ents, and especially the supremely Celtic Elves, have an almost purely "reciprocal relationship with their environment," which is demonstrated clearly in terms of voice: "They speak to their environment and it speaks to them. . . . It isn't just that the natural world hears the Elves, but that the Elves also hear the voice of that world speaking to them."[46] The Ents also treat nature as an equal interlocutor, but even the greatest and eldest of Ents credits the Elves with originating the process: "Elves began it, of course, waking trees up and teaching them to speak and learning their tree-talk," Treebeard tells Merry and Pippin; "They always wished to talk to everything, the old Elves did."[47] Tolkien's Elves, true to their Celtic-influenced heritage, seem able to move at will between the physical landscape and the Otherworldly one overlaid upon it, where everything has something to say worth hearing.

In *The Lord of the Rings* it is Legolas who most often serves as interpreter of such speech, providing his non-Elven companions a partial glimpse into a world whose community of speakers includes everything in that world, animal, vegetable, or mineral. As he and his companions approach the gates of the old kingdom of Hollin, he describes his conversation with the entities of the place: "the Elves of this land were of a race strange to us of the silvan folk, and the trees and the grass do not now remember them. Only I hear the stones lament them: deep they delved us, fair they wrought us, high they builded us; but they are gone."[48] On the edge of Lórien, when the company stops to rest near a stream "flowing down swiftly from the tree-clad slopes that climbed back westward towards the mountains," even Frodo is able to detect a hint of speech: "at length a silence fell, and they heard the music of the waterfall running sweetly in the shadows. Almost Frodo fancied that he could hear a voice singing, mingled with the sound of the water."[49] Legolas identifies the speaker as Nimrodel, who in typical Celtic overlay landscape manner is Elf-maiden and stream both at once.

It is almost trivial to find similar ideas in Muir's writings, as pretty much everything he encounters in the wilderness of the American West becomes his interlocutor. "The shallow pool seems fathomless with the infinite starry heavens in it, while the onlooking rocks and trees, tiny shrubs and daisies and sedges, brought forward in the fire-glow, seem full of thought as if about to speak aloud and tell all their wild stories," he writes in *My First Summer in the Sierra;* he characterizes this encounter as "a marvelously impressive meeting in which every one has something worth while to tell."[50] In the same work Muir celebrates the experience of "the rocks, the air, everything speaking with audible voice or silent; joyful, wonderful, enchanting, banishing weariness and sense of time" and notes how the water of sublime Nevada Falls "does not seem to be under the dominion of ordinary laws, but rather as if it were a living creature, full of the strength of the mountains and their huge, wild joy."[51] It is tempting to reflect on Muir's Scottish heritage in the context of such resonance with Tolkien's Celtic-flavored concept of wilderness. But whether or not any ancient mythic ideas survived Muir's harshly Presbyterian upbringing is almost immaterial in the face of his breathless celebration of a living, almost pantheistic, natural world. Everything—rocks, water, birds, insects, the wind and the storm and the earthquake and the avalanche—speaks to Muir. He spent the latter part of his life interpreting those voices for others and championing a nearly revolutionary idea: that wild lands should be set aside and protected from the ravages of Lord Man.

Much like Emerson (and, for that matter, Tolkien), John Muir's life sits at a crux in the flow of Western cultural and intellectual history. William Cronon opines that "in the myth of the vanishing frontier lay the seeds of wilderness preservation in the United States, for if wild land had been so crucial in the making of the nation, then surely one must save its last remnants as monuments to the American past."[52] If this is so, once the Romantic movement gave wildness a spiritual voice and the American frontier opened up the possibility to experience it in a way long impossible in Europe, it would still require a powerful personality to step into the stream and beat back at least some of the intellectual force being exercised on the transformation of wilderness into civilization. Muir was that personality. His work emerged as an early manifesto that would eventually shift the value judgments of a country famously rooted in materialist and modernist expansion. As one biographer wrote, Muir's life of activism "profoundly shaped the very categories through which Americans understand and envision their relationship with the natural world."[53] In a sense, Muir can be mythically connected to all three of Tolkien's wilderness ideas: he had the strength and endurance to survive the harsh wilderness, the spiritual sensitivity to recognize its uncanny beauty, and the intellectual and political influence to establish a new, more friendly, category of recreational wilderness.

The resonance with all three categories can be clearly seen in the way Muir's life became deeply entwined with Yosemite National Park in California. The Yosemite land grant of 1864 may not have been the very first wild land ever to be set aside by a government for public use (Bogd Khan Uul National Park was established in Mongolia in 1783), but it was certainly a first for the Germanic-influenced and mechanistic Western world.[54] Muir first arrived in Yosemite in 1868. It was not long before he realized the state was not doing enough to protect the stunning natural beauty of the place, and he began to campaign for its transfer to federal control. Muir is now considered the father of the park; he "helped draw up its proposed boundaries in 1889, wrote the magazine articles that led to its creation in 1890 and co-founded the Sierra Club in 1892 to protect it," and it was after a 1903 camping trip with the then sixty-five-year-old Muir in Yosemite Valley that President Theodore Roosevelt expanded the nascent National Park System and unified Yosemite's patchwork of state and federal lands under federal control.[55] It was also Muir's failure to stop the building of the Hetch Hetchy dam inside the park right before his death that "galvanized the American conservation movement to push for the creation in 1916 of the National Park Service and a higher level of protection for all national parks."[56] Through the work of John Muir and others who would follow him, the thoroughly modern idea of a wilderness area set aside for public recreation would enter the Western cultural consciousness.

It is hard to overestimate the significance of this ideological shift. Importantly, wild places did not lose their connotations of danger—danger was still inherent in their wildness, almost by definition—but it was the danger of challenge rather than the danger of malevolence. As William Cronon observes, "once set aside within the fixed and carefully policed boundaries of the modern bureaucratic state, the wilderness lost its savage image and became safe: a place more of reverie than of revulsion or fear."[57] Lurking within the dangers of the wilderness there was no longer any inherent evil. In Tolkienian literary and mythic terms, wilderness in the American experience had moved from *Beowulf* to Shakespeare, from the evil blackness of Mirkwood to the friendly wildness in certain corners of the Shire.

Although this shift is undeniably a positive development, it—like the shining city beaming the light of civilization into the darkness of the Germanic wilderness discussed above—has a dark side. This shadow concept is simultaneously more overt and more subtle than the racism and exceptionalism of thinkers like Bradford or Winthrop, to which it is nevertheless related. On the obvious side, for all of his luminous prose and foundational position in American Wilderness Philosophy, many of John Muir's early writings on the Native Americans who inhabited his beloved Sierra Nevada are problematic at best.[58] Indeed, it is a painfully sad irony to reflect on how the "untrammeled" wilderness so beloved of the American inheritors of the nineteenth-century Romantic view of nature was created by murdering or evicting entire populations of "savages" (somewhat less noble in reality than in idealized philosophy) from their ancestral lands. This fact, as clear as it is when pointed out, is still not quite strong enough to dampen the Romantic enthusiasm for the mythological conception of wilderness as a place of sublimity and salvation. But in actuality, the sense of a pure, virgin land untouched by man is an utterly unnatural idea, and—much like the Celtic wilderness idea it echoes—it presents a more indirect spiritual danger for those who enter into it unawares.

Lydia Millet has famously observed how the beautiful pinup calendars of nature preservation organizations can serve as a sort of "ecoporn" that, "tarted up into perfectly circumscribed simulations of the wild . . . serve as surrogates for real engagement with wilderness, the way porn models serve as surrogates for real women."[59] In contemplating the soaring beauty of a carefully crafted, perfectly lit, artificially enhanced photograph of Yosemite's Half Dome bathed in a golden sunrise, or the jagged silhouette of the Grand Tetons thrusting into a multicolored sunset sky, it far too easy to conflate the unnatural and idealized image (and the deeply spiritual sublimity it can induce in a viewer steeped in Romantic thought) with the imperfectly mundane and sadly endangered reality of the dirt and trees and rocks of the actual place. Such aesthetically enjoyable experiences are subtly dangerous; "at best they elicit a regretful nostalgia for a never-known past of unspoiled landscapes; at worst, they reassure us disingenuously that the last great places are safe and sound."[60] The long contemplation and worship of such images can also often render the actual experience of the place rather a disappointment, especially when the weather turns out to be other than picture-perfect and the insects bite, never mind when the campsites are overcrowded and the traffic is snarled. It can sometimes be more pleasant to retreat back into contemplation of the snapshots in time framed in the undeniably glorious photographs than it is to expose oneself to the inconveniences involved in any real experience of a beautiful but nonidealized wild place.

The Tolkienian echoes of this dark side sound clearly enough if one is willing to listen for them. Dickerson and Evans reflect that the failure of the Elves in the context of their existence as a fallen race in a fallen Middle-earth resides in their "effort to resist all change, stemming from their prideful, selfish desire to have things as they once were."[61] Gabriel Ertsgaard, following Dickerson and Evans, notes that the undeniably good Elves "can still be tempted by the imperial fantasies that trigger in other beings ecologically-destructive pursuits of domination," that their preserving enchantments "always risk entanglement with darker magics," and that the "last vestiges of the Elves' earlier imperial greatness are entangled with Sauron's Ring" in the fallen world of Middle-earth.[62] These vestiges, the soaringly beautiful monuments to the Celtic wilderness idea in Rivendell and Lothlórien, partake of the dark as well as the light in this philosophical context.

Galadriel's Lothlórien is a particularly good example; the Golden Wood is a clear reflection of the Romantic ideal, a sublimely beautiful forest realm fenced off completely from grubby reality. But it is in a sense just as unnatural as the glorious photos that adorn an ecoporn calendar. Like the national parks it reflects, which are protected by the science and technology of the modernist juggernaut that made them necessary in the first place, Lórien is sustained by a power so deeply entangled with Sauron's evil that it must fade away once that evil has been defeated. Also, much as the land on Rohan's borders was not Aragorn's to give to the Drúedan (who were there long before the Númenorean exiles established the kingdom he ultimately came to rule), Middle-earth and its forests are not truly Galadriel's to preserve.[63] She was born in a land across the sea and, echoing the American settlers, came into Middle-earth "seeking to rule a realm of her own will."[64] At the end of the Age, her wisdom and undeniable goodness return to her a grace she had once chosen to forfeit, the option to leave Middle-earth and return to the Earthly Paradise of Valinor from whence she came. But for those who must remain, for whom that escape is unavailable, only loss and sad memory remain. The image of Arwen laying herself down to die alone amid the winter-dead leaves on deserted Cerin Amroth is one of the saddest moments in Tolkien's tale, and its sadness is all the greater for the memory of the beauty and joy that once reigned in the Golden Wood.

And yet—and yet. While it is undeniably important to recognize that the bright spiritual light of the Celtic/Romantic/frontier wilderness casts an often-unacknowledged shadow, none of this should be read as denying in any way the spiritual power present in the aesthetic arrest induced by experiencing the stunning beauty of such wild landscapes, real or imagined. That power has incredible mythic force. It should also not be read as arguing that the problematic philosophical implications of the idea render the effort to preserve and protect such places a worthless endeavor. It is not. Even if preserving something creates in the act of preservation an unnatural idea, it does not follow that such preservation is pointless, if only for the fact that the idea retains its power to inspire positive action going forward. It is simply that even the most sublimely Romantic ideas partake of the ambiguity of humankind's relationship with the natural world.

As Tom Shippey has observed, "the forest, and Middle-earth, can turn into Mirkwood, 'where the trees strive one against another and their branches rot and wither', or into Lórien, so beautiful that in it no grief has power."[65] These two opposing concepts, the archaic Germanic idea of wilderness as evil and the Romantic Celtic one of sublime beauty, are fully present even today in the Primary World. But these competing concepts do not fully reflect everything that is included in the internally ambiguous word *wil-*

derness. When the ideological shift between conquering the wilderness to protecting it occurred, the inherent evil that once imbued wild lands did not disappear from the world. In the minds of those for whom wilderness had become an important issue, the mythological enemy simply stepped over the wilderness-civilization boundary and took up a new residence within the protection of the seductive and nearly unlimited power that had been a proximate cause of the shift in the first place. Instead of savages (removed to facilitate the white man's ideal wilderness) and wild beasts (also, much as had happened in England centuries before, systematically eradicated so that newly untrammeled wilderness could be safely enjoyed), wilderness heroes began to array their forces and establish a new idea, one that stood in direct opposition to the insatiable and unstoppable modernist industry of Isengard and Mordor.

Once the wilderness had been tamed and the frontier erased, once the idea became established that the public good was served by setting aside areas of great wildness for recreation, the question largely became one of government policy. But the problem with any government is that those with the power make the policy. The cultural juggernaut of modernism was without a doubt the dominant power in early twentieth-century America—and it still maintains such momentum that it determines in large part the course and speed of wilderness management even today. The mythological disruption caused by the changing story about wilderness set off a deeply contentious ideological debate. Battle lines soon arose between two major ideas regarding the management of protected federal lands. On one side stood thinkers like Muir, who championed preservation, the "protection of nature from use," and on the other policy makers who sought to prescribe conservation, the "proper use of nature."[66] In a world of lawyers and businesses, of lucrative resource exploitation and new possibilities of exploitative wilderness tourism, the spiritual, almost ecstatic, attitude toward nature of transcendentalists like Thoreau and Muir—no matter how beautifully poetic or inspiring—was not on its own an effective enough force to contend with the confusion it had itself caused.

An important wilderness philosopher of this ideologically transitional period is the ecologist and author Aldo Leopold. A 1909 graduate of the newly minted forestry school at Yale, Leopold's early career with the US Forest Service in the Southwest set him up as one of the great practitioners of conservation. However, dismayed by the largely human-caused Dust Bowl conditions of the 1930s, and heavily affected by his work to revitalize a barren patch of land in central Wisconsin in the years before his death, he eventually came to reject the purely utilitarian attitudes of that philosophy. It is in his writings, so sad and luminous, that the gap between preservation and conservation first began to close. Roderick Nash notes that before Leopold "the source of American respect for nature had been more sentimental and spiritual than scientific," and argues that in Leopold's lifetime the science of ecology enabled human beings to "conceive of nature as an intricate web of interdependent parts, a myriad of cogs and wheels each essential to the healthy operation of the whole."[67] But even as he approached wilderness from a scientific perspective, Leopold still managed to hold onto the sentiment and spirit that moved his more Romantic predecessors, and as a result his thinking draws on the mythic power of the ideas present in both the conservationist and preservationist traditions.

Oelschlaeger usefully sums up these two opposing traditions in ecology during Leopold's time. He posits an Arcadian tradition associated with men like Thoreau and Muir, who "resonated with the wilderness, with the birds and animals, the grass and the sky, feeling themselves to be a part of the larger and enveloping whole" in opposition to an imperial tradition in which foresters like Leopold sought to "dominate and manage wild nature," and he suggests that Leopold "used the tools of an imperial ecologist . . . but had the feelings and perceptions of an Arcadian ecologist—that is, he affectively bonded with wild nature, a relation that produced intense aesthetic and ethical responses."[68] Such responses, an echo of the spiritual ecstasy of the preservationists arising out of the mind of a man with a long and respected career in the poorly organized and often frustrating trenches of conservationist wilderness management, proved to be critically influential in the continuing development of the wilderness idea.

Leopold, much like Muir, connects with all three of Tolkien's concepts of wilderness. He was an avid outdoorsman and hunter with a deep love of the harsh, beautiful, Germanic wilderness. In his final plea for changing the conservation story, he describes wilderness as "the raw material out of which man has hammered the artifact called civilization" and argues, Ranger-like, that "public wilderness areas are, first of all, a means of perpetuating, in sport form, the more virile and primitive skills in pioneering travel and subsistence."[69] He was also supremely sensitive to the complex natural dramas, small and great, that occur daily within the Celtic overlay of landscape normally unseen by human eyes. As he examines the slow process of the yearly transition from winter to spring, Leopold enters seamlessly into the lives of the nonhuman inhabitants of his sand farm; he describes a mouse as "a sober citizen who knows that grass grows in order that mice may store it as underground haystacks, and that snow falls in order that mice may build subways from stack to stack," but also notes that the rough-legged hawk thinks differently; that returning visitor "has no opinion why grass grows, but he is well aware that snow melts in order that hawks may again catch mice."[70] It is clear from his writings that Leopold knows as much as Muir does about Germanic and Celtic wilderness ideas (even if neither man would describe them in those terms). But where Muir in the end esteems the heart-rending beauty of the Romantic Celtic wilderness over all others, Leopold's ultimate ideals more closely echo Tolkien's third, English, semitame concept of wilderness.

Although it carefully acknowledges the many real benefits of human progress and includes many deeply beautiful passages about the simple pleasures of life, a deep vein of inescapable sadness runs throughout Leopold's final work. Nearly every page of *A Sand County Almanac*, published a year after his death, is colored with a very Tolkienian regret for lost beauty, for wildness sacrificed on the altar of progress and industry. Leopold reflects somberly on the irretrievability of things lost in the civilization process: "Man always kills the thing he loves, and so we the pioneers have killed our wilderness. Some say we had to. Be that as it may, I am glad I shall never be young without wild country to be young in."[71] At the end of some reflections on a visit to a Canadian marsh, he waxes elegiac about how "the marshlands that once sprawled over the prairie from the Illinois to the Athabasca are shrinking northward. Man cannot live by marsh alone, therefore he must needs live marshless. Progress cannot abide that farmland and marshland, wild and tame, exist in mutual toleration and harmony."[72] He condemns the trends in outdoor recreation activities of "more and more mechanization, with a corresponding shrinkage in cultural values."[73] Painfully aware of the mythological roots of the problem, he begs for a change in humanity's story about its relationship to the world: "Conservation is getting nowhere because it is incompatible with our Abrahamic concept of land. We abuse land because we regard it as a commodity belonging to us. When we see land as a community to which we belong, we may begin to use it with love and respect. There is no other way for land to survive the impact of mechanized man."[74]

In the end Leopold proposes as the only remaining hope his famous "land ethic," an idea that has become the unofficial Golden Rule of ecology: "Examine each question in terms of what is ethically and esthetically right, as well as what is economically expedient. A thing is right when it tends to preserve the integrity, stability, and beauty of the biotic community. It is wrong when it tends otherwise."[75] This quiet, and quietly radical, concept has determined the direction of nearly all subsequent wilderness philosophy. Despite the almost certain lack of any direct connection, it is impossible to imagine Tolkien, who began and ended *The Lord of the Rings* in the integral, beautiful, and stable community of the Shire, would disagree with such a charge.

In the final reckoning, Tolkien presents his hobbits as his ideal human community. The grandeur and nobility of Rohan and Gondor are admirable, certainly, and the wisdom and greatness of the Elves are awe-inspiring, but these peoples sing a more mythical, heroic, even archaic song in his ultimately modern tale. Such greatness is the greatness of antiquity, of a golden age when humans measured themselves against harshly beautiful wildernesses given in Germanic or Celtic terms. But in a world where the forces of modernism have irretrievably reshaped the physical and cultural landscape, it is with the down-to-earth, likable, and very English little people that Tolkien's readers are most easily able to identify. It is significant, therefore, that the most important defining characteristic of the hobbits involves their relationship with their well-cultivated but still-healthy agrarian home.

Tolkien's Shire is undoubtedly a pastoral or Arcadian vision, a static snapshot of an idealized time and a people who "do not and did not understand or like machines more complicated than a forge-bellows, a water-mill, or a hand-loom" and yet still somehow enjoy anachronistic luxuries like folding umbrellas and fine silk waistcoats with gold buttons.[76] It is a country with twice-daily post services and lawyers to conduct estate auctions but somehow "hardly any 'government,'" a place where the inhabitants had always been content that "growing food and eating it occupied most of their time" but a limited collection of small farmholdings seems to easily produce enough for everyone with plenty to spare.[77] It is an agrarian paradise with "rich and kindly" land, "well tilled" with "many farms, cornlands, vineyards, and woods."[78] For all of that, however, or perhaps even because of it, the Shire still feels very real to modern readers. It often feels much more real than the archaic realms rising out of medieval legends to thrill adventure-seekers with tales of a world lost; it serves as a "familiar landscape—in the imagination, if not in reality—to English and American readers captured by the idyll."[79] This anachronistic but very tangible sense of reality lends great power to the Shire as a mythical example of an ideal community in the Leopoldian mode.

In her analysis, Susan Jeffers argues that the hobbits of the Shire stand alongside Ents and Elves as examples of the most admirable relationship a people can have with its environment. She notes that they are "motivated, consciously or not, by a deep love for their home, a love that is rooted in a relationship with the Earth," and she argues explicitly that "the existence of Hobbits and their relationship to the Shire is . . . indicative of Tolkien's own ecological perspective."[80] It is interesting how close that perspective comes to that of Leopold (as well that of Leopold's successors like the cantankerous Kentucky agrarian Wendell Berry). The hobbits "do not expect food to fall from the sky; they work to fill their pantries,"[81] and in this they show themselves free from certain "spiritual dangers" against which Leopold warns: "One is the danger of supposing that breakfast comes from the grocery, and the other that heat comes from the furnace."[82] Leopold also argues that "every farm woodland, in addition to yielding lumber, fuel, and posts, should provide its owner a liberal education. This crop of wisdom never fails, but it is not always harvested."[83] Tolkien's approving description of Farmer Maggot, with "earth under his old feet, and clay on his fingers; wisdom in his bones, and both his eyes are open" makes it easy to imagine that certain Shire farmers have undertaken a similar course of study.[84]

The despoliation of the Shire by modernist forces of industry and collectivism has a Leopoldian feel to it as well. Leopold sadly chronicles the ugly "epidemic of ditch-digging and land-booming" by which his farmland in Wisconsin had come into its current marginal condition: "Peat beds dried, shrank, caught fire. Sun-energy out of the Pleistocene shrouded the countryside in acrid smoke. No man raised his voice against the waste, only his nose against the smell."[85] After spending several luminous pages describing the glories of White Mountain in Arizona, he admits regretfully that he will likely never visit it again because he would "prefer not to see what tourists, roads, sawmills, and logging railroads have done for it, or to it."[86] It is easy to imagine his commiseration with Merry's lament that "Shire-folk have been so comfortable so long they don't know what to do," and he could have quite a conversation with the stout hobbit farmer Tom Cotton about the ugly new mill "always a-hammering and a-letting out a smoke and a stench" in Hobbiton.[87] Leopold would likely have found the profiteering and bad sense of Lotho Pimple all too familiar.

The Scouring of the Shire episode in *The Lord of the Rings* is a perennial favorite in Tolkien ecocriticism, and for good reason. If the Shire feels very real to modern readers, that only makes its peril strike closer to home: "We catch a glimpse of this form of evil penetrating the Shire and immediately think of our own homes. We see the destruction of old houses and the construction of new ones, not because there is anything wrong with the old ones but simply because, according to the standards of innovation and progress, the new are supposed to be better and therefore preferable."[88]

The emotional concordance between these observations and Leopold's sad commentary on marshless living quoted above is undeniable. Liam Campbell's analysis of the incident is equally resonant: "Many, even today, consider the environmental crisis to be someone else's problem, something that could never really manifest itself with any serious consequence in the 'Shires' of their own homeland. Meanwhile the Sharkeys of big business capitalism pedal [*sic*] their wares all the time assuaging us that Mordor will never find its way to our homes."[89] When Leopold remarks on an ostensible policy of good business that "there might be more than one definition of what is good, and even of what is business," he shows himself to be profoundly distrustful of similar assurances.[90] Although he certainly could never have read about the Scouring of the Shire, it is satisfying to imagine how much he would have approved of it.[91]

Indeed, Tolkien's resolution of his cautionary parable can be seen, in expressly Leopoldian terms, as significant, perhaps even hopeful; for in the end, it is not through the efforts of any external actors that the Shire is restored. Pippin's "silver and sable" livery and his claim to be "a messenger of the King" notwithstanding, the Shire is not saved by any actions of Aragorn on his faraway throne, however honorable and noble he may be.[92] Even the great Gandalf, whose stewardship encompasses all things on earth "that can still grow fair or bear fruit and flower again in days to come," contributes little more than a bit of encouragement.[93] The restoration of the Shire comes about through the efforts of the Shire-dwellers themselves, strengthened and inspired by the return of hobbit heroes from far countries (who, not incidentally, bring painful firsthand knowledge of how bad things can actually get in lands under destructive regimes). This echoes quite clearly the ideals regarding the "conviction of individual responsibility for the health of the land" and "the capacity of the land for self-renewal" espoused by Leopold's still-influential land ethic.[94]

This striking resonance between the idealized Shire and the agrarian traditions of Leopold and the modern wilderness philosophers who followed him has been noted by many ecocritics. Dickerson and Evans are quite explicit: "The idea informing both modern thinking on the subject and Tolkien's perspective, exemplified in the Shire, is that of *sustainable agriculture,* which Tolkien portrays as an implicit concern in the societal mores of the people who live there."[95] Lucas Niiler suggests that Tolkien's work underscores Leopold's "through its attention to escape of what was for him a society too dependent on industry and technology," and carefully examines the character arc of the hobbit heroes as they "complete a paradigm shift in which they recover a sure sense of themselves as members of a vast ecosystem."[96] When Jeffers observes how "Tolkien offers a model—to readers, to ecocriticism, to humans generally—in which a place and its inhabitants connect in mutually beneficial ways, in which neither the human . . . nor the land have to claim dominance to gain validity," she is tapping into a mythological stream whose still-current flow, if not its direct content, has been shaped by the influence of Leopold's wilderness philosophy.[97]

Considering that this locally oriented and semiwild concept of wilderness grew out of the earlier archaic/Germanic and Romantic/Celtic ones, it should come as no surprise that, like them, it casts a shadow that must be acknowledged, one that resonates as deeply with Tolkien's work as the more positive aspects do. As a product of a later time than the early American colonists or the frontier-era philosophers, Aldo Leopold's thinking is more developed than theirs, but it is not significantly less problematic in its normative assumptions. Consider the opening to a 1924 article he published in *Sunset* magazine: "Pioneering a new country is hard labor. It has absorbed the best brawn and brains of the Nordic race since before the dawn of history. Anthropologists tell us that we, the Nordics, have a racial genius for pioneering, surpassing all other races in ability to reduce the wilderness to possession."[98] For a modern reader, aware of to what use such thought was put less than a decade later in Europe, such unironic statements ring painfully odious notes on the fascist dog-whistle scale.

This questionable article was admittedly a product of Leopold's earlier career before he shifted from the imperial to the Arcadian traditions. It was published in a time before the widespread disgust with Nazi propaganda rendered such blatantly racist statements distasteful to the American public, and Leopold's later work reflected sensitively on how semiwild lands in the Southwest had been radically transformed for the worse by the removal of the Native Americans to reservations. But he also explored attitudes about human population growth in his writings, which ended up serving other, less-nuanced, thinkers as inspiration for some very distasteful ideas. As Miles A. Powell describes, "the vision of wilderness Leopold inherited and refined . . . set the stage" for the reception of writers such as William Vogt and Henry Fairfield Obsorn Jr.[99] Vogt, explicitly citing Leopold's work, "demonstrated a callous opposition to providing medical assistance to individuals in developing countries" because such assistance allowed the human populations to grow.[100] Osborn explicitly endorsed the virulent racism of the American eugenics movement, which argued, among other unsavory things, that "charity and government interference had allowed inferior individuals and races to reproduce with greater frequency than ideal Nordics," and supported sterilization laws that were ultimately adopted at the state level in more than two-thirds of the United States.[101] In defense of Leopold, as he wrestled with the implications of human population control, he came to significantly more-nuanced conclusions than those who followed him, and he never publicly advocated for eugenics or sterilization.[102] But there is no doubt that his concept of an ideal, sustainable, local human relationship with semitame wild lands was based on the casual assumption of the superiority of white Northwestern European peoples prevalent in most writers of his time.

This is of course true of Tolkien as well. The not-insignificant nonwhite imperial population of early twentieth-century England notwithstanding, his archetypally English hobbits are absolutely and incontrovertibly coded as white. Today, though, such white-normative ideas of racial superiority are much less acceptable in general public discourse, and educated readers are getting better at navigating the unconscious but still violently racist assumptions that undergird the work of those who were writing in less-inclusive times. While it is important to acknowledge the unsavory past from which they spring, such ideological pitfalls are reasonably avoidable for those willing to do the uncomfortable work of looking for them. But this Leopoldian dark side can also manifest in an explicitly nonracial (but still dangerous) way. In championing the small, sustainable communities whose relationship with their local semiwild lands make up this English-inspired ideal of wilderness, it can become quite easy to fall into the trap of selfish parochialism.

A dirty truth embedded in the modern climate change movement is that First World nations, whose gluttonous enjoyment of the spending spree of capitalist consumerism caused most of the problem, are now self-righteously insisting that people of developing nations who didn't get to enjoy the feast must nevertheless make the sacrifices necessary to pay for it. When a person—who perhaps considers turning down the air conditioner a laudable sacrifice for the climate, or who smugly shames those who do not use government-provided recycling services—rails against emerging economies building coal-fired plants to extend electricity to hundreds of communities who have never enjoyed it, the entitlement is downright breathtaking. Localism and sustainability and all of the land ethic ideals in the Leopoldian mode are undeniably a positive thing when examining the human relationship with the natural world. But the opposite side of the localism coin is that, even if divorced from explicitly racist or othering attitudes,[103] a too-insular focus on the local can cause people to dismiss the experiences and concerns of other humans living outside their protected enclave.

Tolkien's Shire explicitly (and probably intentionally) demonstrates how unpleasant such parochialism can be. While the issues with the sort of globalization that defines today's worldwide supply chains was not yet a factor in the thinking of his time, he still manages to touch obliquely on a related idea when he presents the hobbits as mistrustful of strangers, blissfully unaware of the sacrifices in blood and lives made by those very strangers. "Travellers scowl at us, and countrymen give us scornful names," grumbles Aragorn; "'Strider' I am to one fat man who lives within a day's march of foes that would freeze his heart, or lay his little town in ruin, if he were not guarded ceaselessly."[104] Here Tolkien is acknowledging that the idealized and perfectly sustainable relationship with their land enjoyed by the Shire hobbits and the Breelanders has a cost that is completely invisible to those living within those peaceful borders. A loose comparison might be drawn here between this self-absorption and the human suffering inherent in cheap sweatshop clothing, disappearing rainforests caused by palm oil plantations, or the carbon impact of shipping out-of-season produce halfway around the planet. These contributing factors to the environmental crisis writ large are not always included in the calculations of shoppers virtuously patronizing the locally owned shops in their neighborhoods.

On a personal level, Hobbiton folk characterize the Bucklanders as queer, the Shire-hobbits "referred to those of Bree . . . as Outsiders," taking "very little interest in them, considering them dull and uncouth. . . . *Strange as News from Bree* was still a saying in the Eastfarthing," while in Bree they say "there's no accounting for East and West . . . meaning the Rangers and the Shire-folk."[105] All of this mutual mistrust elicits knowing chuckles because it mirrors perfectly the stereotype of the small-minded small town with its regional myopia. Even the sturdy and lovable Sam demonstrates what Tolkien himself describes as "that quality which even some hobbits found at times hard to bear: a vulgarity—by which I do not mean a mere 'down-to-earthiness'—a mental myopia which is proud of itself, a smugness (in varying degrees) and cocksureness, and a readiness to measure and sum up all things from a limited experience, largely enshrined in sententious traditional 'wisdom.'"[106] It is not hard to see how such insularity and parochialism can make these hyper-local places, and the semiwild wildernesses that they tend to nurture and support, feel very unwelcoming to outside visitors, whatever their country or race.

This is not to say that focusing on protecting and experiencing one's own local wild places is bad. In fact, it is probably one of the best and most impactful actions available for those seeking to shift the human relationship with the natural world. But, while working tirelessly to sustain their own Shires, and hopefully to move beyond the institutional racism that created them, it is important for people to consciously remember that there are Shires everywhere. All places are ultimately interconnected in a globalized world; small communities in the Leopoldian mode must make "think globally, act locally" more than a pious platitude if they are to be successful in shifting destructive stories about the natural world in ways that benefit everyone and not just themselves.

American Wilderness Philosophy has undoubtedly continued to develop since Leopold's milieu of the early twentieth century. As much could be said about the Tolkienian resonances in the work of Wendell Berry, Arne Naess, and William Cronon as could be noted about the differences between the environmental philosophies of Tom Bombadil and Treebeard, and much indeed has already been said on these topics by critics applying the newly expanding field of eoccriticism to Tolkien's great myth. The vast amount of cultural raw material common to the United States and Great Britain in the nineteenth and twentieth centuries means that such shared imagery and mythological ideas are certainly not unexpected—but considering that Tolkien was consciously and quite explicitly not writing a "nature" work, the fact that the ethical values of what would become the environmental movement appear so clearly in his successful tale is worth exploring.

Tolkien's Germanic concept of wilderness is consonant with the dark and dangerous place that loomed beyond the American colonial frontier; his royal pedigree notwithstanding, it is likely that Aragorn would have found the danger and beauty of a place like James Fenimore Cooper's idealized frontier woodlands a familiar and congenial landscape through which to adventure. The same Romantic impulse behind the stunning beauty of

Tolkien's Celtic Elven Otherworlds shines out from the flood of American nature writing luminously celebrating the wilderness treasures of the American West, and if John Muir were ever to visit Middle-earth he would likely go into raptures over the beauty of Rivendell and Lothlórien and find kindred spirits in the tough, wise, and protective Elrond or the sensitive but quietly powerful Galadriel. Tolkien's English wilderness, the friendly semitame corners of wildness hovering on the edges of well-ordered farmland, echoes strongly much of later American environmental thinking; it grows out of and celebrates the same pastoral impulses as the agrarian writers pleading sadly for a better relationship between people and the land. Aldo Leopold would be absolutely in his element roaming over the Shire with gardener-cum-forester Samwise Gamgee or commiserating about the dangers of progress over a good farm meal, perhaps with Farmer Maggot or Sam's sturdy father-in-law Tom Cotton. Upon inspection, Tolkien's wild places turn out to be especially familiar terrain in terms of the ideals of American Wilderness Philosophy.

For better or for worse, this twentieth-century philosophical tradition is still the dominant force in wilderness thinking in the twenty-first century. But, as important as philosophical frameworks are, and as foundational as they are to the Zeitgest of their times, most people interact with their ideas in ways that do not involve examining the nuances of their creation. In the story-based mythological context of today, the indirect influence of such philosophy is mostly experienced through the much more direct impact of its manifestations in the powerful myths of popular culture. Tolkien's three wilderness ideas, so resonant with those making up the philosophical undercurrent of American Wilderness Philosophy, are thankfully still present as an undeniable cultural force in the enormous pop-culture juggernaut known as the "Tolkien phenomenon."

CHAPTER EIGHT

Tolkienian Wilderness in the Information Age

The original components of the Middle-earth legendarium are printed works of literature, the products of an artistic technological paradigm that has improved in capacity and efficiency but not significantly changed in structure since the days of Gutenberg. But, although print remains a vital element of the modern media environment, it is no longer the only (nor arguably even the principal) vector for the distribution and exchange of cultural ideas. The later years of Tolkien's life overlapped the early years of the rise of electronic mass media, from the radio broadcasts of the 1920s through the beginnings of broadcast television and then to the increasing installation of cable television systems in the 1950s and 1960s. Later, satellite distribution and more interactive media such as computer and console games developed, and at the advent of the Information Age in the 1990s, these last evolved into networks of players connected via digital communications technology into massive multiplayer online role-playing games. In the early part of the twenty-first century, these enterprises have developed into coherent cultural groupings in their own right, with functioning economies, mythic experiences, and all the trappings of human culture shared between like-minded individuals living across the quickly flattening but still fractured world.

The place of Tolkien's mythology in this new media world is deeply rooted, even foundational. While tabletop sports simulation and military tactics games were popular as early as the 1940s and 1950s, the explosion of the Tolkien phenomenon onto the American cultural scene in the 1960s provided game players an opportunity for a fuller and much more mythically satisfying experience than obsessing over at-bat statistics or pushing painted miniatures across a map. In a study of the history of gaming, Matt Barton observes how Middle-earth, "a fictional world so vivid and detailed that it seemed to many readers to be a real place, an alternate reality that they longed to visit," created a phenomenon so powerful it "paved the way for a new type of game, one that would allow fans to go beyond reading and actually enter exciting worlds of fantasy to play a role in their own adventures."[1] The original pen-and-paper role-playing game of *Dungeons and Dragons* was heavily influenced by Middle-earth, as its creator Gary Gygax explicitly acknowledges: "Just about all the players were huge JRRT fans, and so they insisted that I put as much Tolkien-influenced material[2] into the game as possible."[3] Considering that the earliest computer games, many created by college students in the 1970s for illicit use on university mainframes, were direct adaptations of *D&D* with explicitly Tolkienian names like *Moria* and *Orthanc*, it is by no means an exaggeration to argue that "to say that the works of J. R. R. Tolkien have influenced the [computer role-playing game] is akin to saying that the Big Bang influenced the universe. The influence is deep, profound, and fundamental."[4] While the original sports and military games would certainly become a part of the new industry as it developed, it was the Tolkien-inspired dungeon crawling that started it all.

Although something like the massive, interactive, worldwide experience of the multiplayer game *The Lord of the Rings Online* would likely be quite beyond Tolkien's personal ken, this expansion of Middle-earth beyond the covers of *The Hobbit* and *The Lord of the Rings* into the digital Information Age can ultimately be considered a fulfillment of his original vision. He once wrote in a letter, a bit wistfully, that he hoped his mythic cycle "should be linked to a majestic whole, and yet leave scope for other minds and hands, wielding paint and music and drama."[5] The popularity of his twentieth-century texts certainly shows no signs of waning, but today they represent only one of the many pathways of cultural transmission bringing the stunningly powerful myth of Middle-earth to more and more people around the world.

Since *The Lord of the Rings* was published, there have been several attempts to capitalize on its popularity and open the story to wider audiences via broadcast-style audiovisual media such as radio, television, and film, but most of the early attempts met with mixed success at best. Tolkien did not initially seem averse to audio adaptations of his work; after his first dubious encounter with a portable tape recorder in 1952,[6] he wrote to his publisher to say that he had "recently made some tape-recordings of parts of the Hobbit and The Lord (notably the Gollum-passages and some pieces of 'Elvish') and was much surprised to discover their effectiveness as recitations, and (if I may say so) my own effectiveness as a narrator. . . . Could not the BBC be interested?"[7] Nothing really came of these early recordings, but a few years later, when the BBC did broadcast a series of radio dramatizations of *The Lord of the Rings,* Tolkien apparently did not enjoy them at all. In a 1955 letter to a friend, he comes across as bitterly dissatisfied with the effort, stating that he had come to believe his work "quite unsuitable for 'dramatization,'" thought the BBC's presentation of Tom Bombadil "dreadful," and was annoyed that the scriptwriters had got wrong such basic things as Tom Bombadil's relationship to Goldberry.[8]

In 1957 Tolkien received a proposal from Forrest J. Ackerman, Morton Grady Zimmerman, and Al Brodax, which was "the earliest serious attempt to write a screenplay for *The Lord of the Rings*."[9] Initially he seemed positive about the project and compared it favorably to the BBC's efforts; he told his son Christopher that "this Mr Ackerman brought some really astonishingly good pictures (Rackham rather than Disney) and some remarkable colour photographs" and admitted to his publisher that personally he should "welcome the idea of an animated motion picture, with all the risk of vulgarization; and that quite apart from the glint of money. . . . I think I should find vulgarization less painful than the sillification achieved by the B.B.C."[10] But when he reviewed the film's storyline the next year, he evidently found it to be very bad indeed. In a private letter to his publisher, he expressed his "grave anxiety" about the dialogue and complained of "the extreme silliness and incompetence of Z[11] and his complete lack of respect for the original (it seems wilfully wrong without discernible technical reasons at nearly every point)."[12] In the lengthy critique eventually sent to Ackerman, Tolkien takes issue with a great number of words and phrases and overall structural elements of the film treatment, eventually thundering that its third part was "*totally unacceptable to me, as a whole and in detail.*"[13] Negotiations eventually broke down between Tolkien's publisher and the Hollywood executives, and in the end the Ackerman film was never made.[14]

As early as 1943,[15] Tolkien had been contending that to introduce into the "quasi-magical secondary world" of drama "a further fantasy or magic is to demand, as it were, an inner or tertiary world. It is a world too much.

To make such a thing may not be impossible. I have never seen it done with success."[16] This sentiment seems to have hardened in him over the years; he growls in a 1968 interview that "you can't cramp narrative into dramatic form. It would be easier to film *The Odyssey*. Much less happens in it. Only a few storms."[17] However, this irascibility did not prevent him from selling the film, stage, and merchandising rights of *The Hobbit* and *The Lord of the Rings* to United Artists in 1969 for £104,602, reportedly to "ward off the taxman."[18] After Tolkien's death, the rights were subsequently sold to a division of The Saul Zaentz Company operating under the name Tolkien Enterprises. The American television studio Rankin/Bass developed for Tolkien Enterprises a fairly faithful animated musical adaptation of *The Hobbit* in 1977, which would prove to be much more well received than Ralph Bakshi's incomplete *The Lord of the Rings* in 1978 or their own animated treatment of *The Return of the King* in 1980. Other international adaptations followed, from a 1985 Soviet Russian film to a 1993 Finnish mini-series, but it was not until the turn of the twenty-first century that a film adaptation would prove successful enough to match the wild popularity and mythic power of the books.

There is no doubt that Peter Jackson's vastly successful and critically acclaimed films changed everything. The films were technical triumphs, with every prop made from scratch and mostly by hand, some of the most detailed sets ever developed, and groundbreaking new computer graphics technology that included a massive database allowing every single frame of film to be manipulated digitally as necessary.[19] Much as Tolkien had done for novels of the fantastic in the twentieth century, the success of these films in the twenty-first kicked off what one critic called a "geek film renaissance," demonstrating that "fantasy was no longer for a niche audience."[20] After the success of Jackson's trilogy, other fantasy films and television series based on critically disdained but popularly successful novels and comic books (of the superhero, boy wizard, fairy tale, and swords-and-sorcery variety) subsequently began to appear in increasing numbers—and a decade later, when Jackson reunited much of his cast to make films based on *The Hobbit*, the concept was no longer considered risky or even terribly unusual.

Along with their foundational position in bringing fantasy to a new audience, the films also share with their literary progenitors a sort of critical polarization; people seem to either adore them or detest them. W. H. Auden once remarked of *The Lord of the Rings* that "I rarely remember a book about which I have had such violent arguments. Nobody seems to have a moderate opinion: either, like myself, people find it a masterpiece of its genre or they cannot abide it, and among the hostile there are some, I must confess, for whose literary judgment I have great respect."[21] The responses to Peter Jackson's first trilogy proved to be similarly divided, and similarly emotional. Interestingly, while some criticism of the films does tend to mirror the visceral dislike of Tolkien's tale, which characterized the mainstream literary critical response, it is often the most devoted fans of the books who have the harshest opinions of the films. In a testament to the emotional power of Tolkien's legendarium, some of these describe themselves as literally shaking with rage at what they perceived Jackson had done to a story that had been so important in their lives.

The response of the Tolkien family to Jackson's work is also rather mixed. Tolkien's executor and literary heir Christopher famously disliked the films intensely. His general policy was to maintain a stern media silence regarding any licensed adaptations of his father's work; when in 2001 a media frenzy started over a reported rift with his son Simon over the estate's involvement in the films, Christopher submitted to the press a careful lawyerly comment: "My own position is that 'The Lord Of The Rings' is peculiarly unsuitable to transformation into visual dramatic form. . . . On the other hand, I recognize that this is a debatable and complex question of art, and the suggestions that have been made that I 'disapprove' of the films, whatever their cinematic quality, even to the extent of thinking ill of those with whom I may differ, are wholly without foundation."[22] However, in 2012 a French reporter caught him in an unguarded moment, observing that "Ils ont éviscéré le livre, en en faisant un film d'action pour les 15–25 ans,"[23] and sadly stating that he believed his father "est devenu un monstre, dévoré par sa popularité et absorbé par l'absurdité de l'époque."[24] However, J. W. Braun reports[25] that "after the London premiere of *The Fellowship of the Ring*, one of Tolkien's relatives approached Jackson and said her uncle would be very happy. It meant a lot to Jackson."[26] Also, Tolkien's great-grandson Royd, who works in the film industry himself, made cameo appearances in both *The Return of the King* and *The Desolation of Smaug*, describing the opportunity as a "huge privilege" and remarking that he was "incredibly proud" of how the stories had been translated into film.[27] All things considered, despite a sort of purist blowback, the overall reaction to the first three films was generally positive in the end. They were critical successes as well as commercial blockbusters—*The Return of the King* won every Academy Award for which it was nominated, and tied with *Ben Hur* and *Titanic* to become one of the most honored films in history—and the general consensus is that Jackson managed a fitting and faithful adaptation of a twentieth-century myth for a twenty-first century audience.

While the three films of *The Lord of the Rings* generally met with more popular and critical success than approbation, Peter Jackson's second trilogy of Middle-earth films based on *The Hobbit* seemed to tip some unspoken scale of authenticity a bit too far. Despite their similarly successful box-office numbers, the voluble dislike registered by critics and fans alike swelled into a raucous chorus that made the attacks on the first set of films seem almost muted. The main complaints against the second trilogy were not dissimilar to those levied against the first: flat or pointless or unbelievable storylines, overuse of technological wizardry and CGI for its own sake, blatant unfaithfulness to Tolkien's original vision, the perception that greedy Hollywood executives distorted the shape and length of the story in a cynical grab for money. Whereas these arguments had been generally balanced by the critical and popular appreciation of Jackson's groundbreaking efforts in the first films, the same complaints sounded much louder against the new landscape of fantasy filmmaking, whose very contours had been so shaped by Jackson's own earlier successes. Setting aside valid differences in opinion about the relative quality of the films, there are some very interesting points that can be discerned in the general response to the second trilogy.

From a mythological perspective, the more negative response to the *Hobbit* movies can be seen to stem from an underestimation of the inescapably powerful and relentlessly one-way movement of the flow of the mythological river, as well as a fundamental misunderstanding of exactly what Peter Jackson was trying to do. At the time of its publication, *The Hobbit* was a children's book that had only barely brushed up against the more tragic and serious events of Tolkien's larger mythology. After *The Lord of the Rings* met with publishing success, however, Tolkien himself went back and made many changes to the text of his first book, in order to update it and bring it in line with his still-developing mythological ideas, which had become significantly more expansive over the years.[28] The legendarium continued to evolve over the next three decades, and indeed was growing and changing in Tolkien's mind until the very last days of his life. Since his death, the dedicated editorial work of his son Christopher has allowed his myth to continue this growth and change in the minds of its fans; with the publication of *The Silmarillion*, the *Unfinished Tales*, the twelve volumes of *The History of Middle-earth*, and stand-alone tales such as *The Children of Húrin* and *Beren and Lúthien*, the fullness and richness of Tolkien's tapestry have come into much clearer public focus than it ever could have been in the very early (and relatively simple) children's book published in 1937. Peter Jackson's three *The Lord of the Rings* films created for this tapestry a coherent, richly evocative, and stunningly beautiful cinematic setting.

The three *Hobbit* films were made many years after Jackson's original setting and treatment had established itself in the public consciousness as the modern incarnation of Tolkien's world. To make a film using the much less developed Middle-earth setting of *The Hobbit* would be to try and turn back time, to intentionally reblur what had been so carefully brought into focus by more than a century of work by Tolkien himself and those who followed him. Filmgoers who had thrilled to Hugo Weaving as the masterful Elrond or felt the creepy fascination of Andy Serkis's Gollum would not have understood or appreciated a filmic throwback to the relatively undeveloped characters of the friendly host/loremaster or the odd riddle-gamer of *The Hobbit*. The very existence of appendix B to *The Lord of the Rings* ("The Tale of Years"), from which Peter Jackson took much of the "new" material he added to his storyline for *The Hobbit*, is a testament to how clearly Tolkien saw how far his work had grown beyond its original boundaries. Jackson essentially created films that dramatized the modern and fully developed concept of the entire Middle-earth legendarium, not the initial and undeveloped children's story that began it all. Now, two decades after the first films and half a decade after the second, the television series forthcoming from Amazon Studios will have to operate in a context that has grown and changed along with the continuing cultural and mythological development of Tolkien's original ideas.

Because of the deep emotion and strong power flowing beneath Tolkien's mythic world, various arguments about how faithful or unfaithful Peter Jackson's characters and storyline were to Tolkien's original work are likely never to be resolved to anyone's satisfaction. But, in the end, this ecocritical study is concerned about landscape and wilderness and the ways that humans relate to them. From that perspective, Tolkien's themes concerning the importance of the natural world are presented by Jackson quite unchanged. Indeed, in many cases they are highlighted and even augmented by the deeply aural and visual experience of the film medium. The ecocritical words of one film critic, although reacting to the details of dialogue and events in the screenplay, are just as valid when applied to the original books: "Nature is sentient; it has history and language. Legolas tells Gimli that the 'forest is full of memory and anger.' Treebeard writes and recited poetry and mourns the death of trees that 'had voices of their own.' The landscape speaks to, or is read by, the characters: Aragorn listens to the ground and reads the terrain to find Pippin and Merry; Gimli discerningly tastes Orc blood; Legolas reads the sky and senses that 'blood has been spilled.' The Landscape is a language."[29] The characteristics of this language are, with one or two exceptions, scrupulously faithful to those of Tolkien's own textual Middle-earth landscape.

If Middle-earth itself is a character in the books, it is an even more developed one in the films: muscular, powerful, possessed of nearly unimaginable beauty, bathed in golden light or bleak darkness, and traveled over in a visible and concrete way that the most luminous prose in the world would fail to capture. A word picture can by its very nature never be completed. There is always another small detail to be described, and because a writer must balance completeness of description against the flow of the narrative, in the end there are as many different and equally valid visual interpretations of a word picture as there are readers of the text. But photographic imagery, moving or otherwise, captures a single interpretation; it collapses the waveform, as it were, and selects a single option to present as reality. In this process, deep clarity is gained but at the expense of broad applicability.

Tolkien knew this well. In *On Fairy Stories* he insists that "in human art Fantasy is a thing best left to words, to true literature," and suggests that "the visible presentation of the fantastic image is technically too easy; the hand tends to outrun the mind, even to overthrow it."[30] In a long note, he goes on to discuss in detail the generality of literature as set against the specificity of the visual arts. He notes that "the radical distinction between all art (including drama) that offers a visible presentation and true literature is that it imposes one visible form," and describes the difference thusly: "If a story says 'he climbed a hill and saw a river in the valley below', the illustrator may catch, or nearly catch, his own vision of such a scene; but every hearer of the words will have his own picture, and it will be made out of all the hills and rivers and dales he has ever seen, but especially out of The Hill, The River, The Valley which were for him the first embodiment of the word."[31] Accordingly, every reader of Tolkien's books will have her or his own conception of Middle-earth, while viewers of the films are limited to experiencing Jackson's vision.

In human terms this specificity can manifest in something as controversial as the pale blond hair of Orlando Bloom's Legolas; in terms of setting, it solidifies the many different possibilities of Elven architecture into the graceful Art Nouveau knotwork of the filmic Rivendell. Just as the cast of the film visually substantiates Tolkien's characters "simply by concretely embodying them, by giving them face, form, and voice," the stunning landscapes of the New Zealand countryside (a place Tolkien himself never saw) provide the contours and lines of a concrete reality for the world through which those characters walk.[32] Regardless of critical or popular approval or disapproval, for good or ill, the characters and settings of the films have become the definitive visual picture of Tolkien's Middle-earth in the broader popular consciousness of the early part of the twenty-first century.

All three of Tolkien's wilderness concepts appear in completely recognizable form in Peter Jackson's world, and in some cases they are amplified by the clarity and emotion of cinema to a point that they become even more important in the films than they were in the books. Tolkien's Germanic concept of wilderness especially resonates with some of the main connotations surrounding the modern word, and the films' presentation of the wildernesses of monsters and Rangers is accordingly the most fully realized of the three. Still, the Celtic heritage behind the Elven lands is also prominent in the visually striking treatments of the Elvenking's halls, Rivendell, and Lothlórien, and the way all of those realms blur the line between natural and built elements highlights the uncanny wildness of Tolkien's second concept of wilderness. His third, more friendly, concept is admittedly difficult to spot in the films, but it does appear to those who look at the presentation of the Shire through eyes attuned to its more subdued wildness.

The emotional amplification of film is most obvious when considering the Germanic concept of wilderness; some of the most breathtaking visual effects of the films rely on this concept and its pitting of humankind against the overwhelming power of the natural world. Steven Woodward and Kostis Kourelis point out how viewers "often discover the protagonists only after the camera has scanned along the ridges of sheer-faced mountains or surveyed bleak, frozen expanses. Dynamic boom, crane, and helicopter shots work to maintain the sense not only of diminutive heroes pitted against the landscape as much as against their enemies, but of a deeply unsettled reality of the verge of cataclysm."[33] The visceral visual experience of film certainly heightens this sense of danger and smallness against the vast power of nature, but it also highlights the incredible, almost painful, beauty that is part of the reward for showing courage in the face of that power.

The mountains in the films, whether the harsh alpine peaks of the Misty Mountains or the stark solitude of the Lonely Mountain, especially reflect and often amplify Tolkien's ideas surrounding the beauty and danger of mountainous terrain. The stoutly *Beowulf*ian Edoras is in the films "a hilltop city crowned by the Golden Hall of Meduseld . . . like an island rising on a rocky outcrop from a broad, desolate valley between two spectacular mountain ranges."[34] The Germanic-inspired monsters—from the wraithlike Nazgûl gathering to attack on Weathertop to the bloated spiders filling the trees of Mirkwood—are fully realized and utterly terrifying. The howling wind and driving snow of the blizzard on Caradhras inspire a feeling of a viscerally present danger when served up to filmgoers in full audiovisual detail, right down to the ice in Gandalf's beard. Even the Germanic sense of shelter in woodland is present; very early in the story, as they hide from the terrifying Black Riders, Frodo and his hobbit friends find themselves embraced by the huge and friendly trees along the roads of the Shire. The episode where Pippin and Merry escape from the Orcs into Fangorn forest also presents that grandly Teutonic place as both more frightening and more sheltering than Merry's brief remark in the book manages to do.

While the emotional impact of the Germanic wilderness is significantly amplified in the films, the uncanniness of the Celtic one feels slightly lessened by the specificity of a photographic medium. Visually, the striking beauty of the Elven lands is completely realized on-screen. Especially notable are the intricately beautiful halls of Thranduil's stronghold in Mirkwood, which appear in *The Hobbit* films as fully fleshed-out spaces whose kinship to the beauty of Rivendell and Lothlórien is unmistakable, and which are a far cry from the sparsely described cave-like holes readers are given in the text of *The Hobbit*. Film scholar Steven Woodward and art historian Kostis Kourelis describe the filmic versions of this Elven landscape mode as "naturalistic," involving "a dreamy stylized world set in the woods and vegetative in form" that "is not folksy or vernacular; its reference comes from cosmopolitan Europe at the end of the nineteenth century, from the exuberant designs of Art Nouveau."[35] But, while the breathtaking beauty of this wilderness concept has survived the media transition perfectly well, the sense of a magical overlay landscape is more difficult to evoke without disrupting the flow of the cinematic narrative.

The movie versions of Lothlórien and Rivendell, with their hazy gold lighting and soft crystalline music, do have a magical and ethereal quality about them, but the necessity for solid and completely realized sets for the actors to inhabit make the Elven places feel somehow more grounded on the screen than they were presented in the books. Still, the overlay landscape does manage to gleam through in places. The visions and dreamlike shimmer of Arwen's interrupted journey to the Grey Havens in Jackson's *The Return of the King* imply another world into which she peers at the last possible moment to see the consequences of her choice. Jackson's startling visual transformations of Galadriel in *The Fellowship of the Ring* and *The Battle of Five Armies* into a darker Otherworldly form suggest that there is more to this most powerful of Elves than can be easily seen in the blonde simplicity of a white-clad Cate Blanchett. Even the timelessness of the Celtic wilderness realms, which would seem almost impossible to portray on-screen, can be glimpsed after the fact in the presence of Hugo Weaving's never-changing and never-aging face in the flashbacks of *The Fellowship of the Ring;* the films visually provide a young Bilbo in Martin Freeman and an old one in Sir Ian Holm, but Elven timelessness means that Elrond at the end of the Second Age can look on screen exactly the same as he does two thousand years later.

If the harshness and beauty of Tolkien's first wilderness concept is vastly more powerful than its film incarnation, and the overlay landscape of his second is subdued but still discernible, the subtle wildness of his more friendly English concept is not fully present in any concrete way—but it is still visible in glimpses, largely through strong implication, because Peter Jackson's world lavishes such a great deal of exquisitely faithful attention on the pastoral paradise of the Shire. In a vast production so reliant on CGI animation that new technologies had to be invented to support it, the set designers nevertheless had crews plant a complete vegetable garden in the area that would become the set of Hobbiton a full year before filming began, so that it would appear mature enough to "make the domestically gifted Hobbits look at home."[36] In both film trilogies, after the vaguely threatening exposition of the prologues, the beginning of the actual story is clearly signaled by a series of camera pans, which wander leisurely through the diffuse green light and homey music of the "place of pastoral bridges, water mills, and above ground and underground houses, all nestled cozily in a lush and rolling landscape" of Tolkien's idealized English country village.[37]

The specific episodes that largely define the friendly English woodlands of Tolkien's third concept of wilderness, particularly the walking-party from Bag End to the house in Crickhollow, are replaced in the cinematic storyline with faster-paced and more dangerous (and hence more Germanic) chase scenes. Still, in their flight, the smaller-than-human film hobbits more than once hide among gnarled trees of greater-than-human scale, in whose friendly roots they find a place of at least partial safety. Although there is more than a touch of the Germanic idea of shelter in woodlands in this sequence, these are not the deep woods of the Teutobergerwald or Beowulf's dragon country but an evocation of wildness within the purportedly tame landscape of the Shire. The Black Riders may be much more fully realized and terrifying, but this tiny slice of the idyllic English greenwood proves equal to their menace, if in a typically—and indeed almost unbelievable—cinematic way.

In a sense Jackson's Shire is even more idealized than Tolkien's, because it is never truly threatened by the forces of evil. In the films, the story "starts and ends in a place of innocence; the refusal to include the scouring of the Shire in the film reaffirms it as some sort of Eden to which the heroes can safely return."[38] This elision, made for arguably valid storyline-based reasons, nevertheless weakens a theme that can be seen as an activist-oriented lesson on how ordinary people can fight and win against the despoliation of nature by industrialization and modernism. Viewers of the films miss out on the visceral horror experienced by the four adventuring hobbits on their long-awaited return home. In the books, instead of rest and welcome, Frodo and his friends discover their streams befouled, their trees cut down, and a burgeoning Orwellian dystopia overtaking the Shire, with new schemes of gathering and sharing, the reporting of hobbits on other hobbits, and many other modernist horrors. Tolkien's own idealization can be seen in the fact that all of these are rather quickly and easily swept clean by the returning heroes, and the Shire is returned to its former glory in just a few pages.

Jackson's decision to leave the Shire unspoiled does strengthen its archetypal power as the perfect nostalgic idealization of the English countryside, however, and it allows him to sensitively explore some ideas of exile and return, which were somewhat muted by all the shouting and escapades that accompanied the textual hobbits' homecoming. The emotional impact of the destruction of the Shire is not completely missing from the films either; in the books it is Sam who sees an apocalyptic vision of the Shire in Galadriel's mirror, but Jackson's story translocates the image to Frodo as a warning of what will happen to his beloved home should he fail in his quest.

This translocation echoes other instances where Tolkien's dialogue was reassigned, otherwise unchanged, by the screenwriters from one character to another. Extending this concept just a bit, it can be argued that the theme of the Scouring of the Shire episode, that despoliation of a green paradise by the fires of industry, is not lost but instead shifted to another place: the ruining of Isengard. Gandalf's observations about how Isengard "had once been green and fair" but was now "filled with pits and forges" appear in Tolkien's text but are passed over quickly in favor of the more human drama of the Council of Elrond.[39] The emotional impact of the change is observed only much later, and somewhat more distantly, in Treebeard's anger at the felling of his trees and all the "smoke rising from Isengard."[40]

In the films, the transformation of Isengard is a much more immediate and emotional experience; Gandalf's initial ride through the beautiful green circular valley is seen in real time, and its transformation into an industrialized wasteland is a visual and visceral episode instead of a dispatch from the front lines of a regrettable but distant war. Augmented by the disgust evoked in viewers by the slimy visages of the Orcs, the violent uprooting of venerable trees (seen clearly on-screen in the angry red light of forge fires and ordered and overseen by a delightfully malevolent Sir Christopher Lee as Saruman) is presented as a proximate example of true evil. The compressed timeline of the films also makes the spoiling of Isengard, and the subsequent cleansing deluge engineered by the angry Ents, feel as breathtakingly fast as the single-chapter Scouring of the Shire in the books. So, while removing this episode weakens one of Tolkien's important environmental themes, that theme is partially strengthened elsewhere, in the more complete treatment of the travails of another part of the landscape of Middle-earth.

Jackson's steady faithfulness to Tolkien's ecological themes is clearly visible in the presence of all three wilderness concepts in the world of the films. It is also visible in the ethical underpinnings of the film's storyline. This is generally true of most of Tolkien's values—the honoring of ancient wisdom and ancient things over new knowledge and modern creations is one example, the somewhat anachronistic celebration of the "good and faithful servant" in Sam's heroic dedication to his master is another, and there are certainly many more—but it is so clear in the presentation of the relationship between humanity and the natural world that sensitive ethical criticism of the film in this realm applies without qualification of any kind to Tolkien's original text. Woodward and Kourelis note that, in the films, "the hobbit houses of the Shire are molded under the contours of gently rolling hills; the Elven habitation of Rivendell is enshrouded and interpenetrated by trees, cliffs, and rivers; and the human city of Minas Tirith takes the logic of its form and defenses from the rocky pinnacle it encircles."[41] Goodly creatures, hobbits and Elves and noble men, are clearly presented as living in harmony with rather than warring against the powers of the natural world.

A film critic who "had not even read the book" when asked to comment on the films notes that, in contrast to all of this goodly harmony, "it is oppressive power and control over subjects and the natural world that constitutes the monstrous in *The Lord of the Rings*."[42] This same ethical marker distinguishing between good and evil characters is clearly present in the books, and had certainly not gone unnoticed by literary critics, long before Jackson began filming. Patricia Meyer Spacks observes that, in Tolkien's books, "goodness is partly equated with understanding of nature, closeness to the natural world" while "the Enemy's territory, even its outskirts, is physically and morally a wasteland; the implication is strong that the barrenness of nature here is a direct result of the operations of evil," and she simplifies her observations into the bald statement that "the good love nature, the evil destroy it."[43] Susan Jeffers, following Spacks, notes that the heroes of Tolkien's books "all connect in some positive fashion to the world around them, while the villains all disregard it or attempt to exploit that connection" and that "Tolkien's work illuminates ways of seeing what is good, evil, and in between in part by showing the relation of each to landscape."[44] It is clear that, whatever storyline changes appear in the screenplay, the ethical orientation regarding wilderness and the natural world in Middle-earth is one thing that has been faithfully realized in Peter Jackson's world.

In areas where significant changes have been made to the storyline, these ethics manage to survive the transition, even when other important elements do not. One example is the subtle but critical change in the circumstances behind the Ents' decision to march to war on Isengard. In the books, the decision is made as a result of long and careful deliberation at the Entmoot; for nearly three full days "the voices of the Ents at the Moot still rose and fell, sometimes loud and strong, sometimes low and sad, sometimes quickening, sometimes slow and solemn as a dirge," and Merry and Pippin learn of their decision only when Treebeard swoops them up to join the thrilling last march of the Ents.[45] Conversely, the filmic Ents in their deliberation explicitly choose not to intervene; Treebeard solemnly informs the dejected young hobbits that "The Ents cannot hold back this storm. We must weather such things as we have always done."[46] Pippin, in a moment of inspiration, convinces the old Ent to journey south past Isengard rather than west in his effort to transport them out of his domain. It is not until Treebeard (along with the audience) sees the mangled and smoking destruction at the edge of the forest—"as if he would not already know: he, the shepherd of the trees"—that he reverses his dedication to the Ents' noninterventionist principles and rouses his kindred to attack.[47]

This characterization stands in stark contrast to the textual Ents, who were slow, thoughtful creatures deliberate to a fault and who would certainly not have been so easily manipulated by a too clever (and far too hasty) hobbit. As critic Martin Barker complains, the Ents, "from being embodiments of long wisdom, became foolish, grumpy, diminished creatures. Instead of reasoning their way to a decision, and accepting the fate this imposed on them, they became servants to others' wills."[48] The end result is the same: the unstoppable power of natural forces of good is brought to bear against the destructive symbol of evil modern industry. But the circumstances of the film episode significantly undermine Tolkien's complex and complete characterization of the Ents as distinctly nonhuman beings with full agency, representatives of the natural world who carefully evaluate the sins of industrial humankind and take deliberate and decisive action to right the wrongs that have been done to the forest.

Despite this weakening of Tolkien's generally strong nonanthropocentric sensibility, however, it is important to note something that did not change: the assignment of good and evil in regard to wanton destruction of a green and growing landscape. Saruman's actions are just as evil, and his downfall is perhaps more satisfying for being complete and final rather than drawn-out and a bit ambiguous as in the text. The visual impact of the final state of Isengard echoes the fiery, Orc-filled scenes presented in real time earlier in the film, and helps to engender in the viewer a sympathetic anger at the wanton destruction of wild lands. Also, in the film episode, it is the landscape, more than the characters who inhabit it, whose suffering must be revenged and repaired. In the text, Quickbeam's sorrowful singing "that seemed to lament in many tongues the fall of trees that he had loved" is presented as his own personal sadness at their deaths.[49] "We never are roused unless it is clear to us that our trees and our lives are in great danger," the textual Treebeard tells the young hobbits, and he hopes that in their last march the Ents "may help the other peoples before we pass away."[50] The result of anthropomorphizing trees into sympathetic characters, even if those characters are clearly representational of the landscape, is the creation of a level of abstraction that takes the narrative one step away from the idea of the landscape itself as an actor. So, while what is lost is a modicum of agency on the part of the natural world, what is gained is a reinforcement of Tolkien's sensibility that the destruction of a landscape is itself enough of a reason to act against evil. It also presents, in Pippin's actions, a powerful lesson about how seemingly small or unimportant actors can have a large impact on more powerful actors (and vast natural forces).

Overall, the tale of Peter Jackson's wilderness is a positive one, quite faithful to Tolkien's own, and the films demonstrate equal potential to serve as vectors for the myth of Middle-earth to constructively influence people's stories about the natural world. There has been a great deal of well-deserved criticism leveled at the cultural colonialism of Hollywood and the American filmmaking industry over the years, so it is encouraging to note how that vast cinematic force has some beneficial possibilities as well. But films, much like books or audiobooks or radio dramas or television series, are media consumed passively by the people who read, hear, watch, and enjoy them. The rise of computers powerful enough to provide audiovisual experiences in response to real-time input has opened a new, interactive path for people to travel as they seek to find mythic participation in (and hopefully gain positive instruction from) the powerful stories that move them.

Considering just how foundational Tolkien's work was to the entire computer gaming industry, it is odd to realize how thin on the ground decent game properties set in Middle-earth really are. There have been small titles out since the 1980s, when an Australian company released a few licensed text-based interactive fiction adventures, and one or two console games here and there as early tie-ins, but even after Peter Jackson brought the story into wider public consciousness, the space has been oddly fragmented by the legalistic details of licensing agreements and populated with largely disappointing attempts to render Middle-earth in interactive form. It wasn't until Warner Bros. obtained licenses with access to both the books and the films in the 2010s that any interactive media property could hope to represent the full scope of the twenty-first-century version of Tolkien's powerful myth—but even today, no official Middle-earth game has ever achieved anything like the grand success of other fantasy franchises, from *The Legend of Zelda* to *World of Warcraft* to *The Witcher*.

Choosing a game to examine for this study, then, was not a simple matter of judging a popularity contest. But this freedom from relying on market success permitted a nuanced choice that allowed for full consideration of the mythological value to be found in the new medium. Examining a direct tie-in property, in which players act out a known plot as a known character (Vivendi's 2003 *The Hobbit* is an early example, or the charming Warner Bros. *Lego*-themed games), feels in such a context as though it would miss out on the main difference between the active experience of a game and the passive one of reading books or watching films. In order to provide a fair look at Tolkien's wilderness concepts as presented in an interactive medium, it was important to select a game reflecting a reasonably faithful facsimile of Middle-earth. In order to fairly argue that the game partakes of the mythological power of Tolkien's grand tale, the game would have to authentically access all of the satisfying psychological identification available while providing an adventure separate from a simple rehashing of familiar plots. And in order to permit real ecocritical analysis, it would be useful if the game's simulated natural environment was one that could be "engaged with semiotically—that is, audio-visually and discursively—as well as ludically."[51] All of these criteria were met to some extent in the Warner Bros. 2011 title *Lord of the Rings: War in the North*.

This game was admittedly not a huge commercial success. Part of this was probably due to the timing of its release in November 2011, which not only competed with the hugely anticipated *Dark Souls* (September 2011) but was also impacted by the release of several sequels in widely popular blockbuster game franchises; 2011 was the year of *Dragon Age II* (March 2011) and *The Witcher 2: Assassins of Kings* (May 2011), and *War in the North* debuted only ten days before the juggernaut that was *The Elder Scrolls V: Skyrim*. Even setting aside this unfortunate timing, though, *War in the North* broke no new ground for the genre. Its overall quality, even at its release, was at best average in a very competitive space, and replaying it in the context of today's advanced and seamless synthetic worlds only highlights its many limitations. It does boast an excellent cooperative system baked in that permits rollicking social Middle-earth adventures on the couch with friends, but even this benefit is also a detraction because the limitations of the artificial intelligence engine driving the unplayed characters create brutal difficulty walls at points for players who attempt the campaign solo. It embraces the repetitive hack-and-slash gore-fest typical of an action role-playing game. There is very little in the way of player-led exploration and absolutely zero in the way of development for the playable characters, who are cardboard cutouts straight out of Tolkienian central casting.[52] The storyline is utterly linear, with only a few deviations permitted to go back and finish side quests, and the combat system is a repetitive grind of breaking bones for experience and barrels for loot.

But none of this matters. The game's unyielding fidelity to Middle-earth makes it deeply mythologically satisfying, despite its faults. "The narrative compels you to play on, particularly if you're an avid fan of the *Lord of the Rings* universe and lore," writes reviewer Uros "Vader" Pavlovic for *Actiontrip;* after panning the outdated visuals, repetitive combat, and "little freedom and little choice" of the game, he concludes that "what keeps this thing afloat is the story, the characters and the adaptation of Tolkien's compelling lore."[53] Reviewing the game for *Escapist* magazine, Greg Tito explains more fully:

> When I sat down to play *War in the North,* I was not expecting a journey into Tolkien's Middle Earth on par with the books or movies. The voice-acting, art style and dialogue feel so authentic, that it's easy to forget the action RPG skeleton of whacking orcs and collecting loot is merely average. In some ways, the standard gameplay only focuses the player firmly on the world that Tolkien built. Nowadays, I can kill orcs and break crates in any old game, but only *War in the North* lets me feel like I'm walking with the great heroes I'd read about since I was a kid.[54]

Even the game's detractors acknowledge this fidelity; one reviewer for *Kotaku,* who calls the game "a bog-standard dungeon creeping action RPG loot-athon with an unconvincing cast" and criticizes its "cynical undertone," grudgingly admits that the game "does render a mostly convincing portrait of Middle-earth."[55]

As the first property to have adaptation licenses with access to both text and films, *War in the North* could embrace a visual feel more representative of the shape and color Peter Jackson has given to today's Middle-earth than any of its predecessors, while still providing an opportunity to interactively explore canonical landscapes not seen in the films (such as the undead-haunted Barrow-downs). But the game designers went out of their way to include the philosophical and psychological elements that make Middle-earth unique, right down to the idea of the landscape as a character in itself. An early interview reports art director Philip Straub's insistence "that 'environment is character' is an encouraging philosophy he's used to create hellish 'big characters who act as environments' which decorate the spookier locations in the game."[56] The fact that the game feels so true despite its average technology and gameplay speaks volumes in testament to the incredible power of Tolkien's original vision.

When launching the game and at the end of every level, players choose one of three playable characters: Eradan, a Ranger under the command of Aragorn's kinsman Halbarad; Farin, a Dwarf of the Lonely Mountain; and Andriel, an Elven loremaster of Elrond's household. This small but archetypical multiracial fellowship embarks on an adventure whose plot is carefully woven into the events of both the books and the films. As the game's opening narration (spoken in the sonorous, instantly recognizable voice of Gandalf)[57] explains, "Of the great War of the Ring many songs have been sung and many tales told. The names of heroes like Gandalf the Grey, Aragorn the King and Frodo the Ring-bearer are greatly revered. And rightly so. Yet Sauron's grasp stretched much further than the lands of Gondor and Rohan alone, and his forces might have done great evil in the North of Middle-earth had a handful of heroes not stood in his path. Their stories too, deserve to be told."[58]

The incidents of the game were inspired by the mention in appendix A to *The Lord of the Rings* that "with his far-stretched right hand Sauron might have done great evil in the North" were it not for the valor of the Dwarves and men of Erebor.[59] Game producer Ruth Tormandl explained in a 2010 interview that "the fact that the whole world was at war is what we're drawing on for *War in the North*. Tolkien's work mentions Dwarves living in the Grey Mountains, and that the Orcs had a capital city at Mt. Gundabad, and that the Witch-king of Angmar had once ruled a large part of the North, so we're using that canon as the foundation of our story."[60]

The game opens in the Prancing Pony, where the three heroes meet with a mysterious yet familiar-looking hooded Ranger seated in a shadowy corner. Aragorn tasks them with distracting forces of the enemy gathering at Fornost in order to allow a certain very important hobbit bearing a great burden to safely make his way to Bree. After rescuing the Great Eagle Belaram from his Orc captors and fighting through legions of enemies at Fornost, the three return to Halbarad at Sarn Ford, who asks them to look for a pair of missing Rangers in the Barrow-downs on their way to Rivendell. At Rivendell, Elrond sends the trio out on a scouting mission to the Ettenmoors, where Belaram joins them again for a fight against Orcs and a renegade stone giant waging war on the Eagles. Elrond then tasks the small fellowship to travel to the Grey Mountains, where they encounter Dwarves seeking an ancient weapon to destroy the once-fine halls of Mount Gundabad. The heroes help the Dwarves and are welcomed at the hidden Dwarven city of Nordinbad, whence they depart to Mirkwood to rescue the wizard Radagast the Brown, to the lair of the dragon Úrgost, and finally, after defending Nordinbad from a vast assault, to the ancient fortress of Carn Dûm to confront Agandaûr, the Black Númenorean lieutenant of Sauron behind all the trouble.

The three Tolkienian ideas of wilderness appear pretty much unchanged in the environment of the game. The heroic monster-battling genre of this typical action title means that the Germanic wilderness of the Rangers is much in evidence throughout; players find themselves contending with the dangers of quintessential cruel mountains (the exterior areas of the Mount Gundabad map are full of deep snow blowing around in an endless storm) and dark forests (Mirkwood is positively crawling with monsters, from wargs and Orcs to all sizes of great spiders), as well as other less archetypal but even more *Beowulf*ian wilderness landscapes like the troll-infested Ettenmoors. But the landscape rendering also successfully evokes the beautiful side of the beauty/danger Germanic wilderness coin, allowing the game to at least partially draw on the ambiguity in the modern idea of wilderness. As Tormandl points out, "Middle-earth is a beautiful place, but it's also a very dangerous place, and it's important to stick with your allies and protect your home from your enemies. J. R. R. Tolkien didn't sugarcoat that, and we're not either."[61] The surprising blue flowers that pop up around Mirkwood are a continuous delight, especially considering that they are not gatherable as potion components or in any way interactive but serve only to add a touch of beautiful visual interest to the forest. The gray-green pines scattered among the boulders and waste of the Ettenmoors are as majestic and calming as their real-world equivalents in similar highlands, and there is a subterranean lake hidden behind the Dwarven stone walls of Viking-feeling Nordinbad that is downright spectacular.

The game shares with the films the difficulty of rendering into a concrete visual experience the timeless, Otherworldly Celtic Elven landscape, and wilderness areas of this type appear mostly by implication. But the visual resonance with the films evokes a consonant (if subtle) perilous beauty, especially in the sense of wild mystery captured in the softly blurred chiaroscuro backdrop of mountains and waterfalls surrounding the haven of Rivendell. This somewhat hazy visual sense is extended to a small glimpse of the soaring *mellyrn* of Lothlórien in some downloadable content added to the game after its release.[62] But genre-wise this game occupies a position one step to the left along the archaic/Romantic/modern spectrum of the books and the films, and consequently the muted Celtic wilderness idea of the films is merely implied here, and the English wilderness that appeared by implication in the films is in this game almost wholly missing.

There are a few scattered exceptions. The story begins in charmingly quaint (if endlessly rainy) Bree, and at one point the player can move to the edge of the map in Sarn Ford to catch a glimpse of some hobbit holes up on a hill overlooking the pleasant currents of the Brandywine River, but otherwise there is little rest and recreation to be had in wild areas anywhere. Even the hobbits themselves are scarce throughout. A riddle-gamer and a shopkeeper in Bree and cameo appearances from Frodo and Bilbo at Rivendell are basically the only connections the game provides to the anachronistically modern hobbits and their English wilderness. Still, even these small references are enough to evoke in a player who has read the books and seen the movies the pleasant green beauty of the Shire, in protection of which many of the game's missions are ostensibly undertaken—a fact that resonates well with Tolkien's thematic use of the Shire as a touchstone of home and safety far away.

The designers were just as careful to remain true to the less physical foundations of Tolkien's grand tale. Unlike the later, more successful, but rather morally questionable *Shadow* series,[63] whose tone is "frequently cynical and oppressive where Tolkien's books are hopeful and humanistic,"[64] *War in the North* is an unabashedly "good guy" game. Tormandl admits this openly in a 2011 game preview segment: "There's a very clear line between good and evil in Tolkien. . . . There are odd grey areas, but mostly the heroes are good. Eradan isn't going to be a dick to a shopkeeper. . . . We've been working with the license holders to ensure that this really respects the franchise in a way they want it to, and one of the things they told us is that they want our heroes to be good guys."[65]

Overall, from the crystalline waterfalls of Rivendell to the black tower of Carn Dûm, from the high style of the characters' speech to the instant apologies available to follow even the mildest of negative or dismissive dialogue options, from the many opportunities to help good folk and satisfyingly slice through bad ones, *War in the North* does an excellent job of evoking the physical, philosophical, and moral aspects of the commitment to "traditional views of good and evil" that so annoyed Tolkien's modernist, relativist critics and yet so underlie the still relevant mythic power of the story he created.[66]

In the context of ecocriticism, the mechanism of player choice in interactive media makes examining game properties a bit less straightforward than literature or films. The way that the experience of a game reacts to such choices opens up a third dimension for analysis of a game's representation of the relationship between humans and the natural world, which expands an already wide pool of options into nearly infinite territory. Hans Joachim Backe has adapted theories from Lawrence Buell's book *The Environmental Imagination* in order to propose some questions to help narrow the examination of ecological ethics in computer games, and his framework provides some interesting insight into the ecocritical strengths and limitations of *War in the North.*

Backe's first question, whether the environment is a semiotic as well as a ludic experience for the player, is mentioned above. The answer here is generally an affirmative one. Admittedly, Alenda Chang's observation that game environments "tend to lean heavily on clichéd landscapes" that "may give players the disorienting and somewhat anaesthetizing sense that *this could be anywhere or nowhere at all*" is not completely inapplicable to the comparatively bland visual spaces in *War in the North,* but on close examination, the problem seems to be more of a technological limitation than anything else, because her related accusation that such environments are also guilty of "abandoning any attempts at regional specificity for prepatterned and ultimately generic scenes" is much less applicable.[67] Compared to the smooth and endlessly variable landscapes of more modern open-world games, visuals in *War in the North* suffer from the sort of one-note repetitiveness typical of earlier technology. But the game designers clearly relied on Tolkien's own very specific landscape descriptions to create their various maps, and the skillful deployment of audiovisual cues like plants and weather are detailed enough to successfully provide each area with an overall feel that is quite distinguishable from each of the others. The overall results are more than good enough to permit a player familiar with Middle-earth to mythologically accept a prepatterned repetition of deep green trees as a representation of Mirkwood, or misty hills as the Barrow-downs, or sere pine uplands as the Ettenmoors. The fact that licensing agreements also permitted the game to produce close representations of Peter Jackson's well-developed audiovisual landscapes means that places like Rivendell and the glimpse of the Shire as seen from Sarn Ford add to the verisimilitude enjoyed by players who have seen the films.

The rest of Backe's ecoethical questions are less binary criteria than vectors for discussion, and in such a discussion the game's overall score comes out somewhat mixed. Notably, there is little "friction" created through engaging with ecological topics;[68] while the dialogue possibilities are all fairly positive ones, choosing sharper or more negative responses has no impact on gameplay, and players are only once forced to reckon with any differences between acting for their own benefit versus that of the natural world, and even then only by implication. Ecological topics feel more on the "implicit and peripheral" side than the "explicit and central" one, but here the results are a bit more encouraging as there are a few points where the dialogue does go out of its way to remind the player of natural processes.[69]

An example might be the eggs laid by the spiders of Mirkwood; they are not directly relevant to any gameplay, but Eradan remarks ominously on the great size and quantity of the eggs (leaving unspoken the implied warning of enemies to come), and one cutscene depicts a troll snacking on a handful of the glowing white orbs.[70] Such entomological detail provides a glimpse into the fantasy life cycle of these more "natural" monsters that is ignored for bipedal enemies such as Orcs or undead warriors. Also, near the end of the game, the players enter the final citadel through a sewer. "Ugh!" grouses Andriel, "This channel drains the refuse of the fortress." As they proceed, the players move around and through veritable geysers of red liquid pouring out from all directions. "Is this . . . blood?" asks Eradan incredulously, but Farin in his Dwarven wisdom knows better: "No, not blood, it's rust. Much of this fortress is clad in iron."[71] Sewer adventures are a common trope in fantasy games (all three of the *Witcher* titles in particular spend quite a lot of time in the muck), but dialogic acknowledgment of waste management provenance and construction is rare.

The careful distinctions in landscape described above do provide a treatment of the natural world that can reasonably be characterized as "specific and informed."[72] The "treatment of ecological topics" in the game is also generally affirmative rather than critical or ironic, as evinced by explicit mentions in dialogue establishing ethical judgments regarding environmental actions.[73] The game's area of Mount Gundabad, a once-great Dwarven hall fouled by Orcs, visually echoes in color and shape the ugly industrial pits that replaced the green circle of Isengard in the films. As the player gazes on the fiery, machine-haunted repulsion, Farin observes bitterly that "the Orcs are like maggots teeming in the corpse of once great Gundabad," and Andriel replies (with characteristic Elven sententiousness) that "they delight in marring the works of others and twisting them to their own foul purpose."[74] Whether in book, film, or game, Orcs serve as shorthand for all the evils of destructive modernity, and their effect on place is universally a despoiling one.

This obvious ethical judgment is strikingly juxtaposed with the next area, the still-great Dwarven hall of Nordinbad, where the goodly Longbeards tend to their spectacular underground lake. The player learns how good beings treat areas of natural beauty in a very Tolkienian conversation with Gorin, the ruler of the city:

> FARIN: I have beheld many an underground lake, but never one as large and beautiful as this. Is this the work of your kin?
>
> GORIN: Nay, my ancestors discovered Azan-zâram even as you see it. We have worked with care to enhance what we found. A chip here, a tap there, fashioning bridges, halls and tunnels, but always we have taken care to preserve the great gift we were given.
>
> PLAYER: Tell me about this Nordinbad of yours.
>
> GORIN: My great, great grandsire was the first to enter the caves of this mountain where he discovered the Hidden Lake we call Azan-zâram. He was awed by its beauty and led some of his kin here. Slowly, over many long years, with loving hands and careful chisels we created the halls you see before you. Nordinbad was never rich in gold or jewels but its beauty would move even the most cold-hearted Dwarf.[75]

The visual landscape beheld by the player, combined with Gorin's words here, together provide a clear reference to the textual Gimli's description of the Glittering Caves of Aglarond. That breathless Dwarf enthuses for two full pages about the beauty of the caverns, where "still lakes" mirror columns, which "spring up from many-coloured floors to meet the glistening pendants of the roof" and a "glimmering world looks up from dark pools covered with clear glass," and he assures Legolas that his people would "tend these glades of flowering stone. . . . With cautious skill, tap by tap—a small chip of rock and no more, perhaps in a whole anxious day—so we could work, and as the years went by, we should open up new ways and display far chambers that are still dark."[76] It is interesting to observe that, in both text and game, these sentiments are not expressed (as stereotype might demand) by the tree-hugging Elves, but instead are put into the mouths of Germanic, greedy-delving Dwarves. Patricia Spacks's observation that "The good love nature, the evil destroy it" is clearly just as valid for this game as it was for the books and the films.[77]

Backe's question asking, "Are game mechanics or semantics anthropocentric, or do they offer alternative perspectives?" is perhaps the most interesting one to use in examining *War in the North* because of the centrality to the story of the admittedly anthropomorphic but nevertheless very nonhuman Great Eagles.[78] There is admittedly a certain philosophic danger in providing a player with the ability to use a consumable item (a Great Feather) to call Beleram from the air to devastate enemies in a single attack, never mind the trope of Eagle-back travel to move characters around Middle-earth willy-nilly, which the creator of Middle-earth himself so disliked. In his detailed written response to the 1958 Zimmerman storyline proposal, Tolkien condemned the "intrusion of the Eagles" as a "major mistake" and their use as a transport mechanism as "*a wholly unacceptable tampering with the tale.*"[79] But the game designers try almost a bit too hard to avoid the artillery-cum-transport-service into which the Eagles' presence might have easily devolved. While it cannot be honestly asserted that they are fully developed as literary characters, this is balanced by the regrettable fact that the main heroes are equally flat. The writers pay at least as much attention to (and actually provide a bit more in the way of backstory dialogue for) Belaram and his winged compatriots Armenel and Baranthor as they do to Andriel, Farin, and Eradan.

Belaram in particular is consistently referenced in dialogue as the companion of the active player character. The game reinforces this idea not only in story but also visually in the ludic framework of the game mechanics; in the lower right corner of the game screen, where stylized icons represent the health levels of both the active character and his or her bipedal companions, the game inserts an equivalent eagle-shaped symbol next to the others when the players travel through landscapes above which he is flying. One co-op reviewer calls him as "the fourth, non-player-controllable member of the party," and his centrality to the storyline extends to the very last battle.[80]

The conversation explaining the motivations of the Great Eagles is worth quoting at length because dialogic repetition is one of the things that so firmly establishes the ethics on display regarding the player's relationship to these noble representatives of a wild natural world. In Rivendell the player has the chance to approach Beleram, by this midpoint of the game a friend and comrade of many adventures, to ask about the other Eagle characters.

> PLAYER: I thought it a rare thing that you offered your aid to us, and hardly expected two more Eagles to do the same. What can you tell me of them?
>
> BELARAM: Armenel is a seasoned warrior. He knows full well what he faces and accepts it gladly. Baranthor is young and eager to prove himself, but he has deep courage and few can match his swiftness on the wing. But you need not take my word. Ask them yourself. They will gladly speak with you if you so desire.[81]

If the player takes his advice, the resulting interactions provide a fully contextualized characterization of the Eagles as beings with agency and both individual and cultural history:

> ARMENEL: Elrond is a generous host, but it is long since I rested in my own aerie.
>
> PLAYER: What can you tell me of your leader, Gwaihir?
>
> ARMENEL: Gwaihir is the Lord of the Eagles. He can outfly the North Wind and his word is law. Long ages of the world have passed since ancient Thorondor, first and greatest of Eagle-lords, soared over Middle-earth, but Gwaihir is the mightiest descendant of that line. He is wise and sees much that others miss.
>
> PLAYER: Are you close in friendship to Radagast?
>
> ARMENEL: Ragadast has been a true friend to the Great Eagles since he first appeared in Middle-earth with the other Wizards many hundreds of years ago. I have called him friend since I was a fledgling. Gandalf, too, is a valued friend, but only Radagast has devoted himself entirely to the welfare of birds and beasts. By doing so, Radagast has also won the loyalty of my kind. . . .

> PLAYER: Were you one of the Eagles that took part in the Battle of Five Armies?
>
> ARMENEL: So I was. When the allied armies found themselves set upon by goblins who had stealthily scaled the mountain slopes, I was among those who set upon the enemy and cast them from the cliffs to perish.
>
> PLAYER: An Eagle rarely offers to carry another on his back. Why do you offer us this rare privilege?
>
> ARMENEL: It was enough for me that Beleram wished to join you. but there is also this: one of the Eagles the Stone-giant slew was my own father. You avenged him, and for that act alone I would bear any of you to the farthest ends of Middle-earth. And though Bargrisar is gone, I still burn with the need for vengeance against the master that sent him against us, Agandaûr. Your enemy is my enemy. I will not rest until he is brought down.[82]

Note the direct mention and detailed justification of Armenel's choice to carry the characters. This recalls the textual friendship of steeds like the great Shadowfax, whom "you do not ride . . . he is willing to carry you—or not," and it also directly references Gandalf's conversation with the Windlord at the utmost pinnacle of the tale: "Twice you have born me, Gwaihir my friend. . . . Thrice shall pay for all, if you are willing."[83] The same motif of choice appears in the second conversation:

> BARANTHOR: It is a fine day for flying, don't you think?
>
> PLAYER: Are you kin to Beleram?
>
> BARANTHOR: No, but he has always guided me. Beleram taught me tricks of the air and secrets of the wind. We often hunt together. He's shown me the fine art of snatching a wild sheep from the side of a mountain and how to dive upon a wolf and pluck hairs from its tail. Wherever Beleram leads, I will follow.
>
> PLAYER: Are you one of the Eagles who came to Bilbo's aid in his quest?
>
> BARANTHOR: I haven't met Bilbo, though I've heard much about him. My father was one of those who carried a Dwarf and later fought in the Battle of Five Armies. I was considered too young and inexperienced to take part in a battle. I have much to do if I'm to match my father's fame and valor.
>
> PLAYER: Great Eagles are not built to carry burdens, Baranthor. I would not have you continue to carry us against your will.
>
> BARANTHOR: I am more than willing! I had long begged the Windlord for a chance to prove myself. I don't fear Orc, goblin or troll. Let's

> return to the air and put the fear into the hearts of our enemies. It is a grand adventure![84]

All of this repetitive insistence on the Eagles' free choices to help the characters is almost certainly intended to address Tolkien's bitter criticism quoted above (of which the game designers must have been aware). But it also has a beneficial side effect of providing the player with a chance to encounter an explicitly nonhuman perspective. Armenel's reminiscence of being a fledgling or Baranthor's description of the thrill of hunting mountain sheep from the air jolt the player into at least a brief moment of imagination about what it must be like to be an awkward eaglet or soar on the wind.

The Eagles, like the Ents, display quite familiar human values despite their nonhuman bodies. The high style of Belaram's speech and the refined accent and sonorous tones of his voice actor evoke a sense of almost overwhelming nobility, and it is specifically a very human concept of nobility, one wholly steeped in the great Northern tradition of which Tolkien was so fond. Some of Armenel and Baranthor's words quoted above could easily have been spoken by Beowulf or Gawain themselves, and both of those Great Eagles perish heroically in battle at the bloody siege of Nordinbad.

Belaram continues the aquiline display of grim Northern courage at the end of the game when, gravely wounded, he flies in to save his friends from Agandaûr's winged fell-beast. He wrestles in the sky with the formidable creature, barely manages to impale it on a spike of the great iron tower, and then crashes to the ground at the player's feet, torn and bleeding. "I could not remain in safety while you three risked your lives, yet again," he explains when the heroes chide him for leaving the Dwarven healers; "I wish to be a part of the final stroke against Agandaûr. The blood of my kin . . . and the bonds of friendship demand as much." If the player presses him to depart, he refuses: "It is not my way to abandon friends in the face of danger . . . and much less so, great-hearted friends who beg me to leave them." At a point in the final battle when the player is most hard-pressed, Belaram offers his aid: "Death would be acceptable if it meant an end to Agandaûr."[85] Players can accept his help, which results in a thrilling cutscene depicting his inevitably heroic death, or they can fight on without him. Those who choose not to sacrifice their friend receive a clear reward for considering the great-hearted winged warrior to be equal to the other members of the small fellowship: a game Achievement titled "Eagle Savior." This is arguably the only instance that the player's desires might conflict with that of an ostensibly environmental actor, but the way that the game encourages the player to embrace a nonhuman character as a companion makes the choice a fairly easy one in the end.

Overall, the sensitive treatment and integral presence of Great Eagle characters, nonhuman in shape but with familiar human values, provide a specific set of mythic circumstances that can be set alongside the carefully developed visual landscapes as an argument for a generally positive ecocritical evaluation of *War in the North*. The game's environmental fidelity to Tolkien's vision, physical as well as moral, allows it to unambiguously reflect the environmental ethics so prevalent throughout the entire Middle-earth legendarium. Indeed, as an interactive property, it arguably goes one step beyond evoking such ethics to providing an opportunity for players to psychologically "try on" how it feels to develop a relationship with a nonhuman character, or fight against overwhelming odds in order to save a carefully preserved place of stunning natural beauty. All of this allows the game to stand solidly in the company of Tolkien's books and Jackson's films as stories that reflect the vastly popular myth of Middle-earth.

It is a hopeful sign that even the most modern technological incarnations of this great tale demonstrate at least some potential for positive environmental influence. Such mythological possibilities will only multiply as Middle-earth continues to expand beyond its simple beginnings between the covers of Tolkien's books. Film and game adaptations have taken their places in the overall universe of Middle-earth, and are now at least as prevalent in the growing online and real-life communities coming together around the ever-increasing number of people who find deep meaning in Tolkien's compelling mythic universe. Considering the fact that mythology is not simply a cosmological or personal experience but a communal one as well, it is perhaps worthwhile to examine how Tolkien's myth has been experienced within, and directly influenced the environmental stories of, such communities of like-minded devotees.

The enthusiastic following enjoyed by the popular culture phenomenon of Middle-earth is in today's critical landscape referred to as a *fandom*. Although this word is a product of early twentieth-century America, and its root *fan* (short for *fanatic*) was used for loyal enthusiasts as far back as the seventeenth century, there is no doubt that groups of people have always enjoyed experiencing mythic delight in social ways.[86] From secular writers in medieval England producing what would today be called Bible fanfiction to the wave of "musicomania" that swept post–Civil War America, "acting in fanlike ways is probably as ancient as culture itself."[87] In today's fractured mythological context, a fandom can be viewed as a "specifically chosen personal myth" that helps its fans fill the gap left by the decline in traditional mythological cycles.[88] For people who find deep mythic identification in a fan object, it becomes as important in their psychological and ethical foundation as any of the more traditional mythological influences present in their cultural stream.

There is no doubt that there is tremendous power in such identification. Outside of stereotypical "geek" myths like *Star Trek* or Harry Potter (or, for that matter, Tolkien), there are the crowds of committed sports fans whose behavior is so heavily influenced by whether their team or fighter wins or loses that both riotous and celebratory mobs have become staples of the nightly news after big games in sports-obsessed places. As the world grows flatter, fan objects continue to expand beyond their original scope to capture the imagination of people vastly removed from their geographic, ethnic, or cultural origins. The UK Premier League team Manchester United has legions of fans around the world, many of whom have never set foot in the United Kingdom. Other examples abound, from the K-pop or anime invasions into the Anglophone cultural sphere, to the statue of Rocky Balboa in Žitište, Serbia, to the huge success of the very Tolkienian high-fantasy *Witcher* franchise in bringing Slavic myth to a wider audience through books, some incredibly popular computer games, and its own Netflix television series.

Tolkien's mythic universe serves as the basis for one of the most powerful and cross-cultural fandoms in existence today. The branches spreading out from the trunk of *The Hobbit* and *The Lord of the Rings* bear fruit in multitudes: all of the various adaptations of the original story mentioned earlier grow there, from radio dramas and audiobooks to Peter Jackson's films to interactive games to the forthcoming television series, but also an entire academic field interrogating the details of the original texts as carefully as others consider Shakespeare or Jane Austen (of which this book is an unabashed example); fan conventions and social media spaces where people of all colors and cultures come together to cosplay as Elves and hobbits; Web site archives collecting and distributing absolute reams of unofficial fan-penned stories set in Middle-earth;

and vast commercial ventures tied in with the films, from official merchandise to a privately owned Tolkien museum in Switzerland to the nascent but growing Middle-earth tourism industry in New Zealand (which actually minted a series of legal tender gold and silver coins commemorative coins bearing images of the filmic Bilbo, Gandalf, Thorin, Elrond, and even Gollum[89]). A quick browse through the Tolkien section of any online bookseller turns up entries in every imaginable genre; there are pop-psychology titles like *The Individuated Hobbit* by Timothy R. O'Neill, the Tolkien edition in Open Court's Popular Culture and Philosophy series cleverly titled The Lord of the Rings *and Philosophy: One Book to Rule Them All,* and even Middle-earth–themed food books with delightfully ridiculous names like *An Unexpected Cookbook* or *Medium Rare and Back Again.* This ubiquity in the popular market speaks volumes about the power of Tolkien's myth to capture the imagination of its fans.

Interestingly, such power often has the potential to place the myths of modern fandoms at the forefront of much societal change. Critics using feminist, ethnic, and queer perspectives to interrogate modern fan objects have contributed, with not a little success, to the positive shift in overall public stories surrounding gender and race inclusivity. From *Star Trek*'s interracial kiss to Jesse Owens's embrace of second-place German long-jumper Luz Long in front of Hitler, from Joss Whedon's long list of unapologetic female warrior characters to celebrated Olympic decathlete Caitlyn Jenner's high-profile gender transition, pop-culture controversies surrounding fandom myths have long been helping to shift the standards of ethical behavior in today's world.[90] Similar examples in the environmental sphere are also not hard to find: a former captain of the Manchester United club cofounded the United Kingdom's Sustainability in Sport initiative; the art-rock band Radiohead completely overhauled their equipment to reduce their carbon footprint and consciously attempted to influence their fans to do the same; and celebrities as diverse as Arnold Schwarzenegger, Prince Harry, Leonardo DiCaprio, Emma Watson, and Natalie Portman have spoken out on climate issues.

Critics from all manner of fields have participated quite enthusiastically in this process of deriving ethical guidance from the mythic properties of Tolkien's pop-culture phenomenon. Popular Christian writers in particular seem to find deep and endless inspiration in Middle-earth; Bible-themed Tolkien books for general readers range from the fairly scholarly and theological *Tolkien's Sacramental Vision* by Craig Bernthal to pleasantly chatty devotionals like *Walking with Bilbo* and *Walking with*

Frodo by Sarah Arthur or the straightforward *A Hobbit Devotional: Bilbo Baggins and the Bible* by Ed Strauss. Some of the ecocritical works important to this study might also overlap a bit with such a list, particularly Susan Jeffers's *Arda Inhabited* or *Ents, Elves, and Eriador* by Matthew Dickerson and Jonathan Evans. (Dickerson is also the author of *A Hobbit Journey*, a broader study of Tolkien's ethics from a generally Christian perspective.)

Unfortunately, writers with darker designs are just as able to access this inspirational power to create change, and some of these find Middle-earth to be fertile ground in which to sow their dangerous seeds. David Ibata observes that "For years, Tolkien scholars have waged a fight on two fronts: against an academic establishment that for the most part refused to take the author's work seriously, and against white supremacists who have tried to claim the professor as one of their own," and it is distressingly easy to dig up questionable sympathies hiding in some of the darker recesses of Tolkien criticism.[91] Examples abound; a particularly illustrative one resides in Tolkien biographer and literary critic Joseph Pearce. A former member of the National Front who participated in several violent protests and was imprisoned in the United Kingdom on two separate occasions for "publishing material deemed likely to incite racial hatred," he is the author of *Tolkien: Man and Myth* and *Tolkien: A Celebration* (as well as a book on Merrie England mentioned in chapter 6 above).[92] He has since converted to Catholicism, a conversion he attributes to reading Catholic writers such as Tolkien and G. K. Chesterton in prison. Although he has publicly renounced both the National Front and all forms of overt race hatred, he still holds such quieter views as the condemnation of the multicultural effects of immigration on Britain as "an unmitigated disaster."[93] These days his writings are less inflammatory but they nevertheless share space with the shadowy areas of extreme cultural conservatism to which racists have retreated in the face of changing public attitudes. The fact that he distances himself from white nationalism today does little to discourage others in the movement from citing his work, particularly his Tolkien criticism, in support of their cause. But this unpleasant fact only highlights the vast potential of Tolkien's powerful modern myth to capture the public imagination and shift cultural stories for good or ill.

Because of its undeniably positive environmental themes, the fact that Tolkien's work serves as a deep well of mythic instruction for its fans can be a very encouraging thought to anyone concerned about the destructive stories surrounding modern humanity and its relationship with the natural world. Brian Rosebury suggests that "of all the sceptical responses to the modern world which are manifest in Tolkien's work, this romantic protest against the despoliation of nature is the one which has gained greatest retrospective force since his death, as well as the one which has the deepest roots in his personal life, and the one which most comprehensively informs his work."[94] While environmental philosophy can be heavy going for nonspecialist readers, and self-professed nature writers often lack a compelling story to bring their work to a greater audience than those already inclined to appreciate their poetically Romantic ramblings, the broad appeal and mythic power of Tolkien fandom offer a tremendous opportunity to bring a positive shift in stories about the environment, and an associated change in behavior, to a much wider audience.

The mythic link between Middle-earth and committed environmental activism clearly visible today was established quite early in the history of the movement. In her book *Fantasy, the Bomb, and the Greening of Britain*, Meredith Veldman discusses in detail the common origins and influences shared by the culture of protest of the 1960s and Tolkien's Middle-earth. She asserts that "both grew out of a reaction against the triumph of industrialism and empiricism in British thought and culture. Fundamentally romantic, they both asserted the primacy of the suprarational and the nonmaterial," and argues that Middle-earth's "romantic attitudes toward the environment, technology, and the role of the individual and the community within society matched the context of the culture of protest."[95] Such resonance probably goes a long way toward explaining the curious attraction of the work of a stuffy Oxford don, so conservative as to be nearly reactionary, to the notoriously freewheeling and postmodern culture that arose in the West in the second half of the twentieth century.

Explicit examples are easy to find. Canadian Maude Barlow famously describes the horrors of the Alberta tar sands as "Canada's Mordor": "Like the fictional barren land, home to the evil Sauron in JRR Tolkien's Middle Earth, the tar sands are vast, destructive and represent the real-life death of nature. The air is foul; water is being poisoned and drained. Large tracts of forest and wetlands are being torn from the earth, and in the gaping holes where life once thrived sit giant ponds of toxic waste."[96]

Robert Hunter of Greenpeace described in explicitly Tolkienian terms the "mythical overtone" of the nuclear protests that launched that organization: "We are like Bilbo Baggins and the dwarves attempting to get to the lair of Smaug. No—more like the Fellowship of the Ring—the Ring of Power, which for us is the closed-circle ecology symbol—and we are on our way to the dread dark land of Mordor, and Amchitka is Mount Doom, and Cannikin is the very Crack of Doom. Somehow we have to hurl the Ring of Power into the fire and bring down the whole kingdom of the Dark Lord."[97]

David McTaggart, on another Greenpeace sea voyage a year later, was just as explicit: "I had been reading *The Lord of the Rings*. I could not avoid thinking of parallels between our own little fellowship and the long journey of the Hobbits into the volcano-haunted land of Mordor, home of the dark Lord who lived in his fortress surrounded by fierce armies, his Evil Eye scanning, scanning, scanning for intruders."[98] Such conscious awareness of the relationship between a myth and the behavior it inspires is unusual, but activists often have a deep understanding of how stories can be used to inspire people to overcome community scruples and take actions bordering on the criminal.

Unfortunately, that border has often been crossed by those using Tolkien as justification for their actions. The infamous The Earth Liberation Front (ELF), an anarchic offshoot of the already-radical Earth First! organization, conducts severe ecotage and sanctions extreme violence in defense of Mother Earth, and they cite Tolkien just as explicitly as Greenpeace does. The claim is not a tenuous one, either. Tolkien wrote to his son Christopher in 1943 asserting that "My political opinions lean more and more to anarchy. . . . There is only one bright spot and that is the growing habit of disgruntled men of dynamiting factories and power stations; I hope that, encouraged now as 'patriotism', may remain a habit! But it won't do any good, if it is not universal."[99] Writing in the *Earth First! Journal* in 2002, James Bell explicitly cites this letter in support of his assertion that "Tolkien would have approved of today's 'elves,' those of the Earth Liberation Front. It is a fact that Tolkien was deeply troubled by the impact of modern industry and technology on the world's environment," and goes on to argue that "Tolkien's heroes turn the tool of the enemy against itself, tossing it into the fires of the Crack of Doom like a monkeywrench thrown into the gears of a machine."[100] Political scientist Jonathan Matusitz, in a book discussing terrorist symbolism and motivation, noted the presence of two main myths in the inspiration of the ELF, both of which are important to the mythological wilderness ideas under discussion here: the life, achievements, and writings of Aldo Leopold, and the life and writings of J. R. R. Tolkien. "The ecoterrorist movement exalts Tolkien as a true role model of environmentalism that everyone should emulate," Matusitz asserts; "to the eyes of ELF activists, the mythological characters created by J. R. R. Tolkien and the philosophical foundations that characterized his environmentalism have offered those activists concrete ideas based on which they can take action."[101] This association with ecoterrorists is nearly as problematic as that with white nationalists and rather more germane to the mythological and ecocritical goals of this study.

The truth is that activists, violent or otherwise, are by definition deeply committed to their ideals, so their appreciation of Tolkien is just as likely to be a supporting resonance as a proximate cause of their activities. Tolkien's text is nearly biblical in its diversity of sentiments; both the soldier deployed in a combat zone and the peace-loving protestor can legitimately find mythical instruction and ethical validation in *The Lord of the Rings,* and those who believe in the necessity for radical action in the first place will easily find justification for their activities if they look for it. But it is possible to categorically condemn violent terrorism (or, for that matter, white nationalism) while acknowledging the skillful way such organizations tap into and operationalize the mythic power of Middle-earth to influence people's behavior.

One very important point rises out of all of this: the idea that good people have just as much right as evil ones to access this cultural power for change. In a sense, this is the whole point of this mythological study in the first place; if the stories that people tell themselves about the natural world make them act in destructive ways, then pulling those unconscious stories into consciousness, and consciously replacing them with less-destructive ones, has great potential to shift people into less-destructive behavior.

But there is a danger here. Tales of angry activists certainly demonstrate the vast power of mythic influence on communal behavior, and the presence of Tolkien's myth in the cultural stream of many environmental agitators, from arsonists invoking Treebeard as they set fire to a Maryland housing development[102] to vandals scrawling "another bit of Mordor" on ugly construction projects,[103] is absolutely crystal clear. But there are many more fans of Tolkien beyond small groups of anarchic Elves firebombing logging trucks or alt-right white power devotees haunting the dark reaches of Stormfront or Parler online. Especially considering how attacks on people or property or associations with distasteful movements can make nonactivist fans feel threatened or defensive, focusing too heavily on such radical connections can be ultimately counterproductive in the context of trying to change people's stories.

Thankfully, the wider mythological momentum is shifting. Support for wilderness preservation is growing. Scientific fields like ecology are beginning to encourage the more utilitarian conservation movement to take into account value-oriented concepts such as ecosystem sustainability and biodiversity. Trends from community recycling to ecotourism are on the rise, and as the cost of human destruction in the guise of progress becomes less and less easy to ignore, more and more people may become receptive to the positive environmental ethics and ideals in Tolkien's work. The three concepts of wilderness in Middle-earth collectively draw deep cultural legitimacy from the ancient springs that nourished them as well as powerful current authority from the twentieth-century myth they animate. Consequently, they present several intriguing possibilities for powerful mythic instruction in the minds of the vast majority of ordinary, nonviolent, nonactivist fans of Middle-earth, who may nevertheless be concerned about the continued primacy of destructive environmental stories.

CHAPTER NINE

Tolkienian Courage and Wilderness Today

From a mythological point of view, the modern environmental movement can be seen as an effort set up in opposition to the dangerous stories underlying the human activities causing widespread natural devastation around the world. The power of those stories to cause breathtaking destruction is undeniable and has been exhaustively detailed by the many fields emerging under the rubric of green studies. It is almost too easy to find millions of words describing in exact and overwhelming detail what humanity has done wrong over the years. Sometimes it can feel like every one of those words, however well intentioned, only adds more energy to the ever-increasing forces arrayed against the concepts ostensibly being defended. The recognition that the stories of the environmentalists themselves might be part of the problem is rather less well recognized—but, slowly, that too is beginning to change. An oft-quoted line in Michael Shellenberger and Ted Norhaus's controversial 2004 polemic "The Death of Environmentalism" concludes that "environmentalists need to tap into the creative worlds of myth-making, even religion, not to better sell narrow and technical policy proposals but rather to figure out who we are and who we need to be."[1] Similarly, philosopher Kathleen Dean Moore notes that "If it is critical to engage the public in ethical arguments about our relation to the land, and if the usual forms of philosophical prose are utterly unable to do this, how do we philosophers raise the quality and quantity of public ethical discourse? One answer is through ripping stories, powerfully and beautifully told."[2] A despairing ecocritical mythologist can certainly find hope in such statements.

Unfortunately, such hope is often disappointed. What little creative work extant today actively undertaken to counteract destructive environmental stories tends to be heavy-handed and painfully preachy. As ethically sound as the rhymes of Dr. Seuss's *The Lorax* or the cliché-bound treatment of the sweeping and endangered jungle paradise of James Cameron's film *Avatar* may be, their mythic power has proven limited, mostly attracting an audience who already subscribes to the values those works espouse. The major problem with such explicitly allegorical works is that, well, they are allegory. Much like the wooden didacticism of old-fashioned children's stories weighed down by too much moralizing, they reek of the "purposed domination of the author" that Tolkien cites as the reason behind his own dislike and distrust of allegory.[3] A work whose message is more important than its story is no real story, and this is as true of today's explicitly green fiction as it was of insipid Christian allegory in Dark Ages Britain, where authorities complained that Christians were listening to harpers and heathen songs instead of attending to the word of God. *Quid enim Hinieldus cum Christo* indeed.[4]

A partial solution to this problem, and one that the best of modern ecocriticism is beginning to provide, is the act of highlighting and promoting positive environmental themes in stories that are genuinely popular in their own right. As has been extensively discussed above, Tolkien's Middle-earth legendarium lends itself well to such an analysis. Considering the positive light in which the various concepts of wilderness are portrayed in Tolkien's stories, and considering that the broad appeal of the Middle-earth legendarium overlaps and in many cases extends far beyond the subset of environmentally minded individuals in the general population, greater exposure to the ethical elements of Tolkien's environmental themes may help to counteract at least some of the more destructive elements of other current stories.

One of the most important such elements, one so fundamental to Western civilization that it arguably lies at the root of all truly destructive myths, is also one that Tolkien's work arguably addresses quite well: the concept that the human animal is somehow separate from, rather than a part of, the environment in which it lives, breathes, eats, breeds, and dies. It is not just antienvironmental industrialist trolls who hold such a belief; the separation story is the inheritance of all intellectual children of Aristotle and Descartes, and even the most ardent defenders of wilderness can fall prey to it. As William Cronon suggests, it is a paradox: "wilderness embodies a dualistic vision in which the human is entirely outside the natural. . . . To the extent that we celebrate wilderness as the measure with which we judge civilization, we reproduce the dualism that sets humanity and nature at opposite poles."[5] The environmentalist version of this dualism is inverted from that of the modernist, to be sure, but in neither case are humans considered part of the natural world. Susan Jeffers articulates both the problem and Tolkien's place in helping to solve it: "The political goal of greater environmental awareness, sympathy, and legislation ties in closely with a particular morality favored by those in 'green studies,' which at its most reductive turns into 'Nature equals Good,' 'People equals Bad,' and 'People do not equal Nature.' Tolkien's representation of Middle-earth is an antidote to this oversimplification as it demonstrates the falseness of this separation and the danger implicit in supporting such a division."[6] As the modern environmental movement inevitably arises out of the same mythological grounding as the problem it seeks to address, it is not surprising that it finds such dualism much easier to invert than to escape. Tolkien's work is, as Jeffers argues, well suited to counteract such dualistic dangers, especially in the admirable mythic examples of human action it provides.

It is definitely important to remember that all of Tolkien's wilderness ideas have their shadow sides, and to acknowledge that the shadows cast by Tolkien's work darken other realms besides the wilderness one. The fact that Tolkien's entire œuvre is incredibly popular in white nationalist circles—not to mention the disturbing overlap between those circles and some environmental ones, to the point that "the menace of ecofascism" is entering the awareness of environmental thinkers—is something that could stand to be addressed more directly, both in Tolkien criticism and ecocriticism in general.[7] But the danger of these dark ideas lessens the more they are brought into the light of consciousness. The fact that racist skinheads use Tolkien's work for their own destructive purposes does not invalidate its power to inspire people who are not racist skinheads, and it does not automatically follow that good people will become racist skinheads if they find inspiration in Middle-earth. It is possible to acknowledge the racist and reductionist and parochial elements in Tolkien's resonance with the three aspects of American wilderness philosophy under discussion here while also taking advantage of the positive mythic guidance they can provide.

Once people become conscious of how the stories they tell themselves about the wilderness influence the way they interact with the natural world, they become able to consciously choose to identify with the positive examples in the stories that inspire them, and it is these positive examples that have the greatest potential to shape positive human behavior. This chapter will therefore intentionally focus on ways that identifying with characters representative of Tolkien's wilderness ideas can inspire people to act in positive ways.

So, with due acknowledgment of problematic pasts and cautious hope for better futures, the important question arises: What might the Middle-earth legendarium, with its clear belief in the inherent value of wildness and wild places, be able to contribute to the mythic vocabulary of ordinary people seeking to improve the overall human relationship with wilderness and the natural world?

Before proposing any answers, it is worthwhile to stop and reflect on the true immensity of the problem. Broadly examined, environmental issues—whether more subtle ones like climate change or aggressive ones like the reckless destruction of an acre and a half of rainforest every second of every day—are utterly overwhelming to consider, and become more so the longer and more carefully they are considered. Even if those great problems are set aside and the focus reduced to a narrower one, like the accelerating decline of wilderness lands more relevant to this study, the outlook is grim at best. The harsh reality of environmental science, set next to the desperate denial its hopelessness tends to evoke in people willing to consider it in the first place, creates an intellectual and emotional atmosphere of turmoil and gloomy despondency, so much so that one environmental psychologist has called this "the most psychologically trying time in all of human history."[8] Small acts like recycling or paying to plant trees to offset a cross-country flight feel like applying Band-Aids to a sucking chest wound. The steps that everyone knows they should be taking are uncomfortable, even painful, and a normal rationalization impulse inflates them immediately into great hardships: give up travel, give up meat, give up the taste of tropical fruit, give up climate control and running water, give up all the benefits of modern life? No. Much easier to ignore the problem, argue it away, or simply remain in denial, guiltily kicking the can down the road for a generation (or two, assuming the human race lasts that long). The most likely emotion waiting at the end of the line for anyone who pays too much attention to environmental crises is one very familiar to anyone living in the modern world: despair.

Tolkien had definite opinions about despair—and about the only right and true way to combat it, which he overwhelmingly presents as a certain kind of courage. Tolkien argues in his famous lecture on *Beowulf* that "it is the strength of the northern mythological imagination that it . . . put the monsters in the centre, gave them victory but no honour, and found a potent but terrible solution in naked will and courage," and goes on to assert his firm belief that this imagination "has power, as it were, to revive its spirit even in our own times."[9] Tom Shippey concentrates Tolkien's many arguments on this point into the concise, if slightly dismal, statement that "even ultimate defeat does not turn right into wrong."[10] It is clear that Shippey believes this to be one of Tolkien's most important themes; various discussions of courage in the face of despair are a strong current running through nearly all of his critical commentary on Tolkien's work.

Shippey claims that "a major goal of *The Lord of the Rings* was to dramatise that 'theory of courage'" proposed in the *Beowulf* lecture, and he explores the possibility elsewhere that Tolkien may have even believed such courage to be "ethically superior to the Classical if not to the Christian world-view, in that it demanded commitment to virtue without any offer of lasting reward."[11] He asserts quite firmly that, while "it may not be possible to draw any certain *correct* conclusion from the confusions and bewilderments of Middle-earth, it is possible to see one always marked as unequivocally and permanently *wrong*: which is, that there is no point in trying any further."[12] In a personal essay for a general newspaper audience, Shippey boils down Tolkien's guidance even more simply: "the one thing definitely wrong is giving up, losing hope."[13] This, then, Shippey might argue, is Tolkien's message, not just for environmentalists but for all good peoples engaging in battles with destructive evil: no matter how desperate the odds, no matter how certain the failure or how utter the coming defeat, it is morally inexcusable to give in to despair.

This is certainly a rather harsh and uncompromising statement. In a different context, one of championing specific government policies, or defining specific actions to be taken against specific physical threats, it might even be considered a pointless one, akin to suggesting an uplifting song to the bandleader on the sinking *Titanic*. But this study is more concerned about the stories behind destructive actions than the actions themselves, and seeks only to highlight how the myth of Middle-earth might provide different stories that might help inspire different actions. Climate scientists, government policy makers, and corporate boards all have a part to play in the defining crisis of this age. To shore up research and legislation and sustainability initiatives, a mythologist can only offer stories; a vain endeavor, perhaps, or even an absurd one, but (following Shippey, and ultimately Tolkien) preferable to submitting without a struggle to the emptiness of hopeless resignation.

All of this grim Northern bleakness might seem to indicate a priority of Tolkien's Germanic wilderness over the others as a source for mythic guidance on modern environmental issues, but in truth all three of his wilderness concepts have something to add to such a discussion. All three of them depict lands that are wild, and even the harshest can be understood as portraying that wildness in a positive light. All three are deeply linked with memorable and beloved characters who have taken up residence in the cultural mythos of the twenty-first century. By examining those representative characters with the aim of understanding how they manifest Tolkien's particular breed of courage, it may be possible to gain some ideas about what a "manful deed within their measure" might look like to modern humans attempting to face the overwhelming dark forces of this late Fourth Age.[14]

Inclusivity aside, it does still make sense to begin where Tolkien himself did, in the dark and monster-hunted forests of the North. Tolkien's first concept of wilderness is mythically the deepest-connected one, as well as the one he developed most completely. In seeking an evocative personalization of it to emulate, readers have many options from which to choose. One of the earliest and most obvious is the hard-bitten Dwarves (especially Thorin and company in *The Hobbit*), with their Norse names, grim heroics in the face of certain doom, and unquestionable origins in the darkest of Northern European myth cycles. But the general relationship between the Dwarves and the natural world of Middle-earth is almost too archaic, even for Tolkien; theirs is the world of darkness and danger only just beginning to be mitigated by the Romantic beauty, or even the Anglo-Saxon concept of shelter in woodlands, which, while not strictly Eddaic, are still integral to Tolkien's first wilderness concept. Also, the Dwarves of Middle-earth are the creations of Aulë, the great smith and craftsman of the Valar, and Aulë's gifts to the Children of Ilúvatar lie in the fields of knowledge, skill, and invention. From an ecocritical perspective, the heroic Dwarves almost feel more like a positive personalization of technology in the world rather than any personal evocation of wild places.

The Ents would be another eminently logical choice. Treebeard and his people are quite literally an anthropomorphic representation of the deep strength of dark Germanic forest powers; they are trees that walk and talk and, much as might be expected of such beings, have their own perspective on things—a perspective that is completely outside the petty affairs of humans and Elves. The Ents certainly have much to teach modern humans about the validity of considering nonhuman perspectives, and as a consequence they have been popular topics in a good deal of existing Tolkien ecocriticism. Rather than restate the large amount of general agreement in the research and analysis of scholars like Jeffers or Curry or Dickerson and Evans, however, this study will refer readers to their excellent work, and consider instead the guidance to be found in a third group, an admirable subset of Tolkien's race of humans: the hardy, strong, brave, and noble Dúnedain.

Reassuringly familiar in their humanity, and drawing on the full breadth of Western cultural narratives, Tolkien's Rangers are the kind of thrilling action heroes with whom even nonfantasy readers can find space to identify. Aragorn, *the* Dúnadan and the quintessential Ranger, manages at one point or another to tick off pretty much every quality expected of heroic protagonists in modern genre fiction: he is variously portrayed as a skilled solitary woodsman and a brilliant leader of armies, a master of lore and a master of weapons, a killer and a healer, a kind friend and a dangerous enemy, a Ranger and a paladin, an outsider and a king. As Strider, he is associated with what would today be termed *wilderness experience*, protecting the Shire from wandering monsters and guiding the hobbit heroes through the wild lands of Eriador to Rivendell and beyond. As leader of the Grey Company, he has the strength and fortitude to journey through the darkest of wild lands and inspire his followers to do the same. As ruler of Gondor he represents (and is represented by) the restoration and renewal of the White Tree in the court of the kings, and the flowering of the golden age of humanity at the beginning of the Fourth Age. Aragorn serves the tale as a convenient mythological shorthand for the positive Germanic hero-king, and by extension the concept of wilderness within which such heroes stand.

So what does this inexhaustible Ranger of Rangers and dauntingly majestic King of Gondor have to teach less stupendous modern Westerners about relating to wild nature? The courage of Aragorn is the courage of fortitude, that most Germanic of heroic traits. Verlyn Flieger describes his archetypal attributes thusly: "Strider—silent, watchful, road weary—

is an attractive figure. His steely presence, his air of being someone dangerous to cross, his resourcefulness in crisis, evoke a character out of the mythic American West—the stranger in town—cool, alert, alone. He has that quiet toughness we associate with our folk heroes."[15] Importantly, like many such folk heroes, Aragorn was not forced into a life of adventure. The young fosterling Estel, named by Elrond for a mysterious trusting hope that cannot be "defeated by the ways of the world, for it does not come from experience, but from our nature and first being," was the orphaned descendant of a line of kings.[16] He could have stayed safe and comfortable in Rivendell, married a nice third cousin from Eriador, and ensured the survival of his bloodline; indeed, prudence would dictate that he had the obligation to do exactly that rather than to go endangering himself with many decades of monster hunting and perilous journeys in the wilderness. But, as pleasant a place as Rivendell was, Aragorn knew he would have to leave its boundaries if he wanted to become the person he was meant to be. "He went out into the wild," Tolkien says, and in doing so he "became at last the most hardy of living Men."[17] He made his heroic choice.

This, then, might be Aragorn's mythic instruction to people concerned about wilderness issues today: Get outside. Go out into the wild. Leave the safety of the comfort zone illuminated by the circle of civilization's light and experience real wildness on its own terms, humbly, with preparation and respect, and—most importantly—seek there the attribute of fortitude. One who ventures out in this mythic mode can expect to become a stronger and better person as a result.

Ecologist and environmental biologist Peter Kareiva finds cause for alarm in a 2008 study (using data from Spain, Japan, and the United States), which demonstrates a widespread decline in nature-based recreation; he suggests that this trend "ultimately may be far more foreboding for the environment than even declining tropical forest cover or increasing greenhouse gas emissions" and concludes grimly that, assuming "successful nature conservation and sustainable ecosystems will require a battle for the hearts and minds of people," it could be that "the pervasive decline in nature recreation may well be the world's greatest environmental threat."[18] This concern echoes the research and associated activism of people such as Richard Louv, author of the best-selling book *Last Child in the Woods* and originator of the term "nature-deficit disorder," who argues fervently that "a reconnection to the natural world is fundamental to human health, well-being, spirit, and survival."[19] There are certainly many possible causes and influences behind such a trend. Kareiva cites increasing urbanization as a factor,[20] Louv condemns the "electronic bubble" of video games and constant connectivity,[21] and economic or racial inequities in access to nature experience are in many places not insignificant. But whatever the cause, the result is the same: an increasing number of people lack personal experience of real wildness in its natural state.

In this kind of world, where electricity and internet access are elevated to equal status with food and water as necessities for life, it would seem that more and more people are choosing not to travel to places where their electronic tethers do not reach. To do without social media or air conditioning feels a great hardship, even before the possibilities of unpleasant physical exertion or biting insects or getting rained on arise to make a proposed natural experience seem even more distasteful. However melodramatic it might seem, it does take a solid amount of courage for such people to consider venturing outside of their comfort zones. Going on a quest to the nearest national park or other wilderness area, or even out for a walk in the local woods, may not seem like much compared to daring the gaping black door to the Paths of the Dead—but the difference is more one of degree than substance.

It could be argued that there are those for whom identifying with the admittedly overachieving Aragorn may feel like a stretch. There are increasing numbers of people in the Western world who have never been outside at night beyond the reach of artificial lighting; for them, the idea of venturing out into dark and wild places might feel only slightly less fantastic than battling a dragon. But even here the Rangers provide good guidance, and not only in metaphorical terms. Critics overwhelmingly agree that the hobbits serve Tolkien as anachronistic stand-ins for modern humanity navigating the ideals and challenges of the ancient heroic world, and this situation is no exception. It is not without purpose that Tolkien takes the time to comment approvingly on how venturing out of Bree in Strider's care expands the idea of what is possible in the minds of Frodo and his friends:

> The hobbits felt refreshed, as if they had had a night of unbroken sleep. Already they were getting used to much walking on short commons—shorter at any rate than what in the Shire they would have thought barely enough to keep them on their legs. Pippin declared that Frodo was looking twice the hobbit that he had been.

> "Very odd," said Frodo, tightening his belt, "considering that there is actually a good deal less of me."[22]

Bilbo, too, is clearly changed for the better by his adventures, and hobbits doing nothing but staying inside would hardly be a story worth reading. Who would consciously choose Fatty Bolger's fate of languishing in the lockholes over all of the wonder and excitement that Merry and Pippin got to see and experience after they left the Shire with Frodo and Sam?

Such Ranger-inspired encouragement to seek wilderness experience does not need to be imagined as some sort of huge Germanic hero-quest (although for those with the inclination or means, it certainly can be). That all-important internet access does more than download cat pictures and enable online gaming; it also connects outdoor enthusiasts of all conceivable persuasions, making it much easier to find town park maps or birding resources or local hiking groups than it ever was in the preinternet age. The power of social media can connect anyone to a nearly unlimited number of free resources to help them experience the natural wildness even in the most urban places. As modern-day hobbits get more comfortable with traveling, there are wilderness outfitters willing to provide logistical support for and expert guidance through every imaginable outdoor adventure, covering the full continuum of excitement (and expense) from exploring coastal tidepools to climbing Mount Everest. Those who cannot imagine being Rangers can still take small steps toward participating mythically in this wilderness concept by finding Rangers to guide them.

There is a small but growing movement of outdoor education initiatives beginning to make a mark on modern Western culture, from once-a-week experiments with forest schools to middle-grade field trips to national parks to virtual and augmented reality experiences specifically engineered to encourage the technologically obsessed to go outside. There is also the continued proliferation and success of early twentieth-century wilderness experience programs like Outward Bound (whose motto of likely Tennysonian provenance, "To serve, to strive, and not to yield," could nevertheless hardly be more Tolkienian). These initiatives are encouraging, certainly, but in the grand scheme of things they are still quite rare or even financially or physically inaccessible to large swathes of the Western population. If more Tolkien fans could be encouraged to notice the mythological link between programs like these and their wilderness-wise heroes, it might help expand awareness of and desire for the programs, and perhaps even bring their well-attested benefits to people who might not otherwise consider such things to be for them. But even without any organized activities or external structures, the example of Aragorn can still serve as at least a small story-based nudge to get humans out into nature; until that happens on a wider scale, as the research on recreation cited above so clearly warns, it is possible that progress on any other environmental lines of effort will only continue to stall.

One of the most significant and defining characteristics of Tolkien's Rangers is their close association with Elves. In the long years between the death of Isildur and Aragorn's triumph, the line of heirs is protected by Elrond, whose sons often ride "out upon errantry . . . with the Rangers of the North."[23] Similarly, listening to the speech of the "Dúnedain of the South, men of the line of the Lords of Westernesse" who make up Faramir's company in Ithilien, Frodo is amazed to discover that "it was the elven-tongue that they spoke, or one but little different."[24] Throughout the story the Dúnedain are presented as greater and wiser than other courageous human peoples such as the Rohirrim, and Tolkien implies quite strongly that this greatness and wisdom is due as much to their less complete estrangement from the Elves as to the purity of their bloodline.

The courage of the Elves differs somewhat from that of the Rangers, or perhaps more accurately goes beyond it, in the same way the Elves differ from and are beyond humans. For while there is no doubt that the fortitude of Tolkien's Elven heroes is equal to or greater than that of the greatest of his human ones, the immortal Elves all have the gift (and curse) of memory. Gimli describes, a bit wistfully, how the memory of Elves "is more like to the waking world than to a dream."[25] This means that in temperament the Elves are generally "overburdened with sadness and nostalgic regret."[26] Still, although many Elves do fall into a sort of depressive hopelessness and choose to leave Middle-earth, this nostalgia also breeds the deepest of resolve in those who choose to stay. The Elves live long enough to truly experience the unceasing and inescapable decline of the world, and yet—despite their perfect memory of what has been lost, and their full knowledge of their ultimate failure—they still work tirelessly to preserve what beauty remains. This is courage of a higher sort: the courage not only to face evil and destroy it, but to watch it grow again despite all of the blood and pain spent to defeat it, and then spend more blood and pain to defeat it again only to see it rise again, over and over and over. It is a psychological fortitude every bit the match of the physical courage of Tolkien's human heroes.

Tolkien frequently chooses Elves as his mouthpiece to express the thematic core of his idea of courage in the face of despair. Despite the long memory of Elrond, who had "seen three ages in the West of the world, and many defeats, and many fruitless victories" before the events of the War of the Ring, or the even longer memory of Galadriel, who tells sadly how "ere the fall of Nargothrond or Gondolin, I passed over the mountains, and together through ages of the world we have fought the long defeat," these two great warriors and loremasters are the most ardent and powerful foes of the Dark Lord.[27] It is they who speak the strongest words in support of continued resistance. "There is naught that you can do, other than to resist, with hope or without it," Elrond grimly informs the emissary of the Dwarves to his council.[28] "The love of the Elves for their land and their works is deeper than the depths of the Sea, and their regret is undying and cannot ever wholly be assuaged. Yet they will cast all away rather than submit to Sauron," Galadriel tells a confused and irresolute Frodo.[29] Both of these great characters are portrayed as sacrificing everything, including the sum total of the creative work of their impossibly long lives, to defeat the great enemy—and even as they do this, they know that even that victory will not stand. They will eventually be obliged to pass forever out of the Middle-earth they love so much.

If, among all of Tolkien's hard-handed heroes, the Ranger of Rangers is Aragorn, the most Elven of his Elves is Galadriel, whom he explicitly describes as the "mightiest and fairest of all the Elves that remained in Middle-earth" in the Third Age.[30] She is, like Aragorn, a being of monumental physical courage. *The Silmarillion* tells how she was among the Noldor treacherously abandoned by Fëanor; that valiant host "wandered long in misery, but their valor and endurance grew with hardship; for they were a mighty people . . . not yet weary with the weariness of Earth. The fire of their hearts was young, and led by Fingolfin and his sons, and by Finrod and Galadriel, they dared to pass into the bitterest North; and finding no other way they endured at last the terror of the Helcaraxë and the cruel hills of ice. Few of the deeds of the Noldor thereafter surpassed that desperate crossing in hardihood or woe."[31]

To those familiar only with Cate Blanchett's gently graceful film portrayal, or even the distant Marian figure or target of courtly love the less observant reader of *The Lord of the Rings* might take her to be, this description of Galadriel's physical fortitude may come as a bit of surprise. So also might the tale of her leaving Valinor with her kinsmen, "standing tall and valiant among the contending princes" because she "yearned to see the wide unguarded lands and to rule there a realm at her own will."[32] The steely resolve of the White Lady of Lórien is built on a foundation of wilderness trials far surpassing any mere child of men.

Still, despite the fact that she is heroic and does rule, Galadriel's mythic legacy in the Middle-earth legendarium is not that of the heroic ruler archetype so clearly presented in Aragorn. She is instead a preserver, a healer, a powerful and inspiring, almost religious, figure of distant beauty and all-knowing wisdom. "I owe much of this character to Christian and Catholic teaching and imagination about Mary," Tolkien admitted of Galadriel, but she also draws more than a little upon sovereignty goddesses associated with the Celtic overlay landscapes of which her timelessly beautiful realm of Lothlórien is a direct evocation.[33] As such, she is an illuminating choice for a character to serve as a mythic shorthand for Tolkien's second concept of wilderness.

In the context of wilderness philosophy, the difference between Aragorn and Galadriel reflects the typical conservation/preservation split. Aragorn's character reflects the sort of rugged, outdoorsy type common on the conservation side, while Galadriel's is more in line with the Romantic spiritual attitudes of preservation. In the extended version of Peter Jackson's film *The Fellowship of the Ring*, there is a brief scene where Aragorn returns to camp with a smallish buck deer slung over his shoulders; while there is almost zero direct textual evidence for this episode, it fits the modern Ranger character archetype to a *T*, and would look perfectly at home alongside the hunting tips and fishing lure ads of a publication like *Field & Stream* or *Outside*. The Sorceress of the Golden Wood, however, walking gracefully among the soaring trees and unstained rivers of her Otherworldly home, would be much more likely to grace the pages of an ecoporn calendar sent out by Muir's Sierra Club or Leopold's Wilderness Society. Despite these differences, however, the two concepts are less opposing than complementary ones, and Tolkien does an admirable job of marrying them in Middle-earth. If Aragorn's example mythically encourages people to get outside into the wild, Galadriel's might be seen as exhorting them to seek out and work to preserve the beauty that can be found there.

In 2016 a group of Australian scientists published an article in the journal *Current Biology* with the alarming and unequivocal title "Catastrophic Declines in Wilderness Areas Undermine Global Environment Targets," which quantified "alarming losses comprising one-tenth . . . of global wilderness areas over the last two decades" and assessed that what increases in wilderness protection policy had occurred were "failing to keep pace with the rate of wilderness loss."[34] Their analysis enumerates a laundry list of familiar enemies of wild lands: "industrial forestry, oil and gas exploration, anthropogenic fire, and rapid climate change."[35] Even allowing for some politically expedient quibbling about the last one, these threats to wilderness are overwhelmingly related to human activity.

Two years later, in the more well-known and prestigious journal *Nature,* some of the same scientists published an even more alarming article detailing the ways that humans are destroying the remains of the only thing that may help protect them from their destructive selves. Watson and his colleagues warn that "Earth's remaining wilderness areas are increasingly important buffers against the effects of climate change and other human impacts," and propose significant international policy changes to "prevent Earth's intact ecosystems from disappearing completely."[36] They also lament that "Wild places are facing the same extinction crisis as species," note that five countries—Russia, Canada, Australia, the United States, and Brazil—account for more than 70 percent of the world's remaining wilderness areas, and argue persuasively for local and national action to "limit the expansion of roads and shipping lanes, and to rein in large-scale developments in mining, forestry, agriculture, aquaculture and industrial fishing."[37] Their message is clear, and their voices are only a few among the growing chorus of scientists sounding alarms about the catastrophic loss of wild places—and such alarms are based on solid, scientific, physical evidence and reasoning quite apart from any aesthetic or spiritual Romantic appreciation for transcendent natural beauty.

Such loss of wilderness areas to the encroachment of civilization is hardly a new development of the twenty-first century. Tolkien himself was so painfully aware of it in his era that he wrote it into the pages of *The Lord of the Rings.* Elrond's remark that "Time was when a squirrel could go from tree to tree from what is now the Shire to Dunland west of Isengard" was quoted earlier, and Treebeard voices a similar lament for the corresponding woodlands east of the Misty Mountains, right down to his use of the same slightly archaic and nostalgic phrase: "Aye, aye, there was all one wood once upon a time from here to the Mountains of Lune, and this was just the East End. . . . Time was when I could walk and sing all day and hear no more than the echo of my own voice in the hollow hills. The woods were like the woods of Lothlórien, only thicker, stronger, younger. And the smell of the air! I used to spend a week just breathing."[38]

The old Ent here seems to be suggesting that Galadriel's protected realm represents, or at least is emblematic of, the once-vast forests of Rhovanion, which also included both his own forest of Fangorn and the now-dark reaches of Mirkwood. Frodo's earlier observation that "evil had been seen and heard there, sorrow had been known; the Elves feared and distrusted the world outside: wolves were howling on the wood's borders: but on the land of Lórien no shadow lay" supports both Treebeard's characterization as well as the idea that the tireless efforts of Galadriel and her people are all that protect the shrinking remnants of their unspoiled wild place.[39]

Just as with Aragorn above, Galadriel—supremely powerful and immortal daughter of a line of kings and wielder of one of the greatest magical artifacts ever created—might seem to set an example impossible for ordinary people in the Primary World to emulate. But the lesson she has for modern humans relates less to her means (which are inarguably fantastic) than to her ends (which are painfully and alarmingly real) and to the quality of her courage (which, in the best of worlds, is universal). For Galadriel's courage is ultimately the courage of memory, and even those who cannot fight can remember.

Tolkien explicitly presents Elven memory as an important contribution to mending the heartbreaking destruction caused by the forces of modern industrialism. This link is most obvious in Galadriel's gift to Sam when he passes through Lothlórien. With her characteristic foresight, she provides him with the means to restore his ruined home and, in the process, preserve at least some small remnant of her fading one: "Though you should find all barren and laid waste, there will be few gardens in Middle-earth that will bloom like your garden, if you sprinkle this earth there. Then you may remember Galadriel, and catch a glimpse far off of Lórien, that you have seen only in our winter. For our Spring and our Summer are gone by, and they will never be seen on earth again save in memory."[40] People with the space and inclination for gardens may not be able to plant a *mallorn*, but depending on their climate zone, they could perhaps plant a Torrey pine, or a Georgia aster, or any of a number of imperiled plant species, or they could simply choose to avoid invasive or resource-hungry plants in their landscaping.

The small wildness resident within a Shire-like garden is a worthy aim, certainly, but the power of such memory can extend much further. A 2015 article on human-caused species extinction argues that "the loss of biodiversity is one of the most critical current environmental problems, threatening valuable ecosystem services and human well-being," determines that "the average rate of vertebrate species loss over the last century is up to 100 times higher than the background rate," and concludes grimly "that modern extinction rates are exceptionally high, that they are increasing, and that they suggest a mass extinction under way—the sixth of its kind in Earth's 4.5 billion years of history."[41] Contemplating one of the most famous of modern extinctions, that of the passenger pigeon, Aldo Leopold, one of the most well known of American conservationists, observed that "Men still live who, in their youth, remember pigeons. Trees still live who, in their youth, were shaken by a living wind. But a decade hence only the oldest oaks will remember, and at long last only the hills will know."[42] Here Leopold couches the extinction debate in melancholic words of remembrance that would not be out of place in the songs of Lothlórien, but he also notes that there is hope in the very existence of the sorrow: "For one species to mourn the death of another is a new thing under the sun. The Cro-Magnon who slew the last mammoth thought only of steaks. The sportsman who shot the last pigeon thought only of his prowess. The sailor who clubbed the last auk thought of nothing at all. But we, who have lost our pigeons, mourn the loss."[43] Indeed, the timing of the extinction of the passenger pigeon, and the sense of loss that accompanied it, arguably added great force to the earliest American conservation efforts. In 1900, when John Muir at sixty-two was still lobbying to protect Yosemite and Aldo Leopold was only a boy of thirteen, Congressman John Lacey of Iowa introduced America's first wildlife protection law: "The wild pigeon, formerly in flocks of millions, has entirely disappeared from the face of the earth. . . . We have given an awful exhibition of slaughter and destruction, which may serve as a warning to all mankind. Let us now give an example of wise conservation of what remains of the gifts of nature."[44] This, then, is the courage memory can inspire: the courage to remember faithfully what has been lost, even if the memory is painful, and to work to preserve what remains, even if the work is likely to prove futile.

Recession models in a 2015 international nonprofit report[45] predict that there will be no active glaciers left in Montana's Glacier National Park by 2030.[46] It is extremely unlikely that there is any intervention capable, at this late date, of preventing this loss, but it is easy to imagine what melancholy-but-resolute advice Galadriel would have for Americans wrestling with its sad truth. She would remind anyone with the courage to hear her that inevitability of loss does not equate to an absence of value in working to protect, preserve, and enjoy the wild beauty of the glaciers that still exist. The powerful sorceress who laid bare the pits of Dol Guldur and opened them to the cleansing forest would likely applaud efforts to remove environmentally destructive industrial projects like aging, deteriorating, or species-destroying dams. One of the most beautiful evocations of the Celtic wilderness in modern fantasy fiction is created by Galadriel's long memory of lost beauty and her resolute steadfastness in continuing to fight what she knows in her heart will ultimately be a long defeat. For Tolkien fans who can see the link between her imperiled but beautiful forest and the few remaining and similarly imperiled wild places of the Primary World, her courage of memory can be an inspiration to support their protection.

Not everyone can pursue a career in conservation, or even materially support such efforts through financial support or local volunteer work. But everyone can remember. Those who remember the reckless destruction of rainforest biodiversity to create the barren monoculture of industrial palm oil plantations can allow that memory to guide their choice of food products at the grocery store. Those who remember the Mordor-like landscape created by the deforestation and destruction of strip mining and mountaintop removal can let the memory guide their appliance and technology choices and discretionary usage of coal-fired electrical power. Jeffers observes that the Elves, with their strong "power with" relationship to their environment, "see the approaching difficulty and yet remain connected to their places. . . . For the Elves, the mingling of love of Middle-earth and grief over it is not particularly new. Their response is to love their place all the more while they still can and to delay the coming Doom."[47] Such memory and love form the core of the mythic guidance of the Elves in this context; Galadriel's example encourages modern readers and viewers to value what wildness and wilderness still remain, and work to preserve it, enjoy its beauty, and resist its destruction as best they can.

Much like the concepts of wilderness they embody, Tolkien's Rangers and Elves are characters out of an ancient time. They are epic heroes of grand sagas, and their presence in Middle-earth signals both the deep influence on Tolkien of the oldest cultural waters flowing into the Western European stream and the kinship of continuity that his more modern myth shares with those elder days. But a large part of the reason Tolkien's work enjoys wide popular acclaim, while the ancient works that inspired him generally attract a much more specialized and academic audience, is the way that he interweaves and honors much more modern concepts of heroism and virtue alongside the ancient ones. Verlyn Flieger notes how Tolkien presents two kinds of hero in *The Lord of the Rings:* "the extraordinary man to give the epic sweep of great events," which she calls a romance or epic hero, and "the common man who has the immediate, poignant appeal of someone with whom the reader can identify," which she characterizes as a fairy tale or "low mimetic hero."[48] A tale focused only on Aragorn would be more like a Norse saga, and one whose main character was Galadriel might feel more like a beautiful but strangely uncanny Celtic wonder tale. The Middle-earth legendarium draws on the power of such myths, certainly, but as a product of the twentieth century it goes beyond them, acknowledging and reflecting the cultural reality and distinctive challenges of modern life.

There is no doubt that the clearest representatives of modern readers in the ancient world of Middle-earth are the diminutive, mundane, and quite ordinary hobbits. Tolkien himself explicitly acknowledged this; he wrote that he "saw the value of Hobbits, in putting earth under the feet of 'romance', and in providing subjects for 'ennoblement' and heroes more praiseworthy than the professionals."[49] Considering that one of the characteristics of literary modernism is the focus on the ordinary, the very ordinariness of the hobbits—especially for English readers, those most likely to find Bilbo's passive-aggressive middle-class manners, the Gaffer's pub gossip about his employer, and even Sam's longing for an anachronistic dish of fish and chips intimately familiar—is one argument in support of a general critical characterization of Tolkien as a "modern" twentieth-century writer.[50] But, unlike contemporary modernist writings such as Virginia Woolf's patient sifting through the mundanities of daily existence for patterns to elevate into philosophy, or James Joyce's fiendishly difficult minute observations of the details of Dublin life, in Tolkien's work the ordinary is important in addition to (rather than instead of) the extraordinary.

This nonironic inclusion of ancient values alongside the modern ones placed Tolkien rather outside the fashions of the modernist literary establishment of his time, which tended to reject the old heroic values in favor of the new, the mundane, even the disgusting, and champion the literary concept of the existentialist and alienated antihero. Nevertheless, it is key to understanding why his work has such power. In a letter, Tolkien wrote that he was "personally immensely amused by hobbits as such, and can contemplate them eating and making their rather fatuous jokes indefinitely; but I find that this is not the case with even my most devoted 'fans' . . . hobbits are only amusing when in unhobbitlike situations."[51] This reads like a bit of donnish self-effacement; it is hard to imagine anything more "unhobbitlike" than *Beowulf* or *Gawain* or the many other ancient works that Tolkien spent his academic life championing against the onslaught of ordinary fatuousness. Tolkien knew very well the power of this contrast, and he deployed it often and with great skill.

For all their mundane modernity, the ordinary Shire folk are characterized by a truly extraordinary courage. Tolkien insisted that "the Hobbits are just rustic English people, made small in size because it reflects the generally small reach of their imagination—not the small reach of their courage or latent power."[52] The courage of the hobbits, great as it undeniably is, seems to be of a generally different quality than that of the Rangers or the Elves. This is not to say that they do not occasionally demonstrate purely epic courage; they do and earn the respect of both Rangers and Elves for doing so. But they are not really epic characters in the action hero mold. Instead, they are Tolkien's best channel for demonstrating what Shippey calls "that style of courage—cold courage, 'moral courage', two-o-'clock-in-the-morning courage—which our age is most prepared to venerate."[53] The hobbits are generally presented as ordinary people who, if they are brave, are brave in ordinary ways.

Bilbo's self-doubt in the dark tunnel leading to Smaug's lair is the classic example of Tolkien's take on this modern idea. The old, epic courage of Thorin Oakenshield, who at the Battle of Azanulbizar cast away his broken shield in the face of a horde of Orcs and "hewed off with his axe a branch of an oak and held it in his left hand to ward off the strokes of his foes," seems rather uncharacteristically to fail at this point.[54] He prevaricates importantly, describing Bilbo as "a good companion on our long road, and a hobbit full of courage and resource far exceeding his size,"[55] but then "for all his heroic name, sends Bilbo down the tunnel, and the rest do little but look embarrassed."[56] Tolkien's narrator informs his readers of Bilbo's heroism in unequivocal terms: "Going on from there was the bravest thing he ever did. The tremendous things that happened afterwards were as nothing compared to it. He fought the real battle in the tunnel alone, before he ever saw the vast danger that lay in wait."[57] Despite the terrible dragon, Tolkien is careful to characterize Bilbo's battle as "a behaviour-model which is not quite beyond emulation (no one can fight a dragon, but everyone can fight fear)."[58] Tolkien clearly values this modern courage highly, but he differs from his modernist contemporaries in that he does not find it necessary to denigrate the ancient sort.

Ultimately, the inclusion of both kinds of courage and the contradistinction between the hobbits and the greater folk in Middle-earth highlights the value of both. This can be clearly seen in the incident of the Scouring of the Shire, where Tolkien most closely juxtaposes the two. Most of the Shire folk prove easily cowed by the very modern troubles caused by Sharkey and his industrializing and communizing ruffians; although some individuals and small groups bemoan the state of things and longed to take action, nothing really comes of it. Tom Cotton grumbles about how he had "been itching for trouble all this year, but folks wouldn't help,"[59] and even the Tooks hiding in their "deep holes in the Green Hills, the Great Smials and all" where "the ruffians can't come at 'em" only cause more problems for the rest of the Shire: "Tooks shot three for prowling and robbing. After that the ruffians turned nastier."[60] It takes the return of the travelers, "fearless hobbits with bright swords and grim faces" who prove such "a great surprise" to the ruffians, to wake the Shire folk to their birthright of indomitable courage.[61] These fearless hobbit heroes in the epic mode, with their horns and armor and swords and impatience with petty injustice, are able to inspire their countrymen in the same way that they had themselves been inspired by the ancient courage of the greatest folk in Middle-earth—and yet it is Frodo's very modern moral courage that keeps them from sliding completely back into an ancient excess of epic and vengeful bloodshed. Ancient courage tempered with modern sensibilities, not Germanic brutality or weak modern timidity, is what saves and goes on to restore the Shire.

In his book *The Wisdom of the Shire,* Noble Smith dedicates a chapter to "The Courage of a Halfling," where he notes something else that is specifically hobbitic about the quality of modern-but-ancient courage demonstrated by these decidedly unwarlike folk: "How did the Shire produce so many doughty warriors . . . with such a peace-loving atmosphere? Maybe it's because the Hobbits were fighting for something quite different than glory or bloodlust—they were fighting for the love of their friends."[62] The idea that the courage of ordinary people in the face of danger to family or friends can easily reach epic proportions is a deep-seated one in Western culture—who has not heard anecdotes of questionable provenance describing small women facing snarling bears or lifting huge automobiles off their crushed children?—and it appears many times in the adventures of Tolkien's various hobbits.

Frodo in the lair of the barrow-wight is one example. It is here that Tolkien most explicitly describes his conception of hobbit bravery. "There is a seed of courage hidden (often deeply, it is true) in the heart of the fattest and most timid hobbit, waiting for some final and desperate danger to make it grow," the narrator explains; despite Frodo's wild thoughts of escaping by using his magic ring, readers are told that "the courage that had been awakened in him was now too strong: he could not leave his friends so easily."[63] Here readers learn that hobbit courage is deeply buried, slow to wake, and, importantly, manifests to save not just the hobbit but the hobbit's friends as well.

Another example, as well as an interesting demonstration of Tolkien's skillful use of language to highlight the contrast between his conceptions of courage, is Merry's deed of arms at the battle of the Pelennor Fields. Although "such a horror was on him that he was blind and sick," the great Germanic fortitude of Éowyn facing down the Lord of the Nazgûl inspires Merry: "Pity filled his heart and great wonder, and suddenly the slow-kindled courage of his race awoke. He clenched his hand. She should not die, so fair, so desperate! At least she should not die alone, unaided."[64] Éowyn's heroism in this episode is straight out of the sagas, given in language that is direct, forceful, and consciously archaic in form: "Still she did not blench: maiden of the Rohirrim, child of kings, slender but as a steel-blade, fair yet terrible. A swift stroke she dealt, skilled and deadly. The outstretched neck she clove asunder, and the hewn head fell like a stone."[65] The contrast in the language describing Merry's equally heroic deed is remarkable; readers are told that "the Black Captain . . . heeded him no more than a worm in the mud," and his critical strike, which both saves Éowyn's life and gives her the opening for her own fatal stroke, is only mentioned indirectly, in weak pluperfect language, and focuses more on the sword than on Merry's use of it: "Merry's sword had stabbed him from behind, shearing through the black mantle, and passing up beneath the hauberk had pierced the sinew behind his mighty knee."[66] It is ultimately a small deed, performed by a small hobbit, but the courage that inspires it, as well as its ramifications to the story, are every bit as great as Éowyn's heroic fulfillment of prophecy. There are other examples—Pippin stabbing the troll who struck down Beregond before the Black Gate, Bilbo fighting the spiders in Mirkwood to save the Dwarves—but nearly always, when great courage arises in the hearts of hobbits, it is inevitably within the context of great danger to their friends and companions.

Hobbit courage, then, lies not just in the courage of ordinary people doing extraordinary things, but in doing them specifically because of their loyalty to their friends. There is no doubt that this particular concept of courage stems from Tolkien's military experience, which produced in him a deep respect for the "plain soldier from the agricultural counties" with whom he served in the Great War.[67] In a 1956 letter he explicitly acknowledges that his hobbit character is "largely a reflexion of the English soldier—grafted on the village-boys of early days, the memory of the privates and my batmen that I knew in the 1914 War, and recognized as so far superior to myself."[68] It is almost a courage of community, albeit with a distinctly English flair.

To return to the context of wilderness, if Rangers embody the Germanic wilderness and Elves the Celtic one, the hobbits, with their blend of ancient and modern values, are even more deeply intertwined with Tolkien's third, English, concept of wilderness. While most of Tolkien's important hobbit characters have a share in this laudable inheritance, it is easy to choose one who most completely embodies all aspects of the great courage, greater loyalty, and stubborn adherence to what Tom Shippey calls "the notorious Anglo-hobbitic inability to know when they're beaten."[69] Even Tolkien himself admitted that there was one beloved character who was "a more representative hobbit than any others that we have to see much of": Samwise Gamgee, sometime gardener, loyal companion, and longtime Mayor of the Shire.[70]

The above examination of hobbit courage is itself more than enough to establish Sam's bona fides as a courageous character; as the quintessential hobbit, he demonstrates every element under discussion here, from epic, ancient, saga courage in his battle with Shelob, to his stubborn insistence on remembering the Shire in the worst of places, to his fierce loyalty to Frodo through the most hellish of journeys, even to his very modern (and world-saving) courage of mercy in not slaying Gollum at the very last. There is also no need to alleviate any perceived difficulty in identifying with him, as there was with Aragorn and Galadriel; he is easily the most approachable of Tolkien's characters, and yet he is a "jewel among the hobbits" and "the chief hero" of the tale.[71] Sam—as annoying, frustrating, sometimes uncomfortably awkward as he may be, especially to readers not unconsciously steeped in the English social class system he so clearly illuminates—is the real everyday hero of *The Lord of the Rings*.

Fortunately, for an ecocritic considering the values inherent in Tolkien's concepts of wilderness, Sam is nearly the perfect character. He is a down-to-earth individual who is both practical and sensitive, and he experiences with joy and wonder all of the beauty and danger in all three types of wildernesses. He is thrilled by the mountains, looking "with wonder in his eyes" at the snowy peaks of Rivendell, and he is comically delighted in the midst of terrible peril by a glimpse of an exotic (and very dangerous) Oliphaunt.[72] He shouts "Hooray!" at the possibility that he will "go and see Elves and all,"[73] and he is utterly enchanted by the beauty of Lothlórien and the Galadhrim, who meet with a plainspoken hobbit's wondering approval: "Now these folk aren't wanderers or homeless, and seem a bit nearer to the likes of us: they seem to belong here, more even than Hobbits do in the Shire. Whether they've made the land, or the land's made them, it's hard to say."[74] But, despite his genuine delight in the beauty and danger of the Germanic and Celtic wildernesses, in the end his true love is the friendly English wilderness of the Shire. When his adventures are over, Sam doesn't keep moving with the edge of civilization into the wilderness of Eriador (like a pioneer chasing the frontier), and he doesn't make repeated trips to Rivendell or Lórien seeking spiritual fulfillment (like John Muir's endless forays into Yosemite or Alaska). He returns and, much like Aldo Leopold, spends the rest of his life restoring, cultivating, and preserving the wildness and natural character of the home he loved so much. In fact, "The Tale of Years" describes Sam leaving the Shire again only thrice: once to accompany Frodo to the Grey Havens, once to dwell in Gondor for a year with Rosie and Elanor, and one last time on his own journey to the Havens.[75] Bilbo ultimately chooses the Celtic wilderness, retiring to Rivendell to make verses with the Elves, and Frodo ends up drawing a bit on the grimly tragic archetype of the Germanic hero seeking Valhalla because he is too broken by his sufferings to remain, but Sam persists fiercely through everything and to the bitter end, courageously loyal to the "woods and fields and little rivers" of the Shire.[76]

So, if Sam is the ultimate embodiment of Tolkien's third, friendly, concept of wilderness, what mythic instruction can be found for people today concerned about the possibility of scouring their own Shires? If Aragorn's inspiration is to get outside, and Galadriel's is to cherish and protect the natural beauty there, Sam's can be summed up in a plea for people to honor, defend, and live as closely as possible to the wildness in the places in which they make their homes.

Peter Kareiva, the author of the 2008 nature-based recreation study mentioned above, cites "an amusing but unnerving study of British schoolchildren," which reported that "kids between ages 4 and 11 were more than twice as good at identifying characters from Pokémon (a popular card game) than common organisms such as a beetle or a rabbit."[77] A poll sponsored by The Prince's Countryside Fund nearly ten years later determined that, out of young people ages eighteen to twenty-four in the United Kingdom, one in eight had never seen a real cow, less than half knew strawberries grew in the summer, and one in six had never left the city; a third of respondents of all ages believed that less than 30 percent of UK land is used for farming (the actual amount is over 70 percent), but nonetheless "a quarter of those surveyed said they'd give up their day job to become a farmer."[78] Also, just as Sam reckons "there's Elves and Elves,"[79] one might say there are farms and farms, as highlighted by a report sponsored by The Bureau of Investigative Journalism in the same month as the Countryside Fund poll. That report, published in the *Guardian* newspaper, chronicled the increasing use in livestock farming of American-style factory farms in the United Kingdom, observing that "nearly every county in England has at least one industrial-scale livestock farm" and chronicling how the "26% rise in intensive factory farming in six years" is "transforming the British countryside."[80] Tolkien himself was not a farmer, but his brother Hilary was, and it is not hard to imagine what his opinion would be of such a transformation.

If Sam Gamgee were to visit a selection of farms in the United Kingdom or the American Midwest today, he would be guaranteed to find farmers pouring petroleum pesticides on barren fields of lifeless dust to grow monoculture crops as feed for animals trapped in filthy concentrated animal-feeding operations. He might also, if he were lucky in his selection, encounter others using multispecies grazing to rotate cows, chickens, and food crops on land rich with topsoil bacteria and insect life. There is no doubt that Sam would think healthy and Shire-like and which he would think one of the worst perversions of Mordor. Dickerson and Evans observe that "Through the Shire and its farmers and gardeners, Tolkien offers us a vision of the complex interdependencies of people, community, and land comparable to modern environmentalists' recognition that healthy human culture requires responsible agricultural use of the land."[81] There is room and plenty enough in the Shire, both physically and conceptually, for hobbits and foxes, cabbages and corn, sturdy ponies, birds, and bees and even Farmer Maggot's ferocious dogs to live out their lives, and they all work together to form a healthy, working ecosystem. The Shire may be an idealized pastoral idyll, but its basic ideals are sound. Both in Middle-earth and in the Primary World, however, such ideals find themselves under attack on many different fronts, and although the actions necessary might be different, in both worlds the act of defending them requires a certain sort of courage.

The truth is, of the three characters set up as examples here, it is Sam's practical and stubbornly loyal hobbit courage that has the potential to inspire perhaps the most impactful new stories about modern humans and their relationship to the natural world. As critically important as the muscular toughness or spiritual fulfillment produced by the first two concepts of wilderness may be to human happiness, not everyone will be willing, able, or interested in overcoming the sadly common cultural inheritance of isolation from such experiences. But absolutely everyone needs to eat.

Kareiva argues that "people care about what they know, and people need to know something about nature to solve environmental problems."[82] A guaranteed daily point of connection to "nature" in the life of even the most dedicated city-dwellers sits on the table at mealtimes. Hobbits, with their propensity to "eat, and drink, often and heartily" and their desire for "six meals a day (when they could get them),"[83] are already linked with food in the popular consciousness; a Google search for "hobbit mealtimes" turns up any number of social media posts with times and even recipes, as well as heated discussions about whether hobbit dinners and suppers are separate meals. Sam the gardener, Sam the stout friend of Bill the pony (whom he insists "can nearly talk"[84]), Sam the cook who miraculously manages rabbit stew in the wilderness of Ithilien and relinquishes his beloved pans with the utmost reluctance at the very last, has a great deal to teach Tolkien fans about the connections between them and the plants and animals that are intricately linked with the sustenance of their own bodies and lives.

This is not to say that everyone should become a farmer (such an idea is, in the minds of many Westerners, probably equivalent to scaling the Himalayas). Still, there is something growing on pretty much every scrap of dirt on which a detached property is built, even if it is nothing but grass or weeds or spiny desert scrub. It is a much more approachable proposition to suggest that people simply notice, care for, and perhaps even supplement with tasty food the plants with which they are already sharing their homes. Those without much land or living in attached homes can still create, promote, and participate in community garden programs, explore growing food in small containers on a suburban patio, or just put a few herbs in a pot on their windowsill.

For those for whom even this is too much, who lack the inclination or capability to grow even a small amount of their own food, they can at least make good, courageous choices about the food that they buy and eat. In a world obsessed with consumerism and chasing the latest style or gadget, it is somewhat out of the mainstream to choose to spend a lesser percentage of disposable income on flashy consumer goods and a greater amount on quality food produced sustainably. But, just as an Elven-inspired memory of the beauty of the rainforest might give Tolkien fans the nudge they need to avoid palm oil or other ingredients whose unsustainable practices destroy faraway wilderness, cultivating a hobbit-like loyalty might encourage them to support local farmers using sustainable practices, eat more meat-free meals or choose meat from animals raised in free-range (or at least reasonably humane) conditions, and develop a connection to the wildness, however minimal, in their own local Shires.

It takes a certain sort of moral courage to make these choices today because they require people to expand the ethical horizons of human consideration to include animals, plants, and the land itself, and (like most mind-broadening concepts) once the expansion happens, there is no going back. Those unwilling to think too hard about where their food comes from have a much easier time enjoying their shrink-wrapped steaks than those who allow themselves to contemplate the staggering scale of animal suffering involved in cheap, mass-produced meat. Those who have tasted a fresh tomato from their own healthy and well cared-for garden or pot have a hard time enjoying the bland cardboard texture of commodified hothouse plant life bred less for taste than for sturdiness in travel. Concerning the hobbits' strong "power with" relationship to their own environment, Jeffers suggests that "What is at work in the Shire is not so much Hobbits condescending to treat the Shire respectfully as it is the Shire and Hobbits working together to shape each other in the most positive ways possible."[85] Sam's example can encourage everyone to recognize this connection between themselves and their own places, to honor the plant and animal life that supports them, and to fight as fiercely as any loyal hobbit to stop and then work to repair the destruction of the natural world within which and on which they make their homes.

Tom Shippey has suggested that "the whole structure of *The Lord of the Rings* indicates that decision and perseverance—not speculating on what is happening elsewhere, but doing your job and getting on with it, 'looking to your front' like a Lancashire Fusilier—that this mental attitude may be rewarded beyond hope," and he argues that this steadfastness lies at Tolkien's "philosophic core."[86] Tolkien's deep-seated belief that right-thinking people are ethically required to continue to fight the good fight, and that lack of hope is not a justifiable excuse for despair, is a powerful strain in his powerful myth. Accordingly, his many virtuous examples of courage, from Ranger fortitude to Elven memory to hobbit loyalty, are available as powerful mythic guidance for people faced with the evident hopelessness and despair arising out of many of the crises in modern life.

For environmentally minded readers, Middle-earth provides many examples, both positive and negative, of the ways that modern humans can conceive of their relationship with the natural world. The discussion above is focused squarely on the positive examples, but the negative ones, such as the modernist industrial mindlessness of the Orcs or the careful but destructive rationalization of Saruman, are equally valid and enlightening (and have been the subject of much Tolkien ecocriticsm; Jeffers discuses both the Orcs and Saruman in detail, and many other critics have tackled these topics as well). Given the focus Tolkien puts on environmental themes, it is not too much to say that, in his world, good people act less like Orcs and more like Rangers, Elves, and hobbits.

This is not to say that all Rangers, Elves, or hobbits are perfect (or even that Orcs are all bad; Shippey notes that they "recognise the idea of goodness, appreciate humour, value loyalty, trust, group cohesion and the ideal of a higher cause than themselves, and condemn failings from these ideals in others"[87]). All of Tolkien's human analogues have free will and demonstrate a range of character traits, good, bad, and indifferent. The origins of Aragorn's kingly line spring from haughty Númenorians whose hunger for timber caused them to subjugate the native peoples on the coasts of the River Greyflood; their "tree-felling became devastating" and they were "ruthless in their feelings, giving no thought to husbandry or replanting," until the great river "flowed through a land that was far and wide on either bank a desert, treeless but untilled."[88] Galadriel's kinsman Fëanor, the "mightiest in all parts of body and mind, in valour, in endurance, in beauty, in understanding, in skill, in strength and subtlety alike, of all the Children of Ilúvatar," in his hubris ended up serving as the vessel through which the scourges of kin-slaying, betrayal, and darkness first stained the bright morning of the world.[89] Much as it is easier for modern readers to find points of identification with the hobbit heroes, the negative examples of less-than-stellar human character traits among the Shire folk are less cosmological but far more painfully recognizable. How many readers are truthfully more like Lotho Pimple, who owned "a sight more than was good for him; and he was always grabbing more," or Ted Sandyman, who was pleased with the new mill "full o' wheels and outlandish contraptions" and worked there "cleaning wheels for the Men, where his dad was the Miller and his own master," than they might wish to admit?[90]

Both the positive and negative examples Tolkien provides point toward a firmly established set of values and ethics regarding both how humans should interact with the natural world and what they should do when facing the powerful forces of destruction arrayed against them. Those values rest solidly on the high esteem Tolkien awards to the virtue of courage. The human beings today who are intellectually and spiritually honest enough to consider the implications of the environmental destruction caused by their predecessors require a truly vast amount of courage, vast enough to equal the great despair that the grim scientific and cultural reality can engender. But those who wish to move outside of the comfort zone of Western industrial civilization, to recognize instead of deny the place they occupy within the intricate web of life on the planet, or to make ethical choices necessary to preserve rather than destroy that planet, can find inspiration in Tolkien's work to continue past that despair. Even more hopefully, it is possible that those who are inspired by other themes in Tolkien's powerful myth might be encouraged to recognize and possibly even internalize some of his environmental ones as well.

An argument that both crystallizes the necessity for courage in the face of despair and explains the ethical rationale behind it can be found in the words of Gandalf, that greatest of all stewards in Middle-earth, to the council of Lords of the West before they make the desperate choice to march on the Black Gate of Mordor. Gandalf's grim assessment of the situation is one of bleak and ancient Northern courage: "We must walk open-eyed into that trap, with courage, but small hope for ourselves. For, my lords, it may well prove that we ourselves shall perish utterly in a black battle far from the living lands; so that even if Barad-dûr be thrown down, we shall not live to see a new age. But this, I deem, is our duty. And better so than to perish nonetheless—as we surely shall, if we sit here—and know as we die that no new age shall be."[91] These words, which would not be out of place spoken to the *einherjar* on the brink of Ragnarök, are clear reflections of Gandalf's partially Odinic mythic origins. But the reasoning out of which his great resolve arises has a much more contemporary feel to it: "It is not our part to master all the tides of the world, but to do what is in us for the succour of those years wherein we are set, uprooting the evil in the fields that we know, so that those who live after may have clean earth to till. What weather they shall have is not ours to rule."[92] Neither the agricultural metaphor nor the duty good folk have to leave the world better than they found it are accidental here. These very modern ideals—of preserving what can be preserved and finding the courage to carry on—lie at the very core of the mythic instruction of Tolkien's great tale of Middle-earth.

One of the strongest characteristics of good literature is its broad applicability. Those who take the time to sensitively read well-crafted stories often come to see their own lives in a different light, and perhaps even adjust their personal myth based on the lessons they learn in the process. The fractured and unconscious mythical landscape of Western culture today, combined with increasingly challenging times, mean that moving and ethically inspiring tales are more important than ever. Tolkien's work is an excellent example of the powerful inspiration that good, deep-rooted mythic literature can provide. Tolkien explicitly intended his legendarium to be read as a sort of alternate history. "'Middle-earth,' by the way, is not a name of a never-never land without relation to the world we live in," he wrote in a testy letter to his publisher. "Imaginatively this 'history' is supposed to take place in a period of the actual Old World of this planet."[93] This means that the burden laid upon Aragorn and his kindred at the end of *The Lord of the Rings* in some sense still belongs to people today, and the values demonstrated in the story can serve modern readers perfectly well as guides for ethical behavior as they seek the right way to bear that burden themselves.[94]

Susan Jeffers notes that, both in Middle-earth and the Primary World, "an environment is not just the land itself, but all the things living on it, including trees, grass, horses, and people."[95] Approaching this inclusivity from the civilization side of the civilization-wilderness debate, it seems a completely positive ideal, granting trees and horses the same consideration as people, and very few would argue that such expansion of consciousness is a bad thing. But for some reason, when approaching the inclusivity from the other side, some popular wilderness thinking today still sees it in somewhat negative terms. If it is true that humans are part of and not separate from their natural environment, then—while it certainly follows that humans do not have a greater right than other organisms to the necessities for life provided by their environment—it also follows that they do not have a lesser one. The famous definition of wilderness as "an area where the earth and its community of life are untrammeled by man, where man himself is a visitor who does not remain" might include parts of Mirkwood and Eriador, would probably exclude both Rivendell and Lórien, and would definitely exclude even the wilder corners of the Shire.[96] But such a definition would also exclude the very areas it was originally drafted to include, if not for the fact that it denied the humanity of the non-Western human occupants of these ostensibly untrammeled areas. This fact and its implications are the subject of ongoing debates in the academic community, but that debate has largely failed to affect the general concept of wilderness in modern Western culture.

Tolkien's sensitive portrayal of wilderness has the potential to expand this popular understanding into a less binary middle ground. His work draws on deep-flowing mythical currents and presents as valuable in their own right three distinct wilderness concepts, and he has created courageous, compelling, and beloved characters linked to each of those concepts. Accordingly, in the context of wilderness, the overall lessons to be found in Tolkien's work, in that of those who have reimagined his work, and in the places where his work resonates with wilderness philosophy, appear to be threefold. First, wild lands that do not include humans as a permanent part of their ecosystem are valuable as wilderness in their own right. Inaccessible Arctic taiga and tundra or jungle rainforest or lofty mountain peaks are as important in the overall biosphere as places of less wildness but more human utility, and Middle-earth would not be Middle-earth without the Misty Mountains or the Helcaraxë. Second, wild lands that have been shaped to allow humans easier access to the spiritual fulfillment they can provide are valuable as wilderness in their own right. National parks or areas of natural beauty are not invalidated as avenues of wilderness experience by the careful management that permits a broader range of people to enjoy them than places of greater wildness, and Mirkwood or Fangorn or Lothlórien are not lessened by the fact that good beings reside permanently within their borders. Third, and perhaps more controversial, wild lands that wind in, between, and around heavy concentrations of human habitation are valuable as wilderness in their own right. A well cared-for hedgerow can provide shelter and habitat for insects, birds, and small rodents and increase the biodiversity and associated health of a local environment even if it is occasionally trimmed, and the friendly forests of the Woody End in the Shire or Ithilien in Gondor are as important to the wild character of Middle-earth as other places of significantly greater wildness. These three concepts may vary in degree, but they are all wilderness, and as such, they all have something to contribute to the health of the planet as a whole.

Conclusion

The Map of Wilderland

If you want my advice, make for Rivendell.
(Gandalf to Frodo)
—Tolkien, *Lord*, 66

Wilderness is important. It is physically important to the health of the planet and all of the organisms living on that planet. It is also psychologically important, at least for organisms with enough cognitive function to have psychology. Some of those, particularly a certain highly capable simian species now endemic to pretty much every landmass on the planet large enough to sustain it, possess an intellectual capacity so vast that they have been able to separate themselves from their physical environment to an incomprehensible degree. Some members of that species have actually come to believe that the destruction of their physical environment is more of an inconvenience than a catastrophe. The fact that the modern idea of wilderness is itself nothing more than an intellectual construct of that same species does not change its importance; it is so important, in fact, that it is one of the few things that might help that species solve the environmental problems it has created.

If wilderness is a place characterized by wildness, the innumerable nonhuman organisms inhabiting places of even the greatest wildness do not know it; only the humans who enter or dwell there know it, and only if they are humans whose culture has advanced beyond the Paleolithic hunter-gatherer level. But, considering that most humans fall into this category in the twenty-first century, it seems a pointless philosophical quibble to protest that wildness and wilderness do not therefore truly exist. They do. They have been created by the human mind, much like literature and music and transoceanic fiber-optic cables and nuclear fission, and today their reality and importance are all the greater for the fact that they did not exist before humans created them.

One of the things that makes the concept of wilderness so important is its centrality to how Western humans conceive of their relationship to the natural world. To the humans who first began to separate themselves from their environment through the agricultural revolution of the Neolithic Age, wilderness was merely a place where the plants and animals were ones beyond the edge of human control. Then, as humans expanded the area of that control, wilderness became an actively hostile place, the abode of monsters, which were both physical and psychological creatures (and came in both two-legged and four-legged varieties). As the expansion continued, this active hostility transmuted into a more passive resistance against the increasingly powerful civilizing forces of human presence. Eventually the amount of land spoiled by those increasingly destructive forces became so great that wilderness made the shift from something to be opposed to something to be protected. But from its very beginnings, wilderness was intricately entwined with the way that humans saw themselves in relation to the world they inhabited, and over the years the conceptual gulf of that relationship has only continued to widen. Now, today, as the effects of human existence have spread to touch every corner of the planet and people everywhere continue to disconnect, it is beginning to seem like humanity's separation from the natural world may become so complete that they will irretrievably poison the very land that gives them life.

South African wilderness guide and Jungian psychologist Ian McCallum argues that before humans can begin "to heal or to reconcile the Human-Nature split," they must change their perspective on the problem: "First of all, we have to stop speaking about the Earth being in need of healing. The Earth doesn't need healing. We do. Utterly indifferent to human existence, the Earth will thrive—when we are gone. We are the ones who need to redefine our relationship with it. We are the ones who have become ashamed of our wild nature. . . . We are the ones who need to do the reaching out, not to save the Earth, but to rediscover ourselves in it."[1]

Such a shift in perspective might seem impossible in the face of economic realities and government policies and the denial-inducing, hopelessly long response times to any human actions, positive or negative, big enough to have a widespread effect on the environment. But with the death toll rising every time a new destructive storm slams into a coastline or yet another deadly wildfire sweeps through unhealthy forests, even the most ardent deniers of the human role in climate change will eventually have to admit that things are not as they were. The next step will be to recognize that, whatever its origin, the change must be dealt with, or human existence will be imperiled on a much larger scale than anyone ever anticipated.

Mere science or policy will not be enough to make this change. If they stand at odds with the stories humans believe about their relationship to the natural world, their effectiveness will continue to be fatally limited. If the stories do not shift, the best science in the world will not be enough. This might sound unhopeful, but in truth it is the same mechanism by which things came to this juncture in the first place. Each change in the idea of wilderness was associated with a change in the stories humans told themselves about their relationship to their environment. As new stories supplanted the older ones, people's identities (and consequently their behavior) began to change in response. While the overall destruction has continued to increase, some of the more recent human stories about wilderness have at least partially begun to retreat from the purely destructive ones of resourcism and complete separation that have precipitated the many current environmental crises, and the value of wildness as something beneficial to human life is beginning to become more widely accepted. Increasing such acceptance, and introducing the cultural and mythological ideas of wilderness as something important and valuable to more people in a compelling way, would be a valuable weapon in the fight to combat such destruction.

This study has concerned itself with one very powerful and popular modern story that, although not explicitly intended to be a wilderness myth, nevertheless presents several different concepts of wilderness in a positive light. In considering any mythology, it is impossible to separate a story from its context, and Tolkien's Middle-earth legendarium is a product of early twentieth-century Britain. Still, Tolkien consciously drew upon a deep flow of cultural and mythological waters from much older eras, and he updated and recombined them into something compelling and valuable for his own time. Tom Shippey observes that Tolkien's "highly traditional but by no means outdated mythology" has stood solid under the onslaughts of both critics and time; his ideals "have remained perfectly comprehensible to millions of readers: a source of encouragement to one (much larger) group, a challenge, a menace, and even a reproach to another."[2] In the twenty-first century, after nearly a century of cultural and technological change, both the encouragement and the reproach of his work remain powerful, even to people far outside his original English, British, or even Western cultural context. The Middle-earth legendarium continues to provide useful insight into positive ways that people can relate to their natural environment, and its value as a popular and deeply moving story gives it the potential to reach a much wider audience than any grim scientific study or thundering philosophical jeremiad could ever hope to do.

Tolkien's three wilderness concepts are excellent metaphors for the kind of experiences to which people today have access in modern wilderness areas. John Muir's beloved Yosemite National Park is a good and illustrative example. The wilderness of the Rangers is clearly visible in the striking beauty of the mountains, the still-present threat of bears and rattlesnakes and poison oak, and even the relentless steepness and overall difficulty of the long hikes necessary for a modern-day Ranger to climb out of the valley into the boundless breathtaking space of the High Sierra. Camping on El Capitan or Eagle's Rest under an expansive blanket of stars, bathed in moonlight, it is very easy to hear in every rustle and trickle and flutter another, more magical, world that is somehow impossible to discern in places of less wildness, a world where Elven magic blurs the boundaries between here and there. The well-developed but still semiwild areas in Yosemite Valley, with their wide piney paths and slow-flowing river beneath breathtaking walls of gray stone, allow modern city-dwellers to encounter an approachable and friendly wilderness (and to stay in perfect hobbitish comfort, whether beneath the pines of Housekeeping Camp or in the luxurious embrace of one of the finest inns in the world). All three concepts are present for those who know to look for them, and this is true not only of Yosemite National Park but of any similar refuge of wildness, protected or otherwise.

A clear and useful Middle-earth equivalent to Yosemite (or Snowdonia in the United Kingdom, or the Dolomites in the Italian Alps, or any other developed wilderness area characterized by mountains, gorges, waterfalls, and pleasant places to stay amid the beauty of nature) is Elrond's haven in the Misty Mountains, the hidden valley of Rivendell. Imladris, as Gandalf points out, sits at "the very edge of the Wild,"[3] and, as one critic puts it, "doesn't just sit on this boundary; it embodies it. The house of Elrond is the place where the world of quiet comforts and the world of legends come together and coexist."[4] All three of Tolkien's wilderness concepts are powerfully present in this border area. For timid English Shire dwellers approaching Rivendell from the kindly west, it is a wild and Germanic place, full of soaring mountains and deep valleys and the menace of powerful forces beyond human control. For weary travelers approaching from the harsh Germanic wilderness to its east, it is a comfortable English haven, a bulwark and a calm place of healing. Its Elven character gives it a timeless Celtic air of mystery and deep natural magic. Sam tells Frodo that there is no "better place" than Rivendell because it evokes all good places in Middle-earth: "There's something of everything here, if you understand me: the Shire and the Golden Wood and Gondor and kings' houses and inns and meadows and mountains all mixed."[5] The house of Elrond is a place that reflects many different conceptions of the wild natural world.

This liminal position, on the indeterminate border that stretches between the poles of the civilization-wilderness debate, means that Rivendell can partake of the full ambiguity of all human-conceived wild landscapes in all their various manifestations. Here wildness is both powerful and accessible; it is a place where an almost spiritual preservation ethic obtains, where Elves work "to preserve all things unstained," and it is also one where the muscular toughness of conservation ideals are honored, where "Rangers of the wild—hunters . . . of the servants of the Enemy" make their home between their monster-hunting adventures.[6] It also boasts porches, terraces, and "a high garden above the steep bank of the river," where the "light on the faces of the mountains" and the loud "sound of running and falling water" can be experienced in their wild context even by those who are neither hardy Rangers nor starry-eyed Elves, but mere ordinary and comfort-loving hobbits.[7] In the same way that Middle-earth manages to encompass all the various strands of ambiguity around the relationship between humans and the natural world, there is welcome in Rivendell for all who wish to experience the power of wildness on whatever terms they can manage.

At the uttermost end, in the blackness of Mordor on the very edge of Mount Doom, the power of the Ring lies so heavily on Frodo that he reports a complete separation from even the memory of things in the natural world: "No taste of food, no feel of water, no sound of wind, no memory of tree or grass or flower, no image of moon or star are left to me."[8] It is perhaps too much to draw a direct analogy between the malevolent Ring and the technological advances and associated separation between humans and the natural world in the twenty-first century. Still, there are many people today who, whether they know it or not, are suffering variations on the same hopeless theme. It is hopefully not too grand a claim to suggest that, if people can come to recognize their separation from their environment, they may begin to search for a way to reconnect to it. The modern construct of wilderness experience is one of the best ways to open people to the idea that humans are part of a larger ecosystem of planetary wildness that must be maintained in a healthy state if the human race is going to survive.

Tolkien himself created the map of Wilderland present in every edition of *The Hobbit* since 1937. On that map, Rivendell appears just to the east of a clear and dominating boundary line marking the Edge of the Wild and just to the west of the sinuous curve and jagged teeth of the Misty Mountains, in a position to serve both as gateway to and refuge from the landscape of mythic adventure stretching out to the east. Here, on the very edge of many different ideas of wilderness, the Last Homely House stands as a composite symbol for the shifting meaning of wildness in the minds of people today. In a sense, everyone is searching for Rivendell—and the map of Wilderland can show the way. Only by recognizing this need, finding ways to meet it, and then conserving and preserving the places where it can be met will today's adventurers be able to fill the empty spaces in the postmodern soul.

Notes

Introduction

1. Schiffman, "Bigger than Science, Bigger than Religion," 19.
2. Colebatch, *Return of the Heroes*, 92.
3. Carpenter, *Tolkien: A Biography*, 100.
4. Donovan, "Middle-Earth Mythology: An Overview," 92.
5. Abram, *The Spell of the Sensuous*, 273.
6. Abbey, *Desert Solitaire*, 129–30.
7. Nelson and Vucetich, "Value of Wilderness," 5479.
8. Jenkins, "Wilderness Preservation Argument 31," 175.
9. Oelschlaeger, *The Idea of Wilderness*, 321.
10. Schroeder, "The Spiritual Aspect of Nature," 26.
11. De Vries, "Theories Concerning 'Nature Myths,'" 31.
12. Nelson and Vucetich, "Value of Wilderness," 5481.
13. Tolkien, *Letters*, 220.
14. Shippey, *Author*, 89.
15. Dickerson and Evans, *Ents, Elves, and Eriador*, xvi.

Part I

1. Campbell, *Hero*, 3.
2. Paris, *Wisdom of the Psyche*, 81.
3. Odajnyk, "Mandala of the Naropa Dakini," 135.
4. Fisher, "Tolkien and Source Criticism," 40.
5. Tolkien, *Letters*, 147.
6. Tolkien is referring not to Campbell himself here but to his predecessors, probably Sir James Frazer in particular; Verlyn Flieger dates this version of the Kullervo essay to somewhere around the early 1920s (Tolkien, *Kullervo*, 72).
7. Tolkien, *Kullervo*, 103.
8. Tolkien, *Letters*, 418.
9. Shippey, "Why Source Criticism?," 9.
10. Tolkien, *On Fairy Stories*, 39.
11. Shippey, "Why Source Criticism?," 14.

12. Risden, "Source," 17–18.
13. Tolkien, *Letters*, 31.
14. Tolkien, *On Fairy Stories*, 39.
15. Shippey, "Why Source Criticism?," 15.
16. Harrison, *Forests*, 17.
17. Plato, *Complete Works*, 1297.
18. Attenborough, *The First Eden*, 117–18.

1. *Germanic Wilderness*

1. Acocella, "Slaying Monsters."
2. Staver, *A Companion to Beowulf*, 197.
3. Drout, "Preface," xi.
4. Frantzen, *Desire for Origins*, 175.
5. Heaney, *Beowulf*, xi.
6. Tolkien, *Monsters*, 7.
7. Flieger, *Splintered Light*, xxi, 172.
8. Shippey, *Road*, 344.
9. Tolkien, *Letters*, 31.
10. Evans, "The Dragon-Lore of Middle-Earth," 31.
11. Shippey uses this technical linguistic term, which he defines as "the process in which the elements of a compound word are translated bit by bit to make a new word in another language" in a much broader sense, to describe the way Tolkien built on his literary and cultural influences to create something new and yet recognizably related to the old (*Road*, 102).
12. Shippey, *Road*, 124.
13. Shippey, *Road*, 123n1, 127.
14. Honegger, "The Rohirrim," 127.
15. Clark, "J. R. R. Tolkien and the True Hero," 40.
16. Shippey, *Road*, 47.
17. "Literary Society," 20.
18. Tolkien, *Letters*, 31, 134, 150.
19. Tolkien, *Legend*, 23–24.
20. Definitely in extant manuscript age, and likely in mythic provenance as well. The Cotton manuscript in which *Beowulf* appears is dated somewhere near the turn of the eleventh century, while the *Codex Regius*, containing the earliest attestation of the *Poetic Edda*, dates to the end of the thirteenth. Scholars have traced parts of the *Edda* to works from the turn of the first millennium, but *Beowulf* references events in Scandinavia as far back as the sixth century.
21. Tolkien, *Legend*, 39.
22. Nash admittedly begins his etymological analysis with a satisfyingly resonant but unfortunately mistaken claim about *wild* descending from the idea of *will*, but the *OED* backs him up on the *wild-dēor* connection ("Wilderness, n.").
23. Chickering, *Beowulf*, 130.
24. Nash, *Wilderness and the American Mind*, 1.

25. Choosing a *Beowulf* translation for this study proved less straightforward than might be expected. Tolkien completed his own prose translation in 1926; "I have all Beowulf translated, but in much hardly to my liking," he wrote to Kenneth Sisam at the time (*Beowulf*, 2). As Christopher Tolkien points out, "before him lay two decades as the professor of Anglo-Saxon at Oxford, two decades of further study of Old English poetry, together with an arduous program of lectures and classes" (*Beowulf*, 1), and the translation was not published in his lifetime. Seamus Heaney's recent verse translation is well regarded as poetry but diverges more from the original text than Tolkien likely would have approved. Howell Chickering's fairly literal 1977 translation is generally used here, supplemented in places with Tolkien's and Heaney's where the differences seem useful or interesting.
26. Tolkien, *Beowulf*, 106.
27. Heaney, *Beowulf*, 99.
28. Nash, *Wilderness and the American Mind*, 2.
29. Nash, *Wilderness and the American Mind*, 12.
30. Burns, *Perilous Realms*, 37.
31. Magennis, *Images of Community*, 128.
32. Gummere, *Germanic Origins*, 36.
33. Tolkien, *Monsters*, 26.
34. Chickering, *Beowulf*, 113, 115.
35. Chickering, *Beowulf*, 115.
36. Gummere, *Germanic Origins*, 36.
37. Chickering, *Beowulf*, 127, 129.
38. Chickering, *Beowulf*, 131.
39. Chickering, *Beowulf*, 334.
40. Ziolkowski, "Virgil," 173–74.
41. Magennis, *Images of Community*, 135–36.
42. Chickering, *Beowulf*, 334.
43. Chickering, *Beowulf*, 335.
44. Tolkien, *Monsters*, 24.
45. Tolkien, *Monsters*, 23; emphasis in original.
46. *Exemplum optimum* is Tolkien's beloved Gothic language, of which the only extant text is an incomplete translation of the Bible.
47. Chickering, *Beowulf*, 53, 55.
48. Magennis, *Images of Community*, 127.
49. Chickering, *Beowulf*, 67.
50. Chickering, *Beowulf*, 61.
51. Tolkien, *Beowulf*, 180.
52. Heaney, *Beowulf*, 17.
53. Chickering, *Beowulf*, 63.
54. Chickering, *Beowulf*, 83.
55. Chickering, *Beowulf*, 85.
56. Tolkien, *Beowulf*, 491.
57. Heaney, *Beowulf*, 41.
58. Magennis, *Images of Community*, 130.

59. Chickering, *Beowulf*, 205.
60. Chickering, *Beowulf*, 221.
61. "Holt, n.1."
62. Chickering, *Beowulf*, 129.
63. Gummere, *Germanic Origins*, 35.
64. Mattingly, *Tacitus on Britain and Germany*, 104.
65. Gummere, *Germanic Origins*, 37.
66. Tolkien, *Lord*, 459.
67. "dismal wood" (Heaney, *Beowulf*, 99), "joyless forest" (Tolkien, *Beowulf*, 106).
68. Neville, *Representations*, 14.
69. Magennis, *Images of Community*, 142.
70. Chickering, *Beowulf*, 97.
71. Chickering, *Beowulf*, 99.
72. Magennis, *Images of Community*, 142.
73. Chickering, *Beowulf*, 131.
74. Magennis, *Images of Community*, 143.
75. Chickering, *Beowulf*, 131.
76. Neville, *Representations*, 135.
77. Tolkien, *Beowulf*, 118.
78. Neville, *Representations*, 135n192.
79. See Shippey, "Two Views," for more on this Tolkienian private joke.
80. Tolkien, *Letters*, 242.
81. Neville, *Representations*, 73.
82. Neville, *Representations*, 129.
83. Neville, *Representations*, 202.

2. *Celtic Wilderness*

1. Tolkien, *Letters*, 26.
2. Tolkien, *Letters*, 26.
3. Lyman-Thomas, "Celtic," 272.
4. Tolkien, *Letters*, 177; see Tolkien, *Letters*, 219n1; Tolkien, *Monsters*, 197n33.
5. The term *Celtic* is used here in Alfred Siewers's sense of a linguistic "useful shorthand" (Siewers, *Strange Beauty*, 146n8), and should not be read as indicating any overarching ethnic or national identification.
6. Fimi, "'Mad' Elves and 'Elusive Beauty,'" 166.
7. Lyman-Thomas, "Celtic," 273, 274.
8. Tolkien, *Letters*, 12, 213; see Tolkien, *Letters*, 218–19, 289; Carpenter, *Tolkien: A Biography*, 63.
9. Fimi, "'Mad' Elves and 'Elusive Beauty,'" 158.
10. Tolkien, *Monsters*, 189.
11. Carpenter, *Tolkien: A Biography*, 253.
12. Phelpstead, *Tolkien and Wales*, 65.
13. Phelpstead, *Tolkien and Wales*, 67.
14. Shippey, *Road*, 259.
15. Parker, "Hwaet We Holbytla . . . ," 606.

16. Rateliff and Tolkien, *The History of The Hobbit*, 188.
17. Phelpstead, *Tolkien and Wales*, 64.
18. Fimi, "'Mad' Elves and 'Elusive Beauty,'" 161.
19. Flieger, *Green Suns*, 134.
20. Siewers, "Tolkien's Cosmic-Christian Ecology," 143.
21. Siewers, *Strange Beauty*, 55.
22. See Tolkien, *Letters*, 289.
23. Scull and Hammond, *Chronology*, 56, 58, 62, 66.
24. Phelpstead, *Tolkien and Wales*, 60.
25. Tolkien, *Lord*, 14.
26. Day, *Tolkien's Ring*, 79.
27. Gantz, *The Mabinogion*, 11.
28. Davies, *The Mabinogion*, xii.
29. There are interesting similarities here to imagery used by Tolkien in his famous allegory of the tower in his essay on *Beowulf.*
30. Arnold, *On the Study of Celtic Literature*, 61.
31. Siewers, *Strange Beauty*, 56.
32. Lloyd-Morgan, "Narrative Structure in Peredur," 189.
33. Lloyd-Morgan, "Narrative Structure in Peredur," 190.
34. Breeze, "Moor, Court, and River in the Four Branches of the Mabinogi," 311.
35. Compare Patrick Curry's assertion that "it wouldn't be stretching a point to say that Middle-earth itself appears as a character in its own right" in Tolkien's legendarium (Curry, *Defending Middle-Earth*, 50).
36. Siewers, *Strange Beauty*, 56.
37. Bollard, "Landscapes of The Mabinogi," 44–45; emphasis in original.
38. Although Tolkien knew the 1948 Gwyn Jones and Thomas Jones Everyman translation of the *Mabinogion*, a more recent (and less stiltingly archaic) translation by Sioned Davies is used here.
39. Davies, *The Mabinogion*, 58.
40. A cantref was "the basic territorial administrative unit in medieval Wales" (Davies, *The Mabinogion*, 228n3); Davies, *The Mabinogion*, 59.
41. Davies, *The Mabinogion*, 63.
42. Bollard, "Landscapes of The Mabinogi," 45, Fig. 3.
43. Davies, *The Mabinogion*, 226n3.
44. Bollard, "Landscapes of The Mabinogi," 45.
45. This conceptual link between physical landscape and mythical story is somewhat more common in non-Western traditions; Bollard discusses in detail how deeply the description of Apache storytelling in Keith Basso's book *Wisdom Sits in Places* resonates with the relationship between narrative and place in the *Mabinogion.*
46. Siewers, *Strange Beauty*, 5.
47. Neville, *Representations*, 2–3.
48. Siewers, *Strange Beauty*, 7.
49. Davies, *The Mabinogion*, 8.
50. Siewers, *Strange Beauty*, 21.
51. Siewers, *Strange Beauty*, 58.

52. Davies, *The Mabinogion*, 36–37.
53. Siewers, "Writing an Icon of the Land," 207.
54. Davies, *The Mabinogion*, 41.
55. Davies, *The Mabinogion*, 38.
56. Siewers, *Strange Beauty*, 60.
57. Davies, *The Mabinogion*, 36.
58. Breeze, "Moor, Court, and River in the Four Branches of the Mabinogi," 308.
59. Siewers, "Writing an Icon of the Land," 207.
60. Gantz, *The Mabinogion*, 25.
61. Davies, *The Mabinogion*, xxiv.
62. de Troyes, *Arthurian Romances*, 220.
63. His father's name "Efrog" is the Welsh term for York. Davies, *The Mabinogion*, 65.
64. Gantz, *The Mabinogion*, 25.
65. Lloyd-Morgan, "Narrative Structure in Peredur," 203.
66. Davies, *The Mabinogion*, 67.
67. Davies, *The Mabinogion*, 71.
68. Davies, *The Mabinogion*, 72.
69. Davies, *The Mabinogion*, 74.
70. Davies, *The Mabinogion*, 100.
71. Siewers, *Strange Beauty*, 57.
72. Siewers, *Strange Beauty*, 144.

3. *English Wilderness*

1. Schlobin, "The Monsters Are Talismans and Transgressions," 71–72.
2. Shippey, "Gawain-Poet," 213.
3. Flieger, *Green Suns*, 215.
4. Miller, "Of Sum," 345.
5. Lee and Solopova, *The Keys of Middle-Earth*, 327.
6. Rateliff, "She," 146.
7. Tolkien, *Monsters*, 72.
8. Miller, "Of Sum," 362.
9. Shippey, "Gawain-Poet," 216.
10. Tolkien, *Sir Gawain*, 3.
11. Schlobin also disputes the influence of the dragon in *Beowulf* on Smaug in *The Hobbit* because the details of the two cup-stealing incidents are not quite exactly the same. His analysis is well considered and insightful, but it serves here as a good example of the limitations of strictly literary source criticism. A statement like "Tolkien's source for Smaug could have been any number of childhood dragon tales" is certainly true, but using that truth to justify denying any source relationship to *Beowulf* ignores how those tales would interact mythically with Tolkien's long academic preoccupation with the poem (Schlobin, "The Monsters Are Talismans and Transgressions," 72). It also rather misses the point of the kind of blending mythopoeic creation in which Tolkien was engaged in creating his legendarium.

12. Schlobin, "The Monsters Are Talismans and Transgressions," 70, 79.
13. This assertion is supported by the fact that, according to Scull and Hammond, Tolkien delivered his famous lecture on *Sir Gawain* while in the throes of final revision of all three volumes of *The Lord of the Rings* (*Chronology*, 420).
14. Fyler, "Freshman Composition: Epic and Romance," 120.
15. Miller, "Of Sum," 346, 349–50.
16. Miller, "Of Sum," 351, 355, 360.
17. Bowers, *Tolkien's Lost Chaucer*, 1–2.
18. Scull and Hammond, *Chronology*, 169, 233, 244.
19. Tolkien, *Letters*, 39–40.
20. Tolkien, *Sir Gawain*, 8.
21. Tolkien, *Monsters*, 73.
22. Tolkien, *Sir Gawain*, 8.
23. Lee and Solopova, *The Keys of Middle-Earth*, 42.
24. All *Gawain* passages in modern English are from Tolkien's own translation.
25. Tolkien, *Sir Gawain*, 43.
26. Tolkien, *Sir Gawain*, 75.
27. Tolkien, *Sir Gawain*, 77.
28. Lee and Solopova, *The Keys of Middle-Earth*, 329.
29. Rudd, *Greenery*, 119.
30. Tolkien, *Sir Gawain*, 37.
31. Rudd, *Greenery*, 116.
32. Rudd, *Greenery*, 117.
33. Chance, "Sources," 152.
34. Lee and Solopova, *The Keys of Middle-Earth*, 240.
35. Shippey, *Road*, 38.
36. Huntsman, "The Celtic Heritage of Sir Gawain and the Green Knight," 177.
37. Huntsman, "The Celtic Heritage of Sir Gawain and the Green Knight," 178.
38. Siewers, "Green Otherworlds," 39.
39. Fyler, "Freshman Composition: Epic and Romance," 121.
40. Huntsman, "The Celtic Heritage of Sir Gawain and the Green Knight," 180.
41. Siewers, "Green Otherworlds," 39.
42. Tolkien, *Sir Gawain*, 42.
43. Rudd, *Greenery*, 125.
44. Siewers, "Green Otherworlds," 32.
45. Tolkien, *Sir Gawain*, 79.
46. Huntsman, "The Celtic Heritage of Sir Gawain and the Green Knight," 180.
47. Tolkien, *Sir Gawain*, 80.
48. Tolkien, *Monsters*, 75.
49. Shippey, *Road*, 108.
50. Rudd, *Greenery*, 109.
51. Huntsman, "The Celtic Heritage of Sir Gawain and the Green Knight," 180.
52. Rudd, *Greenery*, 111.
53. Rudd, *Greenery*, 110; emphasis in original.
54. Flieger, *Green Suns*, 220.
55. Rudd, *Greenery*, 111.

56. George, "Gawain's Struggle with Ecology," 31.
57. Neville, *Representations*, 25.
58. George, "Gawain's Struggle with Ecology," 39.
59. George, "Gawain's Struggle with Ecology," 39.
60. Westling, "Introduction," 7.
61. Rudd notes that "habitually critics refer to Bertilak's castle as 'Hautdesert', pointing out that the name means 'High Desert' or Wasteland. However, we do not know that Hautdesert is in fact the castle. The term occurs only as part of Bertilak's name . . . and may as easily be a country as a court. If so, Bertilak is declaring his identity as a denizen of the wilderness even as he seems to be identifying himself as a human lord" (*Greenery*, 131n27).
62. George, "Gawain's Struggle with Ecology," 39.
63. Oelschlaeger, *The Idea of Wilderness*, 3.
64. Curry, *Defending Middle-Earth*, 50.

Part II

1. Lunt, "The Climate of Middle Earth," 6.
2. Acks, "Tolkien's Map."
3. Judd and Judd, *Flora of Middle-Earth*, 74–78.
4. Tolkien, *Lord*, 248.
5. Resnick, "An Interview with Tolkien," 41.
6. Tolkien, *Lord*, 1048.
7. Tolkien, *Lord*, 641.
8. Tolkien, *Lord*, 661.
9. Resnick, "An Interview with Tolkien," 41.
10. Tolkien, *Letters*, 212.
11. His defensiveness is perhaps understandable, considering how much critics working in ethnic, racial, and feminist studies had to say even during his lifetime about his failings in this regard. While understanding Tolkien's treatment of race, gender, and other alterities is certainly important in analyzing his impact on the modern mythological landscape, the details of these complex arguments are beyond the scope of this wilderness-based study. Dimitra Fimi concludes in her excellent book *Tolkien, Race, and Cultural History* that Tolkien's Middle-earth is ultimately "a fantasy world that reproduces some of the concepts and prejudices of the 'primary' world while at the same time questioning, challenging and transforming others" (159). It is important to remember that not until the second half of the twentieth century did postcolonial studies even begin to chip away at the unconscious stranglehold on normative culture maintained by the Western educated classes, and that hold has since loosened only a tiny fraction (as the many controversies over Hollywood "whitewashing" illustrate). Tolkien fiercely opposed what he called the "wholly pernicious and unscientific race-doctrine" (*Letters*, 37), and only the most superficial readings of his work and life can conclude that he personally harbored, even in his early twentieth-century time, anything more condemnable than the unconscious male and Eurocentric bias that continues to plague the Western world in the twenty-first.

12. Tolkien, *Letters*, 375; emphasis in original.
13. Tolkien, *Letters*, 376.
14. Tolkien, *Letters*, 376.
15. Snyder, *The Making of Middle-Earth*, 3.
16. Tolkien, *Lord*, 190.
17. Tolkien, *Lord*, 351.
18. Tolkien, *Lord*, 71.
19. Burns, *Perilous Realms*, 26.
20. Dickerson and Evans, *Ents, Elves, and Eriador*, 31; emphasis in original.
21. Jeffers, *Arda Inhabited*, 16–17.
22. Tolkien, *Lord*, 400.

4. *Rangers in the Mountains*

1. Burns, *Perilous Realms*, 26.
2. Tolkien, *Monsters*, 26.
3. Bradford, "From of Plymouth Plantation," 19.
4. Nash, *Wilderness and the American Mind*, 8.
5. Tolkien, *Hobbit*, 13.
6. The Old Norse cognate *Myrkviðr* appears in the *Poetic Edda* as the dangerous border between Muspelheim and Asgard ("Lokasenna," stanza 42). William Morris adapted the word to modern English in his 1889 *The House of the Wolfings;* John Orth also points out that Sir Walter Scott used *Mirkwood* in his 1814 novel *Waverly*, and suggests Scott influenced both Morris and Tolkien ("Mirkwood," 53).
7. Tolkien, *Letters*, 369.
8. Tolkien, *Hobbit*, 45.
9. Tolkien, *Lord*, 43.
10. Tolkien, *Hobbit*, 69.
11. Tolkien, *Hobbit*, 44–45.
12. Tolkien, *Hobbit*, 177.
13. Tolkien, *Hobbit*, 235.
14. Nash, *Wilderness and the American Mind*, 4.
15. Burns, *Perilous Realms*, 52.
16. Burns, *Perilous Realms*, 25.
17. Tolkien, *Letters*, 391–92.
18. Fuegi, "Rivendell in Switzerland"; see Hammond and Scull, *Artist*, 111, Fig. 108; Tolkien, *Hobbit*, 89.
19. Hammond and Scull, *Artist*, 149–51, Fig. 144.
20. Tolkien, *Hobbit*, 256.
21. Burns, *Perilous Realms*, 25.
22. Tolkien, *Hobbit*, 87.
23. Tolkien, *Hobbit*, 88.
24. Tolkien, *Hobbit*, 90.
25. Tolkien, *Hobbit*, 101.
26. Tolkien, *Hobbit*, 104.

27. Tolkien, *Hobbit*, 72.
28. Tolkien, *Hobbit*, 88.
29. Tolkien, *Hobbit*, 100, 101–3.
30. Tolkien, *Hobbit*, 101.
31. Tolkien, *Letters*, 392–93.
32. Tolkien, *Hobbit*, 103.
33. Hammond and Scull, *Artist*, 118, Fig. 109.
34. Tolkien, *Hobbit*, 158.
35. Tolkien, *Hobbit*, 241.
36. Tolkien, *Hobbit*, 242, 255.
37. Tolkien, *Hobbit*, 257–58.
38. Chickering, *Beowulf*, 203.
39. Tolkien, *Hobbit*, 304. Admittedly the riddling conversation Bilbo has with Smaug has a lighter, almost funny sense to it, but it is a comedy of much more deadly seriousness than trolls grumbling about mutton.
40. Tolkien, *Hobbit*, 353.
41. Tolkien, *Lord*, 282.
42. Tolkien, *Lord*, 286.
43. Tolkien, *Lord*, 288.
44. Tolkien, *Lord*, 289.
45. Tolkien, *Lord*, 289.
46. Tolkien, *Lord*, 292.
47. Tolkien, *Lord*, 293.
48. Tolkien, *Lord*, 333.
49. Tolkien, *Lord*, 334.
50. Tolkien, *Lord*, 422.
51. Tolkien, *Lord*, 750–51.
52. Tolkien, *Lord*, 791.
53. The Mercian dialect of Old English; see Shippey, *Road*, 123n1.
54. Tolkien, *Lord*, 508.
55. Magennis, *Images of Community*, 130.
56. Tolkien, *Lord*, 631.
57. Dickerson and Evans, *Ents, Elves, and Eriador*, 187.
58. Tolkien, *Lord*, 631–32.
59. Tolkien, *Lord*, 632.
60. Tolkien, *Lord*, 709.
61. Tolkien, *Lord*, 729.
62. Consider the Norman surname of Bertilak de Hautdesert in *Sir Gawain and the Green Knight*.
63. Nash, *Wilderness and the American Mind*, 2.
64. Mattingly, *Tacitus on Britain and Germany*, 102.
65. Gummere, *Germanic Origins*, 35.
66. Chickering, *Beowulf*, 127, 129.
67. Tolkien, *Hobbit*, 51–52.
68. Tolkien, *Hobbit*, 176–77.

69. Tolkien, *Hobbit*, 186.
70. Douglas Anderson's note on the *Berggeist* examines this mythic influence (Tolkien, *Hobbit*, 189n13).
71. Tolkien, *Hobbit*, 190.
72. Tolkien, *Hobbit*, 191.
73. Tolkien, *Hobbit*, 191, 194.
74. Tolkien, *Lord*, 352.
75. Tolkien, *Hobbit*, 219.
76. Tolkien, *Silmarillion*, 143.
77. Tolkien, *Hobbit*, 194.
78. Tolkien, *Hobbit*, 214.
79. Tolkien, *Hobbit*, 208.
80. Tolkien, *Hobbit*, 217.
81. Tolkien, *Lord*, 110.
82. Tolkien, *Lord*, 110–11.
83. Tolkien, *Lord*, 111.
84. Tolkien, *Lord*, 112.
85. Tolkien, *Lord*, 116.
86. See Tolkien, *Lord*, 130.
87. Tolkien, *Lord*, 133–34.
88. Tolkien, *Lord*, 141.
89. Tolkien, *Lord*, 140.
90. Tolkien, *Lord*, 182, 190.
91. Tolkien, *Lord*, 199.
92. Tolkien, *Lord*, 201.
93. Tolkien, *Lord*, 459.
94. Tolkien, *Lord*, 442.
95. Tolkien, *Lord*, 442.
96. Tolkien, *Lord*, 491.
97. Tolkien, *Lord*, 461–62.
98. Tolkien, *Lord*, 499.
99. Tolkien, *Lord*, 373, 467.
100. Tolkien, *Lord*, 541.
101. Tolkien, *Lord*, 542.
102. Tolkien, *Lord*, 546.
103. Tolkien, *Lord*, 546.
104. Tolkien, *Lord*, 547.
105. Tolkien, *Lord*, 462.
106. Tolkien, *Lord*, 469–70.
107. Tolkien, *Lord*, 479.
108. Tolkien, *Lord*, 485.
109. Tolkien, *Lord*, 486.
110. This assertion is made specifically in the literary-mythic context of genre fiction and role-playing games, where Tolkien's foundational position is unquestioned. But, while Tolkien's Rangers might share some characteristics with uses of the term outside this specific context, such as the elite American military or

policing units, a flow from the same upstream spring of mythic ideas is far more likely than any direct influence from Tolkien.

111. "[Wolves] walk not widely, as they were woont, For fear of raungers, and the great hoont" (Quoted in "Ranger, n.1.").

112. Tolkien, *Lord*, 149.

113. Tolkien, *Lord*, 168, 156.

114. Tolkien, *Lord*, 165.

115. Tolkien, *Lord*, 146.

116. Tolkien, *Lord*, 221.

117. Tolkien, *Lord*, 248.

118. Tolkien, *Lord*, 659.

119. Tolkien, *Silmarillion*, 77.

120. Tolkien, *Children of Húrin*, 53. The posthumous volume *The Children of Húrin* is referenced here because it provides much greater detail on Túrin's tragically heroic tale than is given in *The Silmarillion*.

121. Tolkien, *Children of Húrin*, 60.

122. Tolkien, *Children of Húrin*, 60.

123. Tolkien, *Lord*, 428.

124. Tolkien, *Lord*, 780.

125. Tolkien, *Lord*, 787.

126. Tolkien, *Lord*, 775.

127. Tolkien, *Lord*, 776.

128. Tolkien, *Lord*, 783.

129. Tolkien, *Lord*, 778.

130. Tolkien, *Lord*, 786.

131. Tolkien, *Lord*, 786.

132. Tolkien, *Lord*, 790.

133. Tacitus describes a tribe of Germanic warriors who "black their shields and dye their bodies black and choose pitch dark nights for their battles. The terrifying shadow of such a fiendish army inspires a mortal panic, for no enemy can stand so strange and devilish a sight" (Mattingly, *Tacitus on Britain and Germany*, 136).

134. Tolkien, *Lord*, 164, 861.

135. Tolkien, *Monsters*, 20–21.

136. Shippey, *Road*, 78.

137. Burns, *Perilous Realms*, 60.

138. Dickerson and Evans, *Ents, Elves, and Eriador*, 136.

139. Dickerson and Evans, *Ents, Elves, and Eriador*, 139.

5. *Elves in the Forest*

1. Siewers, "Tolkien's Cosmic-Christian Ecology," 143.
2. Tolkien, *Monsters*, 24.
3. Burns, *Perilous Realms*, 53.
4. Siewers, *Strange Beauty*, 133.
5. Siewers, "Tolkien's Cosmic-Christian Ecology," 144.
6. Siewers, "Tolkien's Cosmic-Christian Ecology," 143.

7. Burns, *Perilous Realms*, 54, 57.
8. Tolkien, *Lord*, 461.
9. Tolkien, *Hobbit*, 198.
10. Douglas Anderson points out that "in Celtic tradition, encounters with white animals (especially white deer) usually prefigure an encounter with beings from the Otherworld (Faërie)" (Tolkien, *Hobbit*, 200n6).
11. Tolkien, *Hobbit*, 199.
12. Tolkien, *Hobbit*, 206.
13. Tolkien, *Hobbit*, 216, 217.
14. Tolkien, *Hobbit*, 219.
15. Burns, *Perilous Realms*, 67.
16. Siewers, *Strange Beauty*, 40.
17. Tolkien, *Lord*, 78.
18. Siewers, "Tolkien's Cosmic-Christian Ecology," 144.
19. Tolkien, *Lord*, 80.
20. Tolkien, *Lord*, 81.
21. Tolkien, *Lord*, 82.
22. Tolkien, *Lord*, 82.
23. Tolkien, *Lord*, 86.
24. Tolkien, *Lord*, 1029.
25. Tolkien, *Lord*, 119; emphasis in original.
26. Tolkien, *Lord*, 91; emphasis in original.
27. Tolkien, *Lord*, 79; emphasis in original.
28. Tolkien, *Letters*, 174.
29. Because he is so broadly presented as an avatar of the natural world, Tom Bombadil is difficult to pin down, and he is quite impossible to slot comfortably within the structures scholars so love to construct. Critics have argued variously that he represents: a Christ figure or a pagan god; a Vala or a Maia; Eru Ilúvatar/God or the first man/Adam; a Green Man or a nature spirit; the author or the reader; see Beal, "Who Is Tom Bombadil?," 15–17, for an exhaustive list. After the publication of *The Hobbit* but before he began *The Lord of the Rings*, Tolkien described Tom Bombadil to his publisher as "the spirit of the (vanishing) Oxford and Berkshire countryside" (*Letters*, 26). More than sixteen years later, he would only admit that Bombadil "represents something I feel important, though I would not be prepared to analyze the feeling precisely" (*Letters*, 178). To avoid falling into the trap of trying to unravel this intentionally enigmatic character, this study will agree with Jane Beal's assertion that Bombadil "must be interpreted at multiple levels of meaning simultaneously" ("Who Is Tom Bombadil?," 2), acknowledge that he stands as separate from this structure as he does from all others, and consider some aspects of his character, which may illuminate the three concepts of wilderness under discussion here.
30. Tolkien, *Lord*, 120.
31. Tolkien, *Lord*, 121.
32. Tolkien, *Lord*, 121.
33. Burns, *Perilous Realms*, 56.
34. Tolkien, *Lord*, 482.

35. Tolkien, *Lord*, 674.
36. Tolkien, *Lord*, 683.
37. Flieger, *Green Suns*, 134.
38. Dickerson and Evans, *Ents, Elves, and Eriador*, 102.
39. Tolkien, *Hobbit*, 88.
40. Burns, *Perilous Realms*, 61.
41. Tolkien, *Hobbit*, 88.
42. Tolkien, *Hobbit*, 90.
43. Tolkien, *Lord*, 212.
44. Tolkien, *Lord*, 214.
45. Siewers, "Tolkien's Cosmic-Christian Ecology," 144.
46. Tolkien, *Hobbit*, 355.
47. Tolkien, *Lord*, 985.
48. Tolkien, *Hobbit*, 97.
49. Tolkien, *Hobbit*, 358.
50. Tolkien, *Lord*, 279.
51. Tolkien, *Lord*, 281.
52. Tolkien, *Hobbit*, 93–94.
53. Tolkien, *Hobbit*, 95.
54. Elrond appears in Tolkien's writings as early as 1926, as a child "part mortal and part elfin and part of the race of Valar" (Tolkien, *Shaping*, 39n7) but it was not until *The Lord of the Rings* that he developed into the wise and powerful character familiar to readers today.
55. Tolkien, *Letters*, 346–47.
56. Tolkien, *Letters*, 158.
57. Tolkien, *Lord*, 222.
58. Tolkien, *Lord*, 223.
59. Tolkien, *Lord*, 226.
60. Tolkien, *Lord*, 239.
61. Tolkien, *Lord*, 239.
62. Tolkien, *Lord*, 239.
63. Tolkien, *Silmarillion*, 142.
64. Tolkien, *Hobbit*, 94.
65. Tolkien, *Lord*, 225.
66. Tolkien, *Hobbit*, 88.
67. Tolkien, *Lord*, 233.
68. Tolkien, *Lord*, 231, 273.
69. Tolkien, *Lord*, 274.
70. Tolkien, *Letters*, 104.
71. Tolkien, *Silmarillion*, 142.
72. Tolkien, *Lord*, 352.
73. Tolkien, *Lord*, 338.
74. Tolkien, *Lord*, 338.
75. This exchange is similar in tone and perspective shift to that of Gandalf warning Gimli he is "beset with dangers" (Tolkien, *Lord*, 499).
76. Tolkien, *Lord*, 338.

77. Burns, *Perilous Realms*, 64.
78. Dickerson and Evans, *Ents, Elves, and Eriador*, 106, 108.
79. Tolkien, *Lord*, 335.
80. Tolkien, *Lord*, 335.
81. Dickerson and Evans, *Ents, Elves, and Eriador*, 107.
82. Tolkien, *Lord*, 339, 341.
83. Dickerson and Evans, *Ents, Elves, and Eriador*, 110.
84. Tolkien, *Silmarillion*, 14.
85. Glorfindel was born in Valinor, but he was not explicitly described in the text as a descendant of Finwé. Elrond is a distant scion of that kingly line, but he was born in Middle-earth and never saw the Blessed Realm until his final journey.
86. Tolkien, *Lord*, 337–38.
87. Tolkien, *Lord*, 337, 346.
88. Tolkien, *Lord*, 346.
89. Tolkien, *Letters*, 63.
90. Tolkien, *Lord*, 349.
91. Tolkien, *Lord*, 350.
92. As the meaning and syntax are totally different, the phonetic similarity of this name to that of the Welsh mound of Gorsedd Arberth might be due to the relationship of the sounds of Sindarin to those of Welsh, or it might be purely coincidental, but either way it is interesting, as both mounds represent an interface for characters between mundane reality and the Otherworld. In Oisín's journey to Tír na nÓg in the Irish Fenian cycle, the hero encounters a surpassingly fair land on which stands a royal mansion, "And in this royal mansion fair / All colors were that eye hath seen—/ The blue most bright, the purest white / With purple and yellow and softest green" (Cross and Slover, *Ancient Irish Tales*, 448). While colors and otherworldly beauty are a shaky foundation on which to build a case for literary influence, in many tales of the Celtic Otherworld the presence of lines extolling an unusual richness of color is extremely common.
93. Tolkien, *Lord*, 350.
94. Tolkien, *Letters*, 221.
95. Tolkien, *Lord*, 353.
96. Tolkien, *Lord*, 354.
97. Tolkien, *Lord*, 338.
98. Tolkien, *Lord*, 351; emphasis in original.
99. Tolkien, *Lord*, 361.
100. Tolkien, *Lord*, 364.
101. Tolkien, *Lord*, 1094.
102. Tolkien, *Silmarillion*, 142.
103. Tolkien, *Silmarillion*, 8.
104. Tolkien, *Silmarillion*, 9.
105. Tolkien, *Silmarillion*, 54.
106. Tolkien, *Lord*, 467.
107. Tolkien, *Unfinished Tales*, 253n5.
108. Tolkien, *Lord*, 362.
109. Tolkien, *Lord*, 379.

110. Flieger, *A Question of Time,* 93.
111. Burns, *Perilous Realms,* 70.
112. Tolkien, *Lord,* 349.
113. Tolkien, *Lord,* 351.
114. Tolkien, *Lord,* 352.
115. Tolkien, *Lord,* 355.
116. Tolkien, *Lord,* 358.
117. Tolkien, *Lord,* 388.
118. Tolkien, *Lord,* 367.
119. Tolkien, *Lord,* 371, 373.
120. Tolkien, *Lord,* 377.
121. Tolkien, *Lord,* 379.
122. Burns, *Perilous Realms,* 70.
123. Tolkien, *Lord,* 434.
124. Dickerson and Evans, *Ents, Elves, and Eriador,* 124.
125. Jeffers, *Arda Inhabited,* 98.

6. *Hobbits in the Shire*

1. Schama, *Landscape and Memory,* 141.
2. Nash, *Wilderness and the American Mind,* 44.
3. Tolkien, born in the fifty-fifth year of Queen Victoria's sixty-three-year reign, was definitely a child of these times.
4. Quoted in Thomas and Hessayon, "The Perception of the Past," 211.
5. Hutton, *The Rise and Fall of Merry England,* 104, 118.
6. Thomas and Hessayon, "The Perception of the Past," 212.
7. Thomas and Hessayon, "The Perception of the Past," 212–13.
8. Thomas and Hessayon, "The Perception of the Past," 213–14.
9. Judge, "May Day and Merrie England," 131.
10. Thomas and Hessayon, "The Perception of the Past," 207.
11. Tolkien, *Letters,* 230.
12. Tolkien, *Hobbit,* 31.
13. Heilbronner, "In Search of the English Psyche," 97.
14. Pearce, *Merrie England,* 5; emphasis in original.
15. Shippey, *Author,* 9.
16. Shippey, *Author,* 11.
17. Flieger, *Green Suns,* 10.
18. Burns, *Perilous Realms,* 27.
19. Tolkien, *Letters,* 288–89; emphasis in original.
20. Schama, *Landscape and Memory,* 183.
21. Schama, *Landscape and Memory,* 142.
22. Schama, *Landscape and Memory,* 143.
23. Schama, *Landscape and Memory,* 143.
24. Tolkien, *Lord,* 1.
25. Tolkien, *Lord,* 5.
26. Tolkien, *Hobbit,* 70.

27. Tolkien, *Lord*, 1.
28. Note the presence of "wild things" in these purportedly tame places. Tolkien, *Lord*, 70–71.
29. Tolkien, *Hobbit*, 52–53.
30. Tolkien, *Lord*, 70, 45.
31. Tolkien, *Lord*, 239.
32. Tolkien, *Lord*, 7, 42.
33. Tolkien, *Lord*, 312.
34. Tolkien, *Lord*, 20.
35. Tolkien, *Hobbit*, 359n4.
36. Tolkien, *Hobbit*, 65.
37. Tolkien, *Hobbit*, 359.
38. Tolkien, *Hobbit*, 45.
39. Tolkien, *Lord*, 71.
40. Tolkien, *Lord*, 71–72.
41. From a fox famously "passing through the wood on business of his own" (Tolkien, *Lord*, 72).
42. Tolkien, *Lord*, 72.
43. Tolkien, *Lord*, 73.
44. Tolkien, *Lord*, 74.
45. Tolkien, *Lord*, 76.
46. Tolkien, *Lord*, 76–77.
47. Tolkien, *Lord*, 86.
48. Tolkien, *Lord*, 88.
49. Tolkien, *Lord*, 88.
50. Tolkien, *Lord*, 88–89.
51. Tolkien, *Lord*, 89.
52. Tolkien, *Lord*, 89.
53. Tolkien, *Lord*, 89–90.
54. Tolkien, *Lord*, 90; emphasis in original.
55. Tolkien, *Lord*, 90.
56. Tolkien, *Lord*, 91.
57. Tolkien, *Lord*, 91.
58. Tolkien, *Lord*, 91.
59. Tolkien, *Lord*, 70, 92.
60. Tolkien, *Lord*, 93.
61. Tolkien, *Hobbit*, 145.
62. Tolkien, *Lord*, 288, also 177, 1089. Harrison, quoting an old English forestry law book, gives an approximate date of 969 CE, and discusses the difference between "ravenous beasts" and "beasts of pleasure" like the hart or the hare (*Forests*, 71).
63. Tolkien, *Lord*, 83.
64. Tolkien, *Lord*, 992.
65. Tolkien, *Lord*, 993.
66. Tolkien, *Lord*, 993.
67. Tolkien, *Lord*, 1000.
68. Tolkien, *Lord*, 1916, 1018.

69. Tolkien, *Lord*, 1022.
70. Tolkien, *Lord*, 1024, 1021.
71. Tolkien, *Lord*, 265.
72. Dickerson and Evans, *Ents, Elves, and Eriador*, 134.
73. Tolkien, *Lord*, 22, 98.
74. Tolkien, *Lord*, 98–99.
75. Tolkien, *Lord*, 99.
76. Tolkien, *Lord*, 99.
77. Tolkien, *Lord*, 5.
78. Tolkien, *Lord*, 110.
79. Tolkien, *Lord*, 177.
80. Tolkien, *Lord*, 129.
81. Tolkien, *Lord*, 130.
82. Tolkien, *Lord*, 109.
83. Tolkien, *Lord*, 103, 107.
84. Tolkien, *Lord*, 22, 109.
85. Tolkien, *Hobbit*, 65.
86. Tolkien, *Hobbit*, 66n6.
87. Tolkien, *Lord*, 182.
88. Tolkien, *Lord*, 182.
89. Tolkien, *Lord*, 182.
90. Tolkien, *Lord*, 182.
91. Tolkien, *Lord*, 650.
92. Tolkien, *Lord*, 649.
93. Tolkien, *Lord*, 649.
94. Tolkien, *Lord*, 650.
95. Tolkien, *Lord*, 650.
96. Tolkien, *Lord*, 651.
97. Shippey, *Road*, 69; emphasis in original.
98. Tolkien, *Lord*, 651.
99. Tolkien, *Letters*, 94.
100. Tolkien, *Letters*, 219, 289.
101. Tolkien, *Letters*, 430.
102. Scull and Hammond, *Chronology*, 6, 814.
103. Hammond and Scull, *Artist*, 17.
104. Carpenter, *Tolkien: A Biography*, 71.
105. Carpenter, *Tolkien: A Biography*, 163.
106. Scull and Hammond, *Chronology*, 208.
107. On these outings Tolkien apparently preferred a more leisurely adventure than his friends. The Lewis brothers in particular, whom he described as "ruthless walkers, very ruthless indeed," complained that he was "a great man, but not our sort of walker" (Sayer, "Recollections," 22) and that he "wouldn't trot at our pace in harness; he will keep going all day on a walk, but to him . . . a walk, no matter what its length, is what we would call an extended stroll" (Quoted in Scull and Hammond, *Chronology*, 340).
108. Scull and Hammond, *Chronology*, 340, 409.

109. Tolkien, *Lord*, 43, 65.
110. Shippey, *Road*, 105.
111. Shippey, *Road*, 104.
112. Shippey, *Road*, 104–5.
113. Shippey, *Author*, 6; emphasis in original.
114. Tolkien, *Letters*, 31.
115. Shippey, *Author*, 48.
116. Shippey, *Road*, 92–93.
117. Tolkien, *Hobbit*, 354.
118. Tolkien, *Lord*, 33.
119. Tolkien, *Letters*, 87.
120. Burns, *Perilous Realms*, 28.
121. Tolkien, *Letters*, 90–91.
122. Siewers, "Tolkien's Cosmic-Christian Ecology," 145.
123. Curry, *Defending Middle-Earth*, 50.
124. Dickerson and Evans, *Ents, Elves, and Eriador*, 142.

Part III

1. The opposite is also generally true—Tom Shippey suggests that Tolkien might have believed the oddly instinctive antipathy with which his work was greeted in the mainstream critical establishment was an ancient one: "people who couldn't stand his books hadn't been able to bear *Beowulf*, or *Pearl*, or Chaucer, or *Sir Gawain*, or *Sir Orfeo* either. For millennia they had been trying to impose their views on a recalcitrant succession of authors, who had fortunately taken no notice" (*Road*, 14). See Lee and Solopova, *The Keys of Middle-Earth*.

2. This somewhat paradoxical combination is also present in other modern Western myths, such as the Sherlock Holmes stories and the Icelandic *Ragnars saga loðbrókar* (both of which have been reimagined as wildly popular television series).

7. Tolkien and American Wilderness Philosophy

1. Oelschlaeger, *The Idea of Wilderness*, 209; emphasis in original.
2. Jones, *Myth & Middle-Earth*, 67–68.
3. Campbell, *The Ecological Augury in the Works of JRR Tolkien*, 2.
4. Harrison, *Forests*, 69.
5. Tolkien, *Letters*, 65.
6. Although there is no conclusive evidence confirming which "Red Indian" stories Tolkien meant here, Tom Shippey discusses several indirect similarities between episodes in *The Lord of the Rings* and the famous nineteenth-century novels of James Fenimore Cooper (*Road*, 127).
7. Tolkien, *On Fairy Stories*, 55.
8. Tolkien, *Letters*, 412.
9. Jeffers, *Arda Inhabited*, 12.
10. It took the folklore revival of the eighteenth century to get the Cotton man-

uscripts copied and studied, and *Beowulf* itself was not published until 1815. The last volume of Lady Charlotte Guest's *Mabinogion* did not appear until 1845.

11. Nash, *Wilderness and the American Mind*, 24.
12. Nash, *Wilderness and the American Mind*, 26.
13. Nash, *Wilderness and the American Mind*, 24.
14. Callicott and Nelson, "Introduction," 4–5.
15. Bradford, "From of Plymouth Plantation," 19.
16. Winthrop, "Modell," 47.
17. Neville, *Representations*, 25.
18. Heaney, *Beowulf*, 23.
19. Tolkien, *Lord*, 430.
20. Of course Númenor at its height was far greater than Gondor ever became, but Númenor is only a distant memory in the most popular segments of Tolkien's modern myth, more a melancholy symbol of lost greatness than a living example of virtuous people in today's world.
21. Tolkien, *Lord*, 451.
22. Reagan, "Farewell."
23. Jeffers, *Arda Inhabited*, 16–17.
24. Jeffers, *Arda Inhabited*, 17.
25. Jeffers, *Arda Inhabited*, 73.
26. Jeffers, *Arda Inhabited*, 73.
27. Jeffers, *Arda Inhabited*, 53.
28. Nash, *Wilderness and the American Mind*, 69.
29. Bradford, "From of Plymouth Plantation," 21–22.
30. Although the popular obsession in the United States with British royalty, from Princess Di to Prince Harry, is evidence that the myths of kingship still speak strongly to American popular culture, whatever the official political stance on monarchy might be.
31. Tolkien, *Lord*, 832.
32. Tolkien, *Lord*, 976.
33. Plumwood, "Wilderness Skepticism and Wilderness Dualism," 660–61.
34. Nash, *Wilderness and the American Mind*, 44.
35. Nash, *Wilderness and the American Mind*, 49.
36. Nash, *Wilderness and the American Mind*, 60.
37. Nash, *Wilderness and the American Mind*, 64, 66.
38. Emerson, *English*, 4.
39. Emerson, *Nature*, 81–82.
40. Emerson, *Nature*, 370.
41. Turner, *The Frontier in American History*, 311.
42. It goes without saying that Turner erased the presence of the Native Americans in his analysis; he also ignored the history of French and Spanish settlement in the New World, as well as the general female and ethnic minority frontier experiences, and his work has come under much-deserved attack almost since its inception. But there is no denying his mythic influence on the American mind.
43. Cronon, "Revisiting the Vanishing Frontier," 160.

44. Oelschlaeger, *The Idea of Wilderness*, 111.
45. Muir, *Mountains*, 162.
46. Jeffers, *Arda Inhabited*, 40.
47. Tolkien, *Lord*, 468.
48. Tolkien, *Lord*, 284.
49. Tolkien, *Lord*, 338–39.
50. Muir, *Summer*, 251.
51. Muir, *Summer*, 155–56, 188.
52. Cronon, "The Trouble with Wilderness," 479.
53. Holmes, *The Young John Muir*, 3.
54. Signed by President Lincoln during the Civil War, this decree gave ownership of Yosemite Valley and the Mariposa Grove of Giant Sequoias to the State of California with the stipulation that "the premises shall be held for public use, resort, and recreation" and "shall be inalienable for all-time" (An Act).
55. Perrottet, "John Muir's Yosemite."
56. Perrottet, "John Muir's Yosemite."
57. Cronon, "The Trouble with Wilderness," 482.
58. Accusations of conscious and outright racism against Muir are often as oversimplified as those leveled against Tolkien, and Muir's later work, particularly that on the Alaska natives, indicate that he partially managed to outgrow some of the worst of his inherited racist thinking. But there is no denying that his work set the early tone for the discussion of wilderness in the West, and like most wilderness writers he maintained a conspicuous silence as Native Americans were removed from their ancestral lands to create the white man's wilderness. See Lankford, "John Muir," for a good overview of Muir's changing thinking throughout his life and a nuanced exploration of Muir's racist past and legacy.
59. Millet, "Ecoporn Exposed," 34.
60. Millet, "Ecoporn Exposed," 34.
61. Dickerson and Evans, *Ents, Elves, and Eriador*, 114.
62. Ertsgaard, "Leaves of Gold There Grew," 217, 218, 220.
63. I am grateful to Martin Simonson for this insight about Galadriel.
64. Tolkien, *Silmarillion*, 74.
65. Shippey, *Author*, 206.
66. "Conservation."
67. Nash, *Wilderness and the American Mind*, 194–95.
68. Oelschlaeger, *The Idea of Wilderness*, 214.
69. Leopold, *A Sand County Almanac*, 188, 192.
70. Leopold, *A Sand County Almanac*, 4.
71. Leopold, *A Sand County Almanac*, 148–49.
72. Leopold, *A Sand County Almanac*, 162.
73. Leopold, *A Sand County Almanac*, 181.
74. Leopold, *A Sand County Almanac*, viii.
75. Leopold, *A Sand County Almanac*, 224–25.
76. Tolkien, *Lord*, 1.
77. Tolkien, *Hobbit*, 32, 360, 9.

78. Tolkien, *Lord*, 5.
79. Dickerson and Evans, *Ents, Elves, and Eriador*, 205.
80. Jeffers, *Arda Inhabited*, 80, 37.
81. Jeffers, *Arda Inhabited*, 33.
82. Leopold, *A Sand County Almanac*, 6.
83. Leopold, *A Sand County Almanac*, 73.
84. Tolkien, *Lord*, 132.
85. Leopold, *A Sand County Almanac*, 100.
86. Leopold, *A Sand County Almanac*, 128.
87. Tolkien, *Lord*, 1007, 1013.
88. Dickerson and Evans, *Ents, Elves, and Eriador*, 205.
89. Campbell, *The Ecological Augury in the Works of JRR Tolkien*, 46.
90. Leopold, *A Sand County Almanac*, 11.
91. Leopold died in 1948; *The Return of the King* was not published until 1955.
92. Tolkien, *Lord*, 1005.
93. Tolkien, *Lord*, 758.
94. Leopold, *A Sand County Almanac*, 221.
95. Dickerson and Evans, *Ents, Elves, and Eriador*, 76; emphasis in original.
96. Niiler, "Timely, Again: Tolkien's Fantastic Ecology," 98–99.
97. Jeffers, *Arda Inhabited*, 38.
98. Leopold, "Pioneers and Gullies," 16.
99. Powell, *Vanishing America*, 183.
100. Powell, *Vanishing America*, 177.
101. Powell, *Vanishing America*, 107.
102. Powell's analysis of Leopold's unpublished paper "In the Long Run" provides some interesting details (*Vanishing America*, 172–74).
103. This is not completely possible, of course, but the thought experiment can help highlight how this local parochialism is dangerous even in homogeneous cultural landscapes.
104. Tolkien, *Lord*, 248.
105. Tolkien, *Lord*, 150 (emphasis in original), 156.
106. Tolkien, *Letters*, 329.

8. Tolkienian Wilderness in the Information Age

1. Barton, *Dungeons and Desktops*, 18–19.
2. The similarities were so blatant that in the mid-1970s Tolkien Enterprises threatened legal action against Gygax, and the Hobbits, Ents, and Balrogs of the *D&D* game world were changed to halflings, Treants, and Balor-demons in subsequent editions (Burdge, "Gaming," 229).
3. Quoted in Tresca, *The Evolution of Fantasy Role-Playing Games*, 23.
4. Barton, *Dungeons and Desktops*, 31–35, 202.
5. Tolkien, *Letters*, 145.
6. Humphrey Carpenter reports the amusing anecdote that Tolkien had "never before encountered a tape-recorder at close quarters" and pretended to regard

the thing "with great suspicion, pronouncing the Lord's Prayer in Gothic into the microphone to cast out any devils that might be lurking within" (*Tolkien: A Biography*, 241).

7. Tolkien, *Letters*, 164.

8. Tolkien, *Letters*, 228.

9. Croft, "Three Rings for Hollywood," 8.

10. Tolkien, *Letters*, 261, 257.

11. The film treatment had been written by Morton Grady Zimmerman, to whom Tolkien refers personally with this initial in his correspondence on the project.

12. Tolkien, *Letters*, 267.

13. Tolkien, *Letters*, 277; emphasis in original.

14. Croft, "Three Rings for Hollywood," 9–10.

15. Or perhaps earlier; the Andrew Lang lecture dates to 1939, but the manuscript record is unclear about whether the paragraphs on drama included in the published essay were part of his original talk.

16. Tolkien, *On Fairy Stories*, 62.

17. Plimmer and Plimmer, "Film My Books?"

18. Harlow and Dobson, "*Lord of the Rings* Is Worth £3bn," 16.

19. Saperstein, "16 Things You Didn't Know About the Making of 'Lord of the Rings.'"

20. Liptak, "Looking Back."

21. Auden, "At the End of the Quest, Victory," 226.

22. Quoted in Susman, "'Lord of the Rings' Widens a Tolkien Family Rift."

23. "They have eviscerated the book, making it an action movie for ages 15–25" (my translation). Rérolle, "Tolkien, l'anneau de la discorde."

24. "has become a monster, devoured by his popularity and absorbed by the absurdity of the times" (my translation). Rérolle, "Tolkien, l'anneau de la discorde."

25. Braun unfortunately does not provide a specific source for this assertion; it is given in a section of his book, which he describes as "behind the scenes information . . . gathered from numerous sources over the years, giving you the inside scoop on the development of the films" (*The Lord of the Films*, xiv).

26. Braun, *The Lord of the Films*, 175–76.

27. "Tolkien Relative."

28. Douglas Anderson's annotations in *The Annotated Hobbit* provide an exhaustive catalog of these changes, some of which were significant.

29. McLarty, "Masculinity, Whiteness, and Social Class in *The Lord of the Rings*," 180.

30. Tolkien, *On Fairy Stories*, 61.

31. Tolkien, *On Fairy Stories*, 82n113.

32. Kozloff, "*The Lord of the Rings* as Melodrama," 168.

33. Woodward and Kourelis, "Urban Legend," 197.

34. Woodward and Kourelis, "Urban Legend," 204.

35. Woodward and Kourelis, "Urban Legend," 202.

36. Saperstein, "16 Things You Didn't Know About the Making of 'Lord of the Rings.'"

37. Woodward and Kourelis, "Urban Legend," 199.

38. Mathijs and Pomerance, "There and Back Again: An Editor's Tale," 10.
39. Tolkien, *Lord*, 260.
40. Tolkien, *Lord*, 474.
41. Woodward and Kourelis, "Urban Legend," 197.
42. McLarty, "Masculinity, Whiteness, and Social Class in *The Lord of the Rings*," 173, 181.
43. Spacks, "Power and Meaning in *The Lord of the Rings*," 55–56.
44. Jeffers, *Arda Inhabited*, 119, 123–24.
45. Tolkien, *Lord*, 484.
46. Walsh et al., The Lord of the Rings: *The Two Towers (Film Script)*, 185.
47. Barker, "On Being a 1960s Tolkien Reader," 84.
48. Barker, "On Being a 1960s Tolkien Reader," 84.
49. Tolkien, *Lord*, 484.
50. Tolkien, *Lord*, 485–86.
51. Backe, "Within the Mainstream," 47.
52. Excepting perhaps Andriel's female gender, of which Tolkien would likely disapprove (although she's arguably not too far off a Lúthien or a Galadriel as presented in *The Silmarillion*).
53. Pavlovic, "*The Lord of the Rings*."
54. Tito, "*War in the North* Review."
55. Maier-Zucchino, "After Nearly 40 Years."
56. Xbox World 360, "*Lord of the Rings: War in the North*," 3.
57. The game credits list Tom Kane as the voice actor, but he sounds enough like the films' definitive portrayal of the wizard to fool Sir Ian McKellen's mother.
58. Snowblind Studios, *War in the North*, chapter 1 (Bree).
59. Tolkien, *Lord*, 1080.
60. Onyett, "*The Lord of the Rings* Meets Diablo."
61. Gamespot Staff, "*The Lord of the Rings: War in the North* Q&A."
62. Unlike Rivendell, the Golden Wood regrettably has no function in the game storyline other than to serve as a location to smite endless waves of undead monsters in a "challenge map" for players who don't get enough hack-and-slash in the main game. What the undead of the Barrow-downs are doing in Lórien in the first place is never actually explained.
63. *Middle-earth: Shadow of Mordor* (2014) and *Middle-earth: Shadow of War* (2017). In these games the player controls Talion, a Ranger possessed by the wraith of the Elven smith Celebrimbor (yes, *that* Celebrimbor—and in this version of Middle-earth, it was he and not Sauron who forged the One Ring. Don't ask.). One positive reviewer notes that the first game "essentially offers you the power of the One Ring," admits "it feels good to seize that power," and suggests this fact is "scary" (Maier-Zucchino, "After Nearly 40 Years"). This feels a bit like arguing that the *Grand Theft Auto* games sensitively explore the idea that stealing cars is wrong.
64. Maier-Zucchino, "After Nearly 40 Years."
65. Xbox World 360, "*Lord of the Rings: War in the North*," 3.
66. Shippey, *Author*, 159.
67. Chang, *Playing Nature*, 22, emphasis in original.
68. Backe, "Within the Mainstream," 47.

69. Backe, "Within the Mainstream," 47.
70. Snowblind Studios, *War in the North*, chapter 5 ("The Shadowed Paths").
71. Snowblind Studios, *War in the North*, chapter 8 ("Carn Dûm").
72. Backe, "Within the Mainstream," 48.
73. Backe, "Within the Mainstream," 48.
74. Snowblind Studios, *War in the North*, chapter 4 ("Mountain's Interior").
75. Snowblind Studios, *War in the North*, chapter 5 ("Nordinbad").
76. Tolkien, *Lord*, 547–48.
77. Spacks, "Power and Meaning in *The Lord of the Rings*," 55–56.
78. Backe, "Within the Mainstream," 48.
79. Tolkien, *Letters*, 273; emphasis in original.
80. Callahan, "*Lord of the Rings: War in the North* Co-Op Review."
81. Snowblind Studios, *War in the North*, chapter 4 ("Rivendell").
82. Snowblind Studios, *War in the North*, chapter 4 ("Rivendell").
83. Tolkien, *Lord*, 596, 949.
84. Snowblind Studios, *War in the North*, chapter 4 ("Rivendell").
85. Snowblind Studios, *War in the North*, chapter 8 ("Carn Dûm Citadel").
86. "Fan, n.2."
87. Fraade-Blanar and Glazer, *Superfandom*, 7.
88. Lehning, "Living Myths in a Living World," 1.
89. Gupta, "New Zealand Issues Hobbit Coins as Legal Tender."
90. Lehning, "Living Myths in a Living World," 14.
91. Ibata, "'Lord' of Racism? Critics View Trilogy as Discriminatory."
92. Pearce, *Race with the Devil*, 1.
93. Pearce, "Letter."
94. Rosebury, "Tolkien in the History of Ideas," 103.
95. Veldman, *Fantasy, the Bomb, and the Greening of Britain*, 107–8.
96. Barlow, "Escape."
97. Hunter, *The Greenpeace to Amchitka*, 31.
98. Quoted in Veldman, *Fantasy, the Bomb, and the Greening of Britain*, 108.
99. Tolkien, *Letters*, 63–64.
100. Bell, "Lord of Machines," 10–11.
101. Matusitz, *Symbolism in Terrorism*, 98.
102. Hernandez, "Arsons May Be Work of Activists."
103. Norman, "The Prevalence of Hobbits."

9. *Tolkienian Courage and Wilderness Today*

1. Shellenberger and Nordhaus, "The Death of Environmentalism," 34.
2. Quoted in Bell, "To the Tenth Generation," 63.
3. Tolkien, *Lord*, xx.
4. "What has Ingeld to do with Christ?" Tolkien discusses this famous lament, penned by Alcuin of York in 797, in his essay on *Beowulf* (*Monsters*, 45n10).
5. Cronon, "The Trouble with Wilderness," 484.
6. Jeffers, *Arda Inhabited*, 11.

7. Phelan, "The Menace of Eco-Fascism."
8. Worthy, "Despair, Courage, & Hope in an Age of Environmental Turmoil."
9. Tolkien, *Monsters*, 25–26.
10. Shippey, *Road*, 120.
11. Shippey, *Roots*, 156, 191.
12. Shippey, *Author*, 111; emphasis in original.
13. Shippey, "Why the Critics."
14. Tolkien, *Lord*, 886.
15. Flieger, *Green Suns*, 143.
16. Tolkien, *Morgoth's Ring*, 320.
17. Tolkien, *Lord*, 1060.
18. Kareiva, "Ominous Trends in Nature Recreation," 2757–58.
19. Louv, *The Nature Principle*, 11.
20. Kareiva, "Ominous Trends in Nature Recreation," 2757.
21. Louv, *The Nature Principle*, 17.
22. Tolkien, *Lord*, 184.
23. Tolkien, *Lord*, 227.
24. Tolkien, *Lord*, 659.
25. Tolkien, *Lord*, 379.
26. Tolkien, *Letters*, 197.
27. Tolkien, *Lord*, 243, 357.
28. Tolkien, *Lord*, 242.
29. Tolkien, *Lord*, 365.
30. Tolkien, *Silmarillion*, 142.
31. Tolkien, *Silmarillion*, 82.
32. Tolkien, *Silmarillion*, 74.
33. Tolkien, *Letters*, 407.
34. Watson et al., "Catastrophic," 2929.
35. Watson et al., "Catastrophic," 2931.
36. Watson et al., "Protect," 27.
37. Watson et al., "Protect," 29–30.
38. Tolkien, *Lord*, 265, 468–69.
39. Tolkien, *Lord*, 349.
40. Tolkien, *Lord*, 375.
41. Ceballos et al., "Accelerated Modern Human-Induced Species Losses."
42. Leopold, *A Sand County Almanac*, 109.
43. Leopold, *A Sand County Almanac*, 110.
44. Quoted in Yeoman, "Why the Passenger Pigeon Went Extinct."
45. And thus less susceptible to political "adjustment"; as of 2020, the official climate reports used for an earlier version of this study have disappeared from publicly accessible US government Web sites.
46. Reuling et al., "Adapting to Change in the Crown of the Continent," i.
47. Jeffers, *Arda Inhabited*, 45–46.
48. Flieger, *Green Suns*, 142.
49. Tolkien, *Letters*, 215.

50. Shippey, *Author;* see Buck, "Literary Context, Twentieth Century"; Rosebury, "Tolkien in the History of Ideas"; Vaninskaya, "Modernity: Tolkien and His Contemporaries."
51. Tolkien, *Letters*, 38.
52. Quoted in Carpenter, *Tolkien: A Biography*, 197.
53. Shippey, *Road*, 79.
54. Tolkien, *Lord*, 1074n1.
55. Tolkien, *Hobbit*, 267.
56. Shippey, *Road*, 79.
57. Tolkien, *Hobbit*, 270.
58. Shippey, *Road*, 79.
59. Tolkien, *Lord*, 1008.
60. Tolkien, *Lord*, 1009–10.
61. Tolkien, *Lord*, 1005.
62. Smith, *The Wisdom of the Shire*, 88.
63. Tolkien, *Lord*, 141.
64. Tolkien, *Lord*, 840–41.
65. Tolkien, *Lord*, 842.
66. Tolkien, *Lord*, 841–42.
67. Tolkien, *Letters*, 54.
68. Tolkien, "Minchin."
69. Shippey, *Road*, 119.
70. Tolkien, *Letters*, 329.
71. Tolkien, *Letters*, 88, 161.
72. Tolkien, *Lord*, 239.
73. Tolkien, *Lord*, 64.
74. Tolkien, *Lord*, 360.
75. Tolkien, *Lord*, 1096–97.
76. Tolkien, *Lord*, 33.
77. Kareiva, "Ominous Trends in Nature Recreation," 2757.
78. "Who'd Be a Farmer Today?"
79. Tolkien, *Lord*, 360.
80. Wasley et al., "UK Has Nearly 800 Livestock Mega Farms, Investigation Reveals."
81. Dickerson and Evans, *Ents, Elves, and Eriador*, 75.
82. Kareiva, "Ominous Trends in Nature Recreation," 2757.
83. Tolkien, *Lord*, 2.
84. Tolkien, *Lord*, 280.
85. Jeffers, *Arda Inhabited*, 38.
86. Shippey, *Roots*, 383.
87. Shippey, *Roots*, 248.
88. Tolkien, *Unfinished Tales*, 261–62.
89. Tolkien, *Silmarillion*, 89.
90. Tolkien, *Lord*, 1012, 1013.
91. Tolkien, *Lord*, 880.

92. Tolkien, *Lord*, 879.
93. Tolkien, *Letters*, 220.
94. "The Third Age of the world is ended, and the new age is begun; and it is your task to order its beginning and to preserve what may be preserved. . . . The burden must lie upon you and your kindred" (Tolkien, *Lord*, 971).
95. Jeffers, *Arda Inhabited*, 62.
96. Callicott and Nelson, "The Wilderness Act," 121.

Conclusion

1. McCallum, *Ecological Intelligence*, 2.
2. Shippey, *Roots*, 95–96.
3. Tolkien, *Hobbit*, 88.
4. Olsen, *Exploring J. R. R. Tolkien's* The Hobbit, 69.
5. Tolkien, *Lord*, 985.
6. Tolkien, *Lord*, 268, 248.
7. Tolkien, *Lord*, 226.
8. Tolkien, *Lord*, 937–38.

Bibliography

Abbey, Edward. *Desert Solitaire: A Season in the Wilderness*. 1st Touchstone ed. 1968. Reprint, New York: Simon & Schuster, 1990.

Abram, David. *The Spell of the Sensuous: Perception and Language in a More-than-Human World*. New York: Vintage, 1997.

Acks, Alex. "Tolkien's Map and the Messed Up Mountains of Middle-Earth." *Tor.Com*, Aug. 1, 2017. https://www.tor.com/2017/08/01/tolkiens-map-and-the-messed-up-mountains-of-middle-earth/.

Acocella, Joan. "Slaying Monsters." *New Yorker*, June 2, 2014. https://www.newyorker.com/magazine/2014/06/02/slaying-monsters.

An Act authorizing a Grant to the State of California of the "Yo-Semite Valley," and of the Land embracing the "Mariposa Big Tree Grove.," Pub. L. No. 159, § 184, 203 Stat. 325 (1864). https://www.loc.gov/law/help/statutes-at-large/38th-congress/session-1/c38s1ch184.pdf.

Arnold, Matthew. *On the Study of Celtic Literature*. London: Smith, Elder and Co., 1867.

Attenborough, David. *The First Eden: The Mediterranean World and Man*. First American ed. Boston. Toronto: Little Brown, 1987.

Auden, W. H. "At the End of the Quest, Victory." *New York Times Book Review*, Jan. 22, 1956.

Backe, Hans-Joachim. "Within the Mainstream: An Ecocritical Framework for Digital Game History." *Ecozon@: European Journal of Literature, Culture and Environment* 8, no. 2 (Oct. 31, 2017): 39–55. https://doi.org/10.37536/ECOZONA.2017.8.2.1362.

Barker, Martin. "On Being a 1960s Tolkien Reader." In *From Hobbits to Hollywood: Essays on Peter Jackson's* Lord of the Rings, edited by Ernest Mathijs and Murray Pomerance, 81–100. Contemporary Cinema 3. Amsterdam: Rodopi, 2006.

Barlow, Maude. "Escape from Mordor." *New Internationalist*, Apr. 2, 2010. https://newint.org/features/2010/04/01/free-trade.

Barton, Matt. *Dungeons and Desktops: The History of Computer Role-Playing Games*. Wellesley, MA: A. K. Peters, 2008.

Beal, Jane. "Who Is Tom Bombadil?: Interpreting the Light in Frodo Baggins and Tom Bombadil's Role in the Healing of Traumatic Memory in J. R. R. Tolkien's

Lord of the Rings." *Journal of Tolkien Research* 6, no. 1 (June 27, 2018): 1–34.
Bell, James. "Lord of Machines." *Earth First!* 22, no. 6 (July 2002): 10–11.
Bell, Jason. "To the Tenth Generation: Homer's *Odyssey* as Environmental Ethics." *Environmental Ethics* 32, no. 1 (2010): 51–65. https://doi.org/10.5840/enviroethics20103215.
Bollard, John K. "Landscapes of the Mabinogi." *Landscapes* 10, no. 2 (Nov. 2009): 37–60. https://doi.org/10.1179/lan.2009.10.2.37.
Bowers, John M. *Tolkien's Lost Chaucer.* Oxford: Oxford Univ. Press, 2019.
Bradford, William. "From of Plymouth Plantation." In *The American Tradition in Literature*, 3rd ed., edited by Sculley Bradley, Richmond Croom Beatty, and Eugene Hudson Long, 1:16–32. New York: W. W. Norton, 1967.
Braun, J. W. *The Lord of the Films: The Unofficial Guide to Tolkien's Middle Earth on the Big Screen.* Toronto: ECW Press, 2009.
Breeze, Andrew. "Moor, Court, and River in the Four Branches of the Mabinogi." In *Rural Space in the Middle Ages and Early Modern Age: The Spatial Turn in Premodern Studies*, edited by Albrecht Classen, 295–312. Berlin: De Gruyter, 2012. https://doi.org/10.1515/9783110285420.
Buck, Claire. "Literary Context, Twentieth Century." In *J. R. R. Tolkien Encyclopedia: Scholarship and Critical Assessment*, edited by Michael D. C. Drout, 363–66. New York: Routledge, 2007.
Burdge, Anthony. "Gaming." In *J. R. R. Tolkien Encyclopedia: Scholarship and Critical Assessment*, edited by Michael D. C. Drout, 228–30. New York: Routledge, 2007.
Burns, Marjorie. *Perilous Realms: Celtic and Norse in Tolkien's Middle-Earth.* Toronto: Univ. of Toronto Press, 2005.
Callahan, Tally. "*Lord of the Rings: War in the North* Co-Op Review." *Co-Optimus*, Nov. 9, 2011. https://www.co-optimus.com/review/928/page/1/lord-of-the-rings-war-in-the-north-co-op-review.html.
Callicott, J. Baird, and Michael P. Nelson. "Introduction." In *The Great New Wilderness Debate*, edited by J. Baird Callicott and Michael P. Nelson, 1–20. Athens: Univ. of Georgia Press, 1998.
———, eds. "The Wilderness Act of 1964." In *The Great New Wilderness Debate*, 120–30. Athens: Univ. of Georgia Press, 1998.
Campbell, Joseph. *The Hero with a Thousand Faces.* Commemorative ed. Bollingen Series 17. 1949. Reprint, Princeton, NJ: Princeton Univ. Press, 2004.
Campbell, Liam. *The Ecological Augury in the Works of JRR Tolkien.* Cormarë 21. Zurich: Walking Tree Publishers, 2011.
Carpenter, Humphrey. *Tolkien: A Biography.* New York: Ballantine Books, 1978.
Ceballos, Gerardo, Paul R. Ehrlich, Anthony D. Barnosky, Andrés García, Robert M. Pringle, and Todd M. Palmer. "Accelerated Modern Human-Induced Species Losses: Entering the Sixth Mass Extinction." *Science Advances* 1, no. 5 (June 2015): e1400253. https://doi.org/10.1126/sciadv.1400253.
Chance, Jane. "Tolkien and His Sources." In *Approaches to Teaching* Sir Gawain and the Green Knight, edited by Miriam Youngerman Miller and Jane Chance, 151–55. Approaches to Teaching Masterpieces of World Literature 9. New York: Modern Language Association, 1986.

Chang, Alenda Y. *Playing Nature: Ecology in Video Games.* Electronic Mediations 58. Minneapolis: Univ. of Minnesota Press, 2019.

Chickering, Howell D., trans. Beowulf: *A Dual-Language Edition.* Garden City, NY: Anchor Books, 1977.

Clark, George. "J. R. R. Tolkien and the True Hero." In *J. R. R. Tolkien and His Literary Resonances: Views of Middle-Earth,* edited by George Clark and Daniel Timmons, 39–51. Contributions to the Study of Science Fiction and Fantasy, no. 89. Westport, CT: Greenwood Press, 2000.

Colebatch, Hal. *Return of the Heroes:* The Lord of the Rings, Star Wars, Harry Potter, *and Social Conflict.* 2nd ed. Christchurch, NZ: Cybereditions, 2003.

"Conservation vs Preservation and the National Park Service." *National Park Service,* Oct. 29, 2019. https://www.nps.gov/teachers/classrooms/conservation-preservation-and-the-national-park-service.htm.

Croft, Janet Brennan. "Three Rings for Hollywood: Scripts for *The Lord of the Rings* by Zimmerman, Boorman, and Beagle." In *Fantasy Fiction into Film: Essays,* edited by Leslie Stratyner and James R. Keller. Jefferson, NC: McFarland, 2007.

Cronon, William. "Revisiting the Vanishing Frontier: The Legacy of Frederick Jackson Turner." *The Western Historical Quarterly* 18, no. 2 (Apr. 1987): 157–76. https://doi.org/10.2307/969581.

———. "The Trouble with Wilderness." In *The Great New Wilderness Debate,* edited by J. Baird Callicott and Michael P. Nelson, 471–99. Athens: Univ. of Georgia Press, 1998.

Cross, Tom Peete, and Clark Harris Slover. *Ancient Irish Tales.* New York: Barnes & Noble, 1996.

Curry, Patrick. *Defending Middle-Earth: Tolkien, Myth & Modernity.* 1st Houghton Mifflin Books ed. 1998. Reprint, Boston: Houghton Mifflin, 2004.

Davies, Sioned, trans. *The Mabinogion.* Oxford: Oxford Univ. Press, 2007.

Day, David. *Tolkien's Ring.* New York: Barnes & Noble, 1999.

De Vries, Jan. "Theories Concerning 'Nature Myths.'" In *Sacred Narrative: Readings in the Theory of Myth,* edited by Alan Dundes, 30–40. Berkeley, CA: Univ. of California Press, 1984.

Dickerson, Matthew T., and Jonathan D. Evans. *Ents, Elves, and Eriador: The Environmental Vision of J. R. R. Tolkien.* Culture of the Land: A Series in the New Agrarianism. Lexington: Univ. Press of Kentucky, 2006.

Donovan, Leslie A. "Middle-Earth Mythology: An Overview." In *A Companion to J. R. R. Tolkien,* edited by Stuart D. Lee, 92–106. Blackwell Companions to Literature and Culture 89. Malden, MA: Wiley Blackwell, 2014.

Drout, Michael D. C. "Preface." In Beowulf *and the Critics,* xi–xiv. Medieval & Renaissance Texts & Studies, v. 248. Tempe: Arizona Center for Medieval and Renaissance Studies, 2002.

Emerson, Ralph Waldo. *English Traits.* Edited by Edward Waldo Emerson. Centenary ed. The Complete Works of Ralph Waldo Emerson 5. Boston: Houghton Mifflin, 1903.

———. *Nature: Addresses and Lectures.* Edited by Edward Waldo Emerson. Centenary ed. The Complete Works of Ralph Waldo Emerson 1. Boston: Houghton Mifflin, 1903.

Ertsgaard, Gabriel. "'Leaves of Gold There Grew': Lothlórien, Postcolonialism, and Ecology." In *Representations of Nature in Middle-Earth,* edited by Martin Simonson, 207–29. Cormarë 34. Zurich: Walking Tree Publishers, 2015.

Evans, Jonathan. "The Dragon-Lore of Middle-Earth: Tolkien and Old English and Old Norse Tradition." In *J. R. R. Tolkien and His Literary Resonances: Views of Middle-Earth,* edited by George Clark and Daniel Timmons, 21–38. Contributions to the Study of Science Fiction and Fantasy, no. 89. Westport, CT: Greenwood Press, 2000.

"Fan, n.2." In *OED Online.* Oxford Univ. Press, June 2020. https://www.oed.com/view/Entry/68000.

Fimi, Dimitra. "'Mad' Elves and 'Elusive Beauty': Some Celtic Strands of Tolkien's Mythology." *Folklore* 117, no. 2 (2006): 156–70. https://doi.org/10.1080/00155870600707847.

———. *Tolkien, Race, and Cultural History: From Fairies to Hobbits.* Basingstoke, UK: Palgrave Macmillan, 2009.

Fisher, Jason. "Tolkien and Source Criticism: Remarking and Remaking." In *Tolkien and the Study of His Sources: Critical Essays,* edited by Jason Fisher, 29–44. Jefferson, NC: McFarland & Co, 2011.

Flieger, Verlyn. *Green Suns and Faërie: Essays on J. R. R. Tolkien.* Kent, OH: Kent State Univ. Press, 2012.

———. *A Question of Time: J. R. R. Tolkien's Road to Faërie.* Kent, OH: Kent State Univ. Press, 1997.

———. *Splintered Light: Logos and Language in Tolkien's World.* 2nd ed. Kent, OH: Kent State Univ. Press, 2002.

Fraade-Blanar, Zoe, and Aaron M. Glazer. *Superfandom: How Our Obsessions Are Changing What We Buy and Who We Are.* New York: Norton, 2017.

Frantzen, Allen J. *Desire for Origins: New Language, Old English, and Teaching the Tradition.* New Brunswick, NJ: Rutgers Univ. Press, 1990.

Fuegi, Aaron. "Rivendell in Switzerland." http://scv.bu.edu/~aarondf/Rivimages/realriv.html.

Fyler, John M. "Freshman Composition: Epic and Romance." In *Approaches to Teaching* Sir Gawain and the Green Knight, edited by Miriam Youngerman Miller and Jane Chance, 119–22. Approaches to Teaching Masterpieces of World Literature 9. 1986. Reprint, New York: Modern Language Association, 1994.

Gamespot Staff. "*The Lord of the Rings: War in the North* Q&A." *GameSpot,* Feb. 1, 2011. https://www.gamespot.com/articles/the-lord-of-the-rings-war-in-the-north-qanda/1100-6296919/.

Gantz, Jeffrey, trans. *The Mabinogion.* New York: Dorset Press, 1985.

George, Michael. "Gawain's Struggle with Ecology: Attitudes Toward the Natural World in *Sir Gawain and the Green Knight.*" *Journal of Ecocriticism* 2, no. 2 (July 2010): 30–44.

Gummere, Francis B. *Germanic Origins: A Study in Primitive Culture.* London: David Nutt, 1892.

Gupta, Prachi. "New Zealand Issues Hobbit Coins as Legal Tender." *Salon*, Oct. 10, 2012. https://www.salon.com/2012/10/10/new_zealand_issues_hobbit_coins_as_legal_tender/.

Hammond, Wayne G., and Christina Scull. *J. R. R. Tolkien: Artist & Illustrator.* Boston: Houghton Mifflin, 1995.

Harlow, John, and Rachel Dobson. "*Lord of the Rings* Is Worth £3bn but Tolkien Sold the Film Rights to Ward off the Taxman." *Sunday Times*, Dec. 15, 2002.

Harrison, Robert Pogue. *Forests: The Shadow of Civilization.* Chicago: Univ. of Chicago Press, 1993.

Heaney, Seamus. Beowulf: *A New Verse Translation.* New York: Norton, 2001.

Heilbronner, Oded. "In Search of the English Psyche." *English Studies* 93, no. 1 (Feb. 2012): 91–105. https://doi.org/10.1080/0013838X.2011.638449.

Hernandez, Nelson. "Arsons May Be Work of Activists." *Washington Post*, Nov. 22, 2005. http://www.washingtonpost.com/wp-dyn/content/article/2005/11/21/AR2005112101621.html.

Holmes, Steven Jon. *The Young John Muir: An Environmental Biography.* Madison: Univ. of Wisconsin Press, 1999.

"Holt, n.1." In *OED Online.* Oxford Univ. Press, June 2020. https://www.oed.com/view/Entry/87829.

Honegger, Thomas. "The Rohirrim: 'Anglo-Saxons on Horseback?' An Inquiry into Tolkien's Use of Sources." In *Tolkien and the Study of His Sources: Critical Essays*, edited by Jason Fisher, 116–34. Jefferson, NC: McFarland & Co, 2011.

Hunter, Robert. *The Greenpeace to Amchitka: An Environmental Odyssey.* 2004. Reprint, Vancouver, BC: Arsenal Pulp Press, 2009.

Huntsman, Jeffrey F. "The Celtic Heritage of *Sir Gawain and the Green Knight.*" In *Approaches to Teaching* Sir Gawain and the Green Knight, edited by Miriam Youngerman Miller and Jane Chance, 177–81. Approaches to Teaching Masterpieces of World Literature 9. New York: Modern Language Association, 1986.

Hutton, Ronald. *The Rise and Fall of Merry England: The Ritual Year, 1400–1700.* Oxford: Oxford Univ. Press, 1994.

Ibata, David. "'Lord' of Racism? Critics View Trilogy as Discriminatory." *Chicago Tribune*, Jan. 12, 2003, sec. Lifestyles. https://www.chicagotribune.com/lifestyles/chi-030112epringsrace-story.html.

Jeffers, Susan. *Arda Inhabited: Environmental Relationships in* The Lord of the Rings. Kent, OH: Kent State Univ. Press, 2014.

Jenkins, Mark P. "Wilderness Preservation Argument 31: The Psychotherapy at a Distance Argument." In *The Wilderness Debate Rages On: Continuing the Great New Wilderness Debate*, edited by J. Baird Callicott and Michael P. Nelson, 170–85. Athens: Univ. of Georgia Press, 2008.

Jones, Leslie Ellen. *Myth & Middle-Earth: Exploring the Medieval Legends behind J. R. R. Tolkien's* The Hobbit & Lord of the Rings. New York: Cold Spring Press, 2002.

Judd, Walter S., and Graham A. Judd. *Flora of Middle-Earth: Plants of J. R. R. Tolkien's Legendarium.* New York: Oxford Univ. Press, 2017.

Judge, Roy. "May Day and Merrie England." *Folklore* 102, no. 2 (1991): 131–48.

Kareiva, P. "Ominous Trends in Nature Recreation." *Proceedings of the National Academy of Sciences* 105, no. 8 (Feb. 26, 2008): 2757–58. https://doi.org/10.1073/pnas.0800474105.

Kozloff, Sarah. "*The Lord of the Rings* as Melodrama." In *From Hobbits to Hollywood: Essays on Peter Jackson's* Lord of the Rings, edited by Ernest Mathijs and Murray Pomerance, 155–72. Contemporary Cinema 3. Amsterdam: Rodopi, 2006.

Lankford, Scott. "John Muir, Eco-Racism, and Finding a Way Forward." *Medium*, Aug. 1, 2020. https://medium.com/@scottlankford/john-muir-eco-racism-and-finding-a-way-forward-322bd2b17834.

Lee, Stuart D., and Elizabeth Solopova. *The Keys of Middle-Earth: Discovering Medieval Literature Through the Fiction of J. R. R. Tolkien*. 2nd ed. Basingstoke, UK: Palgrave Macmillan, 2015.

Lehning, Amber. "Living Myths in a Living World: Mythological Studies and Green Studies Implications of Fandom." In *Multidisciplinary Perspectives on Media Fandom*, edited by Robert Andrew Dunn, 1–19. Advances in Religious and Cultural Studies. Hershey, PA: IGI Global, 2020.

Leopold, Aldo. "Pioneers and Gullies: Why Sweat to Reclaim New Land When We Lack Sense Enough to Hold on to the Old Acres?" *Sunset: The Pacific Monthly*, May 1924.

———. *A Sand County Almanac and Sketches Here and There*. Special Commemorative ed. New York: Oxford Univ. Press, 1989.

Liptak, Andrew. "Looking Back on What Made the *Lord of the Rings* Trilogy Special, 15 Years Later." *Verge*, Dec. 23, 2016. https://www.theverge.com/2016/12/23/14055580/lord-of-the-rings-trilogy-movies-peter-jackson-15th-anniversary.

"Literary Society." *King Edward's School Chronicle* 26, no. 186 (1911): 19–20.

Lloyd-Morgan, Ceridwen. "Narrative Structure in Peredur." *Zeitschrift Für Celtische Philologie* 38, no. 1 (1981): 187–231. https://doi.org/10.1515/zcph.1981.38.1.187.

"Lokasenna." *Old Norse Etexts*. http://etext.old.no/Bugge/lokasenn.html.

Louv, Richard. *The Nature Principle: Human Restoration and the End of Nature-Deficit Disorder*. Chapel Hill, NC: Algonquin Books of Chapel Hill, 2011.

Lunt, D. J. "The Climate of Middle Earth." *Journal of Hobbitlore*, Oct. 3, 2013. http://www.bristol.ac.uk/university/media/press/10013-english.pdf.

Lyman-Thomas, J. S. "'Celtic Things' and 'Things Celtic': Identity, Language, and Mythology." In *A Companion to J. R. R. Tolkien*, edited by Stuart D. Lee, 272–85. Blackwell Companions to Literature and Culture 89. Malden, MA: Wiley Blackwell, 2014.

Magennis, Hugh. *Images of Community in Old English Poetry*. Cambridge Studies in Anglo-Saxon England 18. Cambridge: Cambridge Univ. Press, 1996.

Maier-Zucchino, Evan. "After Nearly 40 Years, Video Games Still Don't Do *Lord of the Rings* Justice." *Kotaku*, May 22, 2019. https://kotaku.com/after-nearly-40-years-video-games-still-dont-do-lord-o-1834901260.

Mathijs, Ernest, and Murray Pomerance. "There and Back Again: An Editor's Tale." In *Introduction. From Hobbits to Hollywood: Essays on Peter Jackson's*

Lord of the Rings, edited by Ernest Mathijs and Murray Pomerance, 1–16. Contemporary Cinema 3. Amsterdam: Rodopi, 2006.

Mattingly, H., trans. *Tacitus on Britain and Germany.* The Penguin Classics L5. West Drayton, UK: Penguin Books, 1948.

Matusitz, Jonathan Andre. *Symbolism in Terrorism: Motivation, Communication, and Behavior.* Security and Professional Intelligence Education Series. Boulder, CO: Rowman & Littlefield, 2015.

McCallum, Ian. *Ecological Intelligence: Rediscovering Ourselves in Nature.* Golden, CO: Fulcrum, 2008.

McLarty, Lianne. "Masculinity, Whiteness, and Social Class in *The Lord of the Rings.*" In *From Hobbits to Hollywood: Essays on Peter Jackson's* Lord of the Rings, edited by Ernest Mathijs and Murray Pomerance, 173–88. Contemporary Cinema 3. Amsterdam: Rodopi, 2006.

Miller, Miriam Youngerman. "'Of Sum Mayn Meruayle, Þat He Myȝt Trawe': *The Lord of the Rings* and *Sir Gawain and the Green Knight.*" In *Inklings and Others,* edited by Jane Chance, 3:345–65. Studies in Medievalism 3. Suffolk, UK: Boydell and Brewer, 1991.

Millet, Lydia. "Ecoporn Exposed." *Utne,* no. 125 (Oct. 9, 2004): 34–35.

Muir, John. *My First Summer in the Sierra.* Boston: Houghton Mifflin, 1917.

———. *The Mountains of California.* New York: Century, 1894.

Nash, Roderick. *Wilderness and the American Mind.* 3rd ed. 1967. Reprint, New Haven, CT: Yale Univ. Press, 1982.

Nelson, Michael P., and John A. Vucetich. "Value of Wilderness." In *The International Encyclopedia of Ethics,* edited by Hugh LaFollette, 5476–84. Wiley Online Library, 2013. https://doi.org/10.1002/9781444367072.

Neville, Jennifer. *Representations of the Natural World in Old English Poetry.* Cambridge Studies in Anglo-Saxon England 27. Cambridge: Cambridge Univ. Press, 1999.

Niiler, Lucas P. "Timely, Again: Tolkien's Fantastic Ecology." *Academic Exchange Quarterly* 7, no. 4 (2003): 97–101.

Norman, Philip. "The Prevalence of Hobbits." *New York Times Magazine,* Jan. 15, 1967. http://movies2.nytimes.com/books/01/02/11/specials/tolkien-mag67.html.

Odajnyk, V. Walter. "Mandala of the Naropa Dakini: Archetypal and Psychological Commentary." In *Varieties of Mythic Experience: Essays on Religion, Psyche and Culture,* edited by Dennis Patrick Slattery and Glen Slater, 135–58. Einsiedeln, Switzerland: Daimon Verlag, 2008.

Oelschlaeger, Max. *The Idea of Wilderness: From Prehistory to the Age of Ecology.* New Haven, CT: Yale Univ. Press, 1991.

Olsen, Corey. *Exploring J. R. R. Tolkien's* The Hobbit. Boston: Houghton Mifflin Harcourt, 2012.

Onyett, Charles. "*The Lord of the Rings* Meets Diablo." *IGN,* Nov. 17, 2010. https://www.ign.com/articles/2010/11/17/the-lord-of-the-rings-meets-diablo.

Orth, John. "Mirkwood." *Mythlore: A Journal of J. R. R. Tolkien, C. S. Lewis, Charles Williams, and Mythopoeic Literature* 38, no. 1 (Oct. 16, 2019). https://dc.swosu.edu/mythlore/vol38/iss1/31.

Paris, Ginette. *Wisdom of the Psyche: Depth Psychology after Neuroscience*. London: Routledge, 2007.

Parker, Douglass. "Hwaet We Holbytla . . ." *The Hudson Review* 9, no. 4 (1957): 598–609.

Pavlovic, Uros "Vader." "*The Lord of the Rings: War in the North* Review," Feb. 20, 2014. http://web.archive.org/web/20140220020454/http://www.actiontrip.com/reviews/the-lord-of-the-rings-war-in-the-north.phtml.

Pearce, Joseph. "A Letter to a Recovering White Supremacist." *Imaginative Conservative*, Nov. 16, 2018. https://theimaginativeconservative.org/2018/11/letter-recovering-white-supremacist-joseph-pearce.html.

———. *Merrie England: A Journey Through the Shire*. Charlotte, NC: TAN, 2016.

———. *Race with the Devil: My Journey from Racial Hatred to Rational Love*. Charlotte, NC: Saint Benedict Press, 2013.

Perrottet, Tony. "John Muir's Yosemite." *Smithsonian Magazine*, July 2008. https://www.smithsonianmag.com/history/john-muirs-yosemite-10737/.

Phelan, Matthew. "The Menace of Eco-Fascism." *New York Review of Books*, Oct. 22, 2018.

Phelpstead, Carl. *Tolkien and Wales: Language, Literature and Identity*. Cardiff, UK: Univ. of Wales Press, 2011.

Plato. *Complete Works*. Edited by John M. Cooper and D. S. Hutchinson. Indianapolis, IN: Hackett, 1997.

Plimmer, Charlotte, and Denis Plimmer. "JRR Tolkien: 'Film My Books? It's Easier to Film *The Odyssey*.'" *Telegraph*, Mar. 22, 1968. https://www.telegraph.co.uk/films/2016/04/19/jrr-tolkien-film-my-books-its-easier-to-film-the-odyssey/.

Plumwood, Val. "Wilderness Skepticism and Wilderness Dualism." In *The Great New Wilderness Debate*, edited by J. Baird Callicott and Michael P. Nelson, 652–90. Athens: Univ. of Georgia Press, 1998.

Powell, Miles A. *Vanishing America: Species Extinction, Racial Peril, and the Origins of Conservation*. Cambridge, MA: Harvard Univ. Press, 2016.

"Ranger, n.1." In *OED Online*. Oxford: Oxford Univ. Press, June 2020. https://www.oed.com/view/Entry/158019.

Rateliff, John D. "She and Tolkien, Revisited." In *Tolkien and the Study of His Sources: Critical Essays*, edited by Jason Fisher, 145–61. Jefferson, NC: McFarland & Co, 2011.

Rateliff, John D., and J. R. R. Tolkien. *The History of* The Hobbit. Boston: Houghton Mifflin, 2007.

Reagan, Ronald. "Farewell Address to the Nation." The White House, Washington, DC, Jan. 11, 1989. Ronald Reagan Presidential Library. https://www.reaganlibrary.gov/research/speeches/011189i.

Rérolle, Raphaëlle. "Tolkien, l'anneau de la discorde." *Le Monde*, July 5, 2012. https://www.lemonde.fr/culture/article/2012/07/05/tolkien-l-anneau-de-la-discorde_1729858_3246.html.

Resnick, Henry. "An Interview with Tolkien." *Niekas* 18 (1967): 37–47.

Reuling, Melly, Shawn Johnson, Sue Higgins, Patrick Bixler, Sam Williams, and Gary Tabor. "Adapting to Change in the Crown of the Continent: An Ecosystem

Scale Approach to Collaborative Management." Bozeman, MT: Center for Large Landscape Conservation, Sept. 11, 2015.

Risden, E. L. "Source Criticism: Background and Applications." In *Tolkien and the Study of His Sources: Critical Essays,* edited by Jason Fisher., 17–28. Jefferson, NC: McFarland & Co, 2011.

Rosebury, Brian. "Tolkien in the History of Ideas." In *Bloom's Literary Criticism,* new ed., edited by Harold Bloom, 89–120. Bloom's Modern Critical Views. New York: Bloom's Literary Criticism, 2008.

Rudd, Gillian. *Greenery: Ecocritical Readings of Late Medieval English Literature.* Manchester Medieval Literature. Manchester: Manchester Univ. Press, 2007.

Saperstein, Pat. "16 Things You Didn't Know About the Making of 'Lord of the Rings.'" *Variety,* Dec. 19, 2016. https://variety.com/2016/film/news/lord-of-the-rings-making-of-backstory-business-1201936646/.

Sayer, George. "Recollections of J. R. R. Tolkien." In *Proceedings of the J. R. R. Tolkien Centenary Conference, 1992: Proceedings of the Conference Held at Keble College, Oxford, England, 17th–24th August 1992 to Celebrate the Centenary of the Birth of Professor J. R. R. Tolkien, Incorporating the 23rd Mythopoeic Conference (Mythcon XXIII) and Oxonmoot 1992,* edited by Patricia Reynolds and Glen GoodKnight, 21–25. Altadena, CA: Mythopoeic Press, 1995.

Schama, Simon. *Landscape and Memory.* New York: A. A. Knopf; Distributed by Random House, 1995.

Schiffman, Richard. "Bigger than Science, Bigger than Religion." *YES! Magazine,* no. 73 (Spring 2015): 18–22.

Schlobin, Roger C. "The Monsters Are Talismans and Transgressions: Tolkien and *Sir Gawain and the Green Knight.*" In *J. R. R. Tolkien and His Literary Resonances: Views of Middle-Earth,* edited by George Clark and Daniel Timmons, 70–81. Contributions to the Study of Science Fiction and Fantasy, no. 89. Westport, CT: Greenwood Press, 2000.

Schroeder, H. W. "The Spiritual Aspect of Nature: A Perspective from Depth Psychology." In *Proceedings of the 1991 Northeastern Recreation Research Symposium: April 7–9, 1991, State Parks Management and Research Institute, Saratoga Springs, New York,* edited by Gail A. Vander Stoep, 25–30. Radnor, PA: US Dept. of Agriculture, Forest Service, Northeastern Forest Experiment Station, 1992.

Scull, Christina, and Wayne G. Hammond. *The J. R. R. Tolkien Companion and Guide: Chronology.* Rev. and expanded ed. London: HarperCollins Publishers, 2017.

Shellenberger, Michael, and Ted Nordhaus. "The Death of Environmentalism." The Breakthrough Institute, Aug. 2004. https://thebreakthrough.org/articles/the-death-of-environmentalism.

Shippey, Tom. "Introduction: Why Source Criticism?" In *Tolkien and the Study of His Sources: Critical Essays,* edited by Jason Fisher, 7–16. Jefferson, NC: McFarland & Co, 2011.

———. *J. R. R. Tolkien: Author of the Century.* Boston: Houghton Mifflin, 2001.

———. *The Road to Middle-Earth: How J. R. R. Tolkien Created a New Mythology.* Rev. and expanded ed. Boston: Houghton Mifflin Co, 2003.

———. *Roots and Branches: Selected Papers on Tolkien.* Cormarë 11. Zurich: Walking Tree Publishers, 2007.

———. "Tolkien and the Gawain-Poet." In *Proceedings of the J. R. R. Tolkien Centenary Conference, 1992: Proceedings of the Conference Held at Keble College, Oxford, England, 17th–24th August 1992 to Celebrate the Centenary of the Birth of Professor J. R. R. Tolkien, Incorporating the 23rd Mythopoeic Conference (Mythcon XXIII) and Oxonmoot 1992,* edited by Patricia Reynolds and Glen GoodKnight, 213–19. Altadena, CA: Mythopoeic Press, 1995.

———. "Tolkien's Two Views of *Beowulf:* One Hailed, One Ignored. But Did We Get This Right?" *LoTRPlaza Scholars Forum,* July 25, 2010. https://web.archive.org/web/20150629165450/www.lotrplaza.com/showthread.php?18483.

———. "Why the Critics Must Recognise *Lord of the Rings* as a Classic." *Telegraph,* Jan. 2, 2002, sec. Comment. https://www.telegraph.co.uk/comment/personal-view/3571458/Why-the-critics-must-recognise-Lord-of-the-Rings-as-a-classic.html.

Siewers, Alfred K. "The Green Otherworlds of Early Medieval Literature." In *The Cambridge Companion to Literature and the Environment,* edited by Louise Westling, 31–44. Cambridge Companions to Literature. New York: Cambridge Univ. Press, 2014. https://doi.org/10.1017/CCO9781139342728.

———. *Strange Beauty: Ecocritical Approaches to Early Medieval Landscape.* The New Middle Ages. New York: Palgrave Macmillan US, 2009. https://doi.org/10.1057/9780230100527.

———. "Tolkien's Cosmic-Christian Ecology: The Medieval Underpinnings." In *Tolkien's Modern Middle Ages,* edited by Jane Chance and Alfred K. Siewers, 138–53. The New Middle Ages. New York: Palgrave Macmillan, 2009.

———. "Writing an Icon of the Land: The Mabinogi as a Mystagogy of Landscape." *Peritia* 19 (2005): 193–228.

Smith, Noble Mason. *The Wisdom of the Shire: A Short Guide to a Long and Happy Life.* New York: Thomas Dunne Books, St. Martin's Press, 2012.

Snowblind Studios. *The Lord of the Rings: War in the North.* XBox 360. Warner Bros. Interactive Entertainment, 2011.

Snyder, Christopher A. *The Making of Middle-Earth: A New Look Inside the World of J. R. R. Tolkien.* New York: Sterling, 2013.

Spacks, Patricia Meyer. "Power and Meaning in *The Lord of the Rings.*" In *Understanding* The Lord of the Rings: *The Best of Tolkien Criticism,* edited by Rose A. Zimbardo and Neil D. Isaacs, 52–67. Boston: Mariner, 2005.

Staver, Ruth Johnston. *A Companion to* Beowulf. Westport, CT: Greenwood Press, 2005.

Susman, Gary. "'Lord of the Rings' Widens a Tolkien Family Rift." *Entertainment Weekly,* Dec. 11, 2001. https://ew.com/article/2001/12/11/lord-rings-widens-tolkien-family-rift/.

Thomas, Keith, and Ariel Hessayon. "The Perception of the Past in Early Modern England." In *The Creighton Century, 1907–2007,* edited by David Bates, Jennifer Wallis, and Jane Winters, 181–218. London: Univ. of London Press, 2009. https://www.jstor.org/stable/j.ctv13qfvgj.13.

Thoreau, Henry David. *Civil Disobedience, and Other Essays*. Dover Thrift Editions. New York: Dover Publications, 1993.

Tito, Greg. "*War in the North* Review." *Escapist*, Nov. 8, 2011. https://www.escapistmagazine.com/v2/war-in-the-north-review/.

Tolkien, J. R. R. *The Annotated Hobbit: The Hobbit, or There and Back Again*. Edited by Douglas A. Anderson. Rev. and expanded ed. 1937. Reprint, Boston: Houghton Mifflin, 2002.

———. Beowulf: *A Translation and Commentary, Together with Sellic Spell*. Edited by Christopher Tolkien. London: HarperCollins Publishers, 2014.

———. *The Legend of Sigurd & Gudrun*. Edited by Christopher Tolkien. Boston: Houghton Mifflin Harcourt, 2009.

———. "Letter to H. Cotton Minchin." *Tolkiengateway.Net*, Apr. 16, 1956. http://tolkiengateway.net/wiki/H._Cotton_Minchin_16_April_1956.

———. *The Letters of J. R. R. Tolkien*. Edited by Humphrey Carpenter and Christopher Tolkien. 1st Houghton Mifflin pbk. ed. 1981. Reprint, Boston: Houghton Mifflin Co, 2000.

———. *The Lord of the Rings*. 50th Anniversary ed. 1968. Reprint, Pymble, NSW: HarperCollins ebooks, 2009.

———. *The Monsters and the Critics and Other Essays*. Edited by Christopher Tolkien. London: HarperCollins, 2006.

———. *Morgoth's Ring: The Later Silmarillion Part One, The Legends of Aman*. Edited by Christopher Tolkien. The History of Middle-Earth 10. London: HarperCollins, 1994.

———. *Narn I Chîn Húrin: The Tale of the Children of Húrin*. Edited by Christopher Tolkien. Boston: Houghton Mifflin, 2008.

———. *The Shaping of Middle-Earth: The Quenta, the Ambarkanta, and the Annals, Together with the Earliest "Silmarillion" and the First Map*. Edited by Christopher Tolkien. The History of Middle-Earth 4. London: Unwin Paperbacks, 1988.

———. *The Silmarillion: The Myths and Legends of Middle-Earth*. Edited by Christopher Tolkien. Boston: Houghton Mifflin, 2004.

———, trans. *Sir Gawain and the Green Knight, Pearl,* and *Sir Orfeo*. 1st American ed. Boston: Houghton Mifflin, 1975.

———. *The Story of Kullervo*. Edited by Verlyn Flieger. Boston: Houghton Mifflin Harcourt, 2016.

———. *Tolkien on Fairy Stories*. Edited by Verlyn Flieger and Douglas Allen Anderson. Expanded ed. London: HarperCollinsPublishers, 2014.

———. *Unfinished Tales of Númenor and Middle-Earth*. Edited by Christopher Tolkien. Boston: Houghton Mifflin, 1980.

"Tolkien Relative Joins Rings Cast." *BBC News*, Dec. 8, 2003. http://news.bbc.co.uk/2/hi/entertainment/3299807.stm.

Tresca, Michael J. *The Evolution of Fantasy Role-Playing Games*. Jefferson, NC: McFarland & Co, 2011.

Troyes, Chrétien de. *Arthurian Romances*. Translated by William W. Kibler and Carleton W. Carroll. Penguin Classics. London: Penguin Books, 1991.

Turner, Frederick Jackson. *The Frontier in American History*. 1920. Reprint, New York: Dover Publications, 1996.

Vaninskaya, Anna. "Modernity: Tolkien and His Contemporaries." In *A Companion to J. R. R. Tolkien*, edited by Stuart D. Lee, 350–66. Blackwell Companions to Literature and Culture 89. Malden, MA: Wiley Blackwell, 2014.

Veldman, Meredith. *Fantasy, the Bomb, and the Greening of Britain: Romantic Protest, 1945–1980*. Cambridge: Cambridge Univ. Press, 1994.

Walsh, Fran, Philippa Boyens, Stephen Sinclair, and Peter Jackson. *The Lord of the Rings: The Two Towers* (film script), 2002. http://www.fempiror.com/other scripts/LordoftheRings2-TTT.pdf.

Wasley, Andrew, Fiona Harvey, Madlen Davies, and David Child. "UK Has Nearly 800 Livestock Mega Farms, Investigation Reveals." *Guardian*, July 17, 2017, sec. Environment. https://www.theguardian.com/environment/2017/jul/17/uk-has-nearly-800-livestock-mega-farms-investigation-reveals.

Watson, James E. M., Oscar Venter, Jasmine Lee, Kendall R. Jones, John G. Robinson, Hugh P. Possingham, and James R. Allan. "Protect the Last of the Wild." *Nature* 563, no. 7729 (Nov. 1, 2018): 27–30. https://doi.org/10.1038/d41586-018-07183-6.

Watson, James E. M., Danielle F. Shanahan, Moreno Di Marco, James Allan, William F. Laurance, Eric W. Sanderson, Brendan Mackey, and Oscar Venter. "Catastrophic Declines in Wilderness Areas Undermine Global Environment Targets." *Current Biology* 26, no. 21 (Nov. 7, 2016): 2929–34. https://doi.org/10.1016/j.cub.2016.08.049.

Westling, Louise. "Introduction." In *The Cambridge Companion to Literature and the Environment*, edited by Louise Westling, 1–16. Cambridge Companions to Literature. New York: Cambridge Univ. Press, 2014. https://doi.org/10.1017/CCO9781139342728.

"Who'd Be a Farmer Today?" The Prince's Countryside Fund, July 31, 2017. https://www.princescountrysidefund.org.uk/downloads/research/whod-be-a-farmer-today.pdf.

"Wilderness, n." In *OED Online*. Oxford: Oxford Univ. Press, June 2020. https://www.oed.com/view/Entry/229003.

Winthrop, John. "A Modell of Christian Charity," 1630. Hanover Historical Texts Collection. https://history.hanover.edu/texts/winthmod.html.

Woodward, Steven, and Kostis Kourelis. "Urban Legend: Architecture in *The Lord of the Rings*." In *From Hobbits to Hollywood: Essays on Peter Jackson's* Lord of the Rings, edited by Ernest Mathijs and Murray Pomerance, 189–214. Contemporary Cinema 3. Amsterdam; New York: Rodopi, 2006.

Worthy, Kenneth. "Despair, Courage, & Hope in an Age of Environmental Turmoil." *Psychology Today*, Nov. 9, 2013. http://www.psychologytoday.com/blog/the-green-mind/201311/despair-courage-hope-in-age-environmental-turmoil.

Xbox World 360. "*Lord of the Rings: War in the North*—A Co-Op Action Game Worth Playing?" *CVG*, Mar. 15, 2011. https://web.archive.org/web/20141211043221/http://www.computerandvideogames.com/293620/previews/lord-of-the-rings-war-in-the-north-a-co-op-action-game-worth-playing/?page=2.

Yeoman, Barry. "Why the Passenger Pigeon Went Extinct." *Audubon*, Apr. 17, 2014. https://www.audubon.org/magazine/may-june-2014/why-passenger-pigeon-went-extinct.

Ziolkowski, Jan M. "Virgil." In *The Oxford History of Classical Reception in English Literature*, edited by Rita Copeland, 1:736. Oxford: Oxford Univ. Press, 2016.

Index